H

TOO SCARED TO CRY

TOO SCARED TO CRY

Psychic Trauma in Childhood

Lenore Terr, M.D.

1817

HARPER & ROW, PUBLISHERS, New York

Grand Rapids, Philadelphia, St. Louis, San Francisco

London, Singapore, Sydney, Tokyo, Toronto

Excerpts from *Children of Hiroshima* by Arata Osada reprinted with permission from Crane, Russak & Co., Inc., New York.

Excerpt from "A Sketch of the Past" in *Moments of Being* by Virginia Woolf, copyright © 1976 by Quentin Bell and Angelica Garnett, reprinted by permission of Harcourt Brace and Jovanovich, Inc.

FIRST EDITION

Designed by Karen Savary

Library of Congress Cataloging-in-Publication Data

Terr, Lenore, 1936–
    Too scared to cry: psychic trauma in childhood / Lenore Terr.—1st ed.
        p.   cm.
    ISBN 0-06-016335-6
    1. Psychic trauma in children. I. Title.
RJ506.P66T47   1990
618.92'8521—dc20   89-46121

---

91 92 93 94 DT/RRD 10 9 8 7 6 5 4 3 2

To the kidnapped children of Chowchilla

The participants in a research study seldom benefit directly
from that study. Instead they give a kind of a gift to others.

I looked at the kidnappers, sort of like . . .
I was too scared to cry.

Billy Estes, age thirteen (1981)

Contents

PART IV: Treatment and Contagion of
Childhood Psychic Trauma

Preface

When I was young my mother allowed me to go to the Saturday afternoon matinee movies at one of two theaters within walking distance of our house. Sometimes I went with a friend. Other times I went alone. One Saturday on an "alone" day I watched a newsreel of the U.S. Army entering Hiroshima. The Americans were wearing space suits not unlike what the actors wore on *Green Lantern* and other such Saturday serials. I remember how Hiroshima looked on the screen—I can see it now as I write. The city was scorched white and leveled to the ground. There was a tower still standing, although that did not impress me. What got to me was a shadow.

The newsreel people had found a foot bridge at ground zero or near to it—and the bridge had been bleached of all color. But a man's shadow lay obliquely across the bridge. He must have been walking there, the movie announcer said, when the bomb vaporized him. (Vaporized!) We know he was there, however, the announcer went on, because the man's shadow had protected the bridge at the instant of highest intensity. (Protected!)

I took it all in. And I understood what I saw. It was either the most horrifying thing I have ever seen—or I was young enough to more fully absorb the horrors. At any rate, Hiroshima entered me by way of the eyes, by dint of a shadow. That shadow still lives today in my mind.

At nine, I recognized a psychological symptom when I had one—and indeed, I did have one then. From the moment I saw that newsreel, if a light was turned on in the middle of the night or if a sudden noise awoke me from sleep, my heart would start pounding at once even before I awoke. I would breathe in gasps, sweat, and say to myself, "This is it. The bomb." I would lie there for a minute—until I could orient myself—and I would wait to be vaporized.

I still have that symptom today. I suppose it's not so bad anymore. I can roll over and touch Ab in bed. I do not sleep quite as soundly as I used to, so the startling is not as intense as it once was. But the symptom still exists

—and at least once a year that same horror comes to me, "This is it! The bomb!"

I do not think I was ever fully traumatized as a child. But as soon as I began my training in psychiatry, I started doing research on childhood trauma—just like that. Part of my quickness to take to trauma, I suppose, was because my very first psychiatric patient was a mother who admitted she had almost drowned her toddler. But part of it, I must confess, was in order better to know myself, the self I had become after Hiroshima.

I write this book as a child psychiatric researcher and a therapist with a couple of pages of professional experience listed on my résumé. But I was impelled to the book as a fourth grader at a Saturday afternoon movie matinee. Some books take a while in the writing. This is one of those books.

Acknowledgments

I wish to thank several people and groups who helped me to organize and execute the research projects that stand at the center of this book. At Chowchilla, Romulo Gonzales, M.D., Mrs. Judy Johnson, Sheriff's Deputy Dale Fore, Alview-Dairyland School Superintendent Leroy Tatum, and District Attorney David Minier helped me start the project and keep it running. In McFarland and Porterville, Donald Duff, M.D., Patty Fiormonti, and Tom Fiormonti enabled me to get started. Three grand ladies of child psychoanalysis reviewed and critiqued the rough draft of my Chowchilla study—Marion Barnes, Selma Fraiberg, and Anna Freud. The Rockefeller Foundation in New York allowed me to work on my publications about the four- to five-year Chowchilla follow-up at their Study and Conference Center, Bellagio, in Lake Como, Italy. The Rosenberg Foundation in San Francisco funded the entire Chowchilla, Porterville, and McFarland project.

The *Challenger* space shuttle disaster field study was funded by the William T. Grant Foundation, New York. My on-site assistant was Mrs. SuzAnne Matayer of Biddeford, Maine. Both John Reinhart, Ph.D., Concord, New Hampshire, and Dan Bloch, Ph.D., Stanford University, consulted to the project. The Rockefeller Foundation allowed me to complete my writing at Bellagio.

This book was aided considerably by two very wise and patient professionals, my agent, Helen Rees, and my editor, Carol Cohen. A number of people in my psychiatric office worked on the research projects or directly on this book. They include Darney Martin, Lesley Chapman, Ellen Creese, Kate Hadley, Lisa Nicola, Marsha Bessey, and Carolyn Bristowe. Several friends critically reviewed the manuscript. They are Evelyne Keitel, Jo Keroes, Rosemary Patton, Joe McGerity, Robert Michels, and my daughter, Julia. Two lifelong friends, Phil and Peggy Wasserstrom, lent me their Hilton Head Island house several times so that I could write. My mother, Esther Cagen Raiken, conducted a massive literature search that is reflected on these pages.

My special thanks to my husband, Abba, with whom I share my office and my life, and my two grown children, David and Julia. Each of them holds a large stake in this book, as do my parents, Sam Cagen, who died in 1982, and Esther Cagen Raiken, my own personal librarian.

Approximately two hundred eighty-five youngsters have left traces of themselves upon the pages of this book. Two hundred nineteen participated in the research studies. Sixty-five saw me in consultations regarding a legal action, psychotherapy, or just an opinion. Each child, in my view, is a hero. Each helped me understand something new about trauma. To each of these unnamed children I send my deepest thanks, my good wishes, and my love.

CHAPTER 1

A First Glance at Childhood Trauma

Goddamn it. Why do I have to tell you stuff like this? Why do I have to go through this? Can't you give me something to shut my mind?
Charlotte Brent, age fifty-three

MOST VISITORS to San Francisco never see the beach. And if they do get the chance to drive by the Pacific on a tour bus or in a rental car, they stop at the Cliff House, look for sea lions on Seal Rock, scan the Farallon Islands far out to sea, and then duck back into the bus or car—a quick jump ahead of the fog.

There is an ocean beach there, though, for the natives—for those dwellers of the deep Richmond or the outer Sunset who moved in during the 1930s and then flooded the back dunes as soon as the postwar developers carried off the sand. But that's not the time we are thinking of right now —we're back at the beginning of 1930, when there were just four big things down at the beach: the Cliff House Restaurant, the Windmill, an amusement park called Playland, and a small Coast Guard compound, fenced off, just waiting for a war. At least, those four things were the landmarks on the beach for little Charlotte Brent.

"Charlie"—as she was called back then when she was two or three— was the daughter of a tattoo artist and his tattoo-designing wife. She was the granddaughter of a sea captain—a lonely child, a creature of the beach. Occasionally as a toddler Charlie stayed by herself while Mom and Dad were off tattooing a group of sailors near Playland. On adventurous days, Charlie might just toddle across the road to the sand. It was safe then. Or so everybody thought.

"I am in a huge room," she tells me on a warm Tuesday afternoon in September. "There are lines of bunk beds against the wall. Rows of clothes are hanging out, and as I step on a bunk, my nose touches the bottom of a

1

shirt. A light beam swings around. On-off-on-off. A man is there. Young. He is going to do something. Something terrible. It's over. Goddamn it," she goes on, "when will this stop?"

"Have you ever been inside the Coast Guard barracks?" I ask. "It sounds like the kind of place you're describing."

"I don't remember," she says, pale blue eyes dull with absence of recall. "What's clearest is the light. On and off. Blinking somehow."

When you walk the San Francisco Ocean Beach, a beam shoots out from the Point Reyes Light, far away but visible nonetheless. There's one much closer over at Point Bonita, but the Point Bonita Light does not seem to hit the condominiums that were put up in the early eighties on the lots where Playland-at-the-Beach once sat.

"I am in a closet. The door is open," she says in November. A fine drizzly rain grays the interior of my office. "A light—a strong one—is going on and off—swinging somewhere over me.

"I am small. Clothes brush the top of my head. I am hiding—I think in a closet—watching something. I hear grown-up voices talking low. Laughing. Hell, I hate this. Why do I have to go through this? A big overhead light suddenly turns on. I'm scared. I am in the Windmill, I think. Upstairs. People shove me out of a closet, where I have been hiding. A woman. A man. I don't know them. The woman shows me her breast—a tiny breast. She wants me to suck on it. I suck. I'm scared. They all laugh."

"Is the woman your mom?"

"God no. My mother had big breasts. No, this is somebody else. A stranger. Something is wrong with the whole thing—very wrong."

The Windmill is on the north side of Golden Gate Park just across from the beach. It recently has been renovated—a lady left money for that in her will. But nobody lives up there now—not since the thirties or the early forties. You never see a light upstairs. I hear, though, that the old place was a spot where some artists and "beach people" used to congregate to have a beer or two with the keeper, who was himself an artist. Could a toddler on the loose have hidden up there? Seen something? Done something? The Point Bonita Light would indeed have been visible from up there in the Windmill. Is this the place where something—"something wrong"—happened to young Charlotte? What happened? Did anything happen at all? How much of the nightmares she relates to me is imagination? Heavily disguised dream symbolism? Frustration?

"I had a different dream Tuesday night," Charlotte says on a Thursday afternoon. It is still November—rainy again. "There was a place at Playland where the guys who started and stopped the rides used to live—like a dormitory under the roller coaster. I'm there. I'm hiding I think. Under a cot. A guy is looking for me. He's going to do something. A bad thing. I'm scared. Terrified. But I can't move. And I think he sees me. That's it. Then it's over.

"I've been trying to will myself not to dream anymore, but it doesn't help. Do you think a person can get control over nightmares? How do I make them stop?"

How do you control dreams? I don't know. Some kids say they can will their dreams beforehand not to come—and some say they can go right back to sleep and end their dreams differently than before. But I can't prescribe a technique or a pill that would work every time.

"My nightmares show up in clusters," Charlotte goes on. "I've had the same ones all of my life, but never as many as I have now. I've been dreaming the most since I started going out with Jim." Charlotte Brent is fifty-three years old. A virgin. She has always preferred men as friends to women, but, also, as long as she can remember, she has felt repelled by the idea of sex. Ever since her school days, Charlotte has avoided anything even remotely romantic. She has been undergoing psychotherapy with me for about two years—because after her mother died, all her hopes collapsed. Charlotte simply could not envision managing alone.

She came up with the first "boyfriend" of her life a year after her mother died. Jim was a bachelor who delivered supplies to Charlotte's office. They had been close friends for years. I was trying to help Charlotte deal with her sexual revulsion, but it was slow going. I doubted we would be totally successful. If Charlotte could establish a good relationship with a man— even at this late date—her desperation might subside. We might be able to get her going.

One evening shortly before Christmas, Charlotte scares herself. She and Jim "park" at the Seal Rock Parking Lot, the point on the ocean that San Francisco teenagers use, always have used, for anything but watching the waves. Charlotte and Jim have ostensibly stopped to chat. They sit—a fifty-three-year-old spinster and her sixty-year-old bachelor friend—in Jim's Ford. They find themselves kissing. Charlotte likes it. "Why hadn't I done this before?" she thinks. And then "Charlie" does something automatic—as if it is something she had always been programmed to do. She unzips Jim's fly and puts his penis in her mouth—an uncharacteristic act from a spinster, a prudish lady who lives alone with her dog. Jim is shocked. He does not, cannot, respond. Charlotte, herself, is mortified and asks to go home. They never speak of it. They no longer are friends—not even talking acquaintances. It's all over.

"Another one today," she hesitates before telling me her dream. It is spring. Jim, granted an urgent request for early retirement, has moved away. "I am running on the sand. The light—the same one—is beaming on and off near me. I am with some guy. He is tall, younger than my parents. His pants—sailor pants, I think (because of all those laces)—are open. He sticks something hard, wet, big in my mouth. I hate it. There is a lady nearby. She is laughing. I think she's the same lady with the small breasts. I hear her laugh. And I hate it. Goddamn it. Why do I have to tell you stuff like this? Why do I have to go through this? Can't you give me something to shut my mind?"

Sex dreams from under the bed—from below the clothes in a darkened closet—from the level of a grown man's leg—these are the nightmares of a fifty-three-year-old virgin. What, if anything, really happened to Charlotte Brent at two or three? We will never know. Fifty years after an event, it is impossible to put the pieces of the "truth" back together. I have a hunch that Charlotte, the toddler, was forced into a series of oral sex acts with adults—perhaps with a group who knew each other—sailors, carny workers, and their girl(s)—at the beach, near the beach, or around the "landmarks" of old San Francisco-by-the-ocean. But there is no way to check out the hunch. "Reality" is gone. Forgotten. What lives on is an inner reality, a trap inside the self from which the adult Charlotte cannot escape.

Charlotte has no waking memories of her disaster. Her repeated nightmares, her fears of sex, and her one odd piece of behavior in a well-known parking lot are the only signs that anything ever happened to her. When Charlotte was placed in a position that she might have—if her life had been more ordinary—assumed as an adolescent, she found herself behaving as if oral sex was the only sex that she knew, the only sex that she wanted, the only sex that ever existed. We can never discover the nature of young Charlie's ordeal. All we can see now is the distorted reflection of that ordeal in a fifty-three-year-old woman's mind.

It is difficult for the psychiatrist to piece together very early events in life from what an adult says. Even though the theme of a particular nightmare repeats itself many times, the dream usually varies enough over the months or years that the "truth" arrives each time wearing a new mask. Furthermore, an adult's waking actions will not exactly duplicate what happened during early childhood, will not precisely repeat the old "truth." The psychiatrist will rarely capture a forgotten event in pure form from an adult. The psychoanalyst Ernst Kris said in 1956, "We are misled if we believe that we are, except in rare instances, able to find [in adult patients] the 'events' of the afternoon on the staircase when the [childhood] seduction happened: we are dealing with the whole period in which the seduction played a role—and in some instances this period may be an extended one. The problem is further complicated by the fact that the further course of life seems to determine which [childhood] experience may gain significance as a traumatic one." Psychiatrists recognized for many years what I had

just seen for myself in Charlotte Brent—that a series of very early childhood shocks might not be fully and accurately "reconstructed" from the
dreams and behaviors of the adult.

But what of the children themselves? If you caught a young person early
enough, could you recognize the aftermath of a terrible event? Could you
find the "truth"? Wouldn't it be easier to pick up the memories of a
childhood trauma while they were still fresh? And if you did, wouldn't you
be able to cut the injuries short by working sooner with the remembrances?

Over the past centuries, children probably were saying quite a bit about
traumas, but few adults seemed to pay attention. Most parents tended not
to ask. Even physicians shied away from examining kids' real experiences.
If nobody said anything during a disaster, maybe a child wouldn't notice.
If children weren't reminded of events, maybe they could forget.

We must look eventually, however, if we are ever going to be able to
understand frightened children. And so let us examine one youngster's
memories of a terrifying event to see how a child's recollections would
compare to the fifty-year-old memories of the unfortunate Charlotte Brent,
to "hear" how a child's reactions sound when told closer to the time that
a terrifying reality actually struck home.

Eight-year-old Alan Bascombe came to me for examination five years
after he was kidnapped for ransom by a stranger, an event that occurred
when Alan was thirty-nine-months old. After almost five years had elapsed,
Alan's parents decided they needed to know what, if anything, Alan had
remembered of it—how he had felt then and, perhaps, how he still felt
about it. Alan was a good student, popular with his peers, and responsible,
though quiet, at home. The Bascombes did not think he had problems.

Alan's parents, leading citizens of their midsized, southern city, believed
it was better to "let the whole thing die." They doubted that their boy still
thought about the kidnapping. A friend of the Bascombes, however, a child
psychiatrist, told them that an expert should hear Alan out. "Did Alan still
remember? Did it affect him? Did he know how close he came to being
killed?" No one, the child psychiatrist told his friends, knew what young
Alan was really feeling. So, on the psychiatrist's advice, the three Bascombes came to see me in San Francisco, and we arranged for a few
appointments over a couple days' time.

"My mom let me take my nap in my blanket tunnel." The nice-looking
boy appears calm, unaffected, and ordinary as he glances about my office.
"I heard footsteps. I woke up. I went into the tunnel thing. I didn't have
time to put my pants on. The man aimed a revolver at Mom. She lay on
the floor. He took me in a car. On a hill I said, 'I want to go back to my
mom,' and the man said, 'You will.' [Alan's voice imitates the voices as
they, then, must have sounded. He had been terrified of losing Mom, and

his emotions begin to sound more immediate as he delivers his now-ancient dialogue.]

"He asked me if I wanted a Coke or 7-Up and I said, '7-Up,' and we went to his apartment. He let me call Mom lots of times. I pushed over his bed. I went to sleep. The next morning he took me to the airport—pushed me out of his car. A lady came. The FBI takes me in. [Alan breaks into present tense here because his release by the kidnapper still stirs up vivid feelings, feelings of immediate danger.] The FBI man takes me in a car. I see Channel 2 News. He takes me to my house. I watched the news. Dad was smoking a cigarette. Then I saw Channel 8 News with my neighbor. Then I went out to play. Nobody let me watch TV after that."

Alan's handsome face recomposes itself. But he now turns directly to me and, unasked, revolves his story once again: "There were regular footsteps on my stairs. I thought it was my dad coming home early from work. I just woke up to see Dad. And it is another man! [The boy seems alarmed. He no longer glances around my office—or really looks at me. He is looking inward, I think.] I was frightened. I didn't know him. I didn't know that this was going to happen. I was trying to put on my underpants. He was scary looking—dark sunglasses, a big coat. He was just real scary. He had brown hair and was about two inches bigger than my dad. [The inches must have been appended to Alan's story later, after he reached school age.] I saw no gun. He said to follow him and I did. He wouldn't give me a chance to put on my pants. [Alan's concern for his state of undress is interesting. At the young age of three years, three months, he was apparently developing some modesty.]

"Before he was about to take me I saw him holding a gun. Mom was in her bedroom taking a nap. He stayed in the hall and asked me to come, and Mom came out and I saw him making Mom get on the floor. I thought he would shoot Mom. I used to play with toy guns. The guy's gun looked like it shot arrows. [Alan is telling a toddler-aged thought. He realizes now that handguns shoot bullets, but at three years of age, he thought they shot arrows.]

"I got in his car. I fell down just before I was going in. I hurt my knees. I was coming down the stairs and I scratched my nose and my fingers, too. I remember my feelings. The man said, 'You'll see your mother,' and I believed him. [Alan sounds surprised that he would ever have believed a kidnapper.] I felt better when he told me that. When he got the 7-Up I felt he had just brought me out to get a Coke. [Alan, at eight, recalls his naive three-year-old hypotheses here, that someone would take you at gunpoint solely to buy you a Coke.] But then when he took me to his apartment, I got scared all over again. I thought, 'I'll never see Mom again.' I was not worried about death. I was afraid that he would injure my arm. He got close to my arm at his apartment. He touched it, pulled at it, because he wanted me to go to sleep. He told me to sleep on the ground. I didn't want to go to sleep. He pulled me. [Alan looks upset again. His sentences are becoming clipped.]

"I wanted to phone Mom. He told me I could. He woke me at 8 or 8:30 in the morning. Took me to his car. I still had no pants on. I was embarrassed. But I didn't tell the man I wanted pants. He had me in a blanket. He took me in the car and said he'd take me somewhere.

"I have a blanket on. It is a short ride. [Both times that this final rescue scene comes up, Alan uses present tense. He is describing a terrible moment for him, a time he knows now, and perhaps knew then, that he was in great peril.] The man stopped, said nothing, and pushes me out of the car —a light push. I walked. Ran. Didn't see anybody I know. Still had on the blanket. Saw two ladies. They asked me my name. I said, 'Bascombe.' She picked me up and the FBI came.

"It felt shorter than a whole day. Felt like a nap, not like a whole sleep. The man did not really talk to me. When the FBI came, I thought *they* were kidnappers, too. When the FBI man first came out, I thought he was trying to put me on an airplane—that he was another kidnapper. He put me in a car and talked to me in the car. I can't remember what he said. He had a gun. His gun scared me. He shotted at the kidnapper. And I was there!" The escape, it seems, was every bit as scary as the abduction itself.

Now Alan gives one of his own motives for willingly, enthusiastically coming to a psychiatrist halfway across the country almost five years after the event had concluded happily—a pressing reason, as a matter of fact. "A boy this year was at the park across town. He was three just like me. A man—or a lady—took him. I don't know why. And then she killed him. [Alan fidgets with some paper clips on my desk.] I felt funny. The little kid had the same first name as me—Alan—and he was the same age, three. At the time it happened to me I thought, 'There will be another kidnapped.' I don't think my thinking caused *that* Alan's kidnapping but I always knew that it would happen again. And the boy died. I think that the kidnapper of that boy got his idea for kidnapping off me—off what happened to me.

"I already know what it's like to die—to be killed. You feel real scared. Can't breathe. I learned that when I was five or six years old and realized that he could have killed me. [Alan says here that he added the fear of death to his memories long after the experience was over. In the same way that inches as measures of the kidnapper's height were added to Alan's memory as he grew older, the idea of death was superimposed onto Alan's remembrance as he came to understand more.]

"I think back now on when I was three and kidnapped. I didn't talk to that kidnapper. I wasn't a talker when I was three—I was a crier. I didn't cry when he took me, though. And I still don't know why."

Alan Bascombe can vividly remember at age eight how an ordeal at three years old feels. He still knows. As opposed to Charlotte Brent, who hates her dreams but no longer can feel her past emotions in the waking state, Alan can still sense it—live it—and, at least, when he is forced to think back, experience it.

An intense, shocking, unexpected incident does to you just what Alan says it does—you can't cry. You are so surprised, so overwhelmed, that you feel lucky not to die with a crazy heart rhythm or a burst blood vessel. However, the overall mechanics of the human body almost always can withstand sudden horrors. Despite the premise of the French movie *Les Diaboliques,* which shows people successfully scaring their victims to death, the body ordinarily appears to recover well from the adrenaline rushes and furious mental activities accompanying emotional shocks (although a recent medical paper indicates that upsetting events may occasionally precipitate damage to the retina in adults). Despite the fact that repeated or sustained externally generated stresses sometimes lead to chronic physical problems, the brunt of single, shocking episodes tends to fall upon the mind alone.

"Psychic trauma" occurs when a sudden, unexpected, overwhelmingly intense emotional blow or a series of blows assaults the person from outside. Traumatic events are external, but they quickly become incorporated into the mind. A person probably will not become fully traumatized unless he or she feels utterly helpless during the event or events.

For many years, from the 1940s through the mid 1970s, the lay public thought it understood "trauma." People tended to use the term in a sloppy, all-knowing, but really unknowing, way—"He was traumatized when his younger brother was born," or "He was traumatized living in that housing project," or "Can you imagine anything more traumatic than breaking up with your boyfriend over the telephone?" Writers regularly put the word "trauma" into their scripts and climaxed their films with pop psychologies of trauma. You may remember *Spellbound,* for instance, in this context. John Ballantine (played by Gregory Peck) uncovers with the help of his lover-psychiatrist (played by Ingrid Bergman) a buried childhood memory of the fatal accident to his brother he witnessed when he was nine or so—something for which the young man had come to feel everlastingly guilty. Repression of childhood trauma leads, Alfred Hitchcock seems to want us to believe, to new episodes of total amnesia when an adult experiences something like the first trauma. This "new" amnesia is the major problem for the character played by Gregory Peck.

But this rarely is a problem for the real victim of childhood trauma. Do you remember how Elizabeth Taylor was forced by her psychiatrist, Montgomery Clift, to recall the cannibalistic, homosexual killing that she had "forgotten" as an adult from just the summer before (in Tennessee William's *Suddenly Last Summer*)? Trauma, according to the movies, is registered and then completely forgotten. This, too, is untrue. Single shocks in adult life are remembered clearly rather than fading out of consciousness.

A major factor underlying the public's misuse and misunderstanding of "trauma" until recently was that psychiatry itself did not know much about the extreme events in childhood. No psychiatrist had followed young victims over an extended period of time and nobody had used a normal control group for comparison. Gregory Peck and Elizabeth Taylor, therefore, couldn't look silly—nobody knew how trauma really looked.

Early in his career, Sigmund Freud was interested in terrible realities, especially childhood seductions, in his patients' backgrounds. But by the late 1890s Freud had found a new point of emphasis, attributing the stories that adults told him to their internal fantasies, fantasies originating with fearful, naughty wishes from childhood. The possibility that a child had really been raped, that he had really watched a baby die, or that he had really ventured too close to a rearing horse—this kind of externally derived "truth" no longer attracted Freud.

In 1983, the psychoanalyst Jeffrey Masson stimulated tremendous flak inside and outside the profession by concluding, on the basis of his readings of Freud's unpublished letters, that Freud had lost interest in actual childhood sexual ordeals because he feared disapproval from his own colleagues. Whether or not Masson was right, it is true that after 1897, Freud, the founder of psychoanalysis, showed only occasional and passing concern for outside events as they affected the childhoods and later lives of his patients. He gave us good definitions for trauma in 1920 ("a breach in the barrier against stimulus") and 1926 ("the sense of utter helplessness"), but he no longer gave the "external" world much standing in his theoretical framework.

One would have thought that the psychiatrists and psychoanalysts who followed Freud might have turned the field's attention back to the external "realities," but they did not. The inner origins of experience held so much fascination for them that the influence of external events stayed relatively out-of-sight. Even during World War II, psychoanalysts who dealt with children were not particularly drawn to psychic trauma. Anna Freud, Sigmund's daughter and herself a distinguished child analyst, set up a young children's "nursery" at Hampstead, England, for preschoolers evacuated during the German bombings of London. The excellent and very moving studies that she and her colleagues accomplished with these youngsters concerned themselves, however, largely with the effects upon children of separations, not with the effects of profound fright. Problems of maternal-child separation were very important in wartime London where many youngsters were evacuated from the city. But so was the Blitz. The Blitz, however, was not studied at Hampstead. Most psychological observations during World War II, as a matter of fact, dealt with the wartime mother-child dyad or with the guardian-child duo—not with the child's subjective experience of terror. From the war, therefore, the lay public arrived at ideas like "children panic when their parents panic" or "children will forget their bad times," while, at the same time, few direct studies of battle-exposed kids were actually accomplished.

The first "breakthrough" scientific project on childhood trauma came after the war, in 1956, when a group of National Institute of Mental Health investigators checked out the psychological aftereffects of a 1953 tornado at Vicksburg, Mississippi. A wind had leveled a movie theater during the Saturday afternoon kiddie matinee. Several young people were killed and everybody was scared. But the Vicksburg study, scientific as it was, threw little light onto the nature of childhood psychic trauma because the investigators interviewed parents only. They did not see the kids. When they concluded, as did their predecessors from World War II, that after traumatic events nervous parents would create nervous children, no other end point could have been reached. The study had been set up that way— the conclusions reflected the researchers' assumptions and methods, not the real experiences of the children at Vicksburg.

After the war most of the "psychology of the external" shifted away from maternal separation, war, and disaster to the more common "life stresses" of childhood. The stress researches of the 1960s and 1970s— much of it interesting and quite good—brought to light a special resiliency youngsters exhibit in their day-to-day lives. Living with psychotic parents or going through ruptures of parental marriages, personal illnesses, and social disruptions seemed to be weathered by most kids. One could reach the conclusion from these studies that no matter what you did to a child, he would manage pretty well.

But life stresses are not psychological trauma. Stress is different from a single overwhelming experience or a series of overwhelming ordeals. Stress is to be expected in an ordinary lifetime. Traumatic events are not. The stress researchers of the sixties and seventies were reporting on day-by-day coping styles developed by children to deal with long-standing life situations, expected ones, chronic ones, and, for the most part, manageable ones.

Despite the fact that childhood psychic trauma was assumed to be understood while simultaneously being ignored through the midcentury decades, however, a few psychiatrists were beginning to listen to children, taking note of what the children themselves were saying about their own personal shocks. David Levy, a gifted child psychiatrist who practiced in midtown Manhattan, observed in 1945 that youngsters fared after surgery similarly to American soldiers who had been evacuated because of "trauma" from the European battlefields. The soldiers had experienced nightmares—so did the kids. The soldiers acted fearful—the youngsters did, too. Levy's report of the traumatic responses in children who had undergone surgery led to an overdue humanism at the hospital. Levy also picked up an eager audience of child psychiatrists, an audience that grows today, years after his death.

Princess Marie Bonaparte and Phyllis Greenacre, both psychoanalysts who worked with adult patients after the war, valued the importance of old childhood traumas as they were expressed in their patient's mental lives. Greenacre argued in the professional literature that psychoanalytic "reconstruction" of real childhood experiences would lead to a better understanding of the adult personality. Marie Bonaparte claimed that finding old traumas would promote better therapeutic results from psychoanalysis. Most analysts, however, were not particularly interested in following Greenacre's and Bonaparte's leads. They were intrigued, instead, with how the subjective experience of an actual event would be incorporated into preexisting fantasy.

A few psychoanalysts who specialized in young people (for instance, Erna Furman, Marion Barnes, and Hansi Kennedy) tried to demonstrate that real events could create real mental effects. Barnes's report about the effects of a young mother's sudden death on her two little girls, as a matter of fact, gave detail upon detail that demonstrated what happens inside young children's minds after shocking tragedy. But these single cases did not fire up much professional enthusiasm. By the 1960s and 1970s child psychiatry had become far too adept at working with the developing drives and childhood fantasies to value the "real." It would take more than the urgings of a few people reporting upon a few cases to turn the attention of the field to terrifying childhood actualities.

Reality, in other words, was being glanced at and then overlooked by the child psychiatrists and psychoanalysts of the midcentury in much the same fashion that reality had come to disappear for the photographer in Cortázar's short story and Antonioni's film *Blow-Up*. The young man of *Blow-Up* enlarges and reenlarges his shot until he can see only his inner fantasy, not the murder that he may or may not have witnessed.

In the 1970s, however, two studies of childhood trauma began to focus everyone's attention upon trauma. The first project was done at Aberfan, Wales, after a slag heap hurtled down a mountainside and destroyed the mining town's elementary school on October 21, 1966. Twenty-eight adults and 116 school children died at Aberfan. Some of the youngsters who had survived (all, of course, were enrolled in Great Britain's National Health Service) came for appointments—as needed—to the local child psychiatrist, a doctor named Gaynor Lacey. Lacey did not think of himself as doing research. He simply reported what he saw in fifty-six young patients who visited him over a five-year period following the disaster. Although he did not put names to what he observed, Lacey described some grim, monotonous play, some changes in developing personalities, and some odd behaviors. Lacey arranged his conclusions to the old World War II "nervous mother, nervous child" refrain, but his fresh descriptions of youngsters' behaviors *away* from their parents forced psychiatrists reading him to think in quite different directions.

The second influential study was done by C. Janet Newman following the collapse of a slag dam on Buffalo Creek. An isolated West Virginia "holler" was inundated one February morning in 1972 by a "crick" flood that behaved like a tidal wave engulfing whole communities with black, muddy water after a man-made dam gave way high above the Buffalo Creek valley. There were 125 deaths. Even those adults who had not been physically present in the valley at the time of the flood were found—later, on examination by members of a University of Cincinnati psychiatric team —to have suffered emotional harm. Newman, a Cincinnati professor, interviewed eleven children who had witnessed the flood and, in several instances, had lost a family member or a friend in the torrent. She wrote about these youngsters' gloomy outlooks, their perpetual mourning, their senses of lost "invincibility," and their daydreams of death and disfigurement. These were new pieces of information. Although Newman's conclusions carried echoes of the old idea that worried mothers forced imitative behaviors from their children, her vivid observations laid a path for others to follow. Newman's traumatized kids were examined away from their parents. She used "draw me a picture" and "give me three wishes" techniques to bring out the children's underlying concerns. The Buffalo Creek children presented themselves as very troubled, indeed, through these drawings, wishes, and dreams. Thanks to Lacey and Newman, then, the traumatized child was finally beginning to emerge as a person in his own right, a person worthy of individual study and treatment.

Such was the situation in the summer of 1976. The public seemed confident that it knew what psychic trauma was—we had seen enough film "psychology" on the subject, to be sure. But psychiatry really did not know much. How overwhelming events would be experienced during the various stages of child development, how they would be felt by kids of various cultural, social, and ethnic backgrounds, how they would be sensed within the larger settings of the family or community, and how they would look over time—all these remained a mystery. A large-scale study was waiting to be done. But first something had to happen. Unfortunately, it would have to be something terrible.

Most drivers zipping down California's Central Valley never catch a glimpse of a place called Chowchilla. As you take Route 99, the commercial route through the San Joaquin Valley, you come to a fig ranch. Dark, shiny leaves mushroom from smooth gray trunks, creating a squat, exotic forest. The figs mark the turnoff. About a half mile back, the town is heralded by a billboard picturing a smiling Indian and the words "Honest Injun. There's a heap of good living here." Otherwise you cannot see Chowchilla at all from the road.

Chowchilla (pronounced Chow-chill-a), with its population of 5,000, spreads out neatly on good, flat ranch land. Most acreage adjacent to town belongs to giant agricultural corporations that specialize in almonds, peaches, apricots, and cotton. In 1976 a cream of tartar factory was providing the local industry, but by 1980 it had closed down and a new roofing plant was taking up the slack. In winter a low-lying "tule fog" lends a bone-rattling chill to the landscape, but by summer the sun blazes steadily for six months and the temperatures reach to the 110s for days on end. As you drive down the palm- and oleander-lined main street you see stores for a few blocks, a couple of "official" buildings, a church, a library, two schools, an old-fashioned town park, and then the houses that become sparser and sparser as your eye scans across the flatlands to meet California's coastal range at the far distance.

Chowchilla is a middle-class farm town. There is some poverty but no affluence. Nobody you meet in town owns any farmland, and farmland equals money in the San Joaquin Valley. The Central Valley itself looks a little poorer around Chowchilla than it does forty to fifty miles north in the lush dairy and apricot country between Turlock and Patterson or forty to fifty miles south near the bustling surrounds of the "Valley capital," Fresno. The Chowchilla people are handsome and healthy looking though: sleekly black-haired Chicanos; nickel-perfect American Indians; olive-skinned Portuguese who came to the Central Valley long ago for now unknown reasons (at least that's what Mr. Donnario, a Portuguese farmer, says); and tanned, bandeau-topped shorts-clad mid-America Americans. At the town park, one table of long-haired, shirtless young people phlegmatically pick at a guitar, drink beer, and occasionally pass around a joint. On Robertson Boulevard, the main street that abuts the park, an unending stream of cars cruises back and forth, back and forth. A funeral occasionally goes by. In general, the traffic is entirely local and easily recognizable by town residents, adults and children alike.

Chowchilla summers are uncomplicated and hot. Teenagers cannot find jobs unless their own families are able to employ them. A local swimming pool meets some of the demand for activity, as does a roller rink and some organized ball teams for both boys and girls. Some families with American Indian blood attend an occasional powwow. But school is the main summer vacation activity for the average Chowchilla kid. It's not a school entirely—it works, in part, like a daycamp. The rural Alview-Dairyland School District runs the program, and since most local children attend the Chowchilla district "town schools" from September through June (funny that such a small place should maintain two separate school systems), the youngsters do not know their summer school teachers and bus drivers as well as they know the "town" school personnel.

It was Thursday, July 15, 1976, a blazing hot and increasingly humid day in Chowchilla, the end of the next to the last day of summer school. Tomorrow it would be all parties. The Dairyland school bus was ambling along a back country road dropping off kids, some of them still wet from the afternoon swim, the final activity of a busy day in which the sixth graders had performed a play called *Born To Be Free,* an irony that later did not escape some of its audience.

The school bus slowed down as it approached a broken-down-looking white van partly obstructing the narrow backcountry road. As Jack Wynne, the bus driver, put on his brakes to get past, a masked gunman suddenly jumped out of the van and ordered Jack to open up. Another man wearing a stocking over his face leaped onto the bus as the doors sprang open, shouting at Jack and the first three rows of children to get to the back. (This, in effect, separated the youngest from the oldest kids. The biggest children at Chowchilla had always tended to sit in the front of the bus, and all others had automatically filed in behind them.)

The new "busmaster" barked at everybody to "Shut up." His buddy took the wheel, and the school bus began to roll. While the new lord of the bus kept his gun trained at the kids, a third member of the gang followed in the white van, which now, of course, did not appear broken down at all. The sorry little caravan of two drove down the country road, past a church, houses, tractors, and ranchers working the fields. Some people said later that they had "seen," but they did not really "look." Nobody really took in that school bus and its strange white escort as they melted into the line of the horizon.

"Hold tight!" a gun-toting masked man ordered. The bus clattered down into a steep rainwater runoff gully, the Berenda Slough. (Chowchillans pronounce it "Brenda.") The doors opened and the leader ordered the group to get off the bus one by one. The oldest children began to file out and, to the eyes of those still on the bus, they seemed to be disappearing into the white van. Suddenly a gun butt slammed into ten-year-old Terrie Thornton's belly. "Stop," the man shouted at her. The van was filled. It drove off and disappeared from sight. Terrie's stomach ached.

Another van that must have been parked in the slough all along, a green one, pulled up next to the bus. Terrie, the younger group of children, and Jack Wynne, the bus driver, filed into this one, one at a time. When the last kid was inside, it too drove out of the slough. The school bus was abandoned, empty.

The kids were a few minutes late. Some Chowchilla mothers started to fret. After about an hour's wait, a number of parents became truly alarmed. Nobody at the school office could say what was happening. There was no word of the bus. Within the next hour the school superintendent and a group of fathers went out searching the bus route for a broken-down bus, a bunch of tired kids, an accident, whatever. Soon it was clear—the children had totally disappeared. The sheriff came. So, eventually, did the FBI. And if *that* happens, so does the media. In that way the International News Story of 1976, "the Chowchilla School Bus Kidnapping," was on its way, rolling along parallel to, but not at all in sync with, those two boarded-up vans full of kids.

The children pitched about at extremely close quarters on hard wooden benches for hour after hour. They had no idea what had happened to the other half of the group. It was totally dark inside of each van. A barrier built between the front seat and the back portion of the vehicle prevented anyone from communicating with the driver. The youngsters were hungry, but no one gave them a bite. They complained of thirst, but there was nothing to drink. They desperately needed to go to the bathroom and each child discovered that he had a simple choice, to retain urine or to let go.

The youngsters were crammed in so tight that one child's sweat would trickle down another child's arm. A stench of sweat and urine infused the air. Closed-up vans on a California midsummer's eve had become Poe's "pit." Without any light, food, water, bathrooms, or talk with the men who had taken them, the children bounced about for eleven hours—an endless drive to nowhere. Two "lucky" kids in the green van were able to cling to Jack Wynne, who sat between them on their wooden bench. Jack didn't say much, but what was there to say? The younger kids sang "If You're Happy and You Know It, Clap Your Hands—Clap Clap." Nobody clapped. They went on and on with it.

The white van stopped, and some of the older kids inside it smelled gas. They felt the vehicle begin to back up. Three kids told each other the men had put their van into reverse for a free-fall from a cliff. They would die right now, they said. But nothing happened. Another boy was sure that the gas he smelled would be used in another minute to burn them all up. But the white van started forward once more, and the bouncing on the way to "nowhere" started up all over again.

They stopped. This time the vans stayed put. It was about three in the morning. Somebody outside ordered, "Get out when I tell you to." In the older kids' van, the white one, several youngsters jockeyed for the order in which they would get out. The first one and the last one might be shot, several kids figured. Or maybe all of them would be killed one at a time. Hadn't somebody seen an old World War II Battle of the Bulge movie where that had happened to a truckload of GIs?

Each child in turn was placed under a tent-like canopy to be questioned by a masked, illuminated man (flashlight under the chin) while another masked man aimed his gun right at the kid. Nearby there was a ladder that led down into a "hole" in the ground. The spooky, lit-up man demanded the child's full name, and he took away one special thing—a toy, a T-shirt, a bathing suit top, a lunch pail, or the contents of a pocket. The man then ended the interview. "Get down into that hole," he said. Legally blind Sammy Smith threw his shoes at the guy who had just taken away his glasses. But Sammy missed. Luck was never Sammy's strong suit. One shoe hit something and bounced right back into the blind boy's face.

Whatever their ostensible reasons for taking the kids' names and things, these three men were, indeed, stripping their little captives of their identities. Like the most adept of Chinese brainwashers, the Chowchilla kidnappers were forcing their little charges into submission.

Not everybody gave in without comment, however. Six-year-old Benji Banks appointed himself his five-year-old girlfriend's protector. "Don't you touch Susan," he warned the men. Eleven-year-old Johnny Johnson docilely gave up his tennis shoes, but then told a joke: "Now they'll have to smell them, not me."

As the kids descended into the "hole," they finally could see the siblings and friends from whom they had been separated throughout the terrifying eleven hours of riding in separate vans. They felt some relief. For a long time they had had no idea what had happened to their sisters, brothers, and friends. They had made it. So what worse could happen?

After a while, even in such circumstances, any kid can get a little curious. A few of the group began to explore. They found a large rectangular space lit with flashlights and inadequately serviced by a tiny fan. Stale Cheerios, soggy potato chips, and a jar of peanut butter had been left out. Everything tasted "yukky." Everybody drank big slugs of musty-tasting water from the large cans lying about. A stacked-up pile of old mattresses was waiting there, and two places, one marked "Boys" and the other "Girls," looked like primitive bathrooms. While a few kids guarded the others' modesties by holding up towels, all but two of the youngsters were able to relieve themselves. Carl Murillo swore that he heard one of the men say he would return, but nobody else had heard any such promise. A couple of boys recognized the bathrooms to be wheel wells—they were inside a huge truck, they told the others. But most of the kids just went by their first impression. It was the "hole," and it stayed the "hole."

Suddenly the children and their bus driver began to hear the sounds of shoveling above them. Dirt and stones were pelting the ceiling of their "hole." They were being buried alive. They were being killed. Murdered. A few youngsters begged and shouted. A few whimpered. Jack, the bus driver, implored the men to stop, to have mercy. He fell on his knees and prayed to God. But the dirt kept clanging over their heads. Finally, Jack lay down and cried. They were all "goners," he said.

Some children whispered, but after a while the "hole" was quiet. The hours dragged on. Many slept. Others just sat there doing nothing. Few talked. It was almost entirely dark now. Nobody wanted to waste the precious flashlight batteries. After all, how long would they be imprisoned? When would they *really* need a light? How long would their air hold up?

It was quiet. And as the California world slept, the police found an abandoned Dairyland-Alview school bus in the Berenda Slough. It looked like a kidnapping—a mass kidnapping.

One bystander did stay awake most of the night—little Timmy Donnario, a Chowchilla kindergartner. He had been let off Jack Wynne's bus just minutes before it was hijacked. The reason that Timmy had escaped the kidnapping was like "magic." Mrs. Donnario, Timmy's mother, had wondered for weeks why Timmy, who lived the closest of any kid to the summer school, had been let off the bus last each day—on Jack's return trip. So, late in the season, she had asked Jack Wynne timidly to discharge little Timmy first from the bus—not last. Mrs. Donnario made her request just two or three days before the school bus was hijacked. Summer school was already into its final week.

When the children were discovered missing, the director of the Dairyland school system, Leroy Tatum, came over to question Timmy. The young boy felt responsible. *His* bus was missing. The formidable school superintendent was visiting at *his* house. Then the police, too, arrived to question *him*. And they questioned five-year-old Timmy for hours. The humidity increased. The sky blackened. It started to pour. An FBI agent rang the Donnario's front bell. It was late. The exhausted kindergartner needed some sleep. But each of the investigators *had* to have some answers. Thunder rumbled and lightning flickered over the flat landscape. They needed Tim to provide the clues. But the very young boy knew nothing. Absolutely nothing.

Sometime during the day of July 16, 1976, a new crisis developed down in the "hole." Eight-year-old Louis Murillo, a shy, slow learner whose primary language was Spanish, leaned too hard against a tall wooden stake in the center of the "hole," which must have been put there to support the dirt-heavy roof. The makeshift "pillar" suddenly gave way, and the ceiling began to collapse upon the children—much as the Philistine roof had collapsed when the biblical Samson leaned too hard against his pillar.

Some children who realized the seriousness of this newest threat screamed at the bewildered Louis Murillo and cried out in fright to the others. All but one kid woke up.

The crisis of the "hole's" collapsing ceiling was enough of an emergency to evoke some action. The children could plainly see that if they didn't do something soon, they would all die. Flashlights snapped on. Several older boys and the bus driver inspected the sagging ceiling, and they discovered that the kidnappers had covered their entrance to the "hole" with a metal plate. With tremendous effort, the boys and Jack Wynne were able to move the steel plate aside. Two older boys, Bob Barklay, fourteen, and Carl Murillo, ten, then lowered down into Jack's grasp two 100 pound batteries that had been jammed into the small entrance area above the plate. Hispanic American Carl Murillo discovered that he could stand in the newly evacuated space and Bob climbed up to join him. The two boys, squeezed together like pickles in a jar, began to pry open the top of their cubicle. Bob Barklay was the strongest. He found that if he jammed mattress coils up against the wood the kidnappers had hammered together at the entry-way into the buried truck, he could break it up. Eventually Bob and Carl scooped down handfuls of dirt into the "hole." Little by little they were making progress. They were digging a tunnel through the ceiling and the dirt above it back to the outside world.

Bob did most of the digging while Carl Murillo helped. Terrie Thornton held the flashlight for them even though one of the kids had told her that girls weren't supposed to work. Janice Bennett, twelve, did the more traditional girl's job—she "babysat" the littlest ones. Johnny Johnson, who was almost a full year older than Carl Murillo, desperately wanted to help pry up the cubicle, too, but somebody down in the "hole" told him that he was too fat. Grumbling, Johnny removed dirt below. Sammy Smith wanted to help even though he was blind. But when Sammy worked a few minutes in the cubicle, he fainted. Jack Wynne, the bus driver, determined too that he would dig, but, like Sammy, he was forced back down from the cubicle within minutes—defeated.

For hours, Bob and Carl pried and scooped while the other children slept or just sat there. Finally the two boys stopped. The space they had excavated was big enough to allow an adult's body to get by. But nobody was eager to leave the "hole." Maybe something else would happen.

Bob Barklay poked his head out first, keeping it low so that it might not be blown off his body when the guns he was sure were there started to shoot. Bellying like a snake along the ground, Bob dove into some bushes several yards past the "hole." So did his fellow "hero" Carl. Following them, the other children emerged from the hole one by one. Jack Wynne, entirely mobilized now, lifted the youngsters out of the buried truck-trailer and went off to find a phone. It was dusk—Friday the 16th. The group didn't know it then, but the world was waiting for them.

The children emerged into the desolation of a Livermore Valley rock quarry owned by Mr. Frederick Newhall Woods, Jr., a member of a distinguished San Francisco family and a "regular" in Peninsula "society." The Chowchilla children were almost one hundred miles from home. They were in a strange valley, and they still did not know what had happened.

The Alameda County sheriff's deputies arrived within minutes of Jack Wynne's call. They tried to load kids onto buses, but were entirely unable to get a steady head count. The nature of the problem was soon clear. The smallest kids kept squirming off the bus trying to hide. They were slippery as tadpoles. Who could trust buses any longer? A deputy recognized that something was quite wrong.

Finally rounded up, the exhausted children were taken to the Alameda County Prison at Santa Rita for questioning, physical examinations (fifteen minutes each), all the hamburgers and apple pie they could eat, and naps. The two prison doctors who examined the children, a pediatrician and a general practitioner, found the kids to be in good shape. They called for no psychiatrists—no social workers or psychologists either. Nobody. After all, the kids seemed to be making sense and none of them were acting strange. Nobody was hysterical. Nobody shook. Nobody was crazy. Nobody was crying. The doctors did not recognize that something was wrong.

The kids, the doctors declared, were "all right." The world, by now hanging onto every new piece of information about the Chowchilla kids, celebrated. The kids were "all right."

One might want to blame these two frontline doctors for letting all those frightened children go just like that—without any psychiatric help and without even a mental examination—but one has to imagine the state of affairs in 1976, when medicine understood so little about childhood psychic trauma. There were no available medical outlines of trauma-related signs and symptoms in youngsters. The two doctors at Santa Rita Prison had no idea what to look for. As far as the physicians could see, there was nothing abnormal about these kids—nothing that would require any psychiatric intervention. They certainly were not crazy. Nobody was even acting weird.

The children stayed at Santa Rita Prison until the next morning. It was Saturday, July 17, 1976. They had been away from home for more than two days. No officials at the prison mentioned to the kids what was happening back home in Chowchilla, but pandemonium had come to town. Main Street, known in Chowchilla as Robertson Boulevard, was flooded with strangers—FBI men, reporters, and TV "personalities." Farnesi's Safari Motel, the only place in town for transients, was stuffed with visitors, and Merced, a town twenty miles north, was full-up, too. Everybody was waiting for that busload of kids to pull into the parking lot next to the Chowchilla fire station.

The youngsters returned to a bewildering crowd of parents, neighbors, and town officials. Reporters poked microphones into their faces, speaking not only strange American dialects but all sorts of foreign languages as well. Terrie Thornton's older brother became infuriated and broke a reporter's microphone. Paul Sturgis, Sandra's dad, threatened to bop an FBI man. TV and movie cameras whirred, and flashbulbs popped off by the hundreds. The words "kidnap," "kidnappers," and "ransom" flew through the buzzing air, and the kids, who had not used these words themselves, began to think about it. Only two of the children, Leslie Grigson, seven, and Sandra Sturgis, eight, had put the word "kidnapping" to their experience before coming home. Nobody else in the group had known what to call it.

The children had spent about thirty-eight hours away from their community and at least forty-eight hours away from home. They had been driven about in blackened vans for eleven hours and then had been buried alive for seventeen or eighteen hours. They had suffered a terrible shock. They did not know that this series of events was to be called "the Chowchilla school bus kidnapping."

The police, sheriffs, and FBI agents went to work. Under hypnosis, the bus driver, Jack Wynne, was able to remember all but one of the numbers of the license plate on the white van that had blocked his way. A few days later, three young men, Fred Woods, James Schoenfeld, and Richard Schoenfeld, the sons of wealthy Bay Area families, were arrested. Frederick Newhall Woods III, the son of the man who owned that rock quarry in Alameda County, and the two Schoenfeld brothers, sons of a successful podiatrist from Menlo Park, went off to jail. And just about every police department in the United States hired a hypnotist.

The kidnappers would not speak about it. They had smart lawyers—the kind who knew that if their clients said a word, things would go worse for them than if they remained silent. The young men never "talked"—not even in court.

Interesting stories sprang up—after all, nobody really knew the facts from the young men themselves. One tale had to do with long-term planning and, thus, with premeditation. Mrs. Sala Hunter, the mother of Susan, one of the youngest Chowchilla victims, heard somewhere that one late winter night a half year before the kidnapping took place, the watchman of the Woods' Alameda County rock quarry phoned Mr. Woods and complained, "Hey, your son and a couple of his pals are burying a huge truck trailer here!" Old Mr. Woods supposedly chuckled. "Let the kids play," he said.

A couple of the Chowchilla parents thought the kidnappers had come up with the whole scheme from an old fictional mystery, "The Day the Children Vanished," by Hugh Pentecost. Others said that Fred Woods and the two Schoenfelds had been caught speeding near Chowchilla. The "boys" decided, these parents thought, to get a crazy kind of revenge on the town—a Pied Piper caper without the requisite charm.

All kinds of stories develop if perpetrators don't talk. And that's how it was at Chowchilla. Nobody talked. The criminal trial began in October 1977 and it was over before spring of the following year. The three young men waived their rights to trial by jury. Several of the older kids testified at the trial, but the kidnappers did not.

Fred Woods and James and Richard Schoenfeld were convicted of kidnapping with grave bodily harm, a crime that in California carries a mandatory sentence of life imprisonment with no parole. The Alameda County Superior Court judge heard testimony about various small cuts and bruises, bladder infections, and dangerous exposures to heat and cold, but no testimony had been allowed about the children's emotional state. The Chowchilla parents, when they were asked by the local sheriff to let their kids be interviewed by a "defense psychiatrist," had refused. "The kids have been through enough," they said. There could be no prosecution psychiatrist if no defense psychiatrist was allowed. The balanced scales of justice demanded this.

In 1981, the California Supreme Court upheld an appellate court's decision to overturn the "bodily harm" part of the Woods and Schoenfeld convictions. The few small scratches, healed bruises, and minor bladder infections that the children had sustained were simply not enough to convince either the Court of Appeals or the California Supreme Court that grave "bodily harm" had been done. In the entire chain of legal proceedings, no one in the California court system ever "officially" dealt with the *emotional* harm that the Chowchilla victims had suffered, and the only one who may even have considered it in reaching a decision was the Alameda County Superior Court. Unfortunately for everybody except the criminals themselves, the California Supreme Court, in making its decision that emotional harm was not "bodily harm," had neatly lopped off the mind from the body.

At the time of this writing, the three kidnappers still remain in prison, but they repeatedly come up for parole. Thus far, their paroles have been denied. Fred Woods and the Schoenfeld brothers never have said at their hearings why they did it, why they selected these particular children, or why they chose the town of Chowchilla. At a 1983 parole hearing, Richard Schoenfeld told the board, "I can't give you any excuses for the crime. I did it. I did it for the money." But that does not explain much. The police had found a ransom note in one of the kidnapper's homes asking for $3.5

million, but the note never was delivered to the town. Nor was the entire community likely to have come up with that kind of money. The kidnappers' real motives remain a mystery, perhaps buried in the inner reaches of their minds.

Five months after the school bus kidnapping, I was "invited" to see the Chowchilla kids and their families. This "invitation" came in an entirely indirect way. Nobody had been helping the kids—after all, the mayor and all the other officials in town had pronounced them OK. When the parents, themselves, invited a child psychiatrist from the local mental health center to address their group in August 1976, the psychiatrist predicted that only one child in the group of twenty-six would be affected. How could anyone admit that his kid was the only "one in twenty-six"? It is hard to know how this child psychiatrist arrived at his figure, but in so doing, he had inadvertently banged the doors of the mental health center shut.

In early November 1976, Sandy Miller and Gail Tompkins, investigative reporters for the *Fresno Bee,* went out to Chowchilla and learned that the parents were complaining their kids were suffering from fears and terrible nightmares. Miller and Tompkins wrote an article to this effect. A Fresno child psychiatrist I had recently met, Romulo Gonzales, remembering that I had told him I was interested in doing a field study of childhood trauma and that the Chowchilla group was the group that most interested me, forwarded the *Fresno Bee* clipping to my office. I phoned the first Chowchilla parent named in the piece, Mrs. Judy Johnson, the mother of Jackie and Johnny Johnson. In response to my offer of a research project and of very brief psychotherapy, she shocked me. "You are an angel of mercy—an answer to our prayers. Come quickly."

So I arrived in Chowchilla on December 16, 1976. It was 154 days after the kidnapping. I had been waiting for eight years for the "right" field project on psychic trauma in childhood. And I knew this was "right."

I explained to the parents who attended our organizing meeting that the study would include family interviews, child interviews, and brief treatment. I also offered parents a group session once weekly for those who wanted to come. I told why—in a sense—these children would be acting as guinea pigs, explaining to the parents frankly that we would all be exploring together. We would have to find out for ourselves what, if anything, happens to kids who endure terrible frights.

For a while it looked like the Chowchilla district attorney, David Minier, would need my testimony in the criminal case against the three kidnappers. This served as an incentive for kids and parents, who might not otherwise have come into the study, to sign up. As a matter of fact, by late August

1977, every one of the twenty-three children who still lived in Chowchilla had come forward for psychiatric interviews. Unfortunately, when the kidnapped children's parents refused to let any "defense" psychiatrist look at their youngsters, the D.A. could not bring our psychiatric evidence into court to buttress his "bodily harm" case against the kidnappers. And so the legal part of my work at Chowchilla, late in coming, was early to go. But the study had taken hold—I had interviewed every child and family in the group, that is, every family who had stayed in town.

Four years after the first round of interviews, I started all over again. I chose the four-year mark because Bob Barklay, "the children's hero," had just turned eighteen and was about to leave town. The follow-up took almost a year to complete. This time I searched for the three kids who had left town within the first five months of the kidnapping, and I found two of them. (The third had "disappeared," leaving no forwarding address and no school transfer forms.) I also located Timothy Donnario, the kindergartner who had been let off the bus just before it was taken. Many youngsters and their families said they were reluctant to "stir everything up" in order to do this follow-up, and I realized that it would be necessary, as it often is in scientific research, to pay the participants for taking part. With the offer of $100 to each child who completed the entire interview sequence, all but one child willingly saw me at least twice (Jackie Johnson, thirteen, refused to take part in more than one interview).

As part of the four- to five-year follow-up at Chowchilla, I interviewed a normal matched control group of kids from two towns south of Chowchilla, McFarland and Porterville. I also interviewed twenty-five agematched children who came consecutively for first visits to my psychiatric office in San Francisco. Thus, I matched two separate groups to the Chowchilla children—one, a group of normal country kids, and the other, a group of my own urban child psychiatric patients with problems other than psychic trauma.

At the same time as I was working on the Chowchilla field study, I was seeing a number of children, like Alan Bascombe, and adults, like Charlotte Brent, who had experienced real psychic trauma in their childhoods. These were not children who had broken up with boyfriends on the telephone or who had lived in ill-heated, ill-maintained housing projects, but rather, they were youngsters who had been kidnapped, snatched by a parent, or who had survived airplane crashes, dog attacks, auto accidents, rapes, and other sorts of abuses. I was seeing the mental results from such bizarre crimes as the use of infants in satanic rituals or in "child porno" rings— and these children were coming from as far away as the Philippines and Central America. Many of my trauma patients were sent to me by lawyers because their possible emotional injuries were considered crucial to a legal case. Sometimes a lawyer would ask me to see a small group of youngsters exposed to the same shock—a group of witnesses to a terrible death, for instance. These little groups, like the larger one at Chowchilla, particularly helped me to understand psychic trauma. A few trauma victims came for treatment, not just for evaluation, and, of course, I came to understand these patients better than the others. Almost every one of the children I saw who had been traumatized had been "normal" before. Hardly a one had ever been to a psychiatrist. All of these trauma victims helped me to understand what had happened at Chowchilla, and the Chowchilla kids certainly helped me to understand those who had been individually traumatized.

When the findings came in from Chowchilla and from the control groups, I made four huge charts. Each one of these monsters covered my entire kitchen table. Findings were boxed-off in red, and red boxes began marching in certain patterns up and down my table. I could graphically see that every Chowchilla child had been affected by the shocking event both at the one year and the four- to five-year marks. Every single Chowchilla child was the "one in twenty-six" the local psychiatrist had predicted. No one had dared admit it.

I found in 1980 that several control kids were hurting, too, as a result of some previously undiscovered fright. There were ten cases of severe scares and/or full-blown trauma at McFarland and Porterville, a very high prevalence in a group that had been selected ahead of time as having "no known trauma." There apparently was a lot of unrecognized, but real, psychic trauma "out there" in the world of normal kids.

I now looked at the second control group—every consecutively arriving new psychiatric patient coming to my office (*not* for psychic trauma) who fell within the nine to eighteen age range, the concurrent ages of the Chowchilla group in 1980–1981. Eight of the twenty-five children in that group demonstrated that they were still affected by an externally generated terror, a prevalence rate quite similar to that of the McFarland-Porterville control group.

The Chowchilla field study was the first research project on childhood trauma that was controlled, that was prospective (looking at the group forward from near to the beginning), that was directed at a single group that had experienced the identical event, that centered on children (rather than upon parents), and that involved a large number of youngsters at various stages of development, at various levels of educational and economic attainment, and of various kinds of families. The findings at Chowchilla opened up many new avenues of research—for example, it stimulated studies of child witnesses, of child sufferers of simultaneous trauma and bereavement, of child victims of parental abuse or sexual advances, of child victims of parental snatchings, and of child refugees from brutal regimes. It was also possible—using the signs and symptoms of childhood trauma found at Chowchilla—to begin to differentiate children who described experiences that they supposedly had suffered but actually had made up from those who were telling the truth.

It was becoming clear that horrible life experiences could scar the minds of children. Many youngsters were living for years with unrecognized traumatic effects. One could not pick up a newspaper without finding a new day-care center exposé, a child-witnessed shoot-out, or a kidnapping. I began to wonder if a generalized epidemic of psychic trauma was rampant in the world of kids.

I began to wonder something else, too. During my trips to Chowchilla, I had met a few brothers and sisters of kidnapped kids who were "catching" some of the fears, behaviors, play, or dreams of their kidnapped siblings. Was externally generated terror transmissible to kids who had never been directly exposed to a traumatic event? Could books, TV, or the movies also "traumatize" children? Expose them to nightmares? Would normal kids be "traumatized" or "partly traumatized" simply by knowing about someone else's shock? Or even if they never knew directly about the shock, could they be terrified anyway by being exposed to the symptoms?

I began to think about very old traumas, the historical ones—the plagues, seiges, and such. Did the classics, myths, and the old childhood games carry along with them the traces of these old traumas? As I searched Poe, Virginia Woolf, Ingmar Bergman, and others, I began to find some traces of childhood ordeals in their works. I began to see that old disasters could lead to long-standing superstitions. To ghosts. To fortune telling and omens. To horror books and movies. Childhood traumas seemed not to die—nor did they "fade away."

My curiosity about psychic trauma in childhood, thus, started out as a study of the kidnapped kids of Chowchilla, but as time went on it broadened to other victims, like Charlotte Brent and Alan Bascombe, to their families, and their contacts—and then, to literature, folklore, and film. A traumatic event, because it remains so well-impressed in the child victim's mind, may appear later in all sorts of guises—both symptomatic and creative. If one knows the general effects of childhood psychic trauma, one is able to find these effects where they are least expected—in the normal nursery school, on the neighborhood playground, in the bookshelf, and at the Saturday afternoon matinee.

Childhood "psychic trauma" is not so "abnormal." It, or lesser shades of it, plays a part in the ordinary development of any youngster—and it finds a place, too, in our "normal" folklore. There is a "normal psychology" of the external which coexists side by side with the more well-recognized psychology of the internal. This psychology can be discovered once one knows what psychic trauma does.

The mental effects of trauma from childhood can be found both immediately and after a long period of time. It is possible for a parent, teacher, or friend to recognize psychic trauma in a child years after a shocking event is over—that is, if he knows what to look for. As a matter of fact, we can even recognize traumatic effects in our own psychologies. Many post-traumatic attitudes, it appears, are permanent whether or not a child is treated psychiatrically. Others will fade over the years, but in the meantime these post-traumatic effects may spread to others who themselves were never actually victims at all.

Maybe after a traumatic event, a child is still "normal." But the traumatized child is changed—that is certain. All of us get scuffed and bruised by life. There are too many minor frights and horrors out there to count. Perhaps by learning what happened in the minds of the Chowchilla kids, in the minds of young trauma patients who came to my office, and the minds of the normal "control" children who participated in the McFarland and Porterville study, we will come to understand our children's nightmares, fears, and creations. We may, as a matter of fact, begin to understand our own.

The psychology of the external is not "weird science." It is a psychology, ignored but there all along, of ordinary child development. I think that this, in many ways, is the story of us all.

PART I

The Emotions of
Childhood Psychic Trauma

CHAPTER 2

Terror

It was scarier than when I cut my finger deep when I was five years old.
I get a lump in my throat when I go to play my clarinet for people. But
this was a matter of life and death. I was horrified in a way. And also
scared.

Sandra Sturgis, age eleven

SARAH FELLOWS started school in September. At home, like any other
kindergartner, Sarah plays up to her two older brothers who sneer at
"the little pest." In class, like others of her age, Sarah paints her
human beings in three-flowered gardens, under smiling suns, next to trees
with bally tops, and beneath skies that take up no more than one inch at
the top of the page. There is ony one thing about Sarah Fellows in the
kindergarten classroom that is any different from anyone else—all of Sarah's humans are drawn naked. Most of them are not even kids. They carry
the obvious sexual characteristics of adults.

Jack and Susan Fellows had thought everything was OK. A curious little
girl likes to paint people naked—so what? Then, in November, the phone
call comes. A police inspector from their good suburban town wonders—
since the Fellows kids were on a list as having attended the Mary Beth
Hillgard Day Care program sometime in 1978—would Jack Fellows please
drop by some time to look at a few photos.

Jack speeds right over. All three children in the Fellows family had
attended day care at Mary Beth Hillgard's house, but they had been with
her only twelve weeks. ("Maybe nothing could happen in just three
months' time.") Jack and Susan had pulled the children out of day care
because the boys continually complained about Mary Beth's lunches and
everybody seemed to cry on weekday mornings. Jack does not know what
to expect at the police station, but he figures it will not be good.

A detective shows Jack five glossy eight by eleven photos. Sarah—fifteen, sixteen, or seventeen months old—naked, is being touched by an erect, adult penis. There is no means of escape for Jack. Sarah's big strawberry birthmark took the emulsion, too. She has that same mark on her left shoulder today. It is Sarah, all right. No more evidence is needed. Some man is molesting Jack's baby, and Jack must force himself to witness the act. The act is now three and one-half years old.

Jack and Susan Fellows bring Sarah to me. They feel unspeakably guilty. They have not dared expose anything of this to their kids. They have sheltered them from any contact with the police. And they certainly have not "talked" with the boys or Sarah.

In giving me his story, Jack produces a slip of the tongue, referring to five-year-old Sarah as "the woman in the photograph." You can see that Jack's inner picture of his daughter has been tainted by the real pictures he was forced to inspect at the police station.

Leroy Hillgard, the husband of the lady who ran the babysitting operation, has been charged with several counts of child pornography and rape. The Fellowses never suspected a thing. Their little girl (and, it turned out later, the boys, too) had kept their mouths shut. The only clues, at least in retrospect, were those confounded nude drawings—art works that, with the new knowledge at hand, might have been sketched from the Left Bank of the Styx.

Five-year-old Sarah bounds into my office—clean, sparkly, and elfin in a boyish haircut. In response to my question about old babysitters, she says she can remember a little bit about a lady. Sarah's spot memory is a gloomy one. "I kind of feel," she says, "that there was grave danger at a lady, Mary Beth's house." Grave danger? Is that a kindergarten expression? I wonder.

The brick-colored hair glistens as Sarah darts across the room. "I'll draw you a picture," she tells me. She opens the drawers of a small desk and discovers the markers and paper that I leave for the kids who see me. She draws.

The figure is naked. It looks like a baby. "Who is this?" I ask. "My doll. She's laying on the bed naked. I cover her up." Sarah hurriedly tries to scribble a blanket over her doll's nakedness. "I'm playing. I'm yelling at the doll. She was bad! I yell at my doll—well, not really yell. 'You! You bad thing! Get to bed, you!' " Sarah does not know it, but she is really yelling at herself. She is telling me about a baby lying naked on a bed. She feels guilty for actions from age fifteen to eighteen months that she cannot now retrieve in words. This child thinks she is horrid, yet she does not know why.

I ask Sarah if she feels afraid of anything. She answers quickly. "I *am* afraid of some things, but I don't know what they are. I used to be scared of a cow."

"Did you ever see one?"

"No. I never saw a cow. Mooooooooooooo!" She tries to scare me with her sudden bellow. Close to my chair now, she puts her face next to mine and confides, "I thought that part [the udder] was real scary. It looked like some kind of monster to me when I was little."

Sarah is describing projectiles off bodies—metaphoric symbols for the phallus perhaps, or maybe just plain penises, literal ones, from a toddler's eye-view. Her thoughts continue along this line. "I also remember," Sarah says, "we went on a boat in Disney World—an animal boat. Some of the boats on that ride [the Jungle Ride] have stripes. We saw lots of animals. And some little Indians with spears. They pointed their spears at us, and that scared me." She touches her belly. Sarah looks a little scared right now.

"Have you ever been frightened of something someone pointed at *you*, Sarah?" I ask.

"Somebody scared me once—with a finger part." Sarah puts her finger directly onto a spot high up on her belly.

She goes on after a short pause. "I'm afraid of sharp fingernails. I like girls better than boys. Boys are *really* strong. I like girls who are not really strong too much."

"What do you think will happen later—much later—when you grow up?" I asked.

"I will live probably," she says, "until I'm forty or forty-nine. When you get old, you die. I have grandparents who are sixty or sixty-nine and I don't think *they* are ready to die. But I sometimes think I am going to die sooner than other people—I don't know why I think this. I feel bad people will hurt me. I may be killed instead of dying."

The little girl still seems to be guarding her upper abdomen. I inquire. She tells me her tummy feels funny.

A child psychiatrist is used to hearing "displacements," quite common defenses in kids. Sarah, perhaps, has mentally moved up the location of her old sexual assaults to her belly, where the idea probably would create less fear and guilt. It would not be the first time that I had heard such mental anatomical rearrangements. But there is something strange about the exactness, the precision, with which Sarah's finger rests upon the upper reaches of her belly.

The little girl is terrified of males rather than females—of "finger parts" threatening her abdomen—of spears, udders, and fingernails. What would a toddler think that an erect penis was? What words would she apply to her experience at fifteen to eighteen months of age? Something like "finger part," I would imagine, if she were a bright, verbal toddler, that is. The phrase "finger part" sounded genuine and age-specific to the time of the trauma. But why would Sarah sense a threat to her upper abdomen? Would she be able to employ the mental mechanism, "displacement," at such an immature stage of development? That would be young to use such an elaborate defense, I thought.

A few weeks after my meeting with Sarah I go to visit Ron Gordon, Sarah's lawyer, at his Berkeley office. Ron, a bright, young idealist, is handling the civil suit of six youngsters who attended the Hillgard Day Care home. He tells me that Leroy Hillgard has pleaded "guilty" in his criminal trial and is already doing time in prison. Ron keeps the evidence he will use in the children's civil suits in a file cabinet. I ask to see Sarah's photos. The young attorney pulls out a folder and tells me to sit down. "You won't like these," he warns.

I look. First I am arrested by the baby's face. I cannot take my eyes off her eyes and mouth. The most incredible mixture of emotions—of terror, distress, pain, curiosity, seriousness, and, yes, excitement—has infused the features of that baby. There is no way, I feel, that an actor could ever simulate a look like this. I have never before seen such a look.

No tears. The photos, all of them the same in some ways, may have been taken at different times—I cannot be sure. I force myself to glance down the youngster's body. The baby is naked. In each photo the same thing is happening. The baby is being held down by a man's erect penis. It jabs into her upper abdomen. I am looking at the very same spot that the child had repeatedly touched in my office. At age five, Sarah's terrors are absolutely literal. She is afraid of the very same thing that has already happened. She fears "finger parts," her fifteen- to eighteen-month-old word for penises. She worries now that they will threaten her upper abdomen. Her belly feels the discomfort. And that is exactly what the old photos show.

At the instant a terrible event strikes, what does a child do? Does he freeze, run, vomit, defecate, lose his temper, shriek, cry, or become mute? Usually, of course, there are no photographs of a traumatic event to consult after the fact. Unless the psychiatrist were also there in person, he would have to accept a child's remembrances to picture what must have happened.

Before the 1970s there were no published personal accounts from children of their first instants of trauma. We had to depend entirely upon theory. Anna Freud hypothesized, for instance, in 1967, "What I would consider as evidence for the occurrence of a traumatic event is, as an immediate reaction to it, a state of paralysis of action, of numbness of feeling; in the case of a child, a temper tantrum, physical responses via the vegetative nervous system [wheezing, vomiting, defecating, physical shock] taking the place of psychic reactions." That same year, the New York psychoanalyst Sydney Furst, a person who has written a great deal about trauma, theorized, "The acute traumatic state takes one of two forms: the traumatized child may appear immobilized, frozen, pale, becoming extremely infantile and submissive in behavior; or else the trauma may be followed by an emotional storm, accompanied by frenzied, undirected, disorganized behavior bordering on panic. Signs of autonomic dysfunction [vomiting, etc.] may contribute further emphasis to either picture."

Filmmakers have used any or all of these theoretical options to show their "childhood traumas." In *The Memory of Eva Ryker*, a 1980 film starring Natalie Wood, the school-aged Eva, traveling by luxury liner from Europe to New York during the early days of World War II, shrieks in rhythm about ten times and then goes permanently mute when she discovers her mother's murdered body while the ship is sinking from a torpedo attack. Eva, in other words, employs both Sydney Furst's and Anna Freud's theoretical possibilities in sequence following her traumatic shock. She has her "tantrum" and then exhibits her "paralysis of action" and "numbness of feeling." Unsure, perhaps, how to show on-the-spot childhood trauma, Hollywood, in this case, covered all theoretical bases.

At Chowchilla, however, I was able to find out from the children how they really did act during their on-the-spot exposures to the traumatic events. The kidnapped children were quite frank, I thought. They told how they and the others around them had behaved. What emerged was a picture of complete autonomic nervous-system control and of quiet, but directed, behavior. No one vomited, defecated, or otherwise showed problems with the vegetative nervous system. Jackie Johnson and Sammy Smith both fainted several hours into the ordeal, but this happened under the very hot, confined conditions of the vans and the "hole." Several kids urinated on the van ride, but that occurred because for eleven hours the kidnappers had allowed no one a "pit stop" or a drink of water. Two kids, Mary Vane and Alison Adams, later had trouble breathing in the "hole" —one of them, Alison, had been a lifelong asthmatic. But we must remember that all the Chowchilla children knew inside the "hole" that they were buried alive. That particular idea must, to some extent, have influenced Mary's and Alison's breathing problems.

None of the children of Chowchilla shrieked when the gunmen took over their bus. None of them went mute or became "paralyzed." The children moved about, babysat the younger ones, slept, and chatted a little. Nobody carried on as the young actress who played the ten-year-old Eva Ryker had been directed to do in the film.

Perhaps, one might think, preschool children would be more likely to lose control of their bodily functions during disasters than would older kids. But this does not appear to be the case—at least by the retrospective accounts of children who were traumatized as preschoolers. Consider thirty-nine-month-old Alan Bascombe, the kidnapped-for-ransom boy we met in Chapter One, for instance. At no time during his abduction did Alan's body betray itself. True, Alan says he had some trouble going to sleep at the kidnapper's place, but he still drank and digested his 7-Up, slept through the night, responded to a female rescuer, a stranger, by stating his name clearly when she asked. He quietly watched TV on his return. Alan had no tantrums nor did he go mute. He was "not a talker," he tells us, but his actions, speech, and physiology never expressed the out-of-control fright that he was actually feeling.

In the case of Sarah Fellows, I had the unique though horrifying opportunity to view her face and body just as a male abuser was photographing himself in the act of assaulting her. There was no little puddle of urine, no vomitus or feces in any of the several pictures I saw. The child's body seemed tense, but not paralyzed. Her face was the most arresting thing in the photos. I looked at the pornographic photos of two other children under the age of three who were also being abused by the same man, Leroy Hillgard. Each of them, too, showed intense facial expression but no physical loss of control.

At the moment of terror, therefore, young children tend to go on behaving almost as usual, even as their psychological underpinnings are being torn asunder. They sang into the darkness on the youngest kids' van during the Chowchilla kidnapping, "If You're Happy and You Know It, Clap Your Hands—Clap Clap." Nobody clapped. But their voices still could sing.

Occasionally on the television news they show you kids who have just come out of a natural or a man-made disaster. As the TV cameras pan their faces for a few seconds, what you see there is a grave seriousness. Seldom are there any tears. Instead there is an immobility of expression— a failure to move the mouth, a lack of animation in the eyes. Such was the televised look of the youngsters who survived the Cameroon poison lake disaster, of the children who were pulled out of the rubble from the Mexico City earthquake, and of the kids who had just run out of their besieged elementary school in Cokeville, Wyoming. Such was the look of the dazed little Jessica McClure as she came up from her terrible confinement in a backyard Midland, Texas, well. There seems to be little cultural difference in this. The face of horror in childhood is grave and relatively immobile. It may look dazed, but it rarely looks hysterical.

If the outside of the child looks OK (except for those young faces marked by incredible seriousness), what is happening on the inside? The immediate feelings that the Chowchilla children recalled later from their horrible experience were: (1) the fear of helplessness, (2) the fear of another, more fearful event (fear of fear), (3) the fear of separation from loved ones, and (4) the fear of death. Externally generated terrors in childhood appear to raise quite different issues than do the internally activated fears that come up spontaneously during ordinary childhood.

An overwhelmed child immediately feels during a traumatic event that he has no options. His response to this feeling is an awareness of utter helplessness. The child fears the loss of his family connections and, if he is old enough, the loss of his life. He quickly adopts the attitude that worse things will happen. The terror lingers even if the event is happily resolved.

Some of the remarks the Chowchilla children made about their own immediate reactions to the bus takeover showed that, though their faces and bodies must have looked relatively natural, they were, indeed, falling apart on the inside:

I looked at the kidnappers, sort of like . . . I was too scared to cry.

Billy

I had an ashtray in my hand that I made at school. I thought of hitting one of those guys in the head with it. But I couldn't throw it. I didn't know what they might do.

Carl

I was scared more scary things would happen.

Susan

Getting out of the van I thought they'd shoot the first two, the middle two, and the last two, so I went third to get out.

Debbie

I knew guns. I thought they'd shoot.

Mary

I felt a tingle in my back.

Johnny

I thought I'd never see my Mom and Dad again.

Sheila

Externally generated terror, or trauma, often continues to exert a specific, ongoing influence on attitudes and behaviors—sometimes for the remainder of the person's life. One gathers this from listening to adult patients and by studying the biographies of artists who were traumatized as children. An artist's old trauma may create a "theme," permeating his lifetime actions as well as his creative product. Often, this artistic product will carry the tone of terror, even when the trauma is, by now, scarred over by years of living.

On a few rare occasions, adults will give such eloquent words to their own terrors from childhood that we can better grasp how traumatized children feel. The right phrase chosen by an adult expert at phrases makes it easier to empathize with the traumatized young person who has long-since disappeared into linguistically fluent maturity. V. S. Naipaul is one such frightened child, now an adult, a novelist. In a 1981 interview with *Newsweek* correspondent Charles Michener, Naipaul said:

"I have two very early childhood memories of my father being mentally ill and of waking up in a hospital room and being strapped in a bed. Pneumonia my mother tells me. But I have always been fighting a hysteria that plagued me as a child."

"What activates it?"

"The old fear of extinction and I don't mean dying. I mean the fear of being reduced to nothing, of being crushed."

Naipaul puts words to the feelings of childhood trauma. He admits to a "hysteria" that continued to plague him up to the day he was interviewed by *Newsweek*. Most children over five at the time of their traumas are able to put this kind of fear to words, too; that is, unless they're too ashamed to do so. But children in the preschool years—when children are not particularly eloquent, if verbal at all—have much more difficulty finding words to express their traumas. Even though they cannot say so, such very young children are often affected by a lingering sense of terror. They may find a few words years later to express this. Alan Bascombe, for example, who was only three years old when he was kidnapped for ransom and held overnight by his kidnapper, told me at age eight, "I already know what it's like to die—to be killed. You feel real scared. You can't breathe." Alan was affixing new, advanced concepts—death and the cessation of breathing—onto old mental pictures of his toddler-aged ordeal. By age eight, Alan's words were coming to express something for which, at age three, he could not say much at all.

Like Alan, the toddler Sarah Fellows, who was attacked sexually by Leroy Hillgard when she was fifteen to eighteen months old, put more sophisticated words to her ordeal by the time she reached school age. When she was five years old she told me that she had sensed "grave danger at a lady, Mary Beth's house." Sarah must have put these words to her traumatic imagery long after the events were actually taken in and "resting" in memory storage. Perhaps Sarah had seen a television show in which the words "grave danger" were applied to an entirely different, but similarly upsetting situation. We cannot, however, lose our respect for the power of this little girl's terror during her very worst moments in life just because she had discovered new, and therefore phony-sounding, words with which to express it.

Traumatic fright is unique. And it is remembered. The fright from trauma is so special that we don't even have a "right" word for it in English. "Terror?" "Horror?" Stephen King quips that he ranks these words into three stages—terror at the "finest" extreme, horror next down the list, and the "gross-out" when King finds himself unable to horrify or terrify his reader. But none of these words, or even King's sarcastic little ranking, conjurs up exactly what Alan Bascombe, Sarah Fellows, and V. S. Naipaul are trying to tell us.

"Fear of fear itself," one of the immediate fears that springs from psychic trauma, makes arch conservatives out of formerly flexible children. Many of the kids at Chowchilla, for example, told me that their very worst moments in the twenty-seven-hour ordeal came at transfer times—times that they had to move from bus to vans, or from vans to the "hole," or from the "hole" out to freedom. They had lost their tolerance to change. All of the transfers during the kidnapping, including the transfer from captivity to freedom, were, for the children of Chowchilla, new ventures into the unknown. There was no way to grasp, except in retrospect, that when they escaped from the "hole," they had entirely escaped their ordeal. As a matter of fact, Janice Bennett, age twelve at the time she was abducted, told me months later that for her the escape was the most frightening part of the whole kidnapping incident. Her escape plagued her in many a bad dream.

Being psychologically overwhelmed, the sensation of being "reduced to nothing," as Naipaul would put it, is such a hideous feeling that the victim seeks never to experience that sensation again. Fear of further fear, as a matter of fact, keeps victims from trying to escape even when their chances seem good.

I have an extreme example of this. From my knowledge of this case, I began to think of Franklin Roosevelt's famous statement, "There is nothing to fear but fear itself," in a context entirely different from what the thirty-second president had actually meant, referring to the Great Depression. My "case," an adolescent girl who came to fear fear itself, was a bright and pretty fourteen year old, Nancy Columbo. One day after school, Nancy was bound and gagged at home by her psychotic thirty-year-old cousin, Richard. He had forced his way into the girl's apartment, and then waited with an axe for two hours intending to kill Nancy's parents when they came home.

"He was eating in the kitchen," Nancy told me a month after the terrifying incident, "and I was taped up in my room. He had told me all his plans. *I thought I might be able to wiggle free but I couldn't make myself do it.* I was too scared.

"I was talking with him for a while when he took my gag off. And he was talking to me. He had his reasons for wanting to kill my folks, but none of it made sense. He got out some beer and was drinking. He was watching the garage for my parents through the study window. I was alone on the floor of my room. Maybe I could have escaped. For a time, I thought he left the apartment. But I wasn't sure, though, if he had really left. I thought, 'Maybe he's just testing me to see if I move.' And so I was thinking, 'Should I try to get to the phone?' But *I was so confused I didn't move.*

"He ended up coming back," Nancy went on. "I think he put money in his parking meter. [Richard most likely did not do this, no matter how psychotic he was. It was evening by this part of Nancy's story—well after the six o'clock parking meter deadline.] I feel bad about that. I felt really bad about that afterwards. Even now. I feel bad that I didn't do anything. Richard was gone five or ten minutes, and *I didn't try to do anything.*"

When Mr. and Mrs. Columbo and their young son came home, cousin Richard was waiting with his axe to kill them. From the top of the stairs, he struck out wildly, chopping at walls and mutilating Mr. Columbo's forehead and scalp. Mrs. Columbo, finding strength she never knew she had, wrestled the huge man down the long flight of steps. Little Butchie watched, dumbfounded. Richard's leg broke. Mr. Columbo then sent him into unconsciousness with a blow from the axe handle. While the hideous screams, chops, and tumbles resounded throughout the house, the "paralyzed" Nancy, stuck by "the fear of fear itself," could not move. Only in the ensuing silence was she able to struggle free of her bonds. It was so easy to break loose that Nancy realized she could easily have escaped before the mayhem ever started.

Once free, however, the young teenager never left her spot. She sat still in the assigned place on the floor of her bedroom, pretending to be bound and gagged. She silently waited for the victor—whoever that might be—to enter.

This is what I mean by "fear of fear." Nancy, no matter how much psychotherapy she may eventually receive, will probably always feel guilty because she froze while her crazed cousin attacked her parents and little brother. And Nancy's parents, no matter what I tell them, will always blame their teenager. Nancy goes to boarding school now, voluntarily growing up far from the bosom of a family that had planned to be together always. The elder Columbos ended their marriage a few months after the hideous experience.

In 1942 Sandor Rado, a distinguished psychoanalyst from Columbia University, wrote a short psychoanalytic paper about battle fatigue in which he coined the term "trauma to phobia." He was proposing an automatic fear of fear that, he believed, would strike World War II soldiers once they felt psychologically overwhelmed in battle. Rado was proposing a phenomenon that I later found in children—the immediate fear of further fear. Shocked young victims, like Nancy Columbo, tended to stay put under extreme threat. Rather than engineering plans to escape once their immediate instinct for "fight or flight" was discarded, they waited. It took something massive—like the ceiling coming down or the silence after a bloody battle—before a traumatized child might be willing to move.

I think that fear of further fear, "traumatophobia," is one of the reasons that sexually abused children almost universally tend not to talk about what happened while it is happening. They are so afraid of what already took place that the unknown, those things that will happen if and when they tell, terrifies them even more. They are used to what is happening now. What happens next may be even worse than the already known, already expected, sexual "routines."

In the fall of 1979 I attended a small conference on terrorism. Three Federal Bureau of Investigation men, specialists in problems and methods of hostage rescue, gave talks. One of them, Con Hassel ("name freaks" may enjoy this name), spent his time at the Quantico FBI training grounds teaching Special Weapons and Tactics (SWAT) men and women how to rescue hostages. Agent Hassel needed to hear from me what to expect from children during forced confinements, in other words, what child hostages might do in order to effect their own escapes. Adult hostages seemed to stay exactly where they had been put by their captors, Agent Hassel told me.

The FBI's problems with adults were identical to what I was learning from kids. Army rescue teams or policemen would literally have to go in and force young victims from their confinements. They might achieve success by shouting simple step-by-step instructions, one at a time. There was no question, however, that once traumatized, human victims of all ages would naturally tend to stay put. Their utter helplessness, established during the first moments of trauma, would interfere with free thinking and action.

If conditions suddenly change inside a traumatic situation, the trauma victim may suddenly find himself able to shrug off the inertia. A few years ago I interviewed two brothers, Jonathan and James Burgess, eleven and nine years old respectively, who had been held prisoner for eleven hours in their suburban home outside of Phoenix by an escaped convict, "Albert." This murderer on the lam from a federal penitentiary had pulled his car into the Burgesses' driveway, forced his way in at gunpoint while Mother was off doing errands, and ordered the two brothers and their visiting friend to do exactly what he said. The three boys complied for hours until the convict took Jonathan into the bathroom, asked him to take down his pants, and then tried to touch Jonathan's genitals. Within about five minutes of the man's shockingly unwelcome advance, Jonathan was able to mastermind and successfully pull off a dangerous escape for himself and the two other boys.

The same sort of breakout from paralyzing inertia occurred during the Chowchilla kidnapping. Bob Barklay and Carl Murillo did not begin their digging until Carl's little brother, Louis, dislodged the stake holding up the rock-heavy ceiling of their "hole." Knowing that this or any further cave-ins could easily kill them all, several young "heroes" (Bob, Carl, Sammy, Johnny, and Terrie) and their bus driver suddenly sprang into action. The hold of "fear of fear itself" had been broken.

As an ordinary kid grows up he runs an internal handicap course—fears of strangers at age six or seven months, fears of going to sleep at night at age two or three, fears of dogs, bears, alligators, dinosaurs, witches, or monsters at four or five, and fears of becoming a person in his own right at fifteen, or even eighteen or twenty-two, depending, of course, on the particular kid and his particular background. We all know that most children jump imaginary hurdles at certain times in their lives and we go to our doctors or check out our Gesells, Spocks, Kagans, Brazeltons, and Fraibergs to see if, when, and how a kid will pass through a certain, internally generated phase.

How can we tell, however, when a child's fears are trauma-inspired? In other words, how can we tell if the fearfulness is coming from the outside rather than from the inside? One must wonder about potential external origins when a seemingly standard childhood fear lasts too long or becomes too intense. One must also wonder when the fear does not sound so "standard." In this context, let us look at Sarah Fellows, our little child pornography "star" once again, this time considering any fears Jack and Susan might have noticed during Sarah's first five years of development that could have represented clues to the traumatic origin of her problems.

Sarah had started her life cuddly, pleasant, and easy going. When Sarah turned one, Susan Fellows decided to go back to work, sparking a small war between herself and Jack about day care versus in-home babysitting. A truce was struck. Both mother and father heard through the neighborhood grapevine that the Hillgard Day Care Home was "an OK place for kids."

Sarah had whimpered every morning on her way to the Hillgards' house. Then, too, the two older Fellows boys had often complained. They had said they hated Mary Beth's lunches. Maybe Sarah was just imitating her older brothers, whom she obviously admired. Susan and Jack decided, at any rate, to quit the Hillgard program and to get a babysitter. The whole thing was just too much of a hassle.

Some time between Sarah's first and second birthdays, Jack and Susan noticed that the little girl had gone into a "phase." She seemed less friendly, less smiley, and more "closed-up." Everyone knows, however, that the toddler years are tough—kids fall a lot, stick fingers into wall sockets, and run across the street, winding up either spanked or hurt. So Jack and Susan decided just to wait it out.

Jack noticed, though, during the second year of Sarah's life that his little girl was beginning to shy away from him, to avoid his approaches, and even to scream when he would try to diaper her. Jack said to himself that young kids are supposed to go through some sort of problems with people who are not their mothers. Maybe Sarah was just experiencing a little "stranger anxiety." But her whole attitude toward him didn't seem right, Jack thought.

The child improved by age three and four. When she was toilet trained at two and a half, Sarah could take down her own underpants, and as a consequence, there were no more screaming fits at Jack. Thank God. Sarah wasn't the cuddly little thing she had started off to be, of course, but then maybe she was destined to be a bit like Susan's Great-Aunt Myrtle—a little standoffish and self-contained. Sarah might even turn out to be a spinster. Aunt Myrtle didn't like men either, that was for sure.

At age four Sarah entered nursery school. On an afternoon of the first full school week, the preschool teacher came out of the classroom looking for Susan Fellows. The teacher produced three of Sarah's drawings. The pictures—a little difficult to decipher at first because Sarah's technique was so typical of those early scribblings where you're lucky to make out the ears and eyes from the buttons on the coat—showed naked people. You could see the darkly defined nipples, awkward attempts at undercurves for the breasts, oversized penises, and enthusiastically drawn pubic hair. The teacher was appalled.

Miss Percy concluded that Sarah must have seen Jack and Susan naked. That's no big deal in and of itself, she said, but the reaction was impressive in this particular child. Susan, confident that she and Jack had never paraded the halls of their house naked, was confused. Might Sarah have walked in on one or both of them without their knowing it? Maybe they hadn't seen her, but she had seen them. Eventually Susan and Miss Percy agreed. This was probably a phase, but Susan and Jack Fellows must be more careful to maintain some modesty at home. Sarah went on drawing her naked pictures all year. She kept a little to herself, shying away in particular from new and unfamiliar men when one showed up at school. But then, too, Sarah Fellows was bright like Great-Aunt Myrtle, and Myrtle had been a not unpleasant person. Sarah must be doing OK.

A few months after Sarah began kindergarten, Jack Fellows paid his first visit to the police. After that, Jack started jumping at the sounds of any knock, telephone, or siren. He stopped trusting the world, especially the sound of his own doorbell.

Looking back at the whole story, there were just four clues from Sarah that could have warned these parents of the shock awaiting them—a personality change in the child between ages one and two, crying every day on the way to the Hillgards' day-care center, drawing naked people at nursery school, and avoiding Jack, especially whenever he changed her diapers. Could any of these behaviors or fears really have warned Jack and Susan Fellows?

Sarah's shift in personality during her toddler phase was a clue to the possibility of anxiety, but it was not beyond the range of normal. Toddlers become angry, difficult, even pseudoindependent. Parents call these few months of development—maybe even a year or two—"the terrible twos." Susan Fellows had gone back to work and had put the child in day care at the beginning of Sarah's toddler phase. The loss of Mother during the day might have inspired some shifting in personality style. But throughout her life Great-Aunt Myrtle had acted the way Sarah was acting now. There was, thus, a possibility that Sarah had inherited these traits, not to be fully expressed until the second year of life. Looking back at the story, the long-lastingness, the relative permanence of Sarah's shift in behavior, was the most bothersome aspect of this problem—and, of course, a parent might not have realized this to be the case until Sarah turned four or five. At that point the parent might have sought psychiatric consultation for the child, but without the rest of the information that we already know, the child psychiatrist most likely would have concluded that Sarah's personality had changed because of an internal precipitant—a neurotic conflict around separation from Mother or around toilet training, perhaps. A very "modern" child psychiatrist might have set more store on the story of Great-Aunt Myrtle's personality and would have seen Sarah's behavioral change as an inherited trait waiting to be expressed in the second year. But a child psychiatrist would hardly have guessed sex abuse here. There are too many other causes of personality change in childhood to have landed directly on psychic trauma as the operational one.

The second change in Sarah—her whining every day on the way to the Hillgards' house—could have been developmentally determined, too. Young children protest separations from their parents. And they *do* tend to imitate their siblings. This was Sarah's first experience leaving Susan Fellows. She likely could have felt that her mother and father were putting her into this strange place in order to go off and have fun. Any young child might well have protested these daily goings and comings with anticipatory whining—especially when her older brothers were complaining too. As it turned out, Susan and Jack Fellows were convinced after three months that the Hillgard program was not good for their kids—largely on the basis of their children's daily protests. But Susan and Jack never suspected what might be going on inside the "program." "We don't allow our parents to visit here. It upsets the little ones too much," Mary Beth Hillgard had told them early on. Susan and Jack Fellows had taken Mary Beth at her word.

The third change in Sarah—her drawings of naked people—could have been developmentally determined, though I am certainly stretching the point here. During the nursery school years, young children become curious about differences between the sexes, and they spend snatches of time playing "doctor" or inspecting anatomies "behind the barn." Most youngsters of four or five have seen a naked adult, certainly a statue in the park or a girl in a bikini at the beach. And they are interested indeed. It might be assumed that a child would be tempted to draw or paint these sexual differences at nursery school or at the family kitchen table. Although this certainly would have been unusual, the key in Sarah's case was the number of pictures that she drew, not the nature of any particular drawing. If Jack and Susan had taken a few of these curious works of art to their pediatrician, the doctor probably would have found the sketches unremarkable, though good likenesses of the adult physique. It was the quantity, not the quality, of the pictures that would have had to be taken into account if one were to have guessed that something terrible had happened to young Sarah Fellows.

Finally, there is the only behavior—Sarah's frightened avoidance of Jack Fellows, especially of his attempts to diaper her—that cannot be explained away by a knowledge of standard child development. Nor can the avoidance be explained as a neurotic problem—at least, as a common one. There is no phasic root to a terror of one's own parent. From birth on, children readily accept both sexes. They may prefer members of one sex to the other, but they appreciate both. Even seven- and eight-year-old boys, at the height of a supposed girl-hating phase, will tell you that they look forward to love and marriage with a *girl*. A lad might, in a moment of confidence, even whisper the name of some little female he particularly fancies. From "day one," young children allow themselves to be handled by both sexes—to be fed, cleaned, or put to bed. Because of the very helpless nature of human infancy, babies automatically permit others to tend to their needs. They show no developmental fear of care giving—they need the care too much. Sarah's protests when Jack diapered her were unusual indeed. This was post-traumatic fear—the first and, in this case, the only clear danger sign that Jack and Susan Fellows ever noticed themselves.

What was Sarah Fellows saying with her terrified responses to her father's attempts to change her? The child was "telling" her parents a literal, specific, truth—that a man had molested her. Probably, as a matter of fact, she was telling them that a man had assaulted her in the act of changing her diapers. Sarah's fear was so literal and so specific that it encompassed far less territory than the ordinary childhood fear does. Developing youngsters, when they fear dogs, fear *all* of them—not just the large white ones with black spots. Once a fear sounds very literal and very specific, there is a strong possibility that *actual* experience underlies the fear. When you see that old train bearing down on the young boys, for instance, in Rob Reiner's movie *Stand By Me*, you wonder if somebody who made the film had a terrible experience with a train. The engine is so very big, so very menacing, and so very specific.

There is nothing "artistic" or metaphoric about post-traumatic fear. In the first year after the Chowchilla school-bus kidnapping, for instance, twenty of the twenty-three children I interviewed were afraid of being kidnapped again. Twelve were afraid of a fourth kidnapper, six believed that the arrested kidnappers themselves were coming back to get them, and ten thought there would be a second unrelated kidnapping. The hero of Chowchilla, fourteen-year-old Bob Barklay, worried that the kidnappers who took him "did it to let us get out, so they'd get caught and go to jail a couple of years, and then start killing us one by one like in the movies." Bob felt doomed. The specificity of his fear demanded that he continue to believe that more mayhem would come to him at the hands of James and Richard Schoenfeld and Frederick Newhall Woods III.

The children at Chowchilla did not start out afraid of kidnappings, that is, before their own kidnapping. Even though an internally derived fear of being kidnapped is not that unusual in the ordinary school-aged child, the Chowchilla children denied having had that particular fear before. After the kidnapping, several children feared the three young men who were sitting out their young lives in prison. Others feared different people, too, but in particular they feared anybody who resembled one of their kidnappers. The Chowchilla kids were also scared of vans (like those used by the kidnappers), school buses (like the one that was kidnapped), the odor of pot (Sammy swore that he had smelled the kidnappers smoking it), broken-down vehicles at the side of the road (like those used by the kidnappers to block their own after-school passage in July 1976), and caves and tunnels (like the "hole"). In addition, they felt afraid of actions that might be evocative of the old trauma, like slowing down to pass a crawling car up ahead. Although a certain Chowchilla child might carry more fear in the general realm of vehicles and less in the realm of dark caves, many of the post-traumatic fears would remain literal and quite specific.

One summer day I happened to be working in my office wearing a white blouse, a red belt, and a middle blue and white print skirt when an almost three-year-old boy from New Orleans, Nicky Gregory, came to see me. Nicky and his mother had endured a plane crash near Rio on "Brand X Airlines" without physical injury when Nicky was twenty-eight months old. They had flown into San Francisco on "Brand Y," and Nicky's mother told me the child experienced no trouble with the flight. Nicky entered my office looking grim, stepping on and destroying a couple of paper airplanes that he had constructed in the waiting room. "That's how the ball bounces. That's how the cookie crumbles," he was mumbling to himself. Marching in, he glanced up suddenly at me. The boy instantaneously looked horrified and started to scream, trying to bolt out the door. But the handle was just beyond his grasp.

Nicky then turned to me and screeched, "You're wearing bad colors! Why do you put on bad colors?" Usually three year olds don't even know their colors—after all, they're only beginning to speak in well-constructed sentences and there are many other important concepts they must learn. But this little fellow not only knew his blues—he recognized the variegations. Nicky's fear of one particular shade of blue was absolute, literal, and specific. He was right, poor guy. My outfit was all wrong for him. I was wearing the colors of "Brand X Airlines."

There are times that a traumatized child's literal, specific fears take on strange, supernatural proportions. Caroline Cramer, a twelve-year-old sufferer of psychic trauma, was striking in this regard. Four years previously, when she was eight, Caroline's throat had been slashed open by a neighborhood German shepherd dog, Bowser, who attacked her as she roller-skated onto "his" territory, the sidewalk fronting "his" house. Bowser was put to death—the authorities insisted on it. So what did Caroline need to fear after that? "Bowser," of course. Caroline's fears stayed literally and specifically with the dead dog who had attacked her. The child told me four years after Bowser was destroyed, "I'm afraid Bowser could rush through the dog door in our hall and into my room. I know Bowser is dead. But at night I believe he is rushing in. I cover my whole self up with blankets to avoid an attack by Bowser. I check the dog door every night myself. I'm never sure someone else really closed it." What was Bowser now but a ghost dog? A specific, literal monster that absolutely refused to die.

There are times that a kid appears to be experiencing quite ordinary anxieties—"he just saw a scary movie"—but really is dealing, instead, with a specific post-traumatic fear. Faith Goodman, for example, twenty-three months old when she fell face first into the accidentally exposed inboard motor of her dad's boat, could remember for me at age eleven parts of the horrible scene when her mother first wiped off her bleeding, mutilated face in the bathroom. The marvelously repaired Faith still held onto a literal fear nine years after her accident—the fear of facial mutilation. "I have lots of nightmares," Faith told me, "that the guy from the movie *Halloween,* the one who makes bleedy faces, that *he* will come after me. In *Halloween* everybody has a bleedy face."

How many kids were frightened by *Halloween?* Many thousands or more, I would guess. Maybe millions. But Faith Goodman was special. She *knew* how her face had looked in the bathroom and before the plastic surgeon had done his work. She recently had looked at old photographs. "I can't believe how awful I looked," she told me when I interviewed her at age eleven. "I still can't believe it." It was Faith's own "bleedy face" that had stimulated her terror of the movie *Halloween.* For Faith, the film served as a literal reminder of a long-past ordeal. For the untraumatized child, on the other hand, the horror film would serve, perhaps, as an "introduction" to the horrors of others.

After a traumatic event is over, two kinds of fears continue to plague the victim. The first of these is the specific, literal kind of fear I have described in the cases of Sarah, Nicky, and Caroline. The second type is more subtle. "Fear of the mundane" may express itself as a fear of the dark, a fear of strangers, a fear of looming objects, a fear of being alone, or a fear of being outside. Many of us have had periods in our lives during which we have suffered ourselves from "mundane fears"—and *we* weren't traumatized as children. (Or were we?) The main difference, I think, that exists between ordinary childhood fears and the mundane fears of childhood trauma is the passion and the long-lastingness with which post-traumatic fears of the mundane are held.

Traumatized kids bolt at the sight of strangers. They startle at the sounds of unexpected noises. Barbara Bennett, thirteen by the time I reinterviewed her at Chowchilla in 1980, for instance, kept her radio on all night long—she just couldn't stand the dark. Furthermore, she had resolved never to feel "alone" again. Her sister Janice, age seventeen when I reinterviewed her in the follow-up Chowchilla study, crossed to the other side of the road whenever she spotted a new person in town. Carl Murillo had moved to Las Vegas, New Mexico, by the time I caught up with him late in 1980. He hid in the shadows of the small town where he lived whenever he thought he saw a stranger. There he was, a fifteen-year-old middleweight high-school wrestler and the local karate champ, ducking into doorways on the faint chance that an unknown stranger might attack.

The unexpected sounds of someone knocking on the door stirred up quiescent fears of strangers in several Chowchilla kids. Their comments about their own responses to a beckoning at the door made me realize that even four to five years after a trauma, "fear of the mundane" still lived. These fears remained persistent and bothersome. In the five instances I will quote, the knock of a stranger had become something that promised the child utter Naipaulian helplessness:

> The other day I heard someone knocking on my window. I'd rather be dead than hear that!
>
> *Benji, age ten, 1980*

> Johnny [Jackie's fourteen-year-old kidnapped brother] gets a weapon whenever somebody's at our door. He begged Mom for a forty-three-dollar money order and sent for a replica of a pistol—a police revolver with a plugged barrel. He says he'll use it for protection.
>
> *Jackie, age thirteen, 1980*

> I don't trust others. . . . If I'm at home and someone knocks on the door, I go to my room and look out the window 'cause my window is by the door.
>
> *Mandy, age eleven, 1980*

> I'm scared of strangers. I run away. If they knock, me and my sister Lizzie lock the door. . . . I'm afraid people are up to bad things.
>
> *Mary, age nine, 1980*

> I won't answer the door.
>
> *Barbara, age thirteen, 1980*

Whereas an untraumatized kid from one of the two control towns I used for comparison to Chowchilla, McFarland and Porterville, would say something relatively mild in response to questions about their mundane fears—for instance, "I'm afraid of people being wicked" (a fourteen-year-old girl), or "I'm afraid of strangers from out of town giving eyes at you" (a fifteen-year-old girl), or "I might be afraid; it depends on a stranger's appearance" (a sixteen-year-old boy)—the Chowchilla kid would take a far more exaggerated stance—"I saw some hippies down by the gas station, so I dropped my bike right there and ran home" (Sammy Smith, age ten, 1977), or "I thought I heard some strangers back of the house, so I got my uncle to get out his gun, and we went back there, but it was only my cousins. I forgot! I had told them to meet me by the barn at seven o'clock. Thank God, my uncle didn't shoot" (Janice Bennett, age seventeen, 1980).

Not only do trauma victims take extreme positions regarding their mundane fears, but these fears, like the specific, literal fears that follow from trauma, tend to linger well into adulthood. Our old acquaintance from Ocean Beach, San Francisco, Charlotte Brent, demonstrates this. "Charlie" suffered a lifelong, literal, and specific fear of sex—a fear that had been set up by her long-forgotten, traumatic episodes on the dunes. Charlotte broke up with her boyfriend Jim. That "took care" of the specific fear. But she still came occasionally to see me. The most remarkable thing about Charlotte at age fifty-six, once she had, as she said, "permanently put sex aside," was a never-ending "fear of the mundane."

"How is life going, Charlotte?" I would ask her, glad to see her. (I have always especially liked Charlotte. She is plainspoken and painstakingly honest.)

"Terrible," she'd say, looking grim.

"What happened?" I'd ask.

"A series of disasters," she'd say. And then she would launch into a description of quite ordinary things that had kept her from enjoying the past two weeks, month, or season—whatever the interval was since Charlotte's last appointment with me. Charlotte felt uncomfortable being alone, yet she avoided intimacy. At home, she was afraid of the dark, so she kept her dog, a big collie, at-hand and ready-by-her-side at all times. She was afraid of the Democrats—"They'll get us into a nuclear war"—and of the Republicans—"They will eventually rob me of my social security." Charlotte was terrified of making a serious mistake, not even realizing it, a mistake that might cost someone his life. At work Charlotte feared accidental diseases (she was afraid once that some computer equipment she was using might blind her). She could not force herself to fly on airplanes —hijackings and crashes terrified her too much. On the streets of San Francisco, she felt afraid she might contract AIDS. Supposedly safe with her dog at home, she dreaded cancer.

As a matter of fact, I think cancer was Charlotte's second biggest worry, next to sex. Cancer epitomized for Charlotte the loss of control, the helplessness that she had originally felt with some adult or adults on Ocean

Beach. Charlotte's fears of the mundane were almost paralyzing. Talking about them did not help. "Analyzing" them did not do much good. Getting Charlotte to practice overcoming one fear (behavior modification) served to wipe out that particular one, only to have it replaced by another. Valium and its newer, quick-acting "cousins" helped a little.

In 1981, when I checked my normal control group of twenty-five McFarland and Porterville schoolchildren for fears of the mundane, I found that the numbers of Chowchilla children who feared mundane items were almost identical (with the exception of fear of the dark) to the numbers of McFarland and Porterville children who feared those same things:

Fear of the dark: McFarland-Porterville, 3; Chowchilla, 15

Fear of strangers: McFarland-Porterville, 20; Chowchilla, 19

Fear of vehicles: McFarland-Porterville, 5; Chowchilla, 7

Fear of being alone: McFarland-Porterville, 6; Chowchilla, 5

It was not the numbers, or even the kinds of fears, that differentiated best between "subjects" and "controls." It was the intensity of the fears. Five-year-old Susan Hunter of Chowchilla, for instance, "checked" her little sister's bed one morning and ran screaming into her still-sleeping parents' room, "Laverne is dead! Laverne is dead! She's not up yet!" The kindergartner had been terrified she would lose her life during the kidnapping ("In the van, I worried about dying") and she had dreaded separation from her family ("I was worried about my parents"). Her panic of the winter of 1977 expressed both of these underlying terrors. For an instant —until they rushed into Laverne's room and checked—Susan's parents felt the identical panic. It is this kind of panicky intensity that characterizes a traumatized child's fear of everyday things, of the "mundane."

Horror is contagious. Traumatic terror, shock, and the "gross-out" are the feelings with which writers from Edgar Allan Poe to Edith Wharton to Stephen King have titillated their audiences. And why must such writers do this? Because, at least in certain instances, they must release their own childhood horrors back into the external world from whence they originally came.

Alfred Hitchcock is, I think, a good example of this. When "Hitch," as he liked to be called, was quite young, his father arranged for him to be thrown in jail as punishment for some minor offense. The experience in jail, one that was entirely unanticipated by the young lad, lasted only five minutes. But Hitch didn't know at the time how long it would take. And he was sensitive. The effect upon him most likely was traumatic. His stint in jail must have produced feelings of horror and intense suspense, feelings that demanded expression throughout his long career as a filmmaker.

Here is the story of childhood trauma as Hitchcock himself told it near the end of his life. He was the guest of honor at a Hollywood banquet and needed to reminisce, as he so often did, about his time in the local "clink." "When I was no more than six," Hitchcock said (as quoted by his biographer, Donald Spoto), "I did something my father considered worthy of reprimand. He sent me to the local police station with a note. The officer on duty read it and locked me in a jail cell for five minutes, saying, 'This is what we do to naughty boys.' I have, ever since, gone to any length to avoid arrest and confinement."

Hitchcock insisted for years that this incident produced two fears that inspired the majority of his films—the fear of prison and confinement and the fear of pursuit by the law. Hitchcock gave us his variations on these fears with enough originality and visual interest to keep us fascinated. He dished out enough horror to scare us, not only at the movie houses but often—later—in our own houses. Did Hitchcock, however, cure his own fear of wrongful imprisonment by scaring us repeatedly at the movies? Most likely not. After all, he was still talking about this fear at the end of his life, regaling his audiences with that one terrible, true tale from his own childhood. As a matter of fact, there is a story at large about a final ironic tribute to Hitchcock's childhood trauma chiseled into his gravestone. "This is what happens to naughty boys," it supposedly says.

Hitchcock shows us again and again on film the innocent hero hounded by the law. We find him in *The Thirty-Nine Steps* (1935), as the guiltless Robert Donat is pursued for a crime he did not commit. In *Young and Innocent* (1937) the hero, played by Derrick de Marney, a man wrongly suspected of murder, is hunted down by his girlfriend's father, the chief of police. Robert Cummings acts the part of another hounded innocent in *Saboteur* (1942), a film about a young fellow wrongly accused of committing arson on behalf of the Nazis. In 1952 Hitchcock gives us his very frustrating *I Confess,* a film in which a priest (Montgomery Clift) first hears the confession of a murderer and then finds himself pursued for the very same crime. The priest ends up sullied at the trial by a "reasonable doubt" acquittal. At the conclusion of the film, only the priest and the audience know for sure that he is entirely innocent.

Grace Kelly, in *Dial M for Murder* (1953), stands in for the young Alfred Hitchcock, wrongly jailed (again), wrongly tried, and wrongly prepared for execution while the real murderer, Ray Milland, is gleefully getting away with it all. It does not seem to matter to Hitch whether a woman or a man plays his five-year-old self. In 1957, Hitchcock uses Henry Fonda as *The Wrong Man,* arranging that he spend the night in jail mistakenly arrested for armed robbery. This "wrong-man" plot is Hitchcock's most common story line. It shows up in *Strangers on a Train* (1951), *To Catch a Thief* (1955), *North by Northwest* (1959), and *Frenzy* (1972). As a matter of fact, in scanning Hitchcock's best-known films, one finds thirty-seven years of "wrong-man" plots (1935–1972).

In regard to Hitchcock's early childhood trauma, I am especially intrigued with a camera shot he engineered in *Frenzy,* the second to the last film he ever made. *Frenzy* was filmed on location in the place where Hitchcock had grown up, the Covent Garden markets, London. The young Hitch and his father, a greengrocer, had spent hours at Covent Garden wholesaling their fish. The hero of *Frenzy,* Richard Blaney (played by Jon Finch), is taken from Covent Garden and thrown into jail, wrongly accused of a series of hideous sex murders. As Finch settles into his jail cell, Hitchcock takes the camera up high—high, high above the set—so high that the full-grown actor looks like an errant five year old, alone, confined, and utterly overwhelmed in his cell. In this one lingering shot we see the young Alfred's horror, a horror that evidently never left him, even though he was sixty-seven years removed from it.

I'm not finished with Alfred Hitchcock yet, and we will visit him again before this book winds down. But for now, let us pay another visit to little Sarah Fellows, that five-year-old child who, like Hitch, was quite alone in her trauma. I offered to treat Sarah myself—I knew that her early abuses at the hands of the Hillgards had hurt her. She was bright, alert, and motivated enough to benefit from psychiatric treatment. So I spoke to Jack and Susan Fellows about it and suggested we get started right away.

But their lawyer, Ron Gordon, phoned me to ask that I slow things down. "Hold off for a month or two before you start working with Sarah," Ron said. He was worried about the Fellows' marriage. Jack and Susan confirmed that they were in trouble. They needed time to pull things back together. Their horror was just too much for them, they said. They could not foretell whether they would be able to make it as a couple.

The Fellows family left town just a few weeks after that. Jack found a job in the Pacific Northwest that didn't pay as much and didn't help their financial situation in any way. But the job did offer the family an escape. They could leave the place where everything terrible had happened. They could, they thought, get away from it all.

I knew better. Moving doesn't help. It didn't really help anybody from Chowchilla who tried it. I hoped, however, that the move would help Jack and Susan Fellows. Sarah, as far as I know, never entered psychotherapy. Nobody sent for her records. And nobody phoned.

But little Sarah Fellows was gifted. Maybe someday her surrealistically crafted nudes would be shown in the art galleries. Then again, perhaps Sarah would locate a new talent with which to dispell her horror—the novel, perhaps. She was smart enough to write. Or perhaps, yes perhaps, she would go into film.

CHAPTER 3

Rage

I wish they would use a firing squad. It'd be faster, and then it will be over—

Leslie Grigson, age seven

S MALL TOWNS IN RURAL CALIFORNIA don't take up much land. Land is valuable in the California valleys—it is used for crops, not for the backyards and front lawns of a ranch town. Chowchilla is typical in this way. The houses are compact, one-floored, and directly in contact with their neighbors. They sit squat to the earth on long straight blocks with squared-off, small front lawns.

On the stoops of Chowchilla, people keep collapsible chairs. Toward the end of a long, hot day they pull the low-slung awning-striped seats onto their lawns and sit there perfectly still. Come to think of it, I did not see a front porch in the whole town. The yard *is* the porch.

Those front yards of Chowchilla smell good. You can actually smell the wisteria over somebody's front door and fill your nose with lemon blossoms as you walk down Robertson Boulevard past Wilson School and the First Baptist Church heading on over to Red's Market. But my favorite fragrance in all of Chowchilla is the aroma of a late midsummer afternoon. At the end of a long, lazy Saturday the smoke from barbecuing hamburgers suffuses the air. I love those Chowchilla hamburgers.

Chowchilla is nice in many ways—one is the fact that many of the families have kinfolk nearby. You know how it is in too many parts of America—probably worst of all in the big cities of California—where almost everyone is cut off from their cousins, aunts, uncles, and grandparents. Not so with Chowchilla. Several of its families are nestled inside of thick family enclaves, centered at nearby towns like Firebaugh or Los Banos—or within Chowchilla itself. Sometimes a cousin goes off to seek his fortune in the bigger Valley places—say, Merced, Madera, or Fresno—but those "strays" still relate back regularly to their family groups. Clans are big in the Central California Valley.

When the local Indians meet near Chowchilla for their summer powwows, they break up, too, into clan groups—at least, that's what Bev Grigson and Sala Hunter, both Chowchilla Indians, say. But the San Joaquin Valley Caucasians are as family-groupy as the Indians—out and out "clannish," I think. The Portuguese Donnarios go about the Valley exclusively with their Portuguese friends and relatives, and the Dutch Vander-Stynes go with the Dutch. These large family enclaves are "clans"—exactly that—and it can really help to have all those great-uncles and second-cousins once-removed around—especially at a time of crisis.

In eight-year-old Tania Banks's mind, however, her "clan" helped bring on the crisis of her kidnapping. In her way of thinking, they were the cause, not the remedy. Tania's folks, Harry and Lois Banks, belonged to a "cousins group," and every summer, precisely on the middle weekend of July, the cousins—adults between ages twenty and sixty, or so—would camp out in the Sierras. One cousin would select the camping spot for that summer, and a family caravan of pickup trucks, trailers, motorcycles, and campers would take off on a Thursday afternoon for the chosen place, say Red Bud Campground or Indian Flats. Everybody would get there, set up the equipment, talk, drink beer, cook together, play a few games of cards, maybe make love, hike around a bit, perhaps even get up a baseball or volleyball game, and then take down the tents Sunday afternoon and go home. Fun. Good wholesome family-style stuff. "Clan" stuff.

Traditionally, the kids were left home. Even if you had to sign up your babysitter in January, you knew that next July 15th, 16th, or 17th, you'd be taking off again for the mountains with your kin—and the kids knew, too.

The problem was that Harry and Lois Banks had trouble saying "No"—at least to their perky little daughter. As opposed to her younger brother, Benji, who was nothing but problems (Benji was bright, but hyperactive, and he had been medicated with Ritalin-style drugs ever since he was a preschooler), Tania Banks was "easy." And so when Tania asked to go along on the July 15–18 cousins' weekend, Harry and Lois hedged. They were "in charge" of that weekend. They were the chosen kin for the year 1976.

First Harry and Lois told Tania they'd let her go. After all, they were picking the place for the camp out, so maybe they could pick the cast of characters, too. Tania began to envision a triumphant departure from summer school on Thursday, the day before everybody else at school would be able to get out. She would abandon her pesky little brother and hold forth like an adult at that mysterious retreat someplace on a mountainside.

Then the Bankses tried out their idea on a few of their Banks, Petri, Winkler, and Hopper cousins. "No dice," "Hell no"—if Harry and Lois were to break clan rules about children, everybody else would eventually break the rules, too—and who knows, that might end the cousin camp outs forever. Harry and Lois's camping spot was OK. But *no* kids were coming. Period.

Tania was furious. She went off to summer school on Thursday, July 15, 1976, in a rage. An ordinarily happy child, Tania's personality did not suit the sulk. But, oh well—everything would come back to normal by Sunday night—right? Once Harry and Lois returned home, they thought, they'd make it up somehow to their little doll. They hoped, at least, that the campground that they had selected would pan out, that everybody would like it. Those Winkler cousins were sticklers about good sites. Harry and Lois had chosen carefully. The site for 1976 was to be "Jackass Rock."

They never did make it to the "Rock," though, that Thursday afternoon in July. On the way up, one of the Hopper cousins picked up lots of police activity on his CB radio. FBI talk, too. Good Lord, this was something big. Kids? Chowchilla? My god, Benji and Tania! The cousins' caravan turned right around and headed on back. Harry and Lois found themselves surrounded at home by concerned kin on that long miserable Thursday night and Friday.

But in the vans and the "hole" Tania was all alone. Isolated with her anger. Furious. Sulking. As far as Tania knew, her family never heard that she was missing. All of those big cousins up there in the mountains were partying in ways that only adults could imagine, and they didn't give a hoot about her. Not only did the little girl feel angry at the crazy-looking men with stockings over their faces who had held up her bus—she was enraged at her parents, too, and at those older cousins, aunts, and uncles who wouldn't let her come camping with them. In short, Tania found herself angry at everybody. Even the clan.

At Santa Rita Prison, Tania asked Mandy VanderStyne if she would take her back to the VanderStynes' house because no Bankses, she thought, would have yet returned from their midsummer revels. She had been forgotten and abandoned, she thought.

Yes, Tania was surprised at the Chowchilla Fire Station when the bus pulled in from Santa Rita Prison and her whole family—the Bankses, the Petris, the Winklers, and the Hoppers—was waiting "en masse" to greet her. A pleasant surprise. But it was too late. The damage was done. The big sulk had already begun.

Tania arrived home quiet. She would talk that afternoon, as a matter of fact, only to Lois's sister-in-law, Sally Hopper. The child refused to use the word "kidnap" for a month. On the Orange County Lions Club trip to Disneyland, she finally spoke the word for the first time, but after that she rarely said it.

The girl changed. Quite suddenly, they tell me. She turned irritable and a little mean—to everybody in general. A mathematics professor from far across the ocean wrote Tania. He had seen her picture in his local newspaper and had liked her (he probably responded to her gorgeous good looks). He calculated for Tania the extremely low probability that she would ever be kidnapped again. But she ignored the professor and never wrote him back. His numbers meant absolutely nothing to her.

Lois Banks told me shortly after the kidnapping, "We kept stressing to her after she came home that we liked her and cared for her. But you know, there has been a big personality change in Tania. She had been very easy going, easy to get along with. Loving. But when she first came back to us, she wouldn't kiss us, wouldn't sit on our laps. Her Grandma Petri, my mother, pointed out that the child is now fearful of closeness because she knows she might lose it."

Grandma Petri was right. Tania no longer did trust. She did not even want to help the "good guy," Madera County district attorney David Minier, to develop his case against Fred Woods and the Schoenfeld brothers. But in the end, she recanted. "It is the only way to punish those men," she told her mother.

A few months after the kidnapping when she was still eight, Tania ordered me to begin calling her "Tony." She wanted to be tough. The golden blonde child pointedly asked why I was taking notes. "The kidnapping is *not* my family's business," she warned. You see, Tania was still angry at her family because, as far as she was concerned, her parents had abandoned her. Why else would they have gone off camping the day she was kidnapped? Someone was to blame, she felt, and it wasn't her.

"You must be pretty mad at your parents," I pointed out the blatantly self-evident to the eight-year-old little girl. "They were gone the day you were kidnapped."

"Tony" could not make herself agree with me. "I don't hate *them*." Then, turning her exquisite face toward mine, she delivered a steaming list of "displacements," people who by virtue of transference of her feelings had become the substitute butts for her real rage at the kidnappers and her family. "I hate Carlotta," Tania narrowed her eyes. "She's Spanish. Armando, too. It's hard to understand the Spanish kids. . . . I hate my Brownie troop." Her jaw jutted out at me. "Then there's Shana. She's black. She stinks. . . . And Susy. Susy Smithson. I kicked her, who I don't like, and the teacher got mad. Me and my teacher don't get along good either. I don't hate my parents," Tania repeated her original disclaimer, a little softer now. Her defenses were, it appeared, beginning to spare poor Harry and Lois Banks. The child peered through me with cold, bright green eyes. She stared, full-faced, the way a man stares down his enemy before entering into mortal combat. "I haven't made up my mind yet," she said, "about hating *you.*"

Like Tania, Harry and Lois Banks couldn't land much of their anger where it belonged. Harry was obsessed trying to compose a song about the kidnapping. He told me in 1977 that it was almost "all done." Lois was "talking . . . to everybody in town," Wilma and Paul Sturgis told me. The Sturgises, parents themselves of a kidnapped girl, left Chowchilla. They couldn't stand the big mouths in town, they said.

Harry Banks eventually quit his job with the local cream of tartar plant and found new work managing one of those big discount marts at the outskirts of Chowchilla, the kind of store they have all over the Central Valley—for that matter, all over America. First the Bankses found a different house to rent in Chowchilla. But they were still restless, and Harry asked for a job transfer. Eventually they moved to Redwood City, a large suburb between San Francisco and Palo Alto. Harry, Lois, Tania, and Benji Banks didn't seem to be thinking much about it, but they were fleeing everything they knew. Even their own "clan."

I didn't see the Bankses in those years between 1977 and 1980, but I heard about it later. They moved a lot. First to Redwood City, then to Burlingame, then to San Mateo, and then back to Redwood City again. Harry felt pressured. He had a hard time working. He believed that he was physically and mentally falling apart. Lois stopped working. She developed migraine headaches. Nobody knew what caused them. Everybody had problems, but Harry and Lois decided to focus their slim energies and meager finances on Benji, their hyperactive son. They enrolled him in psychotherapy with a "Jungian sandbox analyst." Tania just grew up. She "pubesced." And she sulked.

I drove down Route 101 one beautiful spring morning in 1980 to visit the Bankses in the fourth house they had occupied since I last had visited them in Chowchilla. This place perched on a yellowing hill toward the edge of town. Lois was laid-up in bed with a headache. I said "Hi" to her at the bedroom door and set out to find the kids. Harry was off at his discount mart. I almost crashed into Benji—he was flying about the house. The boy immediately launched into a raving discourse on kidnappers, leading me toward the family room as he talked. At some point during his tirade, Benji screamed, "Boooooooom!" and Tania heard *that*. She popped into the family room the way a champagne cork pops from the bottle into the air. (Tania "startled," Lois told me later that morning, at any loud noise.) And so I saw the newly adolescent Tania for the first time in almost four years.

The first thing that I noticed about Tania was her face. Before, there had been a beautiful child—well-molded features, aristocratic even—framed by a bright halo of hair. But Tania had lost something of her glorious beauty in that precarious transition from early childhood into the double-digits. What had happened? The features—the green eyes, especially—were still absolutely right. No "Roman" bumps or lengthy protrusions had come up to mar the fine lines of the nose. The hair, although by now far too twelve-year-old stylish, each strand feathered and teased to pubescent perfection, was still lovely—silky-fine and absolutely unruinable. What was it then? What had happened?

It was the mouth. Tania's formerly mobile feature was stark still now, and this had cost the girl her stunning looks. The mouth was frozen into a pout. Downward seeking, the mouth had taken on the sullen airs of the French actress, Jeanne Moreau, during her late period.

Tania started with a challenge as soon as I said "Hi." "My name is Tania now, not 'Joe,' or whatever I wanted to change it to after the kidnapping—I didn't like my name then. [It had been 'Tony,' but Tania had 'forgotten']." She moved slowly through the motherless-messy kitchen, ignoring me while idly taking out a piece of Wonder Bread and dropping it into a toaster that sat on the counter dividing the kitchen from the family room. "I don't think about the kidnapping much now," she said, almost as if talking to herself. "So I don't worry."

Benji strolled back in and cracked, "Tania just hates to talk!" Tania didn't like her brother butting in. She started to tease him between bites of toast. "I remember how Benji broke his leg after the kidnapping. It was in a cast a long time. When his leg itched in the cast, he would cry. *Then*, I would tickle his foot."

A lead weight appeared in Benji's hand. I have no idea where he had found it. Big, shaped like the weight in an old clock, the lead started to move a little, propelled by a rope attached to Benji's wrist.

"Bull honkie," "Nigger"—Tania taunted him, spitting out her crumbs. I remembered that Tania had developed prejudices back in 1977 when she began displacing kidnapping-inspired rage onto those kids different from herself. This, however, was going much further. And it was incredibly foolhardy. Tania's hyperactive brother was fiddling with a heavy hunk of lead less than a foot away.

I ordered both kids to calm down. But Tania stepped up her teasing: "I call Benji 'Dummy,' 'Stupid,' 'Retard,' and 'Fag' all the time."

"Then I'll hit you!" Benji started swinging his lead weight. I stopped him, taking the heavy thing away and holding on to it.

The kids settled down. Tania seemed quite eager to tell me how star-crossed, how ill-fated, she felt. "I always wish for a ten-speed bike or somethin'. But I've just got a crummy three-speed. And I want a real monkey when I grow up. I only have stuffed ones now. One night I watched a movie with my Dad," Tania went on. "A man could make animals kill people. [Hadn't Tania just said she wanted a real monkey. Was she hoping for a beast like King Kong?] The movie made me scared, but less scared than the kidnapping did. A movie isn't *really* happening.

"I have dreams about being a movie star," she went on. "But I don't get to be one. People stop me. I do everything wrong. My acting is all wrong. I really want to be a movie star. My dreams started this year 'cause I have pictures of movie actors on my wall. But I haven't wrote any letters to them yet, though. I want to, but I haven't yet."

Jeanne Moreau, yes, that was the resemblance. But Tania would probably have had to move to France to organize her film career—actresses with down-turned mouths are not big in Hollywood. Tania had become overly passive over the four years' time since the kidnapping because she feared the aggressive options to her rage. She was holding back for fear of erupting. "I goof up a lot of things," she went on, "on tests and junk. The moving around has caused me not to have friends, so I do the housework when I come home from school. But I don't clean good. I don't have much faith in the future, I guess. . . . The whole kidnapping—it sort of left me with a down feeling."

Suddenly Tania jumped up. "Oh, oh. I'm supposed to fix Benji some toast. I forgot. I always forget everything I am supposed to do." Tania was expending so much mental energy trying to forget anything connected with her kidnapping that she was forgetting the little things as well.

"She likes boys," Benji started to tease back, but he was about five minutes too late. "Guys surround our house."

"*Before* we moved back to Redwood City, the boys all liked me," Tania corrected him as she handed him the toast. "I like to play boys' games—soccer and stuff. They would always hog the ball though. So I showed them. I made a goal."

Tania looked briefly happy and animated, thinking back to all those San Mateo boys and her wonderful revenge on the soccer field. But she quickly reassembled her gloomy expression. "I wouldn't sign up for special classes [the bright-learners program] this year," she told me, extracting another piece of toast and sticking it into Benji's mouth. " 'Gate' classes are a lot of extra work." Tania's retreat into passivity was costing her dearly. "Gate" programs are a distinct advantage in the California public schools.

"She's a dummy, anyway." Tania's dark little brother belatedly was hitting back for that hideous name calling of moments ago. But Tania could have cared less. She knew she was smart. That wasn't the problem.

Tania returned one last time to her current obsession, the movies. "During the love parts," she smiled—the first full smile of the day, absolutely stunning—"Daddy teases me, and I hate it!" She did not hate Dad's teasing. No psychiatrist was needed here to pick up Tania's feelings about Daddy.

"You love it!" toast crumbs exploded from Benji's lips. Tania's "bratty" little brother had, at last, found his mark. He could get back at his big sister by rubbing her obvious "oedipus complex" in her face.

Tania took off, chasing the black-haired boy deep into the far reaches of the house. I looked over to the counter for the lead weight that I had put down in order to write a little faster. Some leftover toast was stuck to the formica—the lead weight was gone.

Well, the upshot of the Banks story is that it never worked out for the Bankses in Redwood City, or anywhere else they moved in San Mateo County for that matter. Harry, Lois, Tania, and Benji had outrun their roots—they were wilting by the Bay. Harry developed a back problem, a bad one. Lois's headaches didn't get any better. They decided to "retire" —to take some disability pay and move to a tiny farm community on a road into Sequoia National Park—to get closer to the Hoppers, the Winklers, and the Petris, maybe even up the road a piece from some cousins. And so they did. And it was much better. If you're lucky enough to have a clan, stay close. Lois and Harry had learned their lesson.

They kept their new location a secret. I felt lucky to be one of the few trusted with an address. But everybody at the new place still felt discouraged and angry. "Bitter," I guess you'd have to call it. Once in late September, 1981, on our way home from a weekend in the Mineral King section of Sequoia National Park, my husband Ab and I stopped by to say "Hi." While Ab roamed outside, inspecting a new litter of black pups, I chatted with Benji, Lois, Tania, and Harry for a few minutes in their big farm kitchen. Tania knew me—the thirteen year old nodded an acknowledgment and shrugged her shoulders. But no words escaped her mouth. I think she had "decided" at last. I, too, was one of those she hated.

Lois tried to excuse Tania—"She has days like this. Moody with the whole world." Benji spoke a bit, but he was terribly pessimistic. "I know I'm not going to live to ninety. Fifty is my deadline." Instead of registering surprise and concern about his "deadline," Harry and Lois tended to agree. "Yeah," Lois said, "Harry has said, too, he's not going to live to a ripe old age. He's mentioned dying at fifty, himself." Harry assented. "There's a lot of things wrong with me," he said. Benji plunged right ahead. "I'm only ten now," he said, "I've got a long, long time for bad things to happen. . . . I think that other terrible things will happen. Like my dog. I have a wonderful black dog outside this house. I think my dog will be run over."

For the first time since I entered the house Tania said something. "Don't think it," she said, "and it won't happen." She opened the door and slipped out.

I told Lois and Harry that they had to get Tania to the County Mental Health Clinic. It was a must. But Tania must have been listening from outside the door. As Lois started making more excuses for her daughter—"she has two girlfriends now"—Tania came back into the room to convince me how happy, how functional she was. "I have a friend in Menlo Park who I miss—I just keep forgetting to give Mom the letters I write her. . . . And I'm playing cornet in beginning band, and I'll make junior band next year." Tania did not want anybody to think she was doing exactly what she was doing—avoiding important actions while, at the same time, venting small amounts of anger at people disconnected from her kidnapping. She needed professional help. But her family—affected as they were by Tania's moods—did not want the young teenager to see a psychiatrist. After all, Benji was the different one—he needed the help. But Tania was the doll, the family movie star. She was OK.

I looked about the nice, old-fashioned kitchen and glanced at the pretty, two-acre spread beyond the clean window. The Bankses were, indeed, much better off near their clan than they had been for all the years that I had known them. But old angers still lived at their house. Lois concluded as we all stepped out to inspect the new puppies. "Tania has her moody days. We know that. She cries easily." She paused for an instant, winking at me. "OK. So she can be a snot!"

The Bankses were back inside the nest of their family where they belonged—with the other Bankses, the Petris, the Winklers, and the Hoppers. Grandpa Petri was still going great guns at seventy-five—still talking lawsuits against the kidnappers and still writing his poems. But Harry Banks had lost his kidnapping "song." I asked him to sing it for me in that pleasant farm village—just a bus stop, really, on the way up to Mineral King—but he couldn't even remember the first line.

When an animal feels threatened by another, he readies for battle or he flees. Adrenaline circulates, the heart pumps hard and fast, and the muscles tense, enriched by oxygen and nutrients that arrive within a few seconds. Everything is ready for the quick move—fight or flight.

Humans respond this way, too, but of course, they also know how to think or to talk their way out of a jam. The human brain readies itself for emergency, reacting almost instantaneously.

One special human quality is the ability to control the environment, to use long range planning and impulse control to master situations. Children develop this ability—a little at a time, of course—beginning in late infancy from the first moments they are able to wag their heads "no" (a René Spitz concept) or from the time they can waddle on two feet and achieve bladder and bowel control (an Erik Erikson concept). "Autonomy," as Erikson calls it, is a special human attribute. Preplanning, a later development along the autonomy line, is one reason we dominate all other species.

But what happens when a child who already has achieved some autonomy is suddenly robbed of it? When all sophisticated choices are ripped away? Such is the case in rapes, kidnappings, or physical abuses. The same autonomic releases for fight or flight come about—adrenaline is released, nutrients flow quickly to the muscles, and oxygen supply is augmented. But motoric discharge is blocked. The child's body—all ready for taking risks—cannot move. There is no hope of success. The child's mind, thinking overtime and totally on the alert, cannot fashion a plan because the shock of the ambush feels too overwhelming, the attack, too devastating, and the attackers, too powerful. A child, in such circumstances, is totally helpless, and he knows that he is. He has temporarily lost a very human attribute and an early accomplishment, the ability to exert autonomy.

One thing immediately happens when a kid is temporarily rendered "subhuman"—he becomes terrified. But he may also become enraged. The adrenaline, and probably a storm of brain neurotransmitters as well, encourages a buildup of fear and aggression where there is no possible outlet. Anger becomes an important post-traumatic emotion if special circumstances before and/or during the traumatic event inspire the rage (Tania's fury at her family for going camping the day of the kidnapping was one of those special circumstances). Anger may emerge as a problem in trauma if it is clear that man, not nature, created the horror in the first place. Philosophically, even for a child, it is almost impossible to remain permanently angry at God or at the forces of nature. If the horrible events are prolonged and repeated—in other words if the extreme stresses come to be expected and if the perpetrator is well-known to the victim—anger may become especially important. It may even come to dominate the fear.

Tania Banks was not typical of every kidnapped kid at Chowchilla. Although nineteen of these children showed some anger after the kidnapping, only six incorporated the rage into their personalities. The five besides Tania who demonstrated some seepage of anger into their character structures after the kidnapping had also had their special reasons—fights with Mom on the morning of the kidnapping, for instance, or so much fear that they always felt irritable, always pushed. More often than not, however, the Chowchilla children voiced angry fantasies or made statements about their fury rather than exhibiting a full personality change. Bob Barklay, fourteen, the one boy acknowledged by all the other children to be the "hero" of Chowchilla, spoke about his anger only as a fantasy. "I get revenge thoughts," he said. "I'd put the kidnappers down there in the hole where we were. I'd put hinges and a padlock on that metal plate. If they'd done that, we couldn't have gotten out. I'd like to turn them loose in Chowchilla for a day. My dad says, 'They've lived toooooooooooo long!' " Bob showed no personality problems after the kidnapping, but one would have had to say he was angry.

Known perpetrators, those who create repeated, long-standing, ugly experiences, tend to stir up the most angry, the most problematic personalities that one finds among young trauma victims. As a matter of fact, the frequently repeated and the long-standing traumatic experiences of childhood are the ones most marked by extreme rage and its mirror image, extreme passivity. Occasionally, these manifestations of anger swing back and forth in wild, unpredictable combinations after repeated abuses, a picture that is termed, when one sees it, "borderline personality."

Parental abuse is an extremely powerful instrument in creating angry distortions of childhood personality. The physically abused child may be quite open with his rage. Such children may fight back with anything available. One battered infant, for instance, would vomit all over his force-feeding mother whenever she put the bottle to his mouth. As his mother became more panicky and forceful, the baby became more stubborn. Eventually he came close to starving to death and she came close to obliterating him with a throw against the kitchen wall. A preschooler I evaluated long ago used to smear feces on the back screen door whenever her mother would put her outside to play. You would have to say, "that's a pretty angry child." The child was provoked, however. She had been close to death at age two. Her mother had nearly drowned her in the bathtub. Another time the little girl was badly burned when her mother lashed out at her with a kettle full of boiling tea. Which offenses came first? In these two instances, the mothers complained that their babies had been the first offenders. It was clear, however, that the mothers had begun the angry spirals. Were these babies carrying bad, "aggressive" genes? Some would say "yes," arguing that although this genetic connection is not yet worked out, it will eventually be proven. In my view, however, psychic trauma will stay mainly in the province of those interested in how the environment impacts children. Even if genes and/or brain injuries were operational here, it would be difficult to dismiss the strong environmental evidence. Violence leads to more violence. The attack induces the counterattack.

Sometimes the chicken-egg conundrum is almost impossible to pick apart in child-abuse cases. One meets a child who behaves oddly and aggressively, and then one learns that the behavior is coming from the parents' actions. The parents feel justified, in turn, because, in their view, the child originally set up the situation. Janice McGill, age five, for instance, was taking food from other kids' kindergarten lunches, arguing incessantly with peers, and overturning the school garbage pail whenever she had the chance. A school social worker looked into her situation. "Mommy doesn't feed me," the little girl complained. But Mommy did indeed feed Janice. The child was refusing to eat her mother's food. Janice looked like the source of the problem, a liar, a bizarre kid.

The school, however, decided to check further. Janice was taken to a pediatrician. The doctor found old burns on the soles of Janice's feet. "She stepped on the hot air vents," Dad said. "It was a long time ago," said Mom. The pediatrician ordered a series of X rays. There were two old fractures at different stages of healing, almost a sure-fire sign of child abuse (especially if the bones were medically untreated at the time they were broken and if the injuries were unaccompanied by any parental history of what had happened). "That was a long time ago. We don't remember how it happened," said both Mom and Dad.

Janice was sent to me for psychiatric evaluation. The child had always been bad—colicky, disagreeable, temperamental, a "witch," Mom told me. "As a matter of fact," Mom said, "she was born in caul." Mom went on to explain that being born with the membranes intact meant that Janice had been born with "powers." "She's always been like that," Mom said. "She can see right through me."

It was clear by now that the adult McGills, not Janice, had started the abusive cycle. Janice was a terror—a horribly out-of-sorts five year old. But this was reactive, not the source of the problem. Janice's mother had labeled her a "witch" from the moment of Janice's delivery. And "witch," indeed, was what the child had become. The McGills had three girls older than Janice. None of them were abused. Not one turned out to be angry or destructive. It was Janice who had been singled out. She was to be the little "witch." A prophecy asserted at the moment she was born was ful-filled.

A repeatedly abused or sexually misused child may fall upon one of three pathological ways to express anger, that is, if the rage turns out to be the primary emotion stimulated by the abuses. The child may, for one, "identify with the aggressor" or "turn passive into active," leading at its most extreme to a cruel, bullyish, abusive, and even criminal personality. Many child abusers, for instance, were originally child-abuse victims. The abused child may, secondly, retreat into passivity out of habit, a "reenact-ment" of old victimizations, in other words. Such a child may well retain the victim stance for life. The child could, as a third option, continue to act in an acceptable fashion, flaring into wild rages and self-destructive sprees whenever frustration hits. One woman I treat, for example, is a successful banker and a respected community leader, but she occasionally attacks her intimates with fingernails or an open palm. She also cuts herself at unpredictable times with razor blades. The woman feels sexually numb. But she is exquisitely sensitive to small insults and to attempts by others to control her. She told me that for ten years of her midchildhood her father forced her repeatedly into brutal and repulsive sexual acts. At age sixteen she ran away from home, never to return. The main feeling she now experiences is an unquenchable rage. "Can't you give me some medicine to snuff out my anger?" the woman begs me. "We'd have to invent it," I reply.

Whatever configuration the abused child's personality eventually takes, angry children grown-up often turn to alcohol, street drugs, and psychoactive medications in order to dampen their rage. You see, it's true—we have no really good substances at the present time with which to treat anger. Carbamazapine (Tegretol), a drug used primarily to treat epilepsy, holds some hope. It significantly helped the woman of whom I was just speaking. But, thus far, no psychoactive drug has been developed that attacks rage per se. It is amazing how long and how destructively the inner fires set burning during childhood will continue to spark.

Every angry child, of course, does not go on to develop a problem personality or a substance abuse disorder. There are many intervening variables—genetic ones, good life experiences, care and concern from certain family members, social and financial changes in the family's life, a healthy constitution, and luck.

I introduce myself to eight-year-old Roosevelt Long, a resident patient at a midwestern hospital for disturbed children. Roosevelt was repeatedly abused as a toddler by his parents, both alcoholics, who abused each other, as well. But Roosevelt experienced something even worse when he was three. He watched helplessly as his mother stabbed his father to death. Roosevelt's mother went off to prison, and the boy went on to a career of attacks upon other kids, name calling, and self-mutilation. By the time he was eight, Roosevelt found himself hospitalized at a residential treatment center where I had been invited to conduct rounds. A young doctor assigned to Roosevelt was trying to present the boy's case to us. But the lad had burst into our conference room, and there was to be no more privacy for our group.

I introduce myself to Roosevelt. "Might as well make the best of the situation," I think. The boy answers breezily, "Hi, Doc. Hi, Sally, Ernest, Dr. Selcer, Dr. Channing, Dr. Brizard. . . ." Roosevelt proceeds to call off a list of names that must represent just about the entire hospital staff. "Roosevelt," I start to interrupt well into his list. "We want to talk to you today about what you can remember from when you were three years old."

"I don't wanna talk about it. No, no. I can't talk. No can talk. You wouldn't want me to talk. No, no. You wouldn't want that." The lad is effectively keeping his story to himself by indulging in nonstop chatter—rhythmic phrases in cadence that make everything he says nearly meaningless.

"Do you want to tell us what you think of the hospital?"

"Yeah, man. Now you're talking—now you're talking. Like it fine. Like it fine. Man, I like it fine. Good food. Wonderful food. Nice Dr. Selcer, Dr. Channing, Dr. Brizard, Sally, Ernest. . . ." He tries again to rattle off his series of hospital staff names. It sounds like that old camp song "A Hundred Bottles of Beer on the Wall." Once started, there is no stopping it. What subject can attract Roosevelt? What of himself might he be willing to expose?

"Tell me about your future, Roosevelt? What would you like to be?" I interrupt, this time closer to the beginning of the list than before.

Suddenly the child opens up and you can feel his rage pop the room with a horseshoe-stuffed glove. "What I want to be, Mrs. Doctor, is a cop. A cop. Right, that's what I want to be. A cop. A killer cop. I'm gonna kill people. That's what I want to do. Kill people. Be killin'. Be killin'." The boy begins to dance a little. He cannot contain his excitement. Stimulated by his idea of becoming a killer cop (his compromise between his rage and the desire to be good), Roosevelt cannot stop his chant. The chatter goes on nonstop now.

"I'm gonna shoot robbers, killers, anybody do anythin' bad. And they gonna be dead. Dead. They be hurt—bad. Baaaaad. And that be real bloody."

Roosevelt throws himself, back first, onto the seat of a bentwood chair. He lands on the small of his back, all four limbs dangling. I wince for him. But he appears to feel nothing. Wiggling his arms and legs—rhythmically, spasmodically, almost like an epileptic fit, Roosevelt chants, "They gonna die. Die. Die. They gonna die. Die. Die. With blood everywhere. Lots of blooooood." A spasm of excitement jolts Roosevelt's frame. "Like this. They gonna throw out their arms and legs," he jerks about on his back, "and they gonna scream." He screams. He wiggles. He "spazzes," a convulsive series of jitters. Then Roosevelt says, "They gonna move jus' a little then. And then they be still." The boy lets out a long death rattle: "Rghghghorr," and yet another. "They be still—they be still," he hisses. The child whispers the phrase again and again. He looks spent. The room is silent. Roosevelt Long has just reenacted for a group of about forty mental health professionals the bloody family murder he witnessed when he was only three years old. I dread the thought of Roosevelt Long as an adult. Murder is very much on his mind.

The ancient Greeks quivered about their creations the Erinyes, snake-bedecked, female immortals of uncertain number who would ascend periodically from the depths of Earth to drive men mad. These creatures would plague the folk who broke the ancient Greek rules, the most important of which was a prohibition against murder inside the family. No matter what the justification, no one was to kill someone with whom they had blood ties—or the Erinyes would come.

The word "Erinyes" was whispered or avoided, not spoken, in the ancient Greek language. The Romans called these same ladies "Furies." From these names came words like the Latin "furor," for madness, and "maniac," from the Greek place "Maniai," where the Erinyes wore their terrible black robes.

When the parents of Chowchilla waited for word of their missing children, they considered themselves, briefly, a group. A clan, even. Family. Like the stranded aircrash victims of Shangri-La or the members of those real fighting units who rushed the Normandy beaches, the Chowchilla parents immediately became intimates of the other parents through common ordeal. They depended upon each other, spoke personally, and became, in a sense, instant siblings.

Afterward, when everything worked out for the best, they tried to stay brothers and sisters. Judy Johnson, Lois Banks, Sala Hunter, and Cookie Barklay thought of organizing self-help rap sessions for the "family." They didn't quite know what they wanted, but they hoped that the old sense of mutual support could be maintained. So they put together a meeting early in August. They used the Chowchilla Library, a WPA project that still carries some of the old, 1930s American Crafts Movement "class." And that first meeting proved successful.

To the second meeting, however, the Erinyes showed up uninvited. Perhaps they came because a parent or two was beginning to speak ill of the town. Maybe they came because somebody had broken a preordained, ancient, and now unheard-of rule of "family," something like "Nonfamily may not pretend to be family." More likely they came because no mental health professionals were conducting these group meetings—the rap sessions were, in effect, free-for-alls. The Erinyes were there, though, whatever their reasons. Anybody at the "Second Chowchilla Parents' Meeting" would attest to that.

I was not there. I heard about it later. As a matter of fact, I heard about it too many times to recount all the versions I heard. I did not arrive at

Chowchilla until December 1976. The "Second Parents' Meeting" was held in late August. Later, I figured that the whole thing was bound to have happened. By August, there was no one left for the parents to get mad at but the other parents. Fred Woods and the Schoenfeld brothers had been jailed for weeks. The townsfolk were still celebrating the kids' safe return. A bronze shop was still working on a plaque built to last forever, something to nail to a rock near the center of town, something with an inscription that would immortalize twenty-six nice kids and their bus driver. Who, then, could you go after if you still felt furious? It would *have* to be the other families. And so the Erinyes came in advance. They knew what was about to happen.

First, a psychiatrist from the Madera Community Mental Health Center gave a little speech. Lois Banks had invited him. He was supposed to tell the families what to expect of their children, and he said, "One child in twenty-six will be affected." Like a rock thrown into a crowd of nervous warriors, that "one in twenty-six" hurt. Everybody *knew* his own kid was having trouble. That upbeat mental health prediction released a Fury into the crowd.

The psychiatrist left, unchased I assume, for home. Some parents wanted to leave but they didn't. Four years later, the Thorntons asked me if that psychiatrist had been me. They had been there at that meeting, just like everyone else, yet they were so upset that they couldn't even remember whether the "shrink" had been male or female, young or old. Maybe they had spotted one of those hell-raising Furies among the crowd that night.

Somebody at the meeting tried, after the psychiatrist left, to bring up what to do with all the donations coming into Chowchilla. "How much money is there?" "Who has it?" "Do one of *you* have it?" Couples looked hard at other couples. Faces looked mean in the low light. Furies Two and Three sprung up from under the oaken library tables. Almost everybody there could feel the trouble.

But a few people still didn't realize what was happening. "Should we sue?" somebody asked. "The kidnappers are rich kids. Their parents are rich. Maybe we should talk to a lawyer." How could that somebody have been so cut off from the rage in that room? The Furies were laughing aloud by now. Two parents stood up, now three, now five. A few stayed on to make indignant speeches. "How dare this group speak of money?" "How dare we equate lost children with compensation? We refuse to stay here anymore and listen to this!" And ten, maybe fifteen, parents stormed out.

A few folks dribbled out later while the final speeches were being delivered. A few stayed through to the end and hated. One or two of them sat there listening, confused. English was not their first language. "Why was everybody so mad at everybody?" A few of the Greek mythology books on the Chowchilla Library shelves shook. *They* recognized the (whisper when you say it) Erinyes when they came to town.

The "Second Parents' Meeting" was the last self-help attempt ever organized by the Chowchilla parents. It became a focus of rage for many of them. One couple that was there that night, Paul and Wilma Sturgis, were quite verbal about it. Paul and Wilma conveyed feelings that had been building up for more than four years by the first time I met them. You see, Paul and Wilma had left town in 1976, so they did not participate in the first leg of my study. I will go over the results of the "Second Parents' Meeting" from the Sturgises' point of view because it shows what can happen to a family's fury after their child is traumatized. My interview with Paul and Wilma Sturgis took place in the fall of 1980. We were in Visalia, California, a Central Valley town one hundred miles to the south of Chowchilla.

Paul and Wilma Sturgis's daughter, Sandra, had been a kidnap victim. But another child, Bert, had also been enrolled in the Dairyland-Alview summer school and had missed the bus hijacking only because he stayed home sick that day. We met at the Sturgis home, and this was to be the first and only time we would meet. Paul and Wilma were not at all eager to speak with me, they had told my secretary when she made their appointment. As a matter of fact, the atmosphere the Saturday morning I walked into their nice, new-looking, two-story house was a bit stiff, though cordial.

"I've always been concerned about my kids," Paul Sturgis began as we sat down at the dining room table, "and I was the first to discover that the school bus was missing. I was the one worried about the kids' safety from the beginning. I was the first one out there searching for the kids with one of my older daughters. And that's how I found out that a kidnapping was happening."

I explained that I was conducting a research study and would be writing some articles and a book. Paul and Wilma listened without interruption. "We saw the book those two Fresno reporters wrote, and it is not at all interesting," Paul pointedly looked at me when I finished. "It is very centered on some people—the Johnsons, for instance. And actually the Johnsons didn't come into the situation until after *us*." Judy Johnson, the mother of Johnny and Jackie Johnson, both kidnap victims, was the parent who had originally invited me to Chowchilla. Paul Sturgis would speak of her again later that morning. But Paul Sturgis's comments about writers implied that he already was terribly suspicious of me. Would my book be "interesting" enough for him?

"I found the bureaucracy operated so slow," Paul went on without stopping. "I got a very frustrating run around. 'Where is she?' 'Where would the bus be?' 'What route did they take?' I had trouble getting any information. They wanted to kick me out, but my size and my loud voice kept me there." Paul Sturgis did convey a tremendous presence. He was very tall and built like a football player. His deep basso voice suggested a musical career never pursued. "The Dairyland school superintendent was all hush-hush," he went on. "So were the office personnel, and so forth. I went to the school. I had a hard time seeing anybody or getting any information."

Paul's frustration—with nowhere else to settle—had landed on the administrators of the summer school and then had ricocheted onto that old familiar mark, the other Chowchilla parents.

Wilma Sturgis brought up the subject of the "Second Parents' Meeting" at this point. She joined the conversation as Paul paused for breath. "I didn't like what the kids' mothers were doing," Wilma said. "They were forming clubs."

"They were talking at one of their meetings about getting money," Paul had gained enough air to launch another attack. "People were writing books and kids were supposedly going to play parts in movies. There were constant stinking phone calls to our house at all hours. Sandra didn't answer the phone. We wouldn't let her. Some calls were risqué. One was for some written article or something. People were calling us and asking us all sorts of things. They wanted to have meetings."

"We went to a few of those parents' 'club' meetings," said Wilma. "The whole idea—."

"Why would you want to make a social event out of a tragedy?" Paul jumped in again, expecting no answer. "They were talking about electing officers, having parties—."

"*Other* people were OK," Wilma's voice quivered ever so slightly here. She cared about this. "But there was primarily one set—the Johnsons and the Bankses—*they* were so wrapped up in it, it was becoming their life. The rest of us were being drug along for the ride." At that, Wilma Sturgis sighed as she gradually settled back into her meticulously clean, burnt orange dining room chair.

"Mrs. Johnson came over to our house and she called us up all the time," Paul Sturgis's face reddened. Was he embarrassed or just angry? It turned out to be both. "I figured, 'Boy, this lady has a problem,' " he said. "It hurt me to run across those people telling me about the problems their kids were having. We wanted to get on with the business of life and education and stuff. I didn't like my privacy invaded—and Sandra's—with ridiculous questions. Judy Johnson, I think that's her name, actually tried to 'turn me on' by questioning me about stuff like 'Was Sandra molested?' Stuff like that."

I decided to enter an objection here despite the fact that I try not to argue with patients—it's bad technique. I knew Judy Johnson fairly well. Troubled as she was, Mrs. Johnson certainly did not appear to me to be interested in sexually titillating anybody victimized by the Chowchilla kidnapping. She had simply been trying—with Lois Banks's help—to organize the "Parents' Group," that ill-fated "family" or whatever one would call the enclave that had set up the "Second Parents' Meeting." Putting down my pen, I set myself to object, disregarding what many psychiatric colleagues observing the scene would have thought.

But Paul Sturgis did not seem to notice any change of posture or demeanor at my end of the table. "I was doing battle with the reporters," he went right on to the scene of the children's homecoming at the fire station four years earlier. "They were taking pictures of me. Every reporter in the country was there. The school director called twice—he said the FBI had been brought in. I never saw so many fumbling officers in my life—the locals. Thank God they brought the FBI in. But the FBI was late."

There was not a single Chowchilla person or institution that looked good in this South Valley dining room. Four years after the kidnapping, everybody, even I, was the target of Paul and Wilma's anger. "At a certain point people started searching for more than what the kidnapping really was," Paul went on. "The parents kept bringing it up. And they didn't let it go. But they didn't think of any plan to prevent it. [Paul was implying here that he fully expected another mass kidnapping.] As it turned out, the kids got only three hundred dollars apiece and some money for a scholarship fund. Some of the parents at the "Parents' Meeting" thought the city took some of the money. But what could the city do with it? Lawyers came around. Why in the hell do lawyers have to take money for everything? The bank attorney received a fee—I was rapidly becoming disappointed in human nature, and—." Paul was now talking at length about a subject he had previously criticized the other Chowchilla parents for talking about too much, the subject of money. (Two other couples, earlier, had identified Paul Sturgis as the person, they thought, who had talked the most about money at that ill-fated "Second Parents' Meeting." *He* was the reason they had walked out, they said. But who knows whether that was correct. After all, somebody had thought *I* was the psychiatrist at the "Second Parents' Meeting.")

Wilma Sturgis could hold herself back no longer. "I worked at Farnesi's coffee shop in Chowchilla," she said. "It and Pistoresi's Chevy agency were like the town gossip centers. Because of what Judy Johnson was telling people, they'd say at my job, 'I hear you people want to write a book—do a movie.' I was sooooo embarrassed."

"All *I* wanted," said Paul Sturgis, "was my daughter back. I broke through the crowd [waiting at the fire station for the children's return from Santa Rita Prison] and I said, 'I want Sandra.' An FBI agent—he said—I couldn't have her. And I said '*Oh, I can't?*' " Mr. Sturgis made his old threat with renewed flare. His shiny eyes challenged me, defying me to try to take Sandra away from him right then and there. "I took my kid home," he said, quieting quickly when I did not move. "And you can see her now if you'd like."

The scene had come to an end and I would be allowed to interview the young Sandra Sturgis. The girl turned out to be a shy, sweet, polite, and very well-, perhaps too well-, organized person. At this point, however, I will ignore Sandra and list, instead, how many people and groups, both victims and neutrals, were attacked by Wilma and Paul Sturgis four years after their young daughter was kidnapped:

(1) Sandy Miller and Gail Tompkins, the Merced reporters who had written a book about the Chowchilla incident
(2) the Johnson family, particularly Judy
(3) Lois and Harry Banks
(4) the Chowchilla town bureaucracy
(5) the Alview-Dairyland school superintendent and his staff
(6) the mothers of everybody kidnapped
(7) writers
(8) local law enforcement officers
(9) the FBI
(10) lawyers
(11) the bank
(12) "people" at Farnesi's coffee shop and Pistoresi's Chevy agency
(13) human nature
(14) me

There were far too many vectors to the Sturgises' rage to trace any of it back directly to Sandra, the real victim. There were, however, two major omissions from Paul and Wilma's list that, I feel, are worthy of note.

The first omission is the one that might have been expected. The Sturgis-Mooney clan was never once mentioned in anger by Paul and Wilma Sturgis. Clans are usually the one great exception when it comes to rage. Family is the institution you feel you can count on most when things go wrong. And so Paul and Wilma Sturgis, no matter how provoked they were, never turned on kin.

The second omission was a little unexpected, however. Nowhere on the Sturgis "enemies list" that autumn morning, 1980, did the names of the kidnappers, Fred Woods III, James Schoenfeld, and Richard Schoenfeld, appear. Paul and Wilma Sturgis had come to use so much displacement during the four years following the kidnapping that the real perpetrators were entirely spared their wrath. That still surprises me today. But it also shows how "sneaky" the aftereffects of trauma become, that is, if one waits long enough.

Displacement is a very potent, unconscious mental mechanism for moving anger onto others. We have seen how displacement works in psychic trauma as we "listened" to Paul and Wilma Sturgis. "Overgeneralization," on the other hand, is a different mental mechanism for handling the rage inspired by overwhelming events. Overgeneralization takes in whole classes of people. Whereas displacement causes victims and families to attack all sorts of people, animals, and institutions willy-nilly following a terrible experience, overgeneralization will account for a laser-beamed directionality of the rage. Overgeneralized anger focuses upon one single category. It often accounts for racial or cultural prejudice. One hates all workmen in blue shirts—or all Hoosiers—when one overgeneralizes.

Racial prejudice is taught at home—we all know that. But some prejudices begin with the overgeneralizations that are created from childhood trauma. I will never forget, for instance, a black teenager who had been wrongly chased and shot at by a rifle-toting Arab. (Luckily, he escaped uninjured.) Rafael Jones, a boy of the "ghetto," talked to me later about his newfound prejudice. He told me with no intended irony, "All Arab mens look alike. They not to be trusted. They be dangerous. You mus' cross the street to the other side when they be around. 'Stay away from Arabs,' I always say." Rafael, the black, had come to hate the Arabs. He was talking the way some whites talk about blacks, the way a Southeast Asian might speak of the Chinese.

The fright and rage drummed up by the Chowchilla kidnapping eventually landed on me. It had to. Displacement demanded that this happen. As a matter of fact, Jackie Johnson was so angry at me four years after the kidnapping—for nothing that I did or didn't do as far as I could tell—that she allowed me to see her only once. She referred to me that year on network news as "my psychiatrist," yet, at the time, she was actively refusing all appointments with me.

In 1980 Leslie Grigson had to be "prayed over" in tongues Friday nights at a charismatic church in order to "gain enough strength" to come to the park for a Saturday morning interview. All this praying took place more than four years after the kidnapping. In Leslie's mind I was developing more frightening qualities the longer she knew me.

Barbara Bennett eventually came to believe that I was plaguing her, that I was "after" her, that I might even have the power to be in two places at once. Barbara's "displacements" forced her image of me into the world of the supernatural. Barbara was thirteen at the time of the four-year follow-up. She thought, by then, that I was "in cahoots" with the three kidnappers. "Do you know them?" she had asked. "Write them in prison?" "Go see them?" She implied that I "knew" too much about them.

To each of these questions I assured Barbara, "No." I explained she was placing me "in" with the kidnappers because she was feeling so frustrated about the possibilities for any direct revenge at the three young men in jail. Her anger "beam" had deflected onto me. But Barbara shrugged off my explanation. I could tell.

More than a year after the follow-up was finished, Barbara Bennett, by then fifteen years old, phoned me from a small town in the Ozarks. The girl had moved with her mother and sister to an eastern Oklahoma border town when her parents divorced. Nedda Bennett had gone back "home" to be closer to her own Williams clan. And she had brought Barbara and Janice along.

"Hi, doctor!" a cheery voice flew over the plains, the Rockies, the deserts, and the high Sierras. Overbright. Too much. It was about 9 A.M. in California—what was that in Oklahoma? Probably eleven.

"Did you put some stuff into my locker today?" Barbara was asking. Had I invaded that shrine to adolescent privacy, the locker? It was a loaded question.

"What did I put in your locker today, Barbara?"

"Notes. Notes and clippings on kidnappings. Threatening me."

"How long have you been living in the Ozarks?"

"A few months."

"And how long have these notes been coming?"

"A few weeks."

"Did you tell anybody at your new school about what happened at Chowchilla?" I asked.

"Yep. A few people."

"Well, Barbara," I said, "somebody at school who heard the kidnapping story must be trying to tease you—to scare you all over again. The person is probably very worried about your story. And so he or she is frightening you back by putting notes into your locker."

"I don't think a kid did it. There were a couple of newspaper clippings about other kidnappings," Barbara argued. "And the person printed on the clippings, 'Watch out—this is going to happen to you.' Kids don't read the newspapers. They don't clip clippings."

Barbara was wrong. Chowchilla victims didn't read the papers much—they were too scared of what they might find there. But nontraumatized kids, at least many of them, do keep up with the news. The McFarland-Porterville control group certainly did.

"When did the most recent note appear in your locker?" I asked.

"This morning. Between the time I came to school and now."

"So how could I have done it? I'm in my office in California. How would I have been able to put a note into your locker *today*?"

"I don't know *how* you did it. [Pause.] Are you sure you didn't?"

"Yes, I'm sure." I was sure I did not have the power to be two places at once, although I was quite certain Barbara thought I could.

It went on like this for a few more minutes until Barbara Bennett reluctantly signed off. But later that day she phoned my office again. It must have been about two or three o'clock in California.

"Hi Doctor Terr," the upbeat voice sounded its false cheer across the miles. "Are you sure you didn't do it?" "Yes." "A friend of yours?" "No." "Mom wants to talk to you."

"Yeah, hon"—Nedda Bennett joined in—"have you been testing my kid by putting stuff into her locker?" Nedda was trying to be nice and polite, but she meant anything but "hon." The fury and fear of the child had reached the mother. And they had granted me the supernatural speed of the god, Hermes. I would not have been surprised if the other Williamses of east Oklahoma felt a bit miffed and scared, as well.

Remember the Montagues and the Capulets? Shakespeare never did explain why those two ancient families of Verona were at war. From what I remember, Romeo's and Juliet's kin had been "at it" for centuries (Shakespeare says they had battled three times during the Prince of Verona's tenure alone)—and nobody talked in the play about what had originally set off the feud. Two young lovers were shoved, reason or no, into a parade of victims.

At Chowchilla I began to see how traumatic events could stimulate family feuds. Displacements, overgeneralizations, and ongoing wishes for revenge could easily inspire groups to attack one another. Who knows—a traumatic event might have started the troubles between the Montagues and the Capulets, that is, if such families did actually exist in Renaissance Verona.

In another era and place, Paul Sturgis might have challenged Judy Johnson's husband, Elmer, to a duel. The Bankses, Hoppers, Winklers, and Petris might have taken their shotguns to the Newhall-Woods clan of the San Francisco Bay area. And the Oklahoma Williamses might have come after me.

Clan wars have gone on from the time of the ancient Greeks—before then, too, I expect. Some of the great Greek clashes—and the best Greek tragedies—have to do with these terrible, revengeful struggles between families. The *Iliad* does, as do many of the plays of Aeschylus, Sophocles, and Euripides. The ancient Greeks risked death, destruction of their own love affairs, and even madness in order to complete acts of revenge demanded by shocking events. These same sorts of family-enacted vendettas for old traumas still serve as plots for films such as *Deliverance* and popular books such as Stephen King's *It* and *Thinner*.

It is just families? One might look at war this way, too. Years ago, the psychoanalyst Martin Wangh wrote a theoretical paper arguing that war is a consequence of "unconsciously motivated repetitive behaviors following national traumas." Wangh saw the personal vendetta as something that could easily escalate into war.

But I must stop here. War lends itself to foolhardy oversimplification and I am falling into the trap. Let us remember, instead, the small-scale stuff—the lawsuits, petty word-battles, walkouts, and angry obsessions that take place after shocks. I have already mentioned that one of the stories circulating around Chowchilla from the time I first came there was about the kidnappers. "They" were saying that Fred Woods or one of his Schoenfeld friends had been stopped by a traffic cop near Chowchilla for speeding. The ticket, the boys felt, was undeserved. Young Woods, or a Schoenfeld, or whoever, had become angry—mad at the unfairness of it all. "He" had decided to take revenge upon the whole town, to steal the town's kids, to rob the town blind.

So the whole Chowchilla kidnapping—if that story is true—came about because of three young men's fury with a town. A vendetta. A plot to extract the most precious commodities that a town has—its kids. And if this story is just a story, a rumor in other words, then stories of revenge may be "contagious," spreading about towns with the fluidity and mobility of the rage that hatched them in the first place.

Which came first—the chicken or the egg? It's hard to tell when it comes to rage.

CHAPTER 4

Denial and Numbing

It felt weird the times my big brother [ten years older] put his penis in me. Sometimes I was afraid. It hurt like a pencil was hitting me. But I could think other things and forget it. Sometimes I wished to escape this and pretend other things were happening. This is a boring subject. . . . I don't know why this happened with my brother. I say "I don't know" a lot to myself. I say "I don't know" all the time in my mind. On a bad day I say it sixteen times. But I don't really know what makes a bad day. I don't know.

Ginny Bell, age eight

E VERY MAY, CHOWCHILLA PUTS ON A FAIR. "Frontier Days," they call it. The fair celebrates youth. School buses, a whole fleet of them, line the chain-link fence that surrounds the fairgrounds. You can spot yellow, beat-up, battle-scarred snub-noses bearing the exotic names of Central Valley places like Ceres, Crows Landing, Le Grand, Catheys Valley, and Planada. Teenagers in every imaginable kind of band uniform, cheerleading outfit, varsity sweater, or club T-shirt mill about, temporarily off-duty from the baton twirling, roping, riding, singing-along, marching-along, and things equally compelling that make this fair a kids' fair. Scores of young people hang out at the animal pens, just sitting on a fence or mucking-up a stall. In each adolescent mouth sits part of that crazy California health food–oriental–western–Mexican–Pacific Islands potpourri —a taco, some pita bread filled with sesame burgers and sprouts, an elephant ear, teriyaki-on-a-stick, corn dog, stuffed potato, pizza, tempura, fruit salad, egg roll, tamale, juice bar, cotton candy, or a Hawaiian shaved ice.

Next to the kids, the exhibits are the best part. In the pavilion, kiwi preserves, homegrown figs and flowers, crocheted bedspreads, quilts, and home-cured hams vie for the blue ribbons while the bulls, beefalo, steers, swine, and sheep compete at the pens nearby. Most of the stuff exhibited at Frontier Days is done or raised by kids. One cannot escape the mental picture of a bespangled, marching-band or cheerleading type up at 5:30 in the morning, voluntarily tending to a rapidly growing beast. That picture impresses me.

There are commercial exhibits at Frontier Days, too—the usual stuff, encyclopedias, computers, lemon squeezers, potato frenchers, insurance policies, farm machinery, jeans, instructions for crop dusting, and a guy you see at all the fairs who can do an oil painting from start to finish in ten minutes flat. But the sheriffs run a booth, too, in one corner of the commercial area. You can find out from the sheriffs, for instance, how to become a lawman, Madera County style, and even, if you are a kid, how to sign up for a "future policeman" training program. There are booklets telling you how to burglar-proof a house, how to protect a car, and how to safely handle all sorts of firearms. Some bad statistics are available on the deaths and injuries caused by Central Valley drunk drivers and some good statistics are plainly in view touting the record of the county sheriffs. What was missing the day I visited the spring fair, however, was something about kidnapping—mass kidnapping, family kidnapping, solo kidnapping, or any kind of kidnapping at all. There wasn't a thing about kidnapping.

Take those milk carton kids or those missing children posters you see all over America, for instance. There was none of that at the Madera County sheriff's booth when I browsed through their stuff. There were no pamphlets on how to avoid kidnapping, nor was there any tract on parental child-snatching, a sizable contemporary problem. No old pictures of law enforcement men bringing in the Chowchilla victims graced the walls of the booth, nor was there a shot of the three kidnappers being escorted to their arraignment. One might have thought that the Madera County Sheriff's Department would have been proud of its most famous case. After all, from the law enforcement point of view, the outcome was highly successful. But no. No one attending Frontier Days on the day I attended would have known that a bus kidnapping had ever happened in Madera County, unless, that is, the person already knew. The Chowchilla kidnapping was to be denied. Hamelin minus the Pied Piper, the Holy Land minus the Children's Crusaders. The need to forget the disaster, to put it out of heart and out of mind, far outweighed any civic pride in its "successful" outcome. What was left was just a blank spot, a blank spot in group memory and a blank spot in feeling.

"Denial of external reality" is a defense. To my surprise, I discovered that children do not shut off their thinking and feeling during single, unexpected, traumatic situations. Traumatized children over three years old are almost uniformly able to give detailed descriptions of their little brother's murder, their rape, an earthquake they survived, or an accident. At Chowchilla, all twenty-five victims could produce vivid accounts of what happened; and each account, with the exception of some distorted details of perception, supported the other children's accounts. Nobody at Chowchilla was missing a piece of history. Nobody had forgotten. At McFarland and Porterville, too, every frightened or traumatized child could remember extensive details in response to the question, "Can you tell me the worst, the most scary thing that has ever happened to you?" There were no "Marnie's" at Chowchilla, no "John Ballantines."

Children previously unexposed to terror tend not to deny. Traumatized children may later "forget" that they developed a symptom. Or they may become so accustomed to chronic, long-standing, or repeated traumas that they begin to shut-off from their consciousness the, by now, fully expected realities. But school-aged children will almost invariably recall a single shock, a first shock.

This childhood tendency not to deny the reality of a traumatic event makes a striking contrast to the denial one sometimes sees in an adult. The adult may be unable to accept or to remember parts of an incident to which a child responds with vivid, detailed remembrance.

Consider the story of eight-year-old Caroline Cramer and her mother, for instance. As Caroline roller-skated down her block, Bowser, her neighbor's dog, jumped her. Bowser fell upon the little girl, ripping her shoulder and biting open her throat. Caroline's windpipe fell open, a jagged, animal-made tracheotomy. Caroline's jugular vein was probably to be next. But at this point, Hildegarde Cramer came rushing out of the house.

Now appears the discrepancy between the two stories. Four years after the attack, Caroline was able to remember that her mother shouted "Stay!" to Bowser and then moved him by the collar away from the scene. Mrs. Cramer, on the other hand, could not remember how she had quieted the animal. She knew she had rushed out the front door to rescue her daughter, but the rest was a blur from which emerged a vague summation, "I somehow did it." Witnesses were available in this case and they confirmed Caroline's story. Mrs. Cramer had not faced the entire reality. The child, however, had been unable to block it.

Another incident that shows this tendency of young people to face what adults cannot accept took place during a boating accident. Ten survivors of the accident, seven adults and three boys, ages ten, fourteen, and fifteen, came to my office for a three-hour group "marathon" session one week afterward. Each person told his own story. It felt like *Rashomon* several times over. Two boys had been waterskiing, pulled by a large cruiser on which the rest of the party was riding. A speedboat suddenly shot out from nowhere, crashing into one of the boys. The victim, a ten-year-old guest of the youngest child in the group, was instantly killed.

The surviving boy and the two adolescents recalled in turn how quickly each had realized that the young water-skier was dead. Each of the boys had noticed something—the dilated, fixed pupils staring straight into a blinding sun, the lolling tongue, the limp neck. Two of the adults, on the other hand, "thought" that the water-skier might have died but couldn't "accept it." Five other adults told us that it had taken more than three hours to convince themselves that the boy was indeed dead. These five adults could not stop attempting to resuscitate the boy until long after the firemen and paramedics had stopped. And even then, these five adults felt uneasy. "Maybe he was still alive," they fretted. "No doctor had pronounced him dead."

Granted, adults know more about rescue squads, hospitals, and miracles than do children. But the contrast between the adults and children on this ill-fated boating trip was impressive. It appeared, as it did in the case of Caroline Cramer, that children generally accept horrors more easily than do adults. Adults use more immediate denial.

Children begin to develop the ability to deny reality once disasters start piling up. Because second, third, and fourth ordeals can no longer surprise, a battle-weary child finds himself bracing for shocks. He prepares. In an attempt to see no evil, hear no evil, speak no evil, and feel nothing, the youngster starts ignoring what is at hand. His senses go numb and he guards against thinking. Repeated or long-standing disasters, thus, encourage denial and numbing. The worst kinds of disasters will create psychically deadened children.

Lord Byron gives us a moving description of how psychic numbing develops. He wrote a letter from Italy, relating the story of three executions he witnessed. He observed that emotional anesthesia set in once a second and third execution took place. He did not experience this during the first execution. Byron says:

> The day before I left Rome I saw three robbers guillotined. . . . Two of
> these men behaved calmly enough, but the first of the three died with great
> terror and reluctance. What was very horrible, he would not lie down;
> then his neck was too large for the aperture, and the priest was obliged to
> drown his exclamations by still louder exhortations. . . . The first turned
> me quite hot and thirsty, and made me shake so that I could hardly hold
> the opera-glass (I was close, but was determined to see, as one should see
> everything, once, with attention); the second and third (which shows how

dreadfully soon things grow indifferent), I am ashamed to say, had no
effect on me as a horror, though I would have saved them if I could.

Byron, letter to John Murray from
Venice, May 30, 1817

Outrage, terror, thirst, and trembling were Byron's immediate responses
to the first man's death. He employed no denial of reality. As the second
horror took place, however, psychic numbing set in the way Novocain
seeps into a jaw. Interestingly, Byron said he left Rome the next day. Did
the horrors he witnessed near the executioner's block drive him out of
town?

The most benumbed survivors tend to emerge from the most extreme
situations—the Holocaust, Hiroshima, Central American war zones, and
the Cambodian "killing fields." Some American urban ghettos, in which
murders, rapes, robberies, and fires go on with the regularity of the garbage
collections, also qualify. Psychic numbing occurs when horrors are
extreme, long-standing, variable, and repeated—in other words, when a
state of horror becomes predictable.

When the United States dropped the Bomb on Hiroshima on August 6,
1945, some of the children living in or near the drop zone suffered extreme
emotional numbing. The first traumatic event, the bombing itself, was
intensely shocking. But within hours, the horrors that followed became
predictable. Psychic numbing and massive denial came into play. Robert
Jay Lifton concluded in his book about Hiroshima, *Death in Life*, that
psychic numbing was central to the emotionality of the Hiroshima survivor. He told of an "outcast" boy, exposed to the Bomb at age two, who
stated, "As for me, I have a feeling of resignation—but no feeling of anger.
After all—well, I can't put it very well—but because the whole thing was
so huge in scale. . . . " Even a baby exposed to the Bomb appeared to wall-
off his horror, according to Lifton. The infant's mother said, "I don't know
whether such a young baby [age one] can receive a severe shock, but for
about one year, until the following July, he didn't cry, didn't laugh, didn't
make any sound with his voice."

Six years after the atomic bombing of Japan, Arata Osada, a professor
who lived and worked in Hiroshima before, during, and after the Bomb,
collected a number of schoolchildren's essays about their experiences.
Despite the passage of time, the children's feelings, as recorded in their
essays, remained vivid. The large majority of compositions that Osada
collected told tales of terror, rage, and unremitting grief. There were, however, a few essays in the collection that expressed extreme psychic numb-

ing. (There is no way to tell from Osada's book the actual prevalence of this type of benumbed response. An author would not necessarily have included every essay he received.) I will quote seven of Osada's schoolchildren here, the seven that struck me as the most benumbed. Their statements are impossible to read without a shudder.

We heard the sound of an airplane and we could see it, very small, in the southeastern sky. It got bigger and bigger and soon it was over our heads. I was looking at it all the time, I didn't know if it was an American plane or ours. All of a sudden, something white like a parachute fell out from the plane. Five or six seconds later, everything turned yellow. It was like I'd looked right at the sun. Then there was a big sound a second or two later and everything went dark. Stones and tiles fell on my head and I was knocked out for a bit. . . . I felt very thirsty and went to the river to get some water. Many blackened dead bodies were floating down the stream. I had to push them away while I drank. Along the edge of the water were lots of dead people. Some were still alive. A child was calling "Mother, Mother." Already, when I saw dead bodies, I didn't think much about it.

A boy who had been a third-grade
student in 1945

There were people so badly burned, their skin was hanging loose. There was a woman dragging the body of what must have been her child; it was impossible to tell if it had been a boy or a girl. A young man with both of his legs cut off came crawling along. I cannot imagine what state of mind I was in—to see all of those horrors without feeling shocked or frightened, to feel nothing at all.

A boy who had been an eighth-grade
student in 1945

Just the memory of it makes my blood run cold. . . . I thought that everyone on earth had perished, leaving only the five of us here in an eerie world of the dead. . . . At places we were forced to step over them callously, but we apologized in our hearts as we did this.

A boy who had been a fifth-grade
student in 1945

There were seven urns standing in the alcove, the ashes of my grandmother, mother, older brother, older sister, younger brother, uncle, and sister Sadako. When father and I used to kneel before the Buddhist altar, my mind would become completely blank at the enormity of it all.

A girl who had been a fifth-grade
student in 1945

I returned to school for a month at the time of the Bomb [in spring, 1946] and received my diploma. My graduation, which should have been one of the happy moments of my life, left me feeling nothing at all.

A girl who had been in middle school in 1945

Some who came from Hiroshima described the city as being changed into a scorched field by a single bomb. Others compared it to a city of the dead with almost all of its citizens annihilated. I felt more dead than alive.

A girl who had been a third-grade student in 1945

I spent the empty days going to the funerals of my teachers and friends.

A boy who had been a sixth-grade student in 1945

Massive denial and numbing may affect children never exposed to war. Repeated horrifying incidents at home can lead to the same sort of emotional deadening that scars the life of the occasional nuclear bomb victim. Parents have ongoing access to their children. They can, if they are so inclined, perpetrate repeated catastrophes in a child's life. Day-care personnel and babysitters have similar repeated access to youngsters. They, thus, also have the power to create ongoing horrors in the life of a child. Satanic rituals at the preschool carry with them ongoing secrets to be held at the cost of death, terrible witnessings, slow tortures, and traps from which there are no escapes. The horrors of sexual abuse of children, like those of war, become predictable. Psychic numbing may occur in any child as a response to this predictability. Numbing will eventually distort a child's personality. As a matter of fact, a child may arrive at the same kind of disordered personality as an adult by being perpetually numb or by feeling perpetually enraged. During childhood, however, rage and numbing will often create different "looks" from one another.

The numb child may be polite, yet hard to know. Words will not flow easily. Humor may not exist at all. But better than my saying this, let's look at a girl who, I think, was numb. She had been exposed to terrible stresses over a three-month period. They left her indifferent, almost blank.

Florence Chow was eight years old when her mother, who did not hold her custody, dragged the young girl, screaming and fighting, from her California school playground. She bundled the child into the backseat of her car and drove to Miami. Mother and child then went into hiding.

Mr. Chow notified the police and obtained several sworn statements from witnesses who had been at the school playground. The Florida State Police located Florence's mother fairly quickly and arrested her. She would remain in jail, a judge said, until she told the authorities where Florence was hidden. But Florence was in the care of her maternal grandparents by this time. Every few days, Grandma and Grandpa moved someplace new. Florence found herself deep in rural Florida, shifted from abandoned shack, to house-trailer, to run-down motel, to campground, to run-down motel, to abandoned shack, and so on. She could not attend school. She was not allowed to go outside except at night when Grandma and Grandpa would take her to a new hiding place.

Mr. Chow hired private detectives. But it took them three and a half months to catch up with the runaway grandparents and young Florence. When Father brought Florence home to California, she was not the child he had known before. She was quiet. Silent almost. She quickly turned fat. (Mr. Chow showed me photos of how petite and animated Florence had been before the snatching.) Her face took on a motionless quality. Her body became sessile, a barnacle attached to an invisible rock.

From California, the girl kept up contact with her mother by phone, through letters, and, occasionally, with chaperoned visits. Three years passed. The mother decided to demand Florence's custody. Mr. Chow's lawyer asked me to examine the twelve-year-old Florence to help him and his client determine how to respond.

The pubertal girl slumped into my office—obese, expressionless, and painfully slow. She plopped into a chair and her binder notebook opened, disgorging several old letters and cards, stained greasy and dark from hundreds of readings. Florence made no motion to pick up her correspondence, and so I stooped down to get it. "They're cards from Mom," she said as I handed her the pack, "and some letters to Mom I didn't send." She then sat there, silent. I asked Florence what she thought about her custody. "There's nothing to say," she answered without any apparent emotion. A longer pause ensued. A few tears began to drip into the child's lap. She made no move toward the Kleenex box that sat right next to her. "I want to live with Mom," she finally said without a shade of expression. She seemed unable to go on. I then asked Florence about her long episode in Florida on the run with her grandparents. She remembered her terror at the school playground but could remember little from the months in hiding. This was consistent with the blocks in memory a child begins to have if a terrible experience is prolonged or repeated. Despite the unpleasantness of what had happened, Florence concluded, "If Mom went to jail for me, *she* should get me." Again the pubescent girl stopped talking. She sniffed away a few old tears. The small carriage clock on my desk ticked loudly. No expression marked the girl's face.

I shifted to "standard" adolescent topics. Perhaps "teen talk" would help Florence show me some kind of feeling. "Tell me about your friends."

"I don't have any." "Do you like to shop?" "Sometimes. At the mall. Alone. I walk around. Don't go into the stores, though." "What do you like to look at in the store windows?" I asked, a little taken aback that this pubescent girl was uninterested in clothes, makeup, video games, tapes, magazines, and records. "I don't care much," she replied. "How about the styles this year?" "My dad and my stepmother bring clothes home to me." The silence dropped down upon us again. It was as if my heavily sound-proofed ceilings, walls, and doors were asserting wills of their own.

"I imagine you listen to certain disc jockeys," I said, breaking the silence once again. "No." "Do you like any particular type of music?" "Not really. I put on the radio, but I don't care what plays." I mentioned that I had recently seen Steven Spielberg's *Back to the Future* and liked it. She gave no response. I then told Florence a little about the film and asked what she thought about the concept. "I don't go to movies much," she answered. And that, she must have felt, was sufficient. She made no further comment. It became quiet again. "Are you bored a lot?" I asked. "Um-hum." Florence now offered four spontaneous sentences strung together, a precious gift at this point. "I don't like school. I don't bother much with the phone. Dad and my stepmom are a drag. They are boring."

"Do you like anything at all?"

"Not really." No feelings registered on Florence's face—not even sadness.

I told Mr. Chow and his lawyer that Florence needed longer and more frequent visits with her mother—the girl missed her mom. But she also needed a course of psychotherapy—that is, if it wasn't already too late. I was very concerned about the girl's personality. She appeared utterly passive, depressed, angry, and without hope. To the outside observer she looked more dead than alive.

"I don't know about treatment or longer visits," Mr. Chow replied to me. "Trips to her mother would be very risky. She'll hide her again. And psychiatry is very expensive. Anyway, Florence will run to her mother as soon as she's old enough to make it." The implication was clear—why put so much effort into her?

Why, indeed? By the time I met her, Florence carried a poor prognosis. Laboring for three years under frustrated love and perpetual grief for a mother with whom she could not live, the adolescent was deeply discouraged. Laboring for three years with the shocking memories of a scene on a California school playground, the adolescent was afraid to go on with life, afraid of the mundane. But something even more bothersome was evident —a generalized deadening, a numbness, a denial of all human emotion. Florence behaved as if she had been subjected to long-standing, dehumanizing experience. As had some of the child-survivors of Hiroshima, Florence Chow had gone dead.

Florence's hopelessness was best expressed by a little crumb of conversation the last day I ever saw her. (No, she did not enter psychotherapy. Her father must have given up—at least for the time being.) I had asked Florence about her future. She answered, "I have no idea what I'd like to be when I grow up. I have no idea if I'll marry." She had shrugged her shoulders in response to my inquiry whether she expected to have children of her own. I then asked how long she thought she would live. "I don't know how old I'll live. If I get killed—whatever happens—then I die young. If I don't, then I guess I live longer."

Early in life, I have found, it is possible to develop two sorts of benumbed personality styles. These will both follow from repeated childhood traumas. A "withdrawn personality," the style so evident in Florence, is one of these. A "hail fellow well met" personality is the other. Eventually both of these benumbed styles, plus the three angry-style childhood personalities I described in the previous chapter (aggressive, passive, and rapidly fluctuating), probably funnel into disordered adult personality states that cut across those currently termed "borderline," "narcissistic," "antisocial," and "avoidant." Nobody has followed children with personality problems in a good enough long-term study, however, to see in linear fashion if and how this conversion to adult personality disorder comes about.

Withdrawn childhood personalities were first observed in neglected or physically abused infants by René Spitz, the great, early researcher on human infancy. Spitz described a number of these hopeless, unrelating, withdrawn youngsters he had found in an impersonal, unloving orphanage in Central America. This kind of baby, unfortunately, exists in the United States, too. One eight-month-old Cleveland girl, whom I tried to help at the university hospital there, had been ignored and occasionally beaten by her severely depressed mother. In her hospital crib, the infant lay on her back with her little hands clutched at midline. It was difficult to pry apart those tiny, fixed fingers. The baby ignored a brightly colored mobile that had been placed over her crib to keep her busy. She paid scant attention to the nurses who came and went, trying to coax some response from her. Hospital procedures that would have brought shouts of protest from any ordinary child provoked hardly a complaint from this one. Both tears and smiles were rare occurrences in the life of this little girl. There was no brain damage. The damage resided only in the baby's still rudimentary, but benumbed, personality style.

The second set of benumbed childhood personality traits that follows from multiple abuses or repeated, long-standing stress is quite different. I call it "hail fellow well met." Many years ago I applied this informal phrase to a pathological personality style I had observed in physically abused children. There still are no corresponding formalized terms in our diagnostic manuals for this kind of childhood personality. Rather than do away with the idea, which I think is a good one, I have continued to call these youngsters "hail fellow well met," waiting for someone to come up with a better name.

The "hail fellow well met" child almost always has experienced repeated abuse. He makes friends easily. Attractive and seductive, he sidles up to almost anyone. But he, like the withdrawn child, has a fundamental problem with human relationships. He shows little discrimination between people. There are no special ones, no favorite pals. Each person is treated the same. There is no way to get close to this child. The youngster's depths are locked up tighter than Bluebeard's secret room. Or, perhaps (I shudder to think of it), there are no depths at all. This child eventually becomes— because people need to connect with children and will not be able to connect with this one—a grave disappointment. Volunteers cancel their offers. Foster parents give up. Social workers call these kids "agency-wise" because they can manipulate the system and survive any number of shifts in placement. They may move to more than ten foster homes in the course of just one childhood. And they stand a good chance of being abused in more than one family placement. Eventually, many of these "hail fellow well met" children end up in child-care institutions where they may begin to function better. Children and staff at institutions do not demand intimacy. What eventually happens in adulthood to these "hail fellow well met" children, however, remains a mystery. Nobody has prospectively followed this kind of youngster for the number of years it would take to obtain the answer.

Here is the story of a "hail fellow well met" child, one of the prettiest girls I ever saw. This eight year old had been abandoned by her unmarried mother who had been abusive and neglectful before disappearing from the girl's life. The child then lived in several foster homes. In two of these, the "fathers" sexually misused her. At age eight, the girl was adopted by an older woman who had told the adoption workers that she wanted to take on a sexually abused child. The agency did not question this unusual request. They simply gave the child to her "new mother." Mother then went on a campaign to try and break the young girl of her sexuality— something like breaking-in a horse. They played the game "Sorry" every time the girl confessed she felt like masturbating. The woman applied "anti-itch" creams to the girl's genitals at bedtime and after school. She checked the child's labia for redness, too, perhaps two times a day. She cajoled. She talked. Mother also required that the girl suck her old, milkless breasts every night before going to bed—"to correct things."

The girl took all this bizarre parental concern in stride. She did not trust her new mother, so she lied to her. She told Mother whatever Mother seemed to want to hear. She never spoke of a past. She rarely spoke about friends, although she did have a few playmates at school. She rarely talked about her academic work. Mother, who had set herself up as rescuer, controller, academic tutor (and, unconsciously, as sexual abuser), became frustrated. It had been a year and no closeness had yet developed. One evening, following a number of out-and-out lies and subtle evasions on the girl's part, Mother snapped. She administered 226 blows to her new daughter's head and body. As she meted out her punishment, Mother counted—one blow for each offense. She counted everything that the child had done wrong from the time she had come there until the present.

In the hospital, the girl was alert and beautiful, even though she had been beaten black and lumpy. She was extraordinarily engaging. Everybody liked her. She immediately set out to form new "relationships." There was no grief for Mother who was in jail. The girl quickly developed a knack for figuring out which families at the hospital had just received very bad news. She sought them out. Two sets of parents with leukemic children offered to adopt this beautiful girl.

The girl showed no favoritism. She never learned my name, even though I visited her every day while she was in the hospital. She didn't learn other people's names either. She never changed toward me. What I got in the beginning is what I had in the end. All of us at the hospital, I think, were a blur to this child. We were each treated with exquisite politeness and grace. But we were given nothing of value.

This child epitomized the "hail fellow well met" approach. A benumbed, deadened victim, the girl stood a chance of going on to victimize, or simply to "con," others. "Narcissistic personality?" "Antisocial personality?" Whatever one might call her as an adult, the words "hail fellow well met" seemed most appropriate to her demeanor as a child.

We did not allow any parents of dying children to adopt or to provide foster care for this deadened young girl. After Mother lost her parental rights in court, the girl was admitted to a small, well-run institution for neglected and abused children. Our hospital team believed she would have a better chance in a modern, enlightened orphanage than she would inside a family. As for the depths to this pretty little girl, I don't know if they ever developed. There were no real depths there when I knew her.

Psychic numbing will come on normally as any person dies. The dying person will often begin to block off all pain and emotion a few moments before dying. I remember reading in the *San Francisco Chronicle* what a young high school teacher, whom I had known, said after he was stabbed as he waited in line for *The Rocky Horror Picture Show*. "It doesn't hurt." That was all. The teacher died surprised. He had felt nothing.

Some people who have been resuscitated from cardiac arrests later recall that, as they watched their own deaths, they felt neither pain nor fear. As a matter of fact, they felt nothing. These people have reported that they observed their own resuscitations as uninvolved third parties. From somewhere above or to the side of the activity, they uncaringly watched the hospital staff struggle with someone who looked, oddly, like themselves. In other words, they went through an "out-of-body experience" as they lay close to death. This is an extreme, but normal, example of psychic numbing.

Another type of emotional numbing normally occurs during the act of dreaming. The dreamer may feel quite removed from his own personal horrors as they dance about on the dream "screen." When a dream follows trauma, however, the numbing that accompanies the dream state may horrify the trauma victim. The trauma sufferer may, for example, think he actually died in his dream. Or he may feel that he will die soon because the sense of removal in the dream, he thinks, is predictive of things to come. Young Caroline Cramer, the dog-bite victim, believed in both. After Bowser attacked her, Caroline dreamed her own death too many times to count. But what bothered Caroline most about these dreams was her sensation of going numb, a sensation that might mean, she thought, that she had died the night before but also might mean that she would be dying soon.

I have excerpted one of Caroline's post-Bowser nightmares to illustrate how her benumbed dreaming sensations became incorporated into the meanings she put to her dreams. Note how close Caroline's nightmare sounds to an "out-of-body experience."

"It's like I don't know where I was coming from. I was coming home from somewhere, and I walk inside the house, and like, I see my parents. I walk over a little more and I see my brothers and sisters, these dogs, and more and more dogs that look like Bowser. And all the dogs have blood in the same part that Bowser had blood in my accident. And my Mom and my Dad and my brothers and sisters and my own two dogs are all dead. All of them.

"And then Bowser comes walking out. And it's like all the dogs have lined up in a circle surrounding me. I am in the center of the circle and, like Bowser is the only one with a white face. Like there is no blood on it. Like he has saved *me* for himself. And then Bowser starts attacking me and everything. I'm sitting there fighting—trying to fight him off.

"All of a sudden, all the fighting, barking, growling, and screaming stops. I can't hear anything. And there is this floating sensation. I can see my body, the rest of the bodies, the dogs and everything. And everything is still and quiet. And I get, like, this floating feeling. And then I wake up."

The same numbing sensations that would have comforted a dying person at the moment of death or would have provided the sensation of "dreaming" to the ordinary dreamer now terrified young Caroline Cramer. She had been traumatized. She dreaded her "Bowser dreams" because, in her mind, they might be predictive. They might even be real.

In lesser and controlled doses, psychic numbing can be put to useful ends. I suppose one might consider transcendental meditation a healthy form of this. Physicians have found that chronically ill or dying children can be taught to go into self-induced trance states. Doctors at Children's Hospital at Stanford, for instance, taught childhood cancer victims for years to employ hypnotic exercises to wall off their pain and to combat a natural tendency to give up. The children learned to visualize themselves somewhere else or simply to let their minds go blank. These children bravely endured radiation and drug therapies, using their self-hypnotic techniques to mute the discomfort. When called upon, they died with dignity.

A Denver child psychiatrist, Louis Fine, has used self-hypnosis with young victims of Gillian-Barré disease, a paralyzing disorder that often confines a child for months to the respirator. Gillian-Barré disease is frequently self-limited. If you can get the machine to breathe temporarily for a child, his life may be saved. But what boredom and discouragement in the meantime! Louis Fine has bypassed this by training his patients to effect their own mental escapes. He reports that his "students" have shown consistently positive attitudes.

Some children are able, spontaneously, to teach themselves "self-hypnosis." Their trances may be reserved for special circumstances or they may become habit. By peeling off feelings from events, by journeying inside the imagination to other places, by counting, or by simply letting the mind drift, these self-taught self-hypnotizers can put themselves beyond pain.

As a kid, I experimented with this kind of thing at the dentist's office. But it never worked for me. I remember a particularly sadistic dentist who told me, "I see the nerve. We'll hit it any minute now. You'll go through the roof when it happens." In those days, Novocain shots were not routine. So I tried to prepare for, what I imagined to be, a dental disaster. I would count venetian blinds, holes in the soundproofed ceiling, and freckles on my dentist's face. But I could not induce hypnosis in myself, although in those days I had no idea what name might apply to the process I was trying to achieve. Sooner or later I would feel the pain.

But some children are able to teach themselves the art of total mental escape. Their escapes can be effected when the horrors they experience are predictable enough. There must be, in addition, some kind of inborn knack. Self-hypnosis often brings problems along with its use. The length of time "away from it all" and the number of times it happens frequently get out of control. Certain forms of psychic numbing, in other words, cannot be turned on and off with precision.

Frederick Waters, age seven, was one of the best self-hypnotizers I ever met. Even Frederick, however, could not exert perfect control. But let me go back a moment and tell you how I met Frederick. Frederick was a racially mixed (black and white) child who could easily "pass" for white. When he was six, Frederick moved to Biloxi, Mississippi, with a new, black stepfather, Winston Waters. Frederick and his new stepdad were not comfortable together. Winston, in his younger days, had been abused by his father for being too light-skinned. His father had felt doubtful about Winston's paternity. And so Frederick, light-skinned as he was, brought back the past for a man who must have very much wanted the past to go away.

The neighbors began to complain. When Frederick's mother went off to work the night shift, the neighbors could hear the sounds of someone cussing, slamming, and punching somebody else. One neighbor phoned the Child Protective Services agency, but the workers there said they could find "nothing." Then Frederick showed up at his school playground so bruised that the mother of another child playing there took Frederick to the hospital. "Child abuse," the doctors diagnosed, but even though Winston was forced to undergo psychotherapy, he did not improve. Six months dragged by. Frederick began to behave badly at school.

Frederick's mother had tended to believe that her husband was innocent of child abuse. She unconsciously used massive denial. But suddenly the unavoidable proof turned up. Frederick's mother had suspected Winston of having affairs. One night when she went off to work, she left a cassette recorder running in the bedroom. No woman's voice ever graced that tape, however. Instead, the hideous sounds of a man attacking a boy could clearly be heard. Frederick's aunt telegrammed the money at once for the boy to come, one way, to San Francisco. The family agreed to let Aunt Beth raise Frederick. Frederick was brought to my office the very first week he arrived in town.

Frederick's new custodial parent, a widowed, childless schoolteacher, cherished her chance to be a "real" mother to this boy. And she was good at it. Frederick thrived. He quickly stopped misbehaving at school, started to make new friends, and brought home good grades.

But Frederick did not have much to say about his old abuses. He remembered "only two times," he told me. "The others—I forget." Winston had repeatedly threatened to kill Frederick if he ever gave away their secret. The man, however, was two thousand miles away by now. "Does the distance help?" I asked Frederick. But the boy still could not tell his whole story. He could recount but "two times," and the "times" were described quite vaguely.

A month after Frederick arrived in San Francisco, "things" started to happen. Once he accidentally crashed into his aunt's big antique bed, yet he did not cry or say "ouch." A lump the size of a California tomato rose on Frederick's forehead, but the boy never complained. It was rather amazing. Aunt Beth witnessed the impact and said it looked forceful enough to deck a prizefighter.

Two weeks after the bed incident, Frederick glanced down at the schoolyard pavement and saw a small pool of blood. He looked about the playground for a hurt classmate. Gradually it occurred to Frederick that he might be the one bleeding. He fingered his chin and came up with a sticky, red hand. He had been hurt, but he hadn't even felt it. Frederick recognized now that he experienced no pain. He told his Aunt Beth.

I asked Frederick why he was unable to feel pain. "It jus' happens now," he explained. "I used to pretend I was at a picnic with my head on Mommy's lap. The first time my stepdaddy hit me, it hurt a whole lot. But then, I found out that I could make myself go on Mommy's lap [in imagination] and Winston couldn't hurt me that way. I kept goin' on Mommy's lap—I didn't have to cry or scream or anything. I could *be* someplace else and not get hurt. I don't know how many times Winston punched me out. I wasn't always payin' attention. Like I told you, first I'd be at a picnic on Mom's lap. Later I didn't have to think of a picnic—jus' her lap. Now if somethin' makes me bleed I don't think of no lap at all. I jus' don't feel no pain."

Frederick had developed a "routine" for going further and further into bodily anesthesia. But some few children go even further into trance and self-hypnosis than did Frederick Waters. They remove themselves for too long. They remove themselves too frequently. What was done at first by counting, picturing, or letting the mind go adrift becomes absolutely automatic. Psychiatrists term such spontaneous self-removals "dissociations." Dissociative episodes are emotionally and socially costly. The dissociated adult may actually travel far away from home and forget who he is (psychogenic fugue). But children hardly ever do this. Dissociated children more often feel detached from their minds and bodies (depersonalization). This feeling probably is common among repeatedly traumatized children. However, children do not know how to complain about depersonalization. Amnesia, the *Spellbound* phenomenon, is another form of dissociation sometimes seen in children: If amnesia follows from trauma, however, it almost always comes from a long series of terrible incidents, not just from one episode, as the film *Spellbound* would have had us believe.

A relatively rare dissociative condition that may occur after too frequent or too long-lived self-hypnosis is what we call "multiple personality disorder." Rare as it currently appears to be, multiple personality disorder makes up with fascination for its infrequency of appearance. It does affect children. In 1840, Despine described a child patient, Estelle, eleven years old, who appeared paralyzed, but who under hypnosis revealed another personality that could walk and yet another personality that functioned as Estelle's guardian angel. Estelle, thus, had a central, paralyzed personality and two healthier alter egos. She had at least three selves, each one of which functioned separately at different times in the outside world. As opposed to schizophrenia, a serious disruption in emotional and cognitive functioning that has long been misnamed "split personality," Estelle's problem, "multiple personality," did not include blunted emotional responses or quirky thinking. Estelle's problem, instead, was the problem of harboring several different personas inside of one single body.

A hundred years after Estelle's three selves presented themselves to Doctor Despine, three psychiatrists, Cornelia Wilbur from Kentucky, and Corbett Thigpen and Hervey Cleckley from Georgia, wrote up two striking, adult multiple personality cases. Wilbur's "Sybil" and Thigpen and Cleckley's "Eve" were real people whose personalities had fragmented into several alter egos surrounding a weakened host personality. Sybil and Eve shifted from one to another "personality," using wildly variable styles to approach, what for them was, a frightening world. Their personalities ranged from sweet and passive, to angry, to highly sexual. Their various alter egos remained entirely unrecognized by the host personalities. In other words, Eve and Sybil did not know they were "being" other people. They simply knew they couldn't account for a number of minutes, hours, and days. Thigpen and Cleckley hypnotized Eve (played in the movie by Joanne Woodward) and thereby became acquainted with each of her different "faces." Sybil's psychiatrist, Cornelia Wilbur (also played, ironically, by Joanne Woodward in the made-for-television film), also used hypnosis to "meet" Sybil's various personas. In the course of her interviews with Sybil, Wilbur learned that the girl, as a young child, had been repeatedly, horribly abused by her mother. The child had escaped into trances in order to escape the pain and terror. In the trance state, she had taken on several different personas, some capable of expressing rage and others, of exhibiting sexual excitement.

Today, multiple personality disorder is diagnosed far less frequently than the burgeoning statistics on child abuse would lead us to project. As psychiatrists become more aware of the existence of this disorder, however, the numbers of cases may increase. I would venture to guess, though, that far more adults who were abused as children will show disordered personalities of the angry, borderline, narcissistic, or benumbed types than will go on to develop multiple personalities. If a child discovers self-hypnosis, he may use it, as did Frederick Waters, to accomplish bodily anesthesia in order to block out the pain. He may do so without going on to establish a full-blown depersonalization disorder or a multiple personality disorder. The option of bodily anesthesia appears to be a far more reachable one than the more extreme options of emotional removal or the creation of several alter egos.

Let me tell you how young Frederick Waters eventually got over his bodily anesthesia. Frederick showed none of the danger signs of childhood multiple personality—the bouts of amnesia, time losses, mood swings, unpredictable behaviors, and feelings of being subject to outside influences—that the researcher Richard Kluft says children who are going to become "multiples" tend to show. Frederick Waters simply felt no pain. Would I have to hypnotize Frederick to help him?

Frederick's anesthesia was quite recent in origin. It, therefore, carried a good prognosis. I decided to try psychotherapy rather than hypnosis. I explained to Frederick that pain functions as a fire alarm does. Pain warns a person to cry for help, to get a cast put on, or to lie still. I told him that numbing himself while Winston beat on him worked at the time it was happening. But Frederick's self-anesthesia was dangerous to him now. If Frederick went on deadening himself, he might expose his body to danger. Every body needs its pain.

Sounds like a lecture, doesn't it? It was. But this lecture was broken into about two sentences given once a week over a three-week period. At home, Aunt Beth, coached by me, made a few remarks of the same nature. That's all.

The speed of Frederick's response surprised both Aunt Beth and me. Two weeks after my second "lecture," Frederick was screaming in his school principal's office. Aunt Beth came rushing over. Frederick's best friend, Bertram, it seemed, had jumped onto the boy's belly from a rung high up the jungle gym. As Frederick lay on his back looking at the blue California sky, he had been dive-bombed. Frederick would not stop crying. He was sobbing even after his pediatrician gave him the standard OK to "go back to school tomorrow." Aunt Beth was annoyed. The kid had interrupted her school teaching over "nothing." He had made such a big deal of a little thing. Then it struck her. Frederick was feeling his pains again.

Frederick took his aches and pains far too seriously that first month that he allowed himself to feel. His responses looked almost fake, they were so overdrawn. But Frederick settled down soon enough. The jungle-gym Tarzan, Bertram, quickly reinstated himself in Frederick's favor. And most everything else in the young lad's life soon looked the way it does in the life of an ordinary seven-year-old boy.

I still see Frederick Waters once in a while. But he is a little distant now, a little too polite when he comes to my office. He has weaned himself away from me, and that is how it should be. Aunt Beth holds Frederick's legal custody, and I see a bright future ahead for the boy. Frederick never did progress far along the path to multiple personality disorder or, for that matter, to an angry or a benumbed personality. I wonder if he would have, had he stayed longer in Winston's care. I miss Frederick—he was fun. (They should all do so well with a six-sentence lecture.)

Psychic numbing may become a way of life, a debilitating character flaw. The person who lives his life in a place beyond expression, beyond feeling, will present a scary picture indeed. The absent eyes, the blunted responses to another's response, these vacancies frighten anyone who recognizes what they really mean. Who lives behind the empty eyes? Sometimes—too many times—an ordinary child once lived there.

A number of recent films and plays present protagonists who show a frightening absence of feeling. In *The Terminator*, Arnold Schwartzenegger is not supposed to be human at all, although he looks human. His merciless, blank-eyed approach to snuffing out people's lives represents the worst of the benumbed antihero's repertoire. *The Black Widow* tells a similar tale, less gory to be sure, but still a tale of the psychically dead. *Darling* and *Otherwise Engaged* present better functioning people who, though they can manage at work, are isolated from meaningful human contact. The authors of these pieces offer few explanations for their characters' emotional deadening. We are, perhaps, to assume that a numbing of the soul is a sign of the times.

A recent film, *River's Edge*, a horror picture if I ever saw one, tells a benumbed but very true tale of our times. It retells an actual event that occurred in Milpitas, California, a suburban town to the south of San Francisco. In the mid 1980s, a girl at the local high school was raped and murdered by her high school boyfriend. He then showed her nude body, which he had left unburied in a ravine, to a few fellow students. Kids told other kids, and a rumor about the body in the bushes began to spread. Dozens of high schoolers went down to get a look. Two school days passed. For forty-eight hours "everybody" knew, yet nobody reported what had happened. The group's callousness was chilling, to say the least.

The benumbed behavior at Milpitas High School is not well explained in the film. Nor was the kids' motivation given much explanation by the reporters who covered the actual events at the time they occurred. In the film, we are shown that some parents appear too busy to listen to their teenagers. Some parents are too self-absorbed to emerge from their rooms. Hiding because they are overwhelmed with work, divorces, unhappy love affairs, and debt, parents, we are led to believe, cannot manage meaningful relationships with their offspring. This negligent kind of family life may, of course, create callousness in children. But I do not think that negligence, alone, can explain the behavior of the entire group at Milpitas High School. It would not be entirely unexpected to me if it turned out that a few of the "leaders" had been physically or sexually abused. We will never know, however. The Milpitas High School group was not studied.

Repeated or long-standing psychic trauma creates numbing. Lord Byron noted it. The children of Hiroshima gave us further evidence. Abused American children, I think, prove it every day.

Robert Jay Lifton wrote that the world's vicarious experience with Hiroshima changed everyone's emotional state. He said that we are all the benumbed survivors of nuclear catastrophe. He accused the world of going dead. He told us we were passively, dazedly, allowing the proliferation of nuclear weapons, silently co-conspiring in the race to world annihilation.

Lifton's inclusion of the entire world in his concept of psychic numbing is a giant inclusion. Will there ever be proof? I doubt it. Beardslee and Mack interviewed numbers of Boston schoolchildren about their feelings during an intense time of world concern regarding the placement of nuclear missiles in Europe. The children appeared very disturbed by the nuclear threat. But the study was roundly criticized for its methodology. Some children feel there is no future because of nuclear weapons, but the proper study to prove how this comes about has not yet been devised. In the meantime, most of my patients feel quite alive despite the fact that they live their lives under the gathering nuclear cloud. They are not numb. They have not died inside. On the other hand, I have sat for hours with withdrawn, nonreactive babies in big city hospitals. I have tried for hours to get close to "hail fellow well met" youngsters. I have tried to get silent kids to talk, children so depleted of emotion that they cannot even protest their lives with a whisper. These deadened legions of children are the true cousins to the survivors of Hiroshima.

Psychic numbing may be a culturally accepted personality trait in geographical areas where dehumanizing events routinely take place. Recurrent floodings, famines, and mass deaths probably serve to create benumbed characteristics in an entire populace. For instance, the religious striving for nirvana, a state of mind in which no pain is felt and in which a blissful loss of individuality is experienced, may derive, in part, from countless, individual wished-for escapes into oblivion. A society that pursues oblivion as a goal may, indeed, be a repeatedly traumatized one. And this response in such a society may be a "healthy" response.

Psychic and physical numbing, thus, are normal protections for those who must endure pain, those who are dying, and those who must experience disaster upon disaster. Psychic numbing may explain some culturally built-in disregards for human life. It may explain, at least in part, how terrorists brought up in Palestinian refugee "camps" or how dictators, coming from neglected, abused segments of their societies, go about their bloody work.

Scholars say that political, economic, religious, and sociological factors determine the behaviors of societies that tend to devalue life. True. I accept that. But does psychic trauma, especially predictable psychic trauma, darken childhood in such societies? We do not know. But let us try to find out.

In the meantime, a brief note. Remember the film I just mentioned, *River's Edge,* the movie based upon a true, teenaged conspiracy of silence that followed a girl's murder near Milpitas High School? The Milpitas city fathers took action one day after the film had its world premier. They banned it.

CHAPTER 5

Unresolved Grief

Every day I go over to Joe's parents' house to see their faces. I keep thinking I will get a message from Joe through them.
                                                Solomon Wilson, age seventeen

W HEN YOU COME into downtown Baltimore, you are assailed with images of the dead Edgar Allan Poe—commemorative plaques, the place where he drifted toward death in a seamy flophouse, and his grave. But when you visit Richmond, Virginia, you are able to imagine, instead, the living Poe. You see the part of town where he lived as a young man and the places he frequented as a teenager. The story of Edgar Poe as a toddler in the city of Richmond, however, is the one that intrigues me most. It is a story of Eddy and his actress-mother. The way I look at it, a trauma Edgar suffered at age two years, ten months, set the plot and tone for Poe's mature work. It certainly set the direction for his life.

First, one must know the background. David Poe, an actor, had left his wife, Elizabeth Poe, when Edgar was only eighteen months old. Perhaps the point of marital dispute was Elizabeth's pregnancy with, what turned out to be, a little girl, Rosalie. Perhaps David Poe was too sick with tuberculosis to stay with his family (by one newspaper account he died of tuberculosis shortly after abandoning his pregnant wife and son). But, whatever the cause, the little family, mother, toddler boy, and infant girl, were in deep trouble when they arrived in Richmond in 1811. They had farmed out an older boy, William, to relatives. They were poor. Mother had to work as an actress and dancer to support her two little children. An assortment of ladies of the community, including the landlady, Mrs. Phillips, who owned the millinery shop above which the Poes lived, were called upon to watch the baby and Edgar. But worst of all, Elizabeth Poe had tuberculosis. And she was dying. By late November 1811 the theatre where Elizabeth Poe regularly performed put out a Bill of Notice asking patrons to contribute to the impoverished actress who, surrounded by her children, was lingering at death's door. Edgar was about to turn three.

Most of the time, it seems, the mother and her two youngsters were alone in their one-room flat. (Poe probably wrote of this room from a toddler's perspective—"to me it appeared of a size to contain the universe" —in his story "Loss of Breath.") Women of the community would drop by to help. But dying of tuberculosis, as you know, is not pretty. The patient becomes thin, drawn, and ashen-hued. Blood comes up when the person coughs. A child living with such an invalid might find himself horrified. Elizabeth Poe, a pretty woman, was not dying a pretty death.

So little Edgar Poe must have seen some terrible things during his toddler days. We know that children weren't brought much into conversation in the 1800s, certainly not into unpleasant conversation. It was the 1900s that ushered in "The Century of the Child." So we may assume that the ladies of Richmond were not about to ask young Edgar how he was taking his mother's illness. And few people, if any, would have been answering the questions that must have been plaguing this bright toddler who shared a room with his sick mother. Edgar Poe was watching a beloved, beautiful woman fade away. He was seeing blood on her white handkerchiefs, towels, and nightgowns. He was, I think, horrified. Yet he must have been simultaneously fascinated.

Then Elizabeth Poe died. That's all. She was laid out in her room and then buried. And the day after that, Edgar was taken away by the person who became his foster mother and the reason for his middle name, Mrs. Frances Allan. Rosalie went to live with another lady of Richmond, a Mrs. Mackenzie.

But let us return once more to the death scene. I know of no credible contemporary account of it. This makes me think that the only people at home when Elizabeth Poe died were the two-year, ten-month-old boy, Edgar, the baby, Rosalie, and their mother, Elizabeth Poe herself. The ladies of Richmond probably came later. But first there must have been just Death, Elizabeth, Rosalie, and Edgar. All in one small room.

The best way I can postulate how it must have been for little Edgar at the moment his mother died and for the minutes to hours that followed is from Poe's works themselves. Too many times for comfort, Poe describes death the way a traumatized toddler would view it—as an uncertain, transitory state that looks like sleep, were it not so stiff, so ugly, and so quiet. The almost three-year-old Edgar may have lain down with his mother's body, nestled into her, talked to her, shook her, perhaps even tried to open her mouth. He did not understand what death was. But he formed a permanent impression.

There was a trend in the nineteenth century to worry about premature burial. The adult Poe was not alone in his lingering, immature-sounding preoccupations. But Poe's terror most likely derived from an early personal experience with death, an experience that would have given tremendous impact in his mind to the commonly-held, nineteenth century fear of improper burial. As an adult author, Poe tended to kill off his beautiful, fictitious women in such a way that they assumed comatose, sleep-like states, states that must have resembled his own confused, toddler-stage perceptions of his own mother's death (the Lady Madeline in "The Fall of the House of Usher," "Morella," "Berenice," and "Lygeia"). He frequently buried his people alive, again close to perceptions that could have been experienced by a toddler seeing his beloved mother carried away, still beautiful but not moving ("The Cask of Amontillado" and "The Pit and the Pendulum"). Poe repeatedly created dead people who refused to stay put ("The Telltale Heart," "The Premature Burial," and "Loss of Breath"). A few of his male heroes want to lie down inside of tombs occupied by their dead lost loves, much as the young Edgar himself may have lain down in bed with his dead mother ("Annabel Lee" and "Ulalume"). All of these dead, not-dead confusions and longings for reunion sound like the thoughts of a traumatized toddler. They are fascinating feelings, replete with horror, grief, and a sense of confusion.

Poe's works also imply that he might have watched the preliminary preparations of Elizabeth Poe's body for burial. He is just *too* preoccupied with the corporeal disintegration that follows death. He gives us bodies in horrible, gleaming corruption in "The Narrative of Arthur Gordon Pym," a woman's face suffused with blood in "The Murder of Marie Rogêt," and a totally disintegrated, liquified corpse in "The Case of M. Valdemar." Poe presents a hideous plot in "Berenice," telling how a dead woman's smile drives her lover so mad that he enters her sepulchre to extract her teeth. (Of course she comes back to haunt the "hero" anyway. She, like so many other Poe women, refuses to stay permanently dead.)

Poe, the inventor of the mystery story and an early expert at the art of horror fiction, was a simultaneously bereaved and traumatized child. I doubt that he ever recovered from his mother's death. Shock interfered with Poe's mourning. The mourning interfered with his attempts to process the shock. The upshot was that Poe never escaped the effects of his beautiful mother's death. As a young man in his late teens he wrote the following lines in a draft of a poem:

I cannot love except where Death was mingling his with Beauty's breath
—Or Hymen, Time, and Destiny were stalking between her and me.

from *"Preface"* (1829)

Poe's mother was his eternal love. At the same time, she was his horror.

Children very gradually come to an understanding of death. They may realize that death is a different state by the age of five or six, but many youngsters do not grasp the absolute finality of death until much later. At emotional times, even teenagers may not fully realize how irreversible death is. For instance, some adolescents who have actively contemplated suicide may describe their governing fantasy as a wish to see everyone at the funeral cry tears of regret. The dead body in the coffin, in other words, still has its eyes.

Children, partly because they do not fully grasp death and partly also because they process losses slower than do adults, tend to have long-standing difficulties with the deaths of those close to them. A child may roller-skate out on the sidewalk within hours of a death in the family, yet the process of bereavement may turn out to be far more prolonged and difficult for that child than it is for those inside the darkened house. The four stages of bereavement, as outlined by John Bowlby and others, are the same for children as they are for adults: (1) denial, (2) protest, (3) despair coupled with repetitions and reworkings of the relationship with the dead individual, and (4) resolution or detachment, including finding new relationships to substitute for the lost one. Each piece of this four-pronged process is more difficult for children than it is for adults. Adults mourn for about a year. Children, on the other hand, may become stuck for years in just one phase of the mourning process.

Why does this happen? First of all, as Barnes and Furman point out in their studies of nursery-aged youngsters who have lost a parent, grieving adults tend to lack the energy or the inclination to talk with their children about what has occurred in the family. The adults offering support and friendship to families at times of mourning tend to extend this support to surviving adults, not to children. Children, with a sliding concept of what death really is, may have difficulty believing in the finality of what has taken place. They may take years to pass through the denial phase of grief. Their immature cognitive understanding may promote denial of the reality of the death. And their tendency to create daydreams may promote a "denial in fantasy" at the same time. Protest, the second stage of childhood grief, may become reserved for the neighborhood, the playground, or the classroom—after all, the people at home, the children feel, are too upset to be bothered. Thus, children in the second stage of mourning may be labeled neighborhood nuisances, classroom clowns, or "problems." If children enter the third stage of mourning at all, they may be overcome with internal fantasies related to their loss—"Mom died because I told her my secret," or "Dad died because I had wished him dead," or "Mom wanted to die and leave me," or "If I had cleaned up my room every day, all this wouldn't have happened." These fantasies take time, and often professional guidance, to work out. Many of the fantasies are phase-specific, that is, they reflect the inner concerns and thinking styles that characterize certain developmental stages. Fixations may occur at these developmental points if the death of a loved one cements them into place.

The final phase of mourning is, again, particularly difficult for a child. How are youngsters supposed to pick out new parents? Or new siblings? Grieving adults are able to make these substitutions and, thus, to regain some control of their lives. They may choose a new wife and conceive and/or adopt new children. A child cannot do this. Stepmothers are picked *for* children. It may take years—until youngsters get to know camp counselors, teachers, and the parents of their friends—before children can make their own substitutions and put an end to their grief. The child psychiatrist is able to help in this process. But the entire process, if unaided, may take years. Indeed, it may take a lifetime. Now let us add some *traumatic* deaths to the scenario. Mother is run down by a car. Junior watches from the sidewalk. Dad shoots Mom. Junior is peeking from the kitchen doorway. Everybody is flying off on vacation. Junior lives through the plane crash. We can make up unspeakably horrible scripts. And they are true. The family lives in Hiroshima. Junior survives. The family is swallowed up by the Holocaust. Junior makes it out of Europe. The family is dragged off by the Pol Pot Cambodians. Junior and Mother survive. They are put onto boats to flee. Mother is raped on the boat as Junior watches. They arrive in America but cannot speak the language and do not understand the culture. All of these "scenarios" are real. They happen to children.

When shocking surprises are mixed with death, the mourning process, already extraordinarily difficult for children, is now combined with the problems of psychic trauma. Mastery of trauma and its accompanying misunderstandings and misperceptions interferes with the mastery of permanent loss. And vice versa. Traumatically bereaved children may freeze into permanently saddened states or even into deep depressions that, to all purposes, look like major depressive disorders. Traumatically bereaved youngsters may have trouble sleeping through the night or eating normally. Mornings may be impossible times of the day for them, and their behaviors may become unmanageable. The problems of trauma that combine with the bereavement, such as ongoing hallucinations, fantasies, and reenactment, may reach bizarre levels. Traumatized, grieving youngsters may see the ghosts of their lost family members. They may act so strange that they are misdiagnosed as "schizophrenic."

Let us consider some real children stuck in their simultaneous grief and shock in order to fully grasp how painful and difficult the process of recovery from this double condition can be. Because the pain in these cases is extreme, I will tell the stories only briefly. In these tales, one sees how traumatic horror will compound the problems of childhood bereavement.

Muffy Miller came to me as a psychiatric patient at age eleven. The olive-skinned child daydreamed at school, acted silly, sat silently over dinners with her dad, and made but could not keep, girlfriends. She seemed, according to her father, "boring." Muffy was sad. Her initial diagnosis was depression. I learned quite quickly, however, that at age twenty-seven months Muffy sat for two weeks keening at the door to the room in which her young mother lay dying. Nobody had talked to Muffy. Nobody had explained. Her mother was suffering from an accidental poisoning that had impaired the functioning of her brain. She lay in coma. Mr. Miller was frantic. He loved his wife. But in order to protect Muffy from seeing anything, the father locked his dark-haired toddler out of the room. When I learned Muffy's whole story, she received two new diagnoses with a new set of treatment goals. She had been traumatized, I realized. She was also stuck in the process of bereavement. She needed to talk about her early shock and fear. And she also needed help in processing the loss of her mother. At age eleven, Muffy Miller remembered only one part of her ordeal. "I was sitting on a floor outside a closed door." But that was enough. The feelings accompanying the memory had never been worked through.

I have already mentioned that some children who are simultaneously traumatized and bereaved see ghosts and sense presences. The hallucinations come from the trauma; the inability to say a permanent goodbye, from the loss. Let us meet Duane Harrison, age seven, in this regard. Duane had always been very close to his sister, Holly, when she was alive. When she was five and Duane was four, Holly was eviscerated in a freak kiddie pool accident. Duane witnessed the whole thing. Holly died suddenly during transplant surgery two years after her accident. Duane was quite surprised. He had not expected his sister to die. Duane went into mourning. But he was also traumatized by the scenes he had witnessed two years earlier at the kiddie pool. Duane developed two conditions—grief and psychic trauma.

Duane gradually began to "feel" Holly's presence. For him, she was a "poltergeist." Several months after Holly died, Duane told his mother that he was hoping the weather would be nice for a family weekend trip to Disneyland. "But Holly plays tricks," he said. "It would be just like her to make it rain at Disneyland." Duane told me during one of his sessions, "Every time we visit Holly's grave, it rains." Duane believed, it seemed, that Holly was *causing* the rain. I asked Duane once if he was in regular contact with Holly. "She plays tricks on me," he replied. "She makes the doors close behind me when I don't want them closed."

Duane and Holly had been born only ten months apart and were almost like twins. They had shared a secret language and committed frequent pranks during Holly's short lifetime. The close relationship itself and the traumatic circumstances surrounding Holly's injury and death had set up in Duane a sense that his sister still was with him. Duane did not deny the horrible "pictures" he had seen during Holly's evisceration. But he was still stuck in the denial phase of grief for his sister. He wished for a reconnection. By "feeling" her presence, in a sense, Duane Harrison had established this link.

A traumatic death may go so far in the mind as to set up a sense of possession. Stephen King, the horror writer, seems to understand this phenomenon, particularly in his short story "Gramma," a tale in which a young boy's grandmother suddenly dies and in the process takes possession of the boy's soul. Solomon Wilson, a seventeen-year-old patient of mine, was driving on a freeway when his car was hit from the rear. It exploded. Solomon was thrown clear of the car and got up unscratched. What he saw, however, made him wish he never had escaped. His best friend, Joe, was burning alive in the passenger seat.

"I'm daydreaming every day," Solomon Wilson told me ten months afterward. "I still see it. The daydreams are terrible." Solomon went to Joe's parents almost every day for months. He was looking for something, a message, anything on their faces. Two months after the trauma Solomon Wilson began incorporating aspects of what he had remembered of Joe into his own personality. "I put myself in Joe's place trying to think what he's thinking now wherever he is. Sometimes I think he is in heaven trying to help me do what I want to do. Other times I think he is in hell trying to get me." Solomon was, in other words, feeling a bit "possessed."

More consistently, however, Solomon began to project Joe's persona onto his mental representation of Eric, his toddler-aged brother. Six months after Joe's death, Solomon told me, "Sometimes I feel my little brother has received my friend's 'reincarnation.' It's in his eyes. He looks at me funny without smiling. I wonder, 'Could it be?' You never know."

Solomon Wilson could not give up his friend, Joe. Even though he had to reach to such extremes as "possession" or "reincarnation," Solomon was holding on tightly to the mental image of his lost friend.

Do kids see too many movies? Or do the movies "know" more than one would imagine about how kids think? Horror writers seem to understand the connection between childhood trauma and grief. Poe does, although he does not tell his tales about children—he writes, instead, about himself. Some real children, however, provide an answer to the question of whether the movies really plant these weird ideas of possession and ghosts into kids. And the answer in most instances, I think, is "No." Children would get these ideas anyway. The movies help, but "possessions" and "reincarnations" were known to man long before any mass media or any printed books scattered the idea around.

I know one neglected, socially deprived boy who never had a chance in his urban ghetto to go to the movies or to bring home tapes from the local video rental store, yet this boy spontaneously developed his own ideas on possession and reincarnation. In his simultaneous grief and trauma, Douglas Simpson came to these ideas by himself. Douglas was seven years old and very poor. He had watched a great deal of TV. But I don't think Douglas was mature enough to have understood possession or reincarnation, even if he had seen a spooky show or two on his television set. Douglas Simpson, however, witnessed the fatal beating of his toddler brother, Little Andy, at a rundown, inner-city residential hotel. His own stepfather, Big Andy, did it. Douglas watched everything from under a television table. He was distraught at his brother's death. He wanted Little Andy back.

Here is a conversation that Douglas and I had one week after Little Andy was murdered. Despite Douglas's youth and his innocence to the worlds of *The Exorcist,* he had figured out possession and reincarnation for himself.

DOUGLAS: I got nuthin' to worry about. Mama is pregnant anyway. Another baby would be maybe jus' like Lil' Andy. I don't know.

ME: Each baby is different, Doug. Each one is made new by a mother and a father.

DOUGLAS: I'm not so sure about *that.*

ME: You know your Mama had a baby inside her *before* Lil' Andy died. Remember how big her belly looked?

DOUGLAS: Uh huh. [He nods affirmatively.]

ME: So how could Little Andy get inside of her instead of the new baby that was already growing there?

DOUGLAS: [He looks puzzled.] I don't know. But I think Lil' Andy might be able to get inside her anyway.

A life may progress, dragging along its unresolved griefs, hauntings, and terrors as it goes on. Such was the burden of Edgar Allan Poe, beginning with his toddler-aged trauma. The death of his mother, felt as it was by Poe alone, untutored, and amazed at the horror of the thing, set up a pattern of fears and behaviors that plagued him in the life he led away from his art.

The young Edgar was said to be a terrified, mournful child. Once, at age six, he became panicky as he and a foster uncle passed a graveyard. In adolescence he frequently hallucinated a cold, disembodied hand touching his face. He dreamed terrible nightmares of white-robed women coming to get him. (We should note here that women of the nineteenth century wore white nightgowns in bed, even on their deathbeds.)

Edgar Poe needed to witness death—again and again and again. He tended to his older brother, William, from whom he had been separated almost from the time of his own birth, when William lay dying of tuberculosis. He felt absolutely cheated for having missed the dying of his foster mother, Frances Allan, while he was away at West Point. "If she had not died while I was away," he wrote in a letter afterward, "there would have been nothing for me to regret." He set up an almost certain death scene by marrying his thirteen-year-old cousin, the white-faced frail Virginia Clemm. She, like Poe's mother, was already very obviously destined to die of tuberculosis. And Poe almost recreated for himself the toddler-aged "living death" scenes he had observed with his mother by drinking himself comatose and taking opium to the point of stupor. One might say that Poe killed himself by reenacting his trauma.

As Poe lay near moribund from chronic alcoholism in the Baltimore flophouse where he died, he repeatedly hallucinated. He was seeing a white-robed woman coming to get him. She terrified him. But at the same time, she might have brought Poe some relief. Poe's mother, the actress Elizabeth Poe, finally had come to take him away. Poe's simultaneous mourning and shock, established at age two years, ten months, might now come to an end.

Death is not the only precipitant of the kind of grief that stands to complicate childhood psychic trauma. Loss of the sense of self may do the same. If a child is permanently changed in an accident, the youngster must still live with his remembrances of an old, normally functioning self. He must go through the same mourning process we have already outlined for a death in the family. This time, however, the mourning is for the child himself. The traumatically handicapped child must accomplish this same sort of mourning along with one additional piece of mental work—he or she must learn to live with and to accommodate to a handicap. Accomplishing such a feat sometimes makes the tasks of Heracles look easy.

A burned five year old, for example, would not do the exercises ordered by her hand surgeon following three attempts to reconstruct useful fingers for her. On examination in my office, the kindergartner told me that her baby brother had died in the very same burning bed from which she had escaped. Furthermore, she told me, she hated the looks of her own burned face. As a matter of fact she wondered if she really *was* the same person who had gone to sleep in peace the evening of the fire. ("When did she learn about her dead baby brother?" I asked the plastic surgeon. "When she got home. We don't like to give patients bad news on our burn unit," he said. "When did she first see her face?" "At home. There are no mirrors on our unit. Too discouraging," he said.) At home this little girl experienced repeated dreams of fires. She also repeatedly "saw" the last few minutes of her predicament. But the traumatic effects of the fire did not begin to encompass all of her symptoms. Her two most debilitating problems were the unresolved mourning for her dead brother and her continuing revulsion at her own terribly scarred face.

Here is another one. It is the story of Belinda Peck, five years old. The personal adjustments for a child who has been damaged in an unexpected accident are massive—the grief, extreme. Little Belinda Peck was quite like the burned kindergartner I have just described—loving, mentally active, and hurt. Nobody died, however, when Belinda suffered her debilitating trauma. She simply needed to mourn her old self, a self she would never see again.

Belinda's mother's cousin had taken the kindergartner shopping—a jolly midweek holiday with Cousin Meg. Belinda climbed onto a large display table in the lingerie department of a downtown store as Meg charged an item at the desk. The display table fell over. Belinda, at the bottom of the heap, was ruined. Her face was smashed to bits.

Each one of the child's facial bones was put in place and reconstructed with wires and sutures by a gifted plastic surgeon—an artist, really. Belinda turned out quite pretty. But she looked entirely different than she had before. Belinda's school friends no longer could recognize her. The other kindergartners told her when she came back to school, "You must be pretending to be Belinda. You can't really be Belinda."

Belinda, previously outgoing, mischievous, and vivacious, took on a quiet, remote, and perfectly comported style of behavior. At age seven, when I first met her, Belinda told me, "I was a devil before, but I was punished for it. Now I'm good." Despite the fact that Belinda Peck was suffering from bad dreams, was playing alone under dining room chairs, and was mutilating her dolls' faces, the little girl's character change was, by far, the most striking thing about her. Not only did she have a new face now, but she had taken on a new personality. It was a sad one, an inhibited one. Not only had the picture altered, but the underlying substance had massively changed.

It should be obvious by now that the long-standing traumas, the repeated ones, and the ones complicated by death, handicap, or disfigurement are the childhood traumas that will most likely promote deep depressions and major character changes. Despite the fact that psychiatry is becoming increasingly biological and genetic, here is a place that the environment continues to rule. Nobody is born with a genetic diathesis to psychic trauma. If you scare a child badly enough, he will be traumatized —plain and simple. But if you combine the trauma with a death or a new disability, then you will see depression, paranormal thinking, and/or character change—count on it. There may be mitigating factors, an improvement of the family's economic circumstances, a run of good luck, or a nice new stepparent. But most likely the child will make character readjustments in order to meet the long-standing and unresolvable demands of his grief and trauma. He may stay sad. Or he may turn passive. Or he may turn away from relationships altogether because it feels too painful to lose them.

By the time I entered high school, I had read most of the short stories of Poe. I loved Poe best when I was in sixth and seventh grade. I loved him at the very same stage of life in which Stephen King fans mob the movie theaters and deplete the paperback book shelves today. This prepubertal time is the same moment when kids begin to dip into Mary Shelley's *Frankenstein,* or Bram Stoker's *Dracula,* or Robert Louis Stevenson's *Doctor Jekyll and Mr. Hyde,* only to feel frustrated that these authors wrote no sequels. Death—especially the reality of it and the unpredictability of it —fascinates the prepubescent kid.

Death, gradually grasped as an abstract concept some time before a kid reaches age twelve, intrigues the newly initiated. One of the myths about death, the one about how Heracles wrestles Thanatos in order to save Alcestis from her "deathbed," is a special favorite for a few of the literary kids of eleven or twelve years old. The nice thing about the myth of Alcestis is that Death can be foiled.

One wonders about Poe's effect on the prepubescent kid, though. Poe never reassures in the fashion that the myth of Alcestis does. Poe does not put his villains out of the way in the manner of a Bram Stoker, a Robert Louis Stevenson, or a Mary Shelley. Rather, he gives us new information, compelling lessons in what happens to dead bodies in their corruption— lessons in what horrible ways there are to die. Poe does not soothe. Rather, he stirs up. His stories work in the mode of the nightmare. Poe creates new anxiety with each new twist. This is because Poe himself was a childhood trauma victim.

Those of us who read Poe continue to share the horror of a deathbed scene as experienced by a two-year, ten-month-old child. We don't know we are doing so, but we are still enduring Elizabeth Poe's last hours. The desperate dancing of Poe's masquers in "The Masque of the Red Death" conveys to us a sense of childish hysteria, of wild, toddler dancing. Reading Poe, one feels like an out of control three year old wanting to laugh, cry, and scream all at the same time. It is almost too much to bear.

Poe's stories create hysteria, not calm. We learn in "The Cask of Amontillado," for instance, that killers can get away with their crimes. We learn in "The Masque of the Red Death" that wild revels presage wilder attacks from Mother Nature, that color and costume do not fool the blackest of deaths, that people lose their loves in shocking, unfair ways. There is no escape, Poe tells us. We may be one of the unlucky ones. The teeth start to chatter. We have caught Edgar Allan Poe's plague. We are trying to cope simultaneously with Poe's grief and trauma. We *are* Edgar Allan Poe.

Preadolescents love this simultaneous contemplation of death while fearing the loss of control. Many of us continue to court such mixed sensations. We rush to our neighborhood movie houses to see *Nightmare on Elm Street, Cujo,* and even *The Seventh Seal.* We stop by our libraries to borrow as many books on ghosts as we can carry home. As a matter of fact, my mother, a professional librarian, once tried to locate a number of books on ghosts for me at the main branch of the San Francisco Library. Everything on ghosts, spirits, or specters, she told me later, had either been stolen or lost.

CHAPTER 6

Shame and Guilt

No, I don't live in Chowchilla.

Sammy Smith, age fourteen,
to a group of strangers who
had recognized him at Disneyland

T HERE IS A LANDMARK in Chowchilla that you can find without too much trouble. When you come into town on the main street, Robertson Boulevard, you drive over the railroad tracks, pass the Chevy agency, and then drive past three blocks of stores. The last storefront is City Hall. Then left and then make a quick right. You are now at the Chowchilla Civic Center. You'll see a nice group of low-lying red-brick buildings—the jail, the sheriff's office (his main office is in the county seat, Madera, fifteen miles to the south), legal services, and the place where the town's records are kept. Keep going until you see the fire station. Now slow down and pull over. You'll see a rock out on the corner of the front lawn. No need to lock your car. Just park. And keep your windows open. Your car will get too stuffy otherwise, and this will take just a minute.

The rock is quite large—and it probably was hauled down to the valley from twenty, thirty miles up in the foothills where you see lots of polished granite lying around. I think that's how they must have done it. I have never spotted a big natural boulder in the Valley—at least in this part of the Valley. The rock is nicely shaped—big, roundish, but not perfectly so. And one side of it is a little flattened, so that it serves as a perfect surface for the plaque that has been attached to it. The plaque looks bronze to me. On it are listed the names of the kidnapped kids of Chowchilla in alphabetical order. The name of the bus driver is given special prominence because it sits in the middle between two columns of children's names. And, of course, the name of the mayor shows most prominently when you

109

cast your eye over the whole thing. The plaque gives thanks to God for returning the town's children unharmed. And it is dated 1976, so it must have been made in haste for a big unveiling on Chowchilla Children's Day, the day of thanksgiving declared that year by the town mayor.

So that's it. Yes, there's a little irony in all those thanks written on "The Rock." I mean, there's naiveté in the assumption that the kids were absolutely A-OK because they came home alive, in one piece. There's also a naive assumption implied on the rock that the heroism of an adult rescued the kids. But then you can't blame adults for wanting to think that sort of thing. And even in terms of the kidnapper's trial, a "bodily harm" one if you will remember, it was not a terribly politic thing to declare upon a permanent rock monument that the children were completely alright a good year before the sheriff and D.A. would be trying to convince a criminal judge in Alameda County that the children really weren't so fine at all.

At any rate, "The Rock" is a bit of Chowchilla history, and I remember seeing it as a repeated fade-in, fade-out frame between various July 1985 interviews with kidnapped schoolchildren on NBC network news. Now that you've seen it, you might like to cut back onto Robertson and drive further down—maybe half a mile—to Pedro's Mexican food and pizza place for the best chile relleno anywhere (as a matter of fact, the Mexican food is so good I've never even tried the pizza). Don't miss the palms on Robertson either. Somebody planted them one short, one tall, one short, one tall, until—as you drive by watching those waves of palms—you feel a little seasick.

The Thorntons, Terrie's parents, live out past Pedro's in one of those nice, new, two-story houses close to the edge of town. You might ask them what they think of "The Rock." In 1980, when I spoke with the Thorntons last, they didn't think very much of it.

Now, why should anybody dislike a rock monument? After all, your name in bronze probably lasts longer than you do. And you can always take credit for being at the center of a great adventure if your name is put on a marker. It is something special about you, right? Something to mark you off as different. A survivor. Somebody whose face was once seen on every TV screen in America. Somebody who was part of the International News Story of 1976. Somebody who was *somebody*. Right?

Wrong! The kids of Chowchilla hated their notoriety. They hated what had happened to them. They hated their story. And so they hated "The Rock." It served as a symbol of all that. If the monument stood for anything at all, it stood for the children's utter helplessness. It stood for once having been diminished to less-than-human status. As V. S. Naipaul would have said, it stood for "being reduced to nothing, [for] being crushed." The rock marker celebrated something better kept secret. It proclaimed that you weren't as invulnerable as your nontraumatized brother. That you had been out of control. That you were unlucky. "The Rock," in other words, was a marker of "shame."

Early in 1977, when she was only ten years old, Terrie Thornton complained to me, "I feel the kids talk too much. I think some people are trying to get something out of this." And then Terrie mentioned the new monument in town. "I hate 'The Rock,' " she said. "I wish it wasn't there."

Terrie Thornton was expressing a sense of public exposure, of shame. I thought at first that shameful feelings must be specific to Terrie Thornton. But it turned out that she was talking about her own humiliation just a bit earlier than were the other Chowchilla kids. By four to five years after the kidnapping, many of the other Chowchilla youngsters were voicing this same kind of feeling. Carl Murillo, for example, a fifteen-year-old boy, who moved from Chowchilla to El Paso, Texas, to Las Vegas, New Mexico, and back to Chowchilla in five years' time, was known in each community as a hero of Chowchilla. Carl alternated, however, between bragging about his heroism and pretending he never had been kidnapped at all. Carl needed to tell his story in order to try to discharge some of his fright. And he was proud of the part he had played at the kidnapping's end. As a matter of fact, Carl told the kidnapping story to a school assembly whenever he transferred into a new school. Carl felt ashamed, too, however. He ducked the kidnapping issue altogether from time to time. "Everybody makes me talk about it," he told me when I caught up with him in New Mexico. "But I say to them, 'it's not true.' " Carl's sense of shame was hurting his credibility. What was a friend to believe—Carl's school speeches or his private denials?

All of this ducking, bobbing, and weaving around the facts by Chowchilla kids was quite deliberate. Unconscious "denial" of external reality was not at work here. The kidnapped children knew exactly what had happened to them. They were consciously suppressing any talk and even any thinking about their abduction. The Chowchilla victims did not wish to be exposed in public as small, useless, and helpless. This is why the kids fought so hard to avoid exposure. They went so far as to avoid privately exposing feelings to their intimates. No wonder Terrie Thornton so detested "The Rock." It was a bronze announcement of past indignities done to her. "It's embarrassing when people mention the kidnapping," Terrie said. "I don't *want* people to think that I wanted to use it just to get attention and stuff."

Children struggle not to think trauma-related ideas and not to feel trauma-related feelings. They fight any mental picture that might create new upsurges of feeling. They hate the sense of "being crushed," of being less than human. By not thinking about their trauma, by not talking about it, children try to heal their wounds and to look "normal."

"Suppression" is entirely conscious and, thus, not a classic defense mechanism. Yet suppression is probably the most common coping device that people, exposed to external threats, will employ. Suppression functions as a protection against upsetting outside events, the externals. Suppression is often used by normal, healthy people as they try to deal with their world's scuffs and bumps. The renowned psychiatric researcher, George Vaillant, in following a healthy cohort of Harvard men throughout their adult lives, found "suppression" to be a very commonly employed defensive operation.

Eighteen of the twenty-five kidnapped Chowchilla kids eventually showed evidence of "suppression." Although there were many reasons for this deliberate holding down of ideas, the children's shame was the most obvious source. Rachel Mendosa, sixteen, for instance, was able to connect in one statement her tendency to suppress and her feelings of shame. In 1980 she said, "I don't want to be scarred by the kidnapping. I *won't* associate my fears with it. I hate the feeling of helplessness more than anything else. I want to be in control, not to lose control." By day, Rachel did, indeed, feel in control. When she awakened at night, however, she felt impelled to rouse one of her sisters. Once the sun was down, the teenager felt too terrified to walk alone to the bathroom, even inside of her own house. Rachel felt so deeply ashamed of her helplessness both during and after the kidnapping that she considered herself "scarred," despite what she said about her wish to avoid scarring. Thought suppression had not worked well for Rachel in wiping the shame from her repertoire of feelings.

The combination of shame and suppression may force traumatized children to lie. "It's not true," the child utters, "I don't live in Chowchilla" (Sammy Smith). "It's not true," the high school wrestler says in New Mexico a few weeks after telling his kidnapping story to an all-school assembly: "I say to them, 'it's not true' " (Carl Murillo). A combination of shame and suppression may also force a traumatized child to change the course of his life. "I'll never be fat again," said the boy who had been deemed too fat to dig (Johnny Johnson). And he meant it.

Human beings strive to stay in control. People come to believe, in a way, that they can order their lives. Maybe even order the universe. They are God's helpers. Their works are the most magnificent of all creatures'. Children refuse to believe that randomness and disorder can fall upon anyone. It seems that ordinary kids are raised to think they are responsible for what happens, that they will be able to control what occurs. Perhaps people were even genetically selected over the years with those believing in their own powers turning out to be the ones who eventually survived as the "fittest."

But sometimes things do go terribly wrong. The children victimized by these things feel anything but "fittest" afterward. They tend to feel ashamed about their bad luck. Rather than thinking that something wrong "just happened," trauma victims seem to prefer believing that they caused or contributed to the events—that they were responsible.

Everybody has trouble with the idea of bad luck. Inadvertently wandering under a cloud somehow feels disgraceful. Shameful. Often children would rather put together some made-up reasons for tragedies and feel guilty about these made-up causalities than experience the humiliation of being victims to the world's randomness. I think that this is true for adults, too. But children are so clear in the way they look and talk that one "sees" this plainly. As a protection against feeling ashamed, in other words, young people make delayed, unconscious trade-offs—"guilt" for "shame."

Alan Bascombe didn't choose to be in his house on the wrong afternoon, for instance. He was just there, taking a nap like always, and he was kidnapped. He bore absolutely no responsibility for what happened to him at age thirty-nine months. It was a random event. An evil man had been watching him. Casing his house. Waiting. Yet, somewhere inside himself, Alan, as a genetically well selected, well brought up little human being, thought he had to accept some personal responsibility for it. And in so doing, he accepted "guilt." The boy came to believe that other kidnappings in his town were modeled after *his*. There was to be no randomness now that Alan was reordering his universe. But the young man had to pay a price. He came to blame himself for what happened to another little boy, a boy named Alan Banning, kidnapped and murdered five years after Alan Bascombe's own ordeal. Since all kidnappings were now patterned on *Alan Bascombe's* kidnapping (in Alan's mind, of course), the boy had to feel responsible.

Shame comes from public exposure of one's own vulnerability. Guilt, on the other hand, is private. It follows from a sense of failing to measure up to private, internal standards. When others "know" that you once were helpless, you tend to feel ashamed. *They* know. If, on the other hand, you feel you caused your own problems, you cease feeling so vulnerable and blame yourself, instead, for the shape of events. *You* know. But you are the only one.

Exchanges of guilt for shame begin to occur very early in life, too early, as a matter of fact, for a child to possess a fully formed conscience. But if a child has just finished the passage through infancy, the most vulnerable period of life, the youngster will hate having this vulnerability exposed. Rather than risking shame, the toddler will be able to create some guilt to cover over his humiliation. The new "convert" to autonomy, in other words, is the most adamant of converts. No person is more mortified by the loss of autonomy and personal control than is a traumatized three year old. And so, even the relatively young preschooler will make this trade-off —guilt for shame.

Let me introduce a preschool dog-bite victim, Carla McGillicuddy, in order to illustrate what I mean. Carla was a little over three years old when she was attacked by a Doberman pinscher. Yet she unconsciously made the trade, guilt for shame, that almost anybody over two and one-half or so can make. Carla was too young at three to have developed a fully functioning conscience. Yet the child expressed a sense of responsibility about the dog's behavior. An entirely unexpected, random event had caused Carla to lose all personal control. Afterward she felt she could not face those who still had their own controls. And so she created guilt inside of herself. She began to find herself at fault for being bitten by a dog that, as a matter of fact, had been bred for generations to attack.

Carla was only three years, two months, of age when she was slashed by "Gumbo." The animal belonged to two teenaged boys renting riding space on Carla's grandparents' ranch. Carla was visiting her grandparents one day. When she tried to enter Grandma and Grandpa's horse corral, Gumbo spotted the child and knocked her to the ground. He tore open her scalp down to the eyebrows. He would have gone further, had he not been called off by his two horrified masters. The little girl was rushed to the hospital. Gumbo was destroyed by the authorities.

For the first three months following Gumbo's assault, Carla sang a song called, "There Was a Doberman That Bit Me and Now He's Dead." Then, in October, Grandma died. The song stopped. The next June, Carla told her mother a "joke": "Why does the man sit on the chair?" "I don't know. Why, Carla?" "Because he's dead." Carla also asked her mother, "If you smoke, Mommy, will you die?" Mrs. McGillicuddy called the pediatrician. This was too much death from a four year old. The pediatrician sent Carla to me. There was little question, from Carla's joke and her inquiry about smoking, that she felt vulnerable to strange and meaningless death.

Carla looked cute and cunning despite a few lingering facial scars. She did not want to come into my consulting room alone, but I finally convinced her to come in. "When I grow up," she said, "I'll have to walk to kindergarten, but I will take a wrong turn and tell my mother '*You* have to drive me.' I want her to drive me to kindergarten. Mom *has* to come with me. I want her to be with me. I get scared if she's not with me." So here was a formerly independent little girl who used to wander about her grandparents' ranch alone, yet now she was demanding continuous protection.

"There was a dog who hurt me," she started up her story of trauma at my request. "One time I had a dog bite and I went to the hospital. I was in

Grandma and Grandpa's farm to say hello to a horse, 'Josie,' when a dog came and bited me. I wasn't playing with the dog. I was going to go through the gate to Josie, and the dog just came. [This is Carla's statement of randomness.] I thought I was going to die when the dog was on me. And I was starting to cry. [Carla's language is interesting here. She probably could not get her crying started because she was too frightened and too surprised to cry.] He was biting on my head. [This is a terrible, photographic memory shot—a picture of abject helplessness.] I couldn't see his face. I couldn't see nothing. He bled my hands and feet. I ground me. [This means: 'I clung to the earth.'] *And I didn't do anything to him.*" [This is Carla's acknowledgment that she had lost all human control. The animal had emerged as victor without so much as a contest. The child, probably aware by age two or so that she could be master of the beasts, was admitting here to less-than-human status.]

Carla suddenly shifted subjects and activities. When this happens, it is often a sign that a child is about to launch into some sort of defense. "Here, I've got a surprise for you," Carla said. "Close your eyes. [Carla had implied a moment before that she closed her eyes when Gumbo attacked her. She had said, 'I couldn't see nothing.' I closed my own eyes as Carla requested and heard the sounds of mad scribbling.] Open. [I did. Carla was 'controlling' me like a puppet. Carla showed me some indecipherable marks on a piece of paper.] I've made a puppet for you. [Yes, indeed. Puppets were on Carla's mind. She had felt helpless like a puppet when Gumbo jumped her.]

"I was *sneaking* on the farm. That's why Gumbo attacked me. Sneaking is wrong." [This is a confession of guilt. The steps go this way: (1) Carla describes her shame, her less-than-humanness—"I ground me"; (2) Carla attempts to make *me* the one who is less-than-human, a puppet; (3) Carla's displacement of her shame from herself to me fails; (4) Carla conjures up a sense of personal guilt.]

The child went on: "I feel I did the wrong thing and the dog did the right thing. It was the *dog's* farm and the *dog's* gate." [This was not true. The corral belonged to Carla's grandparents and the ranch, someday, most likely, would be hers. Carla had made herself guilty by taking four steps within her own mind.]

Almost anyone, even a three or four year old, would prefer guilt over shame. And so people explain the world's randomness by blaming someone or something. The man-in-the-street wants to know, "What did that child do to make the dog bite?" The public is curious—"How does an industry in the Cameroons cause a lake to give off poison gas?" They ask, "Why would a nice family choose a day-care program managed by an old pig like Leroy Hillgard?" "Why would a young girl dress so provocatively that she would be raped in the street?" "Why did some wealthy family in Winnetka, Illinois, hire a psychotic babysitter?" "Why do so many people go to air shows where they can get killed?"

Nothing is random. Everything must have a cause, a reason. Even an event like the 1981 Hinkley attempt upon President Reagan's life becomes "controllable"—that is, in retrospect. "The president should have been very cautious that day," says an astrologer from my television set in 1988. "His stars were against him." You see—it was Ronald Reagan's "fault," if one looks at things this way. Reagan should have sorted out the randomness of this world in advance. In not having done so, Reagan "neglected" something very important. And so Nancy Reagan hired an astrologer. In the future, Nancy's husband would not be allowed to go about his business without advance "controls."

Then there was Charlotte Brent, who we already know quite well. Charlotte spent her entire life thinking that she was a bad girl. "Sexually depraved," she would accuse herself. Charlotte blamed herself for things she could not remember, for things that people probably had done to her on a beach before she turned three. Charlotte's experiences with sex back in the 1930s caused her to blame herself in the 1980s. Charlotte's guilt was worn like a cloak. It covered up something even worse than guilt. If I had developed a magic "cure" to rid the fifty-six-year-old Charlotte of her guilt, I think she might have retreated into her house, never to emerge again. A guiltless Charlotte Brent would be something less human, less functional than she is today. Without guilt, Charlotte would be left with an overpowering sense of inferiority, of vulnerability, of shame. She might not be fully able to face the world of humans. "My best feature," she often says now at age fifty-six, "is my conscience." A terrible trade-off, that is— guilt for shame. But I think that was the trade-off that Charlotte Brent engineered fifty-three years ago on the beaches of San Francisco.

Stockholm Syndrome is a relatively small point within this bigger subject of "shame and guilt." Stockholm Syndrome, though rare, is occasionally seen in childhood psychic trauma. The name encodes a story from Stockholm, Sweden, a story of a female bank teller held hostage at gunpoint by a bank robber. The captive woman "fell in love" with the man who had taken her. She openly criticized the Swedish government afterward for failing to understand her captor's point of view.

It takes special circumstances to develop Stockholm Syndrome. These conditions rarely come into the world of children. First of all you must be held hostage. Far more adults are taken hostage than are children. Adults are more "valuable" as commodities of trade. Second, the person holding you must be a stranger. Most children held against their wills are taken by known persons—relatives, babysitters, or teachers, for instance—not strangers. Third, the criminal must keep talking to you—relate to you enough, in other words—for you to "fall in love." Obviously, the Chowchilla kidnappers didn't bother talking with their young hostages. They didn't feed, didn't water, and didn't care for them. No one could fall in love with such negligent hostage-takers. And fourth, the criminal must act deadly—he or she probably should have shot someone else or at least demonstrated a frightening arsenal of weapons. It is essential to Stockholm Syndrome that you become convinced that your life is actually in the hands of your captors. Because what lies behind Stockholm Syndrome, of course, is a sense of being less-than-human, the sense of shame. By giving up all your personal choices to the hostage taker you feel totally helpless. You are the slave to the master, the dog to the owner. The criminal is seen as the true human being. He retains control. The hostage is inhuman—out of control. The hostage develops a "crush" on the criminal, based upon the admiration of the "have-not" for the "have." It is a relationship built out of shame and fright.

The closest I have ever seen young children come to exhibiting the Stockholm Syndrome was the case of Jonathan and James Burgess, the eleven-year-old and nine-year-old boys who were taken hostage in their suburban Phoenix home by the convict Albert Drake. Albert kept a gun on the boys for eleven hours.

Once he forced his way into their house, Albert talked, talked, and talked. He used the family phone while the boys listened, giving telephone interviews to disc jockeys and reporters. Albert repeatedly told the boys the story of his life—about his impoverished parents, the unfair accusations he had suffered, a bad rap that was put on him for killing a relative of his, and a crooked judge. There had been chain gangs, knifings in prison yards, and sodomy. "Oh you boys don't know what that is. Let me tell you all about it." Talk, talk, talk. Albert Drake was "on something" while he held the Burgess boys hostage. He couldn't stop talking. Three avid listeners huddled together in the house, the two Burgess boys and their friend Steve Pugwalich. Albert kept pointing his vicious-looking gun at them. And the boys began to identify with Albert's tales of woe. He had been wronged by his family—the boys knew what that felt like. He didn't have any money—nor did they, especially when their parents took away their allowances. Teachers had been unfair to Albert. "Of course." Jonathan and James agreed. "The authorities stunk." "Of course."

Albert then made his mistake with Jonathan. The convict took the elder of the two brothers into the bathroom and tried to fondle his genitals. Jonathan found an excuse to leave for a moment and immediately engineered a daring escape.

The boys ran across the yard from a side door of the Burgess house.

Now nothing could stop the law. Albert emerged from the house almost at once, hands folded across his head—guns ignominiously slung across the lawn—in full, spotlit surrender. It was all over.

But Albert, the convict, had made a couple of lasting "fans" during those eleven hours he held them captive. Even Jonathan Burgess, furious as he felt about the sexual advances he had endured, could not hide his ongoing interest in Albert Drake. I spoke to both Burgess boys together a few months after it happened, and part of the conversation went like this:

> JONATHAN: I tell the story of Albert a lot. Especially in the beginning. James told it twenty times a day. Mostly, we told it because people asked. But we have tapes of the news. [Reporters, of course, had picked up the story and were releasing news bulletins and reporting on-the-spot coverage every half hour or so.]
>
> JAMES: We could hear Albert's voice real clear on the tapes. We listened again and again to Albert's voice the first night we had the tape. Then my father loaned it to somebody. [Mr. Burgess actually had confiscated it. He thought it was "sick" that his boys should be so fascinated with the criminal's voice.]
>
> JONATHAN: We listened together. After we listened to it, we'd get real scared.
>
> JAMES: Somehow we like to hear Albert's voice more than anything else.
>
> BOTH BOYS: [Speaking too quickly to separate the dialogue] We both look at Albert's face a lot, too. We don't know why. He was our friend. We want to see him . . . want to see how he treats us.

So, it wasn't "love," really. It was a kind of friendship and identification with the aggressor that the Burgess boys experienced. But Jonathan and James's father had been right to distrust the boys' interest in their friend, the convict. "Sick," you'd have to say. The boys' need to feel friendly toward Albert Drake overrode his sexual misuse of one of them. It overrode the man's undignified surrender into the floodlit night. It overrode his dumb phone calls to Arizona and Southern California disc jockeys. And it overrode his obvious, drug-induced talkiness. This "friendship" of boys for man was created on the basis of the boys' profound vulnerability, their shame. They had felt for eleven hours that Albert Drake was the only human being in the place. As hostages, the Burgess boys had felt "less-than-human."

Mr. and Mrs. Burgess preferred that I not refer their boys to a Phoenix psychiatrist for treatment. They still were "normal," Mr. and Mrs. Burgess said. And, in one way of looking at it, the boys indeed *were*. They were showing normal responses to terribly abnormal circumstances. I did as the Burgesses wished without arguing. And, after that, the family faded from my professional life. A year after I had last seen them, I phoned Mrs. Burgess to ask when she might be bringing the boys to Tiburon to visit her parents. I wished to see Jonathan and James once more for the purposes of follow-up. Mrs. Burgess agreed. They were planning a trip to California within the month. And so I was afforded one final glimpse of the two young, former hostages.

Jonathan and James's Stockholm Syndrome, I was happy to see, had died its own death. I learned that the Stockholm Syndrome had collapsed on a dramatic note. During Albert Drake's criminal trial, Jonathan Burgess had served as a witness for the prosecution. The young lad had remained quite sympathetic with Albert, and he was trying to give his testimony in the most favorable way he could. When the boy reached the part about what Albert had tried to do to him in the bathroom, Jonathan felt especially ashamed. It mortified him to speak in public of this kind of personal vulnerability.

But Jonathan Burgess had taken the oath to tell the truth, and so he told his story of the sexual fondling without expanding or minimizing it. As Jonathan told the sex story, he watched Albert Drake. Albert was vigorously shaking his head "No." Jonathan stared from the witness chair, transfixed. He watched Albert feverishly writing notes to his attorney. Still shaking his head, "No, no," the convict made a few subtle motions to the spectators in court indicating that the boy must be crazy. Imagining things. Albert's attorney launched into a vicious cross-examination of Jonathan Burgess. Jonathan stood a little outside of himself, watching this courtroom drama. He answered the questions as he watched.

Well, man-to-man, Jonathan knew exactly what had occurred between Albert Drake and himself. He never had had a doubt. His memory was as clear as if everything had taken place yesterday. In a flash, Jonathan Burgess understood. Albert Drake was a pathological liar. A psychopath. Everything he had told Jonathan and his brother a year ago had been distorted. Everything was self-serving. The man, not the boy, was the worm. The man, not the boy, was the less-than-human. In one moment on the witness stand, the boy was able to see it all. He bravely withstood Albert's attorney's attacks. He stood firm. He later shared his revelation with his brother. James Burgess quickly came to see it too. Both boys began hating Albert Drake. And they were far better off for hating him than they had been for liking him.

———

Shame is not frequently depicted in Western literature and film. But I do not think that this infrequency reflects a lack of prevalence. Shame is a very common feeling connected with psychic trauma. Its paucity in literature probably reflects some shame about depicting shame. An audience most likely does not want to witness shame on the movie screen. Nor do creative people want to write about it, even if they feel it. Shame gets almost too close to the center of the psychically traumatized condition for words. It comes from the unspeakably painful sense of being less than human.

There are exceptions, of course. There are a few Western stories that do tell of shameful experience. One German tale, "Rumpelstiltskin," tells of a dwarf with a hidden name (which, by the way, means "crinkled foreskin," a shameful thing to have, I would think). The dwarf makes a proposition —that the virgin, the protagonist of the story, must guess his name. If she misses, she must marry him. The maiden takes the dwarf totally by surprise by proclaiming his shameful name loudly at a public gathering. The dwarf's response is the literal one that a less-than-human person would choose if he could. He stamps his foot and crashes right through the floor, never to be seen or heard from again. "I could have gone right through the floor," one sometimes says. This phrase may come from "Rumpelstilt-skin." But then again, "Rumpelstiltskin" may have evolved from the phrase.

Circe, the sorceress of Homer's *Odyssey,* ambushes her victims in public, again creating a sense of shame. She takes away all choices, drugging the men who want her and eventually turning them into less-than-human beasts. Again, we see in this invention of Homer's the literal loss of human dignity that begins with a psychologically overwhelming experience at the hands of a powerful adversary. Circe does not meet her match until the great Odysseus, forewarned and thereby unsurprised by her, beats her at her own game.

Stephen King begins his novel *Carrie* with a high school locker-room scene of such surprise, of such public disgrace, and, yes, of such psychic trauma that he builds his book to a climax of revenge that any young reader would applaud. King says in *Carrie,* in other words: "Don't trau-matize me, don't shame me, or you will die. And all your sons will die, and your daughters, and all your seed into the generations." That, at least, would be my paraphrase of King's *Carrie.*

One feels this same sense of shame vicariously in the opening scene of Hawthorne's *The Scarlet Letter,* when Hester Prynne is forced to publicly wear the letter *A* because she has given birth to a child of adultery. But Hawthorne is much different psychologically from King. Hawthorne does not seek the solutions demanded by psychic trauma. I saw a needlepoint pillow once that, I think, humorously paraphrases the conclusion Hawthorne draws in *The Scarlet Letter*. "Living well is the best revenge," the pillow says. That is *not* Stephen King's philosophy. King demands annihilation—external havoc. Hawthorne, on the other hand, slowly builds his character back to humanity on the internal level.

A vicariously experienced sense of shame may force groups who should function as helpers to fail. Several months after those large-scale McMartin Nursery School sex accusations began coming to light in Southern California, for instance, the *American Medical Association News* reported that a number of pediatricians and family medicine practitioners, who had been consulted earlier by the alleged victims, had failed to thoroughly examine their little patients. The article suggested that some McMartin students had complained in the past to their doctors of bloody stools, trouble urinating, severe constipation, and/or pain in the anal-genital region. The doctors, according to this news report, had inadequately examined their young patients. After the legal complaints were made, no documentation of injuries could be found in the doctors' charts. The doctors' failure to examine these small children may have been a group-held response to shame. The physicians, in other words, may unconsciously have preferred not to look.

Hopefully, we will begin to look and to see. We cannot respond with our own mortification to the "shame" of others. If we look openly, unabashedly, and then talk with children who have been victims, this, in and of itself, should bring them some relief. Perhaps some sense of being human, after all, might be restored right then and there.

PART II

The Mental Work of
Childhood Psychic Trauma

CHAPTER 7

Misperception

The car that hit me looked like a shark. Big Toyotas and American cars look like the shark.

Natasha Dimmit, age twelve

"And why do I keep talking about that car as if it was a person?" she cried out. Tears had begun to spill down her cheeks. "Why do I keep doing that?"

Stephen King, Christine

WHEN I WAS YOUNG, I listened every Sunday to a radio show that came on a half-hour before those three old classics, "The Shadow," "The FBI in Peace and War," and "Gangbusters." This was a program in which scary, supernatural mysteries were eventually solved in a most sensible manner—of course, only after twenty minutes of terror at the temples and tombs of the exotic world and eight minutes of commercials. Over the years, I have questioned a number of my friends, and nobody I've asked can tell me the name of that program. But the show must have existed in reality because I don't suppose that at age seven or eight I could have hallucinated week after week, Sunday after Sunday, at precisely four in the Cleveland afternoon. At any rate, the "ghost stories, weird stories" on that unnamed radio program were creepy, and one had no choice but to accept all that weirdness, that is, until the last-minute naturalistic explanation was offered. The story line often concluded with the idea that people get things wrong. If you were scared enough, it implied, you might not see straight.

I have always liked naturalistic explanations. And so, despite the fact that my favorite show quickly faded from the air and never became an all-time great like "The Shadow," its premise had staying power for me. It did not seem impossible to me that under extreme stress a person could convince himself of wrong things, of "weird" things.

Then I came to Chowchilla. And I learned that a number of kidnapped kids had immediately perceived incorrectly. They precisely remembered all the events that had occurred to them and around them, but some of them suffered visual illusions. The children had looked directly at the three stocking-masked men, and one had seen a "black man," one had seen a "bald man," one had seen a "lady," and one had seen an "old man who used his shotgun as a cane to support his missing leg." Another Chowchilla child saw her visual illusion a little later, under the terrible stress of the transfer from the vans—it was a "fat, chubby man," she said, describing the person who had sent her down into the "hole."

Three of the Chowchilla victims had hallucinated during the kidnapping. That is to say they had experienced visions where there had actually been nothing at all to see. One of these kids, five-year-old Susan Hunter, saw the kidnappers "lying down to take a nap." This tableau was viewed by Susan from the depths of her burial site—in other words, the kindergartner was reporting what she had "seen" through the ceiling of the buried truck trailer, and what, with her X-ray vision, she had perceived through the overlying layers of dirt and rock.

Those were not all of the missightings reported at Chowchilla, as it turned out. By the time I visited the children for their four- to five-year follow-up interviews, the number of children reporting misperceptions had grown from the original eight to thirteen. Three of the first eight children had given up their mistaken sightings on the basis of talks with me or after receiving updated information from their television sets or in the newspapers. But another eight, seven of whom had probably seen things "right" in the first place, were now exhibiting faulty memories about what originally had been sighted. Among other things, there was now a "man with a long nose," a "man with a pillow stuffed into his pants," a couple of new "girls," a brand new "black man," and a "light blue van" instead of the white one and the green one that the authorities had found at Fred Woods's house. It thus appeared that misperceptions did not stop with a traumatic event itself—they could belatedly appear in memory after a child had thought things through, heard the rumors, or even after he had rerun his own mental "tapes" a few hundred times.

For years psychologists have been particularly interested in how children perceive and register input that can be controlled experimentally. A number of experiments of this nature have been conducted under nontraumatic conditions. If one were to summarize this work, one would probably conclude that, on the whole, children perceive no better nor worse than do adults. In certain ways, however, children do seem to perform better as witnesses in the experimental "lab." Children, for one thing, do not appear to let racial or cultural bias influence their interpretations of what they see. They do not, for instance, seem adept at separating out the races or attributing good or bad traits to certain ethnic groups. This increases children's "fairness" as witnesses. Children are also good at reporting extraneous detail. Since they do not pare down their attention to what they think are the salient points, children may, for instance, pick up the movements of accomplices to the side of a scene or inside a crowd. This childish attention to extraneous detail may actually shed more light upon an experimental scenario of crime than does the more organized, trimmed-down account given by an adult.

There are some weaknesses that children show as witnesses, however, as opposed to adults. When a uniformed person or a strong authority figure like a school principal is shown doing something wrong in a drawing or a photograph, the child looking at the illustration often tends to interpret it as harmless. Adults do not exhibit such blind faith in authorities. Young children also tend to become quite confused when pictures employing face masks or disguises are presented to them. They have more trouble than do adults in locating the key physical characteristics that would penetrate a disguise. Children, in summary, may misidentify strangers, masked individuals, and those posing as authority figures more readily than do adults in the experimental psychology lab. On the other hand, children do not let racial bias or single-minded adherence to a plot line interfere with their perception of what is happening. Obviously, some children will be better witnesses than others, and the youngest children, those under about age four, will not do as well as the older ones. But all of the experiments leading to these conclusions were done under relatively pleasant, nontraumatic conditions. Psychic trauma adds a new element, a crucial element.

Trauma, of course, cannot be studied experimentally in humans. No scientist worthy of the name would want to shock or frighten children to the point of psychological trauma. And even if an investigator did consider doing this, no hospital or university, through its institutional review board, would allow it. Thus, any answers about how misperceptions are formed under psychologically traumatic conditions will have to come from field studies of real events, such as the Chowchilla kidnapping, or from case studies of single children, such as Natasha Dimmit, whom I want you to meet.

When I first met her, Natasha Dimmit was twelve years old. She and her family had immigrated from the Ukraine region of the Soviet Union two years before the traumatic pedestrian-car accident that changed her life. Before her trauma, Natasha had learned to ride the San Francisco buses, to speak fairly good English, to get along passably well with her peers, and to understand at least the basic ways of her adopted land.

Most days after school the young immigrant stopped to buy candy at the "Mom and Pop" grocery store near her house. Oftentimes she carelessly peeled back her candy wrapper, discarding it on the floor or on the front stoop of the shop. Natasha did not realize that the owner of the small store she frequented was himself steeped in the tidy traditions of an immigrant people. And he was becoming silently angry at this sloppy, afterschool customer of his.

The day Natasha Dimmit was hit by a car, she stopped after school, as usual, at the corner store and bought herself a Baby Ruth. Peeling back the wrapper, she discarded the papers with a flick of the wrist. Immediately the quiet, middle-aged man who usually waited on Natasha began to yell: "What's wrong with you, you dirty girl?" Natasha stared at the man. He was an Asian or something. Was he American? He looked Japanese. "Get out of my store. Don't stand there looking. Get out. Don't come back. You're a dirty girl. You always make me clean up after you. Get out."

The child rushed out onto the sidewalk. She wasn't clear about what she had done to upset the man in the store. The man must be crazy. But he seemed angry at her. Had she done something wrong? Natasha recommenced her trek home—just one more block to go. She checked both ways as she came to the crosswalk. No traffic. She stepped out. Just then she heard an enormous screech.

The young girl looked up. A car was coming fast around the corner. It was going to hit her. There was no time to get out of the way. And then, time seemed to go slow.

The car "looked like a shark." Yes indeed, it was a "shark car." Everybody at school had been talking about *Jaws*. There were great white sharks, the kids were saying, in the Pacific Ocean right outside the Golden Gate. In the Ukraine, Natasha had never heard of great white sharks. But here was one of those California ones, a mechanical monster, right here on a San Francisco street.

Natasha glanced up at the driver. What kind of person would speed around corners, driving a shark car and getting ready to hit girls? Middle-aged. Right. Black hair. Right again. Male. Right. Japanese. Wrong. Baaam.

A year after the accident, Natasha was entirely healed—physically, that is. She had suffered a concussion but the neurologist had declared her "OK." Emotionally, well that was a different matter. The toughest thing for the red-headed, blue-eyed Natasha, as it turned out, was that one quick glimpse, that look at a "Japanese" man driving a "shark" machine. You see, the police report stated that the car was a Japanese model and the driver was "Caucasian." I read to Natasha a year later from the accident report. The man had a typically Caucasian surname, I told her. "He could have changed his name when he came to America," she argued. "One of our family friends wanted us to change our name, too, from Dimmit to something more American, like Dunn or Dinisdale."

"But look at this," I showed the early adolescent the police report of her accident. "The policeman who came to the scene of your accident describes the driver as 'white.' "

"I don't know if I believe what the policeman wrote," the teenager insisted. "I *saw* the man. *He sure looked Japanese to me.*"

Natasha Dimmit had experienced two incidents within about five minutes. One was small, the other, big. The small incident, I think, altered Natasha's perception of the big one. It would be difficult, if ever possible, to remove the improperly registered imagery that Natasha had committed to memory. Natasha Dimmit was stuck with her "Japanese" driver. She had set up mental circuitry that seemed burned into place.

Misperception may occur in psychic trauma when a strong metaphor is applied by the victim to the experience. The metaphor and the reality come together in the mind as an amalgam. The end result may feel quite spooky, "supernatural" one might have to say. And the faulty picture may last in memory. Consider Curt Provost, age sixteen, for example. Curt and his best friend, Charley Curtis, had gone joyriding one Sunday afternoon with Charley's irresponsible, but fun, Gramps Mortimer. Gramps drove up to the top of Telegraph Hill that day. The boys thought they might get out and take in the view. But no, that's not why they were there, Charley's grandfather said. He let go of the brakes, and, whee, they were coasting down Telegraph Hill at ever-increasing speed. "Watch out! We're going to crash," one of the boys had hollered. But Gramps Mortimer just sat at the wheel, transfixed. The car bumped one parked car, then another, and another. The last impact sent the old man's car spinning. It dove headlong into a tree and abruptly came to a stop. Curt passed out. He awoke inside a smokey, burning inferno.

"The gas tank! This thing is going to explode any minute," Curt thought. But the teenager found he could not move. Suddenly Charley's face appeared at the car window. Curt's best friend was going to try to rescue him. He was. Charley was saving him. He was prying Curt out of the car. There. They were outside of the burning car now. They were on the grass. There. It was really happening—the car was exploding. It had blown up. "Where's Gramps?"

Gramps Mortimer immediately turned up, dazed but healthy, on the grass across the street from the car. Two months later, Curt Provost came to my office. He had seen something for a second or so inside that smouldering wreck, something that still made him feel uneasy. "I saw Death in Gramps's car," he told me in a monotone. "I saw Death. So whatever comes in the future, it's no big deal."

Curt may have been employing strong metaphor. But, on the other hand, his metaphor was leading him to "see" something tangible, to register something deeply into his mind, something that really wasn't there. A supernatural being. A supernatural experience. Curt had had a personal brush with Death, with a literal Death, with the same Death who had kept an appointment in Jean Cocteau's story "Death and the Gardener" and who had come to fetch the little boy in Schubert's terrifying song, "Erlkönig."

Curt and Gramps Mortimer each walked off from Telegraph Hill alive. Charley Curtis had to deal with some bad burns on his hands, the price exacted for his heroic reentry into his grandfather's car. But Curt Provost was physically unscathed. He, on the other hand, would have to live with his perceptual change, a sense of having been exposed to something weird, perhaps supernatural. Curt's visit by Death was vivid and unforgettable. A metaphor had inspired his misperception. The metaphor had become real in Curt's mind.

Wishing is another operation of the mind that sometimes causes the traumatized child to misperceive. Wishes can be so powerful at moments of overwhelming stress that they color what becomes "seen." When little Susan Hunter, for instance, "saw" her three kidnappers "lying down to take a nap" above the "hole," she was achieving a wished-for connection with them. Rather than experiencing a final, terrifying separation from everything in her known world, Susan believed through her visual hallucination in the "hole" that she was still in contact with the young men who had taken her. By dint of her wish-driven missightings, Susan Hunter could "keep an eye" on her abductors. One boy I know, Jamie Knight, stood in the kitchen doorway and "saw" a gun in his father's hand as his mother shot his dad to death. The police found no such gun on the body. Jamie's wish drove his missighting. He wished his mother was shooting in self-defense. He sided with Mom because Dad had abused both of them too many times to count. His bias toward Mom and his wish that she be innocent allowed him to misperceive at a moment of intense shock.

Traumatic misperceptions may reflect a young person's mood. Bob Barklay, the fourteen-year-old "hero" of Chowchilla, for instance, experienced two mood-related hallucinations, one a vision of despair, and the second, a vision of hope, when he dug the group to safety. Six months after the kidnapping, Bob remembered his hallucinations this way: "I went up there [into the cubicle that had contained the truck-trailer batteries], kicked and tore apart mattresses for tools—got one corner up, and looked through there. It looked like a blue rug, white bedspread, bureau, and a TV. I almost fainted when I saw it. I was positive I was going into the kidnappers' trailer. This happened when I was alone. I didn't tell more than one person."

Bob stopped digging. He was deeply discouraged by what he had "seen." After a while, however, Bob decided to try digging one more time. What did he have to lose? He felt some "second wind," some hope. "I stopped looking there," he said regarding the place where he had "seen" the kidnappers' lair, "and I made a bigger hole. Then I saw rocks and trees, maybe heard a river. This made me dig a lot more."

The fact that Bob had been digging in isolation for hours contributed heavily to the boy's hallucinations. But Bob's moods (discouragement, then encouragement) were what was expressed in the visions. When the mid-adolescent boy emerged from the place where he had been buried, he found himself alone in a desolate rock quarry. "The trees," Bob said, "actually were brown. I had heard [in the hopeful hallucination] running water. But there was no water when I got out. I had seen [in the hopeful hallucination] daylight through the crack. But I actually came out at dusk or dawn."

When in January 1977 Bob Barklay first confessed his hallucinations to me, he told me that he had been afraid for the six months since the kidnapping that he was "insane." "I lost my mind," he said. I explained to Bob that perfectly normal people experience visions under certain circumstances—when they have high fevers, when they are experimentally submerged in tanks for long periods of time (sensory deprivation), or when they are forced not to sleep (sleep deprivation). Bob, I was sure, had hallucinated, in part, because he had dug, either entirely alone or squeezed together like an ant with Carl Murillo, for so many monotonous hours. He had been isolated. He was fatigued. He had hallucinated, also, because he had been scared "out of his wits." But I could assure Bob that he was not insane. Nor had his hallucinations come from being brain-damaged, organically poisoned, or unknowingly drugged. As a matter of fact, Bob and I were discovering something new together—we were finding that pure fright, a nonorganic, nonpsychotic condition, could create visual misperception and hallucination.

What in the young brain enables missightings and misrememberings? One neuroscientist speculated to me that a massive release of neurotransmitters may upset the usual brain functioning during trauma. Such an internal breakdown of chemical equilibrium could account for the misperceptions that are reported afterward. It would be a kind of internal flooding with psychoactive substances. One would not be likely to find these substances in the body because the "blood-brain barrier" would block most trafficking out into the bloodstream. The internally released substances would influence the brain only.

But how would one ever be able to prove this neurotransmitter-release hypothesis? Animal experiment, thus far, hasn't shown much. M. E. Seligman created a laboratory situation, for instance, in which rats, ordinarily water-haters, are forced to swim for long periods of time. The rats develop what Seligman calls "learned helplessness," and this helpless condition will last for hours to days. But learned helplessness experiments, at present, seem to work better as animal models for depression than they do for psychic trauma. Don't ask me why. It just turns out that antidepressant medications behaviorally "cure" rats previously forced into Seligman's "learned helplessness" situation, whereas in humans antidepressants appear not to "cure" psychic trauma unless the condition is dominated by sadness or attacks of panic.

One laboratory experiment strikes me as a relevant one to do if we wish to know what substances the brain might produce and release internally during trauma. We might consider studying the uninjured brains taken from children who died knowing they were in extreme peril (during stabbings, auto accidents, or falls, for instance). If such children realized that at any minute they might die, their brains should contain in the interstitial spaces the neurotransmitters that my friend the neurobiologist guessed about, that is if such substances are really released during traumatic events. Some laboratory may eventually be in the position to separate out, "count up," and analyze these extracellular psychoactive materials from "knowingly" dead children's brains and compare them with "unknowingly" dead children's brains of the same ages and sexes. A ghoulish experiment, yes. But it would not be harmful to living children and it might be of great use to future child-victims. If we could determine which, if any, neurotransmitters were released at the time of life-threatening trauma, we might be able to find a way to block their ongoing release or their continuing influence upon the brain. Perhaps we might find a way to keep these neurotransmitters from coloring a traumatized child's way of looking at the world afterward. Such experiments should be done. But I will not be the one to do them.

When it comes to psychic trauma, the ascendancy of visual representations over all other perceptual memories (with the exception in infants, perhaps, of touch) is an intriguing phenomenon. There appear to be far more missightings, for instance, reported by traumatized children than there are mishearings, misfeelings, missmellings, or mistastings. A few Chowchilla kids, as a matter of fact, continued mistakenly to see Fred Woods and the Schoenfeld boys on their television sets—in cowboy movies or on quiz shows. They knew that the kidnappers were safely locked up in San Quentin. But they couldn't control what they "saw." Yes, many traumatized children are, indeed, bothered by the sounds that they hear in their own backyards. But these sounds are usually identified for what they are —the sounds of "mices and dogs" (Carl Murillo), for instance. Rather than misleading the child into wildly wrong guesses, sounds are usually explainable by children. It is the "visions" that seem to come back most to haunt them.

Seeing apparently dominates all other senses following trauma because it is the sense by which most horrible episodes are recorded and reviewed in the mind. Traumatic "tapes" are almost always replayed by victims in silent video—not in audio or even in "smellovision." Even in cases where a traumatic episode begins in an entirely blinded way—in other words, the child is prevented from ever seeing the episode—the event may eventually transform itself into a "sight." This transfiguration may lead the "see-er" to believe in "weird experience." Here is an example from a child patient of mine:

Betsy Ferguson was nine years old when her grandmother, with whom she was living temporarily, was strangled by Betsy's mother's boyfriend. Betsy had left Grandma's home after breakfast and returned to find the door locked. She called the police. After the police opened up the house, they discovered Grandma's body in the kitchen and covered it with a big blanket. A policeman told Betsy what had happened. The shock, therefore, came by ear, not by eye. Betsy never saw anything. A few months after the murder, however, young Betsy developed a bothersome, repeated visualization—a picture of Grandma being strangled. It was Betsy's imagination, true. But the youngster did not picture herself listening to the shocking news, something that she actually did experience with both eyes and ears. She pictured, instead, what she could not ever have seen—the most awful part—Grandma's murder. Betsy began feeling a little "weird." Perhaps she could "be" two places at once.

I think that another example is in order, but this one will be from a young adult. Henry Hall was twenty years old when his younger brother, Alfie, unexpectedly committed suicide with a gun. At the funeral Henry, in a final gesture of farewell, cradled his dead brother's head in his hands. Henry recoiled. There was no back to the head! The damage was felt, not seen. After the funeral Henry repeatedly drew horrible, misshapen heads. His tactile sensation had been transmuted into something visual, something reproducible in graphic form. Henry began to daydream about the back of Alfie's head. His own hair began falling out—from the back of his head. He began a series of oil paintings—of half-headed monsters. What originally had been touched with the fingers was being reexperienced through the "mind's eye."

What happens if a person, blind from birth, is traumatized? I am sure this does occur. The question intrigues me. Would feels, smells, or sounds predominate? Or would there still be vague sensations of menacing darks and disturbing shades? In sighted persons, the mental apparatus that registers and stores the input from psychic trauma must have some connection to the visual pathways and centers in the brain because vision stays predominant in the memory of the trauma. Therefore, understanding the traumatic experiences of persons blind from birth might help us better understand the underlying mechanisms of psychic trauma.

Were the saints traumatized? They certainly experienced enough "visions" to make one wonder. I heard once from a cleric that the Spanish mystic St. John of the Cross told his fellow mystic St. Theresa of Ávila that he believed his visions to be products of the devil, not of God. In other words, St. John of the Cross did not trust his visual hallucinations. As devil-induced, they were psychological, not spiritual. Saintly visions, as recorded by the Church, include the precision of detail and the vivid colorations that you also "see" in the visual experiences of traumatized kids. Yes, perhaps the saints *were* traumatized—at least some of them.

In this chapter I have given several examples of strong psychological reasons for the missightings and misrememberings of trauma. Curt Provost had ample psychological reasons for accepting death as he woke up unable to move in Gramps Mortimer's burning car. No wonder he *saw* Death at that point. And Susan Hunter could not stand to separate from—to lose contact with—those upon whom she had depended for sustenance and love. No wonder she hallucinated renewed contact with the world above her "hole," even if that had to be the kidnappers.

But some children never demonstrate a psychological connection between what they "see" during trauma and what they have been thinking, fantasizing, or feeling. In many instances of childhood trauma, the psychological "reasons" for a child's traumatic misperceptions do not come to light. Perhaps the brain misfires and that is all. Tania Banks never knew why she had seen a girl with braids in the kidnappers' van. But she still believed in this "girl" four years after the experience. Debbie Mendosa could not connect "a man with a pillow stuffed into his pants to make him look fat" with any prior experience of her life. And Billy Estes "saw" a light blue van—simply that, a light blue van. There was probably no meaning to this—the van was "seen" and remembered incorrectly by Billy, that is all. This sort of misperception without meaning happens commonly under traumatic conditions. And we must keep the point in mind. In Marilynne Robinson's novel *Housekeeping,* two little orphaned girls try to remember what kind of rental car their mother was driving as she purposely ran off a cliff to her death. One child remembers the car as blue, but the other says it was green. Their shock created the perceptual confusion. But there is no particular meaning to these little girls' misperception. I think this is true in many instances of post-traumatic misperception.

If a child has been repeatedly shocked and frightened over a long period of time, in other words if he has been traumatized repeatedly by someone close to him (a parent, babysitter, neighbor, doctor, teacher, etc.), he will usually see things correctly. The traumatic experience has become an expected one—thus, it is not associated with the stormy onslaughts upon the perceptual apparatus that one sees in the single-blow traumas. If a child says, for instance, that the assistant teacher at nursery school has been playing with his "private parts," he is usually quite right. The child knows the teacher. And his experience has become expected, therefore not surprising.

A few situations, however, lead repeatedly traumatized children to become confused about their perceptions. First of all, these children may forget part of their experiences through denial and self-anesthesia. Even so, however, they usually remember the perpetrator. But when perpetators use masks, costumes, or disguises, the repeatedly abused child may become quite confused about what was seen. In child-abusing satanic cults, for instance, the adult members often employ face masks, robes, and even animal suits as part of their rituals. The child victim may not be able to identify these perpetrators even though people well-known to the child actually lived behind those masks. Helen Symes, for instance, a child patient of mine who probably was abused near her preschool a number of times between ages two and three by adult members of a satanic cult, could not identify any of her abusers by the time she reached age four. Helen said to me a couple of times, "they were men in animal suits," and another time, "they looked like Big Bird," and another time, "it was like 'Sleeping Beauty.' " The child, however, had no idea a year after her last abuse what her abusers actually looked like. Helen had frozen in terror at home one day at the sight on TV of a Mayan maiden lying supine on a stone altar. Most likely she had been forced to lie supine. And Helen's parents had found a huge, regularly shaped bruise between her legs when Helen was only two. Somebody had hurt her. A number of Helen's former classmates from nursery school were showing physical problems with their bladders and rectums and mental problems of the post-traumatic type. But what had really happened to Helen Symes over a long period of time? And who had actually attacked her? The bears? Big Bird? The wicked fairy?

The passage of time is another situation that may confuse the perceptions of a repeatedly abused child. Children who endure long-standing abuses tend to keep these repeated experiences secret. They feel dirty. Nasty. The secret often lasts for years. If, for instance, a youngster had been abused over, say, a two-year period by an uncle, and then, if the immediate family severed their ties with that uncle for entirely unrelated reasons, it might be quite difficult, five years later, for a child to identify that uncle. Even though he was "family" once, the uncle's looks no longer can be remembered. Over time, in other words, any child may forget a once-familiar person. People change. If a child is discovered, therefore, years after the fact, to have been repeatedly abused by someone previously well-known to the youngster, the child might not any longer be able to make the identification. The child's mental imagery would be too far removed in time.

A final situation that distorts repeatedly abused children's remembered images of their traumas is the problem of "suggestion." This has become a particularly pressing problem in cases of divorce. But it is also beginning to emerge in civil suits against child-care facilities and schools. If a trusted adult, particularly a parent or a professional person, suggests an idea to a child, the child stands a chance of coming to "see" this suggested idea in his mind. In other words, adults have the power to "plant" mental imagery into children's heads. A child witness, if indoctrinated thoroughly enough by adults, may become convinced of something that never actually happened. He may identify "perpetrators" who never actually harmed him.

The sexually anatomically correct doll is one tool whereby adults, though inadvertently, may suggest visual imagery to kids. Police departments and child-protective service agencies are increasingly relying on this doll today, despite its high potential for suggestion. Because it is a quick, easy way to elicit sex talk from very young children, the doll may bypass years of professional training and expertise on the part of the interviewer. No scientific study, however, has yet proven anatomically correct dolls effective at weeding out definitely abused from definitely nonabused children. There are always "exceptions," children who make serious mistakes with these dolls. The dolls worry me. We do not want to convict people in the American system of justice because of a child's "false positive" identification in response to a highly suggestive instrument. Nor do we want to cut children off from one of their parents because of a session with a strange-looking doll.

Here is an example of what I mean. It is the story of a well-respected day-care operation that stood to lose its license on the basis of one anatomically correct doll interview with a young student, Viola Edwards.

Viola's story comes from the transcript of an interview conducted by a policeman, a social worker, and the five year old's mother. The interview was done in Viola's Southern Oregon home. The youngster had told her mother the night before the interview that she and Uncle Roger, her day-care director's husband, had been playing "Dumbo's Trunk." After being asked by her mother several times, "Did Uncle Roger take you into the bushes?" Viola had answered, "Yes." Mother ran for the phone.

The next morning a police detective-social worker "team" came to Viola Edward's house with a portable TV camera and one doll—a naked male anatomically correct model. They asked Viola to play with the doll. Their tape goes this way:

SOCIAL WORKER: [Giving the naked doll to Viola] Do you know, did you read the story of Dumbo? Remember Dumbo with the long trunk? Do you see anything down here [pointing to the doll's penis] that reminds you of Dumbo's trunk:

VIOLA: [Coughs].

SOCIAL WORKER: Do you see anything here that reminds you of Uncle Roger?

VIOLA: No, that's not *my* blankie. I want my blankie.

SOCIAL WORKER: [Pointing to the doll] Does this look like Uncle Roger? Hmm? Does it look like Uncle Roger?

VIOLA: [Tries to look at the doll's face]

SOCIAL WORKER: [Covering the face] Oh let's don't look at the face. Do you see anything that looks like Uncle Roger down here? Hmmmm? It's all right, sweetheart. It's all right.

VIOLA Yeah, *that's* my blankie.

MOTHER: That's a nice blanket. It's got bunny rabbits on it, doesn't it? We like bunny rabbits, don't we?

VIOLA: Yucky mice. We hate mice.

MOTHER: Yucky mice. [Turning to the policeman and social worker] That's one of the substitutions, one of the terms she has been using [for sexual functions or parts].

SOCIAL WORKER: [To the mother] "Yucky?"

MOTHER: [To the social worker] And "mice." [Turning to Viola] Do you want to talk about that, Cupcake? You want to tell this nice lady about the mice?

VIOLA: Uh-uh. I want to go potty.

That's what I mean about suggestion. I would hate to see the world of children subjected to interviews like this one. If a child was traumatized by a person she knew, the child should be able spontaneously to remember what the perpetrator looked like, that is, unless the abuser used disguises or had lost contact with the child long ago.

How do you think that young Viola Edwards described her alleged abuser, Uncle Roger, when, several months after that anatomically correct doll session, her sworn deposition was taken?

The child offered detail upon detail about a naked man. Her description of the man perfectly corresponded to the anatomically correct doll with which she had been asked to play in her televised and taped interview session. Viola's description, on the other hand, bore no resemblance whatsoever to Uncle Roger.

After traumatic experiences, children repeatedly "see" what happened to them. These visions, accurate or inaccurate, are brought on when the child visits a place where the event occurred, when someone else mentions the traumatic episode, when something connected with the trauma comes to mind through association, and when the smells, the atmosphere, and the season renew a sense of "being there."

Children frequently put their minds on "idle." Daydreaming, with no specific meaning or fantasy, fills up considerable normal childhood time. After a traumatic episode, young victims fill these leisurely moments with visualizations. Traumatized children's visualizations will come, thus, not so much as interruptions, but rather as logical landing sights for the mind upon its return from "Never Never Land."

Leisurely visualization seems to be an important distinction between the responses of those traumatized as children and those traumatized as adults. Remember Clint Eastwood in the film *Firefox*, for instance? Eastwood did not visualize in a leisurely fashion in this movie. *Firefox* tells the story of a Vietnam War–traumatized veteran, the best pilot in America, who goes to Russia to steal the greatest airplane ever made. (It seems I'm always seeing this film on airplanes, and even if I'm not listening to the sound track, those fiery, midair crashes make me feel uncomfortable at thirty or forty thousand feet up.) Because he has been traumatized, Eastwood keeps having "flashbacks": sudden, unexpected, interruptive visualizations of his Vietnam experience. He has these flashbacks at the goddamnedest moments. He's about to leave the Russian pilots' locker room to take over the Soviet plane, for instance, when he starts sweating and seeing his visions. This isn't good. These visions interrupt important actions that Eastwood must take. The poor, traumatized pilot of *Firefox* can barely function. Half of the suspense of *Firefox* is whether the pilot's post-traumatic flashbacks, not the Russians, will defeat him.

The majority of adults traumatized at times of peace do not complain of the interruptive style flashbacks that seemed so common, according to reports from veterans' hospitals, following the Vietnam War. But a few adult civilians *do*. These adults, like the American pilot of *Firefox,* find themselves suddenly cold, sweaty, and experiencing a "tape-review" session at the very worst possible moments. But those traumatized as children or early adolescents do not complain of this. At Chowchilla, in fact, no child experienced sudden, interruptive flashbacks. Everybody "saw" the kidnapping at moments of quiet. Nobody pictured himself kidnapped while doing difficult homework or in the midst of a spelling bee. Flashbacks, variants of daydreaming, appear to be late-adolescent or adult variants. Children, the most practiced daydreamers of all, do not seem to interrupt themselves with visions. Instead, they daydream at leisure.

Bad visions are horrible, however, whether or not they tend to interrupt. If a child sees an ugly death, this visualization will review itself on indestructible tapes. Let us take a quick look at a few of these; but just a quick look because they are horrifying.

Gwendolyn Garcia was thirteen when she, an older sister, two teenaged friends, and a younger brother suffered a terrible automobile accident. Gwendolyn came to consciousness inside an ambulance with her dead younger brother on the next gurney. "I remember waking in the ambulance," Gwendolyn told me, "and I saw my little brother. I saw blood all over his face. I couldn't see his features. I looked away. . . . All along [for the two years that followed the accident] I've had a continual daydream of my brother's face—especially when I see other little kids. I dreamed his face [at night] two times a week for about a year. But now I have different [night] dreams of my younger brother. I see him at home or at a distance. These are not terrifying anymore, but comforting." Gwendolyn Garcia had found some solace in her night dreams. But the girl's daydreams did not veer away from their external origins, that horrible moment in the ambulance.

Solomon Wilson, the seventeen-year-old accident victim we met earlier, whose best friend, Joe, was killed in Solomon's exploding car, had to endure numerous visualizations. "Joe made no sound," Solomon recalled in my office ten months after his disaster. "I saw the outline of his body burning. When I am awake I see the picture of Joe burning over and over. I watch him burn up. . . . I'm daydreaming every day. I still see it. The daydreams are terrible."

Children who live to review their own personal horrors, like those of Gwendolyn Garcia or of Solomon Wilson, feel "haunted." In folklore and in literature, hauntings have traditionally related to houses, not to people. From the ancient Greek writer Pliny (in his letter to Sura), to the modern Argentinian novelist, Cortázar (in his short story "House Taken Over"), we hear of houses that through the bad acts of others have become occupied by spirits. As a matter of fact, Jimmy and Rosalynn Carter live in a Plains, Georgia, house supposedly "haunted" by a young woman ghost who waits forever for her lover to return from the Civil War. (Plains, located a few miles from the notorious Andersonville Prison, may have seen its share of Civil War horrors.) But it is not really the houses, I think, that are the haunted ones. It is the people in those houses. Psychic trauma victims are cursed with an unstoppable tendency to "see" their traumas. They are indeed "haunted."

Traumatized children must live with ongoing daydreams that the ordinary child would avoid at any cost. No wonder we stop breathing as we walk by a supposedly haunted house. This is a place where post-traumatic visualizations were once "shown" several times daily on the big screen. I wonder if Gwendolyn Garcia's or Solomon Wilson's houses have yet been designated by their neighbors as haunted. I know of one house that actually *was*, but the story will have to wait for much later in this book. In the meantime, suffice it to say that by dint of the defense mechanism, displacement, houses, not people, tend to be the ones designated as "haunted."

Spooky, isn't it? But this seems to happen. A tragedy—unexpected and sudden—occurs. Somebody dies. A survivor goes on to hear the screams, smell the smells, or see the terrible sights, day after day, week after week. When the survivor leaves his house or dies, or even sometimes when he stays put, his house becomes the acknowledged repository for all the attendant horrors. As long as group displacement rests upon *this* house, everyone in the neighborhood may rest easy in his own house. After a while, even the traumatized person will be forgotten. But the house will be remembered. And its shocking tragedy, the source of all those terrible visions, will frighten anybody who ventures too close.

Memories of the perceptions experienced during traumatic events will change over time. Inanimate objects may eventually come to look animate. Movies may appear to be directed straight at the traumatized child. Young Natasha Dimmit eventually came to feel pursued by the "shark" car that had hit her. Several months after she was hurt, Natasha's "car" came to get her once again. This is how it went: "I was on the bus Friday. I hadn't wanted to go to school. I got on at 24th Street and I saw *the car.* I was amazed. I did not expect that. Then the bus took off. And I got off the bus two blocks later and walked home." [Natasha refused to try once more to go to school that day. She felt "the car" would hunt her down.] And in another episode with Natasha's malevolent monster: "My stepbrother loves movies about cars hitting people. I turn around and do not look. I saw a movie [probably *Christine*] with my parents. I always want to be with them if they're watching movies. It was about a fifties car going around killing people with the devil in a car. My mother was grabbing me. I left after a half-hour, but I should have stayed to see the ending [because some of Natasha's suspense might have been relieved]. I was sitting there shaking."

When you see horrible, mechanized monsters on film, like the freight train in *Stand By Me* or the car in *Christine,* you can see for yourself how distorted visualizations of an accident may appear firsthand in the mind's eye. Mechanized monsters have been proposed, at least in fiction, since the dawning of the Industrial Revolution. In 1868 Nathaniel Hawthorne wrote himself a note to try to do a story about a malevolent machine. He never did write it. But Hawthorne's simple sketch, as reprinted in his *American Notebooks,* does a pretty good job of raising the goosebumps:

> A steam engine in a factory is supposed to possess a malignant spirit; it catches one man's arm and pulls it off; seizes another by the coattails, and almost grapples him bodily; catches a girl by the hair and scalps *her;* and finally draws a man, and crushes him to death.

I wonder if Nathaniel Hawthorne knew a nineteenth-century Natasha Dimmit—or if he had a scary experience himself with a machine. Hawthorne, as evidenced by his sketch, certainly understood how a traumatic misperception may "look" in the mind. And he seemed to understand that machines could be vested with supernatural powers in their victims' eyes. One hundred years after Hawthorne, Stephen King fills his novels and short stories with similar mechanized monsters—the huge, grinding oil rigs that run people down in *Pet Sematary,* a runaway Coke dispenser that smashes a man like a bug on its glass display window in *Tommyknockers,* the malicious, exploding furnace of the Overlook Hotel in *The Shining,* and the trucks that take over the world in his short story "Trucks." King may have consciously or unconsciously harked back to Hawthorne's sketch about the steam engine for his own tale, "The Mangler." Both Hawthorne and King, it seems, are completely in tune with the perceptual distortions that bother people traumatized by machines.

But mechanized monsters are not the only monsters that hound traumatized children. Human monsters, or even, in some instances, previously human monsters, also afflict them. When gravely frightened, the child may begin to see a familiar person in an unfamiliar light. Consider the experience, for example, of five-year-old Frances Carlson, the daughter of divorced parents and the victim of two attempts by her father, a professional spy, to snatch her. The first time Frances's father tried to steal her away from her mother, several men, all of them colleagues of Pete Carlson's, climbed onto Frances's roof, opened her bedroom window, and called for her to come outside. Frances screamed. Her mother rushed in and slammed the window on one of the men's hands. The child was utterly shocked. The next day Pete Carlson grabbed Frances as she was trying to play at a friend's house. Frances screamed and wet herself. The friend's father, a giant of a man who just happened to be at home that afternoon, heard the little girl's screams and rescued her. He had to wrestle her out of her father's grip.

After a year's cessation of paternal visitations, strawberry-blond, grey-eyed Frances Carlson began misperceiving her father's looks, familiar as Pete Carlson had once been to her. The child began to forget. "I get scared of my father at night," she told me when I met her at age six. "I worry my dad is here in California [Frances knew he was working, by then, on the East Coast]. Sometimes I think I see him. Some people look Chinese. My father looks Chinese or Japanese. My father has black, greasy hair. [Pete had auburn hair that looked clean enough to me.] He wouldn't give back his mustache—he cut it off. We didn't like his mustache cut off." What we had here was man who had metamorphosed in his own child's eyes. In a similar fashion to a Dorian Gray or a Mr. Hyde, Pete Carlson had turned himself into a person of Asian origins. The little girl's belief that she had a Chinese father, beginning with the two incidents of attempted child-snatching, had extruded Pete once and for all from the child's own race.

I met Frances Carlson's mother at a supermarket three years after her ex-husband had tried to steal the little girl. Mrs. Carlson told me that Frances was still firmly resisting visitations with Pete, who by then was, quite ironically, "on assignment" in Taiwan.

Young trauma victims often believe that they spot their tormentors. Even when they know their abusers are gone, they tend to "see" them. Charlene Lu, an eight year old who was picked up from a Chinatown sidewalk and raped with a pair of chopsticks by a crazed, young man, thought she spotted the man at least once a year. When I first met the sixteen-year-old Charlene, she said that her parents had told her years ago that the man had been deported to Asia. But Charlene did not, could not, believe what her mother and father had told her. She believed, instead, what she "saw" with her own "eyes." Here, then, was a man who existed in two places at once—in Chinatown and in the Asian country to which he had been deported. He was a ghost, perhaps, or a powerful, supernatural traveler.

Let me insert a cautionary note at this point. Not every traumatized child misperceives. As a matter of fact, most traumatized kids will get things straight even though the world is falling apart before their very eyes. Half of the kids at Chowchilla *did* see things right. This is important.

A second point to remember is how long the tendency to misperceive, if established in childhood trauma, will last. One of my adult patients, Marcia Henri, began seeing ghosts at age thirty-eight, at a time when her job and her marriage were both in serious trouble. Marcie had almost died in

Nazi-occupied France of diphtheria when she was six years old. As soon as she recovered from her illness, Marcie's great aunt and uncle shocked her one day by announcing they were relinquishing their rights to her. She would live with a foster family. Marcie was traumatized through this experience. The ghosts that came to Marcie Henri at age thirty-eight were French adults dressed in the mode of the early 1940s. They had been transported, firm-bodied and intact, from the small town French hospital where Marcia first had lay dying and then had received the terrible news of her impending abandonment. Ghosts were breaking loose from Marcia Henri's imagination thirty-two years after her childhood trauma. They had just been resting, "waiting in storage" one might say, for the right bout of stress to come along.

In that regard, let us finish this journey into the realm of traumatic misperception with a true story about the American novelist Edith Wharton. Wharton wrote some of the scariest ghost tales ever written, that is, after Poe. Edith Jones, as she was called in her youth, came from a very rich family who coddled her with luxuries and rushed her off to Europe to escape the collapse of the American economy after the Civil War. At age eight, Edith suddenly became desperately ill with typhoid fever. Edith was isolated with a nurse in a separate wing of the spa hotel where her parents, the Joneses, were taking the "cure." The physician attached to the spa came daily. According to a distinguished medical historian, Dr. John B. de C. M. Saunders, the physician would have paused briefly, white gowned and masked, at the little girl's doorway. Then he quickly would have gone his way so that he might avoid catching the dread disease himself. The young Edith would have lain ill in near-total isolation.

The physician who took care of little Edith Jones was not a good one. He corresponded with his son, an army doctor, asking what to do with the gravely ill eight year old. But between the two of them, they failed. Edith would die, the spa physician announced one day.

Mr. and Mrs. Jones did not surrender to the doctor's pronouncement. The day they were given Edith's "death sentence" they heard that the czar of Russia's personal physician would be passing by train through the town, Mildbad, where they were staying. And so they rushed off to the railroad station to see if they could talk him into looking at Edith. Their entreaties prevailed. The czar's doctor came, radically altered the plan for Edith Jones's treatment, and saved her life.

But Edith Jones found herself, as she recovered physically, scarred emotionally. She felt hounded by a strange ghost that followed her everywhere she went, and especially at or near doorways. This is what she says about the experience (from an autobiographical sketch published, for the first time, in a 1985 collection of her ghost stories):

It was like some dark undefinable menace, forever dogging my steps, lurking and threatening; I was conscious of it wherever I went by day, and at night it made sleep impossible, unless a light and a nursemaid were in the room. But whatever it was, it was most formidable and pressing when I was returning from my daily walk (which I always took with a maid or governess or with my father). During the last few yards, and while I waited on the doorstep for the door to be opened, I could feel it behind me, upon me; and if there was any delay in the opening of the door I was seized with a choking agony of terror. It did not matter who was with me, for no one could protect me; but, oh, the rapture of relief if my companion had a latch-key and we could get in at once, before It caught me!

Edith Wharton states in her autobiographical sketch that "this species of hallucination lasted seven or eight years" after her typhoid fever. But the ghost at the doorway actually lasts much longer in Wharton's fiction. In her ghost stories, supernatural creatures consistently attack their victims at doorways or in halls. The ghost in the doorway, thus, spans a time frame from 1870, when Wharton recovered from typhoid fever only to suffer from post-traumatic symptoms at her own doorway, to her death in 1937—sixty-seven years of ghosts at doorways.

Edith Wharton's tales of the supernatural are clearly semiautobiographical. They hark back to her trauma, the old brush with death. The first ghost story begins with the words "It was the autumn after I had typhoid" ("The Lady's Maid's Bell" [1902]). Others include bad bouts of fever from which the protagonists cannot recuperate easily ("The Triumph of Night" [1910] and "Miss Mary Pask" [1925]). In "The Triumph of Night" the sick hero is totally at the mercy of a bad doctor.

But what makes a Wharton ghost tale unique is her reliance upon the doctor-in-white-at-the-doorway, her old "It." This doctor, Wharton's "ghost," assumes the same malignant qualities that Edith perceived at her own doorway during her childhood brush with death. In the story "Afterward" (1909), for instance, an unseen ghost bars a young woman from ever leaving her house, an almost literal repetition of Wharton's terrifying childhood confinement with typhoid. In "Mr. Jones" (1928), the heroine recalls "the uneasy feeling which had come over her as she stood on the threshold after the first tentative ring," a return of Wharton's post-traumatic symptom from her early teens. "Pomegranate Seed" (1931), a frightening tale of how the ghost of a man's first wife invisibly steals him away from the second wife, gives us another unwelcome, unseen specter. This one hangs about the front hallway, leaving notes on the table.

In Wharton's last story, "All Souls," the heroine, an old lady about to die, sees her ghostly antagonist leaving the entryway to her house. Wharton, actually ill with the heart disease that would kill her in a matter of months, was still struggling with that old bothersome perception, that doctor at the doorway. The perception had stayed alive for almost seventy years.

The theme of Edith Wharton's ghost stories reflects what the child Edith visualized from her bed during the most terrible moments of her childhood. Her "ghost" was really just an old, white-robed doctor, and probably a dumb one at that. But her imagery remained powerful for life, fed by the atomic fires of childhood trauma. Edith's post-traumatic imagery retained its zap for an entire lifetime. More than that, it continues to zap us today.

So that is my explanation for a lot of the ghosts that you run into here and there. The "ghost stories, weird stories" that preceded my explanations were probably better than the psychologies offered at their conclusions. Some things may better be left unexplained. Perhaps that's why my old, favorite radio show died such an early death.

CHAPTER 8

Time Goes Awry

If you're happy and you know it clap your hands—uh, uh
If you're happy and you know it clap your hands—uh, uh

> *The kids of Chowchilla, on the*
> *road in the green van*
> *(July 15, 1976)*

And all the way, to guide their chime,
With falling oars they kept the time.

> *Andrew Marvell,*
> *"Bermudas" (1657)*

I WRITE THIS CHAPTER FROM BELLAGIO, Lake Como, the Villa Serbelloni, an uncommonly beautiful retreat for scholars run by the Rockefeller Foundation. I have been here just three days. Each night I have awakened fully alert at 2 a.m. with a bad case of California jet lag. Every afternoon at three I fight the urge to fall into a dead coma. In the mornings people talk about middle-of-the-night news flashes from the 1988 Winter Olympics in Calgary, but these seem impossibly distant. After breakfast, somebody inevitably sits in the study reading the *International Herald Tribune*. It is already a day old, and the stories from America, two days past. Every evening I play the Bechstein concert grand and a group of scholars gather round, singing "Night and Day," "Blue Moon," "Tea for Two," "Shine on Harvest Moon," and "Laura." We do tunes from the junior high school recesses of my brain, yet everyone is at home. Some *scolari* roll up the rug and dance—a tango, a Charleston, the boogie-woogie, a waltz. There is no time here. We are living in the twenties, and thirties—no, the forties and fifties. Day and night are reversed. Calgary is too far away. The news happened two days ago. I am disoriented. Disjointed. But happy. Very happy.

When wonderful things happen, time doesn't seem to matter. Orgasms rarely count themselves out, that is unless one is trying to achieve some long-lasting, superorgastic, californiac state. Good vacations are too short. Good news hits in time-effacing bolts. The kids graduate in nanoseconds. The Villa Serbelloni wipes out time. Maybe I'll never get oriented here. Perhaps I will stay this way and return to the clock only when I return to San Francisco.

But most of us need our clocks. Sooner or later we find comfort in rhythms—sleep, wake; eat, fast; work, rest; socialize, isolate. We pace ourselves to the year's rhythms—the seasonal variations, even to our own stages of the life cycle. We begin to find peace in a life review, a historical perspective, a comparative chronology to the solar ones. We watch for the cherry blossoms, the last oak leaves, the Christmas roses of Bellagio.

I am continuously amazed to observe how early children grasp parts of the idea "time." An extraordinarily bright twenty-four-month-old double amputee (she had gangrene of both feet), who was waiting anxiously for her new artificial feet, asked her parents a couple of times, "What is 'soon'?", "Why is 'soon' not 'now'?" and "What is 'ago'?" If that isn't true "time" concern, I don't know what is. Of course, the artificial feet—the chance to stand up and bear weight—that was the reason little Marcella Stone watched time so closely. But why not an upcoming birthday or a visit from Grandma and Grandpa? Time sense is born in anticipated pleasure as well as in frustration and pain.

Children do not usually fully know and use the names of the days and months or clock time until about seven to nine years old. The great Swiss psychologist Piaget tells us that children do not fully understand "time" as an abstract concept until age twelve or so. But kids orient themselves much earlier than that to time. One can gather considerable time-related information from the average four year old. Preschoolers often know whether an important event happened around Halloween, Christmas, Easter, birthday time, or "when it was hot outside." Questions like, "Did that happen when you lived in your old house?" may narrow down the timing of an event from early childhood further. The answers a preschooler gives won't be perfect. But they won't be bad, either. Young children plug their life events into time slots, though not the same slots we carry about in our handbags or hang up on kitchen walls next to our refrigerators.

I remember an incident from a couple of years ago—a social, not a professional one—in which the very young daughter of one of my friends, a woman pediatrician, said something spontaneous and surprisingly precise about time. Ahna Blessing-Moore was only eighteen months old at the time this happened. The child, a cute little blonde who still didn't have much hair, had come with her mother and dad to Napa for a small weekend medical conference at the Silverado Country Club. We were all sitting around the breakfast table—maybe sixteen of us, lingering over coffee—when Ahna, who had been quiet, suddenly turned to her father and said, "Go horsey." Her dad, a Silicon Valley engineer, smiled and said to us, "It's Saturday. So Ahna wants me to take her to the horses that are boarded near our house. I take her to the pasture every Saturday morning while Joanne makes ward rounds at the hospital.

How could this very small child know it was Saturday? I was amazed. We were in Silverado far from her home. "Did you promise Ahna horses today?" I asked. "No." "Is Saturday the only day that you take your time over breakfast?" "No," said Bob, "breakfast is about the same every day. Joanne makes her hospital rounds at about the same time, including Saturdays, and we both like having leisurely breakfasts at home with Ahna all of the days of the week." "Do you all leave together in the mornings during the work week, but stagger your departures, instead, on Saturdays?" "No. It's the same routine on Saturdays, except for the horses." How, then, had little Ahna Blessing-Moore picked up "Saturday" signals? Was she ticking off the days to herself? It sure looked that way. This toddler was pacing out her week, somehow "knowing" that today, Saturday, was the day for equine delights. "Horsey?" the little girl asked one more time, eyes wide and blue. Ahna was convinced. Something had sparked a sense of "Saturday" in her. At eighteen months of age, without orienting herself to calendar or clock, little Ahna Blessing-Moore was tuned in to "time." She probably would not begin to read the calendar for another five years.

When in 1920 Freud defined psychic trauma as a "breach in the protective shield against stimuli," a number of people asked him to explain what his "protective shield" meant. Freud would only "hint" at an answer. His protective shield, he said, was a discontinuous mode of functioning, a discontinuity that lay at the bases of the concept "time." Somehow, "time" formed a foundation for Freud's protective shield idea, it seemed. But the inventor of psychoanalysis would go no further with his answer.

It's hard to guess, almost seventy years after Freud's "hint," exactly what the great genius meant. But that, of course, won't stop me from trying. Here, in updated language, is what I think Freud's suggestion means. Fitting a frightening event into "time," either personal time or world time, helps a person to cope with that event. Seeing, furthermore, how sequences of events work together and how long events will last also helps prevent any flooding of the psyche. Feeling rhythms, in addition, helps maintain a person's sense of balance. If all of these time awarenesses fail, however, to prevent a person from becoming traumatized, the person's time sense will undergo some damage. This damage will show, just as the flood lines on the walls of Venetian churches show. As a "stimulus barrier," in other words, "time" functions both as a protection against damage and as a marker of the damage.

I think that this is a good "time" to introduce a young psychic trauma victim, Wanda Forrest, in order to show what may happen to a child's time sense following a series of traumatic events. Wanda is a very special little girl, and I think you will like her. Her story is odd, so let me unfold a little background before we get to the main, terrible event and its effect on Wanda's sense of "time."

Wanda Forrest was an only child. Her mother, Becky Sue Livingston, was a runaway from rural Maine who came to California in the early seventies for the usual seventies thing—sex, freedom from parents, sunshine, and an open, communal feeling. Wanda's dad, Ned Forrest, came from a strict fundamentalist, middle-class, southern California background. He never joined the "hippie" movement. He was trying, as a matter of fact, to make it as a construction worker. Fascinated with Becky Sue's flare and good looks (yes, Ned met her on a nude beach at Bolinas), Ned Forrest did his best to get Becky Sue pregnant, hoping that she would marry him. Becky Sue *did,* of course, get pregnant. And she *did* agree to marry Ned. But the rest of Ned's plans were doomed.

The baby, Wanda, was born pretty and intelligent. Becky Sue, however, was not particularly interested in her infant. As soon as the young mother felt well enough, she started spending whole days out with her friends—over in the Haight-Ashbury, or, if she could hitch a ride, on the shoulders of Mount Tamalpais, or at the beach. Neighbors watched Wanda whenever they could. Sometimes Ned would take her to work. She was a good baby. He could leave her in the trailer at the building site, feed her a couple of times, and she'd sleep most of the day.

After a while, however, little Wanda Forrest started to explore. She needed to crawl, to babble with somebody who would babble back, and to play. Ned couldn't carry a playpen along with him while he drove a bulldozer or used the piledriver. Construction sites were no place for a toddler-to-be. Ned fought with Becky Sue, insisting that she stay at home. But Becky Sue Livingston hadn't run away from Maine "for nothin'." Nobody was going to tell her what to do now.

So Ned filed for dissolution of the marriage. Becky Sue didn't contest it at first. She would allow Ned full legal and physical custody of Wanda. Becky Sue didn't even seem to notice that she was giving up her rights to her child. But then came Wanda's first birthday. And there was a scene. By that time Ned was renting a condominium for himself and his baby out in the suburbs. Becky Sue showed up uninvited for Wanda's birthday party, bringing along a couple of stoned-looking hippies, her "friends," she said. Ned told her, "You can't come in." Becky Sue said, "I have my rights. I'll get a lawyer." She did.

For almost a year they fought for Wanda's custody. Becky Sue lost. Yes, she could visit Wanda once a week, if she arranged it in advance with Ned. But no, she had been entirely irresponsible as a mother. She could not hold the custody of her child. Wanda was almost two years old by the time Ned and Becky Sue made their last visit to the court. But their drama was only getting started.

The child was beautiful. She had soft, transparent eyes and unusually silky, ash blonde hair. She giggled, but always quietly. And she spoke a little hesitantly with an ever-so-subtle lisp. Wanda was shy, but she liked both of her parents and she especially loved Becky Sue because she was so much fun. Wanda anticipated her mother's weekly visits with great, though quiet, glee. One Saturday Becky Sue took Wanda out for a "visit" and never brought her back. Wanda was a month short of her third birthday. It would be two years before Ned Forrest would see his daughter again.

When Wanda did not return from her visitation with her mother, Ned did everything he could to find them. He phoned Becky Sue's folks in Maine. Did they know where his little girl was? "No," the Livingstons said. But they were lying. Their runaway baby and *her* baby had come home to stay. Surprisingly, young Wanda Forrest didn't have too much trouble with all this disruption. After all, she knew her mother well and she loved her. She was used to her visits with Mommy. And Mommy was giving her special attention now. As a matter of fact, Becky Sue Livingston had decided to settle down. (It was worth it, as far as she was concerned, just to one-up that jerk Ned Forrest.) Becky Sue told little Wanda Forrest that Ned had gone away for good and didn't want to be with them. Wanda became upset. She grieved. But little Wanda Forrest went on with her life. After about a year or so, Wanda's mother became tired of watching over her shoulder for the police and she decided to settle on an island off the coast of Maine, a place where nobody, she thought, would think to look.

Ned *was* looking, however. He made a trip on his own to Maine and was barred from entering the elder Livingston's house. He obtained a court order, but found no trace of Wanda. Becky Sue was already working as a waitress on her island. Ned hired a private detective. That kid was somewhere around the place. He could just feel it.

Ned's detective eventually came up with an answer. It took him about a year. Wanda Forrest was living on a small island. She had started kindergarten. She was pretty, bright, and happy. She was doing well in school. Her mother had been involved with a man or two, but nothing steady had developed. Becky Sue wasn't doing drugs anymore. She worked from eleven in the morning until eight at night at the only restaurant on the island, the detective said. The kid walked over from her morning kindergarten classes at about noon, ate a sandwich at the restaurant, and then went on to the island's knitting shop where the lady who owned the place would watch her until Becky Sue finished working. Wanda could easily be picked up at the lunch hour on her way over to the daily visit to Mom's restaurant. The walk from kindergarten was the consistent time that the child would be alone.

Ned obtained the necessary court orders in California and in Maine. He spoke to the island police and obtained their permission to pick up his daughter. Ned then joined the local detective at nine o'clock on November 18th and waited for his little Wanda to make that one isolated move that she would make every weekday—that lunchtime trek from school to Mommy's restaurant.

The detective was seven feet tall—a former, well-known, professional basketball star. Ned Forrest had shaved off his beard. He had also lost about twenty-five pounds since his old beefy days as an apprentice construction worker. Ned was successful now—he was a job foreman. He had even made a down payment on a house. He had a new wife, Cynthia, an executive secretary, who had a daughter of her own from a previous marriage. Cynthia and her daughter were waiting back in California for Ned's daughter to come "home."

I answered the phone at the end of my day on November 18th. It was an excellent child-custody attorney I had known for years. "We're bringing in a kid tomorrow from Maine. She's being picked up today. Flown home tonight. You've got to see her tomorrow. I'll bet she's scared to death. She's going to need you. Get her on your schedule."

The Forrest family, including Grandma Forrest, showed up the next morning before I started my regular office hours. And there I was—with a kid who had been traumatized, really traumatized, less than twenty-four hours before. (It was the shortest length of time between a traumatic event and a visit from a patient that I have encountered up to now.)

Wanda thought that she was kidnapped. She *knew* that she was kidnapped. Her *real* kidnapping, the two-year long abduction to the state of Maine, had felt like a visit with new grandparents, a chance to really know Mom, and a rescue from a daddy who, according to Mommy, had told her that he didn't really want her anymore. Yesterday's experience, on the other hand, was different. *This* was a "kidnap." Two strange men—one in a dark green jacket (Wanda completely blanked out on the man's height) and the other, a familiar-looking, clean-shaved, thin guy—took you hard by the hand, told you not to scream, showed you some papers, bundled you into a car, drove you to a helicopter place, stuck you on a helicopter, took off (the green-jacketed man flew the helicopter), landed it at an airport, stuck you onto a big plane, shook hands with each other—and then you went flying off with the clean-shaved man, a guy who said he was your father. You flew to a sunshiny place where the brightness felt funny in your eyes and there was a nice lady there who tried to kiss you and get you to call her "Mommy" and an unfriendly, sulky girl about your age who, they said, was your new sister. And there was an older lady there that you recognized. Something made you run to her. The lady said she was Daddy's Mommy and she held you in her lap and rocked and rocked you until you felt a little better. And then there was this—a new lady who smiled and said she was your "worry doctor." That's a "kidnap," alright.

Well those are my words for Wanda's "events." She actually had very little to say that day herself. A parent and a detective had kidnapped this five-year-old child with all the mechanics of the law on their side, and then the father and his lawyer were telling me to fix it all up. And I felt I needed to fix it.

Wanda looked absolutely bedraggled. Somebody had tried to comb her hair, but she was messing it by scratching her scalp, twiddling her locks, and flopping about on my couch. She was oh-so-sleepy. Her eyelids overshadowed her eyes. She started falling asleep right there as we talked. When she spoke, little as it was, she mumbled. One might have thought the child hadn't received enough oxygen on that helicopter ride with a green-jacketed detective. She looked encephalitic or brain damaged. But it was trauma—very, very early psychic trauma.

The child mumbled something, and this time I caught it. "Mom told me yesterday," she spoke robotically, quietly, "not to leave unless I packed."

"Was it *yesterday* that she told you that?" How could Becky Sue Livingston have anticipated a kidnapping yesterday? Did she have "powers"? If Becky Sue *knew* Wanda would be picked up yesterday, why didn't she guard the kid better? Why did she go off to work at all? Why didn't she keep Wanda home from school?

"I don't know if it was yesterday. Maybe she told me it yesterday," Wanda mumbled. "I don't know." Her voice trailed off. She was mixing up her "times." In an attempt to control the uncontrollable, Wanda was remembering some ancient warning of her mother's. And the warning had assumed a new emphasis—it was something Wanda should, she thought, have taken very, very seriously. Yesterday.

"Wanda—listen to me, Wanda," I said. But Wanda wasn't listening. She was back on her island in Maine. Or in nirvana. She was taking the full responsibility for getting herself kidnapped. She was telling herself that she hadn't heeded some sort of warning, some preknowledge that Mommy had offered her. I knew that Wanda could not have stopped her father and that basketball-playing detective of his, no matter what she thought she could have done. No way. I wanted to tell her so, but Wanda Forrest was too knocked out to listen.

The child opened her eyes. Another thing needed saying, it seemed. "I didn't have a chance to say good-bye to Mom," she intoned without inflection. Wanda was still grasping for some personal responsibility for an entirely uncontrollable event. I asked Ned, as we summed up our session, to let Wanda phone Maine to say "Good-bye." "No," he said. "Becky Sue knows exactly where Wanda is. Wanda has to get to know *us* now. She doesn't even know *me*." And that was that. There were to be no good-byes.

Well, I've just told you about our first session—the first one for Wanda and me. To his credit, Ned Forrest let me see his little Wanda twice a week for a month or so, then once a week, then twice a month, and finally once a month. The child and I worked together for three and a half years—the first year and a half to treat the trauma and the next two years to mourn Mom. Ned really wasn't a bad guy, once you got past all those hard-assed convictions of his. I came to realize that Ned was far "tougher" than he would have been if Becky Sue Livingston had not hurt him so badly.

Wanda began to remember her father. When she watched him at her leisure, he reminded her of old things—a man handy with pliers and wires, a guy who wore a big steel helmet at work, a guy who carried a thermos in a big, black lunch box, a guy who laughed in a gaspy kind of way, a man who liked to bring home tiny presents, things he could hardly hold in his long fingers, things like tiny toy mice, and little dishes, and books with teeny, tiny, gold-tipped pages.

Wanda's new stepmom was a crack stenographer, the best shorthand-taker that I have ever known. "Do you want me to take notes on the things Wanda says and does?" Cynthia Forrest asked me. "I want to help Ned, and I want to help Wanda to get better. I know she's been hurt."

Yes, I thought, taking notes was a good idea. Nobody had ever been willing before to write down exactly what a kid said to herself behind closed doors at home. Wanda's play might be interesting. Maybe we could learn more about the process of a traumatized child's thinking as it evolved. And so Cynthia Forrest began making notes on little Wanda's play and giving them to me—just the way Little Hans's father had given his "notes" about his five-year-old son to Freud.

Several weeks after Ned Forrest and his overgrown henchman picked up Wanda, Cynthia Forrest began to record some new play coming from behind Wanda's bedroom door. Wanda was talking to a group of imaginary playmates, a boy and two or three girls. Wanda had mentioned to me a week before the play started at home that she had made up in her imagination a "Little Wanda," a small, bad younger girl, and a "Big Wanda," an older, good schoolgirl. There were others, too, that she had named as she played—Susan, Harold, Otto, and Yucky Carl, children Wanda had known on her island in Maine. But shortly after starting to play, Wanda Forrest narrowed down her cast of imaginary characters to just two: Little Wanda and Big Wanda. Wanda's imaginary playmates seemed both to be alter egos, a good and a bad self. The child herself served as teacher for these two invisible others. She gave them loud, excited, repetitive lectures that went something like this: "If somebody comes up to you to kidnap you, run away. You hear now, run away. If you're trying to get home from school, do it fast. Don't stop. Don't talk. Run! Somebody might come and take you."

Wanda's games, once set into a regular pattern by about five months after the kidnapping, were totally predictable and totally repetitive. They were recorded and dated by the talented stenographer, Cynthia Forrest. Wanda's lectures to Big Wanda and Little Wanda finally stopped about a year after the kidnapping. I must have made something like twenty or thirty psychiatric interpretations before the stubborn game went its way. Wanda "learned" from me that she had really been lecturing to herself.

Four months after Wanda's play with Big Wanda and Little Wanda stopped, the little girl gave me a surprise announcement. "Do you know? I used to play 'warning games' with Big Wanda and Little Wanda before that man in the green jacket and my daddy took me off the island. If I paid better attention to my 'warning games,' I would not have been kidnapped."

Cynthia Forrest, by this time, had been jotting down every word she had heard of Wanda's play for one year. We knew from Cynthia's transcripts that Wanda's games with her imaginary playmates had started very gradually a few weeks after, not before, the "kidnapping." Wanda's play was in full swing about five to twelve months after the event. The child had "skewed" time, in other words. In order to feel that she could be in control, in order to feel competent and human after her trauma, Wanda had defied the rules of simultaneity and succession. It was better, Wanda felt, to take responsibility for failing to escape despite the "warnings" she had received than it would be to be at the mercy of totally uncontrolled events. Out of shock, in other words, Wanda Forrest had turned "psychic."

I wish I could say something nice about Becky Sue Livingston at this point. She had done a good job with her child those two years that she had kept little Wanda captive in Maine. But Becky Sue suffered from habitually poor attention—"Out of sight, out of mind." She never did visit Wanda in California, despite a number of half-hearted invitations tendered by Ned's lawyer and, in time, one nice one tendered by Ned himself. The child tried to get her mother to come. Poor kid—she loved her Mom, and so she suffered from Mom's absence. I insisted on weekly phone calls so that the relationship could stay alive. But Wanda Forrest could think of fewer and fewer things to say as time went on—her cat died in Maine, and that had been a big thing to discuss for a while—and school in California was good, always good. Becky Sue had habitually drifted in and out of relationships. Luckily, Grandma Forrest was still energetic and totally committed to Wanda.

Wanda's therapy was prolonged because she needed time and help to mourn the loss of her mother. While we were at it, Wanda and I worked on "time" too. It was hard to repair Wanda's "clock" once it went off kilter. But I think we eventually put it back in working order.

All "time" divides into four functions—rhythm, duration, sequence, and temporal perspective. Each function protects children against psychic trauma. But each also serves as a signpost for the scarring that is left after a terrible blow or a series of blows hits the psyche. As we survey how the four functions of time sense are affected by trauma, we will encounter the "paranormal," a supernatural quality. Trauma inspires paranormal feelings; the sense of telepathy, prescience, and powers. Just as post-traumatic visualizations lead at times to ghosts and hauntings, post-traumatic time-distortions create "omens" and uncanny experience.

Rhythm sense, the first and most basic of the time functions, is the most primitive "time" sense demonstrated by human beings. Animals show rhythms, too, in their migrations, their hibernations, and their sexual phases. Infants feel rhythms—both inside themselves (biorhythms) and outside (the rhythms of feeding, cleaning, napping, being held, and sleeping). We take our rhythms so for granted that we rarely mention them in connection to psychic trauma. It seemed almost incidental, for instance, when half of the Chowchilla kids, the younger ones, told me that they had been singing "If You're Happy and You Know It, Clap Your Hands" in their van. The kids had added the extra twist of grunting in rhythm or holding two beats silent at the end of each line. Similar to the way 1960s America buried its assassinated young president to the cadence of a drum, the children of Chowchilla were attempting to give themselves solace with a rhythm, one of the most ancient modes of comfort known to man.

One young paraplegic told me a while ago that he had counted in a ditch during the worst moment of his life. At the age of seventeen, Stanley Sullivan had been driving his small red sports car up a hill, and close to the top his brakes had failed. The little car flipped over. The door popped open and the young fellow rocketed out. Stan's spinal cord was severed and he knew it. He instantly could not move anything from the waist down. Lying there, conscious, all alone, and understanding immediately that he would never walk again, Stan Sullivan began pacing his mind and putting himself into a rhythm. "I counted," he recalled four years after it happened. "I counted because it was the only thing I could think of to do."

Stanley Sullivan was unconsciously doing two things by counting. First, he was putting distance between himself and what had happened—every second that he counted was a second farther away from the crash and a second closer to the future. Second, Stan was establishing a rhythm. Like a quiet song, like a rocking chair on a wooden porch, or a "Pat-a-cake, Pat-a-cake, Baker's man," the sounds of Stan's numbers were rolling off at a pace of approximately one-half a second apart. Stanley Sullivan could, thus, give himself what his mother had given him at the very beginnings of life—expectability, regularity, sequence, and sound. That's rhythm. That's comfort. (And, I think, that is Freud's "stimulus barrier.")

Remember Roosevelt Long, the little boy who repeatedly chanted the names of staff members at the midwestern psychiatric hospital where he lived? Well, Roosevelt couldn't give up all those rhythms, that is, once he had experienced what steady cadencing could do for him. All forces of expectability had abandoned Roosevelt Long at age three when his mother stabbed his father to death. After that, Roosevelt's rhythms had to be rebuilt, reworked, and repracticed—to infinity, it seemed. The boy was not able to strike up enough cadence to suit himself. A beat was dependable. There were two problems, though. Roosevelt's rhythms were restitutive, but so slowly restitutive that they, most likely, would be ultimately useless when one thought of how short a person's life actually is. Roosevelt's cadences also stuck out with the impact of a cymbal crash. They made him sound "weird."

Rhythms occasionally help when trauma is striking somewhere off in the distance. Consider, for example, what happened during the *Challenger* spacecraft disaster of January 28, 1986. The occasional school kid, shocked as he watched the shuttle blow up, kept up the countdown. Co-inciding to NASA's cadences, those few kids who told me about it later went on counting long after NASA had given up. These young people appeared to be entirely unaware of why they had gone on with their countdown. But it looked to me as if they were granting Christa McAuliffe, their heroic shoolteacher-in-space, a few more seconds of life. And they were granting themselves a few more seconds of time to adjust to the horror of it all. They were establishing a rhythm. Time to escape. Wish time. Time to live. Pulse time. Time.

Rhythm and duration seem exact and fixed. Absolute. You set the metronome and it keeps on ticking until you shut it down. When the metronome stops, you know exactly how long it ticked—its duration. The seasons, the movement of the earth in relation to the sun and stars, all of this type of rhythm and duration appears steady and constant. And that constancy provides some comfort. Go through each season once, for instance, and you've completed your cycle of mourning. Go through eighteen cycles and you've reached adulthood in America.

But time, especially durational sense, is also experienced with relativity. Time moves slowly when you're young and more quickly when you're old. Boring things drag on forever, and fascinating ones go too fast. The future is infinite at birth and minutely finite by old age. Yet no matter how highly subjective the states of psychological time are, they still protect a person from overwhelming feelings. Durations, whether experienced as absolute or relative, steady us against too much fright or even against too much joy. When trauma strikes, durational sense will change. One can remember the change long after it takes place.

When a terrible event lasts a short time, for instance, an auto accident or a plane crash, durations tend to expand. A short disaster seems to last longer than the clock indicates. The event may actually be remembered in slow motion. If, on the other hand, an ordeal lasts for a long period, for example, a burial in a well or a day on a stuck elevator, time appears to contract, to race faster than the clock actually moves.

What good does it do a traumatized person to prolong or to quicken time? This durational elasticity may help the person survive. If, in a crash, for instance, time slows down to a crawl, each and every degree of spinout is clearly apparent, the driver has that much more opportunity to take some sort of evasive action. Perhaps the passengers will be able to throw themselves out of the burning car or to duck into a protective posture. If, on the other hand, children are to be stuck in an abandoned rock quarry over, perhaps, the next several days, then they may be aided by perceiving time as racing. By avoiding knowing how many days they have gone without food, water, good air, or comfort, survivors may avoid giving up altogether. The chance of human survival goes down when a mental state of hopelessness is established. Time shortening puts off this kind of ultimate surrender.

Let us consider a couple of concrete examples of traumatic durational distortion, returning to two of our friends from the previous chapter in order to do so. Curt Provost, age sixteen, had spotted Death in the back seat of Gramps Mortimer's burning car. He put his durational distortion quite simply. "Time seemed to go slow," he said. On the other hand, Natasha Dimmit, our young Ukranian friend who was hit by a "shark" car, described her durational slowing more elaborately, more dramatically.

"I get a picture of the accident," she told me a few months after her ordeal in the crosswalk. "I feel real slow. I'm fading. Going away somewhere. [Natasha became unconscious briefly after being hit.] I cross that street [in the mind] very slowly." Natasha could remember how time had slowed down for her as the car had come around the corner. You can't get much more film-like than this. The Russian girl's visualizations, in other words, inclined toward slow-motion cinematography.

Films that tell tales of psychological trauma depend so heavily upon slow-motion camera work that they sometimes verge on the cliché. The shootings, for instance, of Faye Dunaway and Warren Beatty in *Bonnie and Clyde*, or the violent deaths of Ernest Borgnine and his gang in *The Wild Bunch*, are so drawn out and so minutely detailed that they look almost manneristic. Yet audiences do not object to these time-slowing techniques—some viewers must realize that this kind of durational distortion does happen during emotional shocks. Audiences object to the extra violence shown when you slow down the film, but they do not object to the act of going slow.

Four years after the Chowchilla kidnapping, two kidnapped kids told me that the experiences seemed shorter than the actual twenty-seven or so hours that the ordeal had taken by the clock. Two others felt confused about the passage of time. This phenomenon is the opposite of the time slowing that happens during short events. Every once in a while one reads about a person brought out from a very long ordeal in the desert, up at long last from a collapsed mine, or into the light from prolonged captivity in a blackened basement, and that person will tell others that he experienced a condensation, a quickening, of time. Anna Marie Conrad, for instance, a twenty-two-year-old skier who was dug out of a Sierra avalanche five days after she had been buried alive in the snow, said at her news conference afterward: "I may have been unconscious part of the first day. I was conscious most of the time, though I had no sense of time passing. I didn't think it was quite as many days as it was, but it was."

Similarly, one of the Americans who had been held hostage in Iran wrote to me recently to say that he had felt saved during his captivity by the sensation that "time" was passing so quickly. He asked me for any scientific papers I could send him on "time and trauma."

Traumatic durational distortion finds a place in folklore. If one looks closely at these stories there is usually a background of helplessness and/or of terrible fright. It took God only six days to make the world, the Bible says. This may represent the kind of durational collapse that accompanies long, drawn out cataclysms. On the other hand, the ancient Greeks told a tale of the faithfully married mortal woman, Alcmena, who was tricked by Zeus into one night of sex because the god had disguised himself as her husband. In other words, Alcmena was raped. The time that Alcmena, the victim of a relatively short piece of trickery, spent at sex with Zeus, the Greeks say, lasted three times the length of an ordinary night. The Greeks rationalized this considerable amount of time as a necessity for conceiving the greatest hero of them all, Heracles. But how, also, like the time-slowing of psychic trauma does this myth sound. Similarly, in the Bible when Joshua and his warriors tried to fight their way back from the desert into the Promised Land, "the sun stood still, and the moon stayed, until the nation had avenged themselves of their enemies" [Joshua 10:13]. This battle must have felt very, very long to a few young, frightened warriors. Their terror very likely accounts for this biblical durational distortion. The battle may have been quick, but the terrors would have lasted longer. The tale was told. And somebody jotted it down.

I like Nathaniel Hawthorne. I particularly like how he recognized that people were willing to sacrifice the laws of simultaneity and sequence during "marked" events, during glorious events or traumatic events, in other words. In *The Scarlet Letter*, Hawthorne writes:

> We doubt whether any marked event, for good or evil, ever befell New England, from its settlement down to Revolutionary times, of which the inhabitants had not been previously warned by some spectacle. . . . Not seldom has it been seen by the multitudes. Oftener, however, its credibility rested on the faith of some lonely eyewitness, who beheld the wonder through the colored, magnifying, and distorted medium of his after-thought.

How nice—"the colored, magnifying, and distorted medium of his after-thought." That's exactly what happens in psychic trauma. The traumatized child asks himself two questions—"Why?" and then, "Why me?" In his afterthought he rakes through the past, and in so doing he often defies the rules of simultaneity and sequence.

Kids, because of their relative immaturity, are far more able to sacrifice sequential thinking than are adults. After all, in the best of circumstances children cannot easily organize the chronologies or causalities put before them. When put to the test of correctly ordering traumatic events, therefore, children often fail. Through this failing process a child's tale of trauma often becomes a tale in which the uncontrollable might have been controlled. The child, in other words, develops an "omen." The "omen" is a compromise. It takes some of the randomness out of the traumatic event. But, on the other hand, it makes the child feel somewhat guilty for being in the event at all.

Nineteen of the twenty-six Chowchilla kids, including one who had gotten off the bus shortly before it was kidnapped, reordered or reemphasized time sequences. In other words, they invented "omens." By the time I finished my last interviews in 1980–1981, the children's omens were securely appended to their mental imagery of the trauma. The omens at Chowchilla varied from simple warnings to complex reorderings of events. Each omen accomplished the same goal, however. Each developed a part-answer to the "Why me?" question.

Mary Vane, for instance, only five years old at the time she was kidnapped at Chowchilla, explained her experience in terms of a mistaken step she had taken on her way to school the day of the kidnapping. "I stepped on a bad luck square," she said. "If I hadn't stepped on that square, it [the kidnapping] would have happened but it would not have happened to *me*." How many "bad luck squares" does one violate in the course of an ordinary lifetime? A few hundred? Thousands? But that one miserable bad luck square had done the whole trick. It had put Mary Vane into a kidnapping. "Step on a crack, break your mother's back." Perhaps some kid had used Mary Vane–style reasoning to come up with that one.

Kids will retroactively put things that followed a traumatic event into places that precede it. Fourteen children did this at Chowchilla. I call this "time-skew." Our parentally kidnapped friend, Wanda Forrest, showed us how time-skew works. But let's look at a few skewed pieces of time from Chowchilla. They fed into "omens." Take Leslie Grigson, for instance. Seven-year-old Leslie received a crank phone call from someone who had seen her name in the papers shortly after the kidnapping. After Leslie received her crank call, it started her to thinking. Before long, Leslie had inserted the call into a new sequence of events that started before the kidnapping.

"A lady called me up to say there would be a kidnapping," Leslie told me in 1977. "And there *was* one." In other words Leslie had come to believe that she had been warned by a call that really came afterward, not before. Through time-skew, Leslie could now accept partial responsibility for being kidnapped. She had been warned. But Leslie could also feel a little less helpless than she originally had felt. Leslie had constructed a complex distortion of time, one that relied upon a massive mistake in sequencing. I explained the process to her.

But Leslie's mistake lasted through time. In her first follow-up visit with me in 1980, when she was eleven years old, Leslie, accompanied by her mother, told me, "Sometimes I think someone else with those men is after me. Like the lady who called me right before."

Mrs. Grigson interrupted her, "After! It was after the kidnapping that the woman called!" Leslie insisted, "I'm *sure* it was before. It seemed like a warning."

I explained what I thought had happened to Leslie's time sequencings after the kidnapping. And then we veered off to several other subjects, eventually getting ready to conclude. Leslie said good-bye and began walking out. But she suddenly wheeled around and looked back at me. "I still think the lady called *first*," she said.

A thought rather than an action may inspire a trauma-related "omen." Billy Estes, a thirteen-year-old Chowchilla victim, for instance, attributed the kidnapping to an idea. "I was eight years old when I was kidnapped," he told me when I finally located him in 1981 at an aunt's house in Texas. "It was almost the last day of summer school. It was real fun. You could go swimming. That day there was a treasure hunt and candy in a box. And everybody was trying to find it. I didn't find any. And I was thinking, 'Nothing ever happens to me.' Then I got kidnapped."

Perhaps the most amazing "omen" I heard at Chowchilla, however, was Johnny Johnson's. At age eleven, shortly after the kidnapping, Johnny was musing aloud to me about an evening long ago that he had spent at the movies with his father. They had seen *Dirty Harry* together. This is a Clint Eastwood film in which a school bus and its young passengers are held hostage by an escaping criminal. As they watched the movie, Johnny recalled, "Dad kept saying, 'What would you do if you got kidnapped like that?' " But Johnny never had answered his father. He was too busy watching. A few years later when Johnny Johnson was kidnapped, he felt he had been given a warning by his father. He believed, given his opportunity to hear his father's question, that he should have prepared himself for a kidnapping. He spent the next five years preparing. He would never be caught unawares again. He would be a hero. Like Clint Eastwood, maybe. Or like Bob Barklay. Or, perhaps, like himself.

In novels by Stephen King one often finds a hero with special powers—the powers of telepathy, foresight, or mind reading. A King hero receives his powers after a terrible car accident (*Dead Zone*), or the protagonist finds special powers after a public humiliation (*Carrie*). One tiny King hero discovers foresight after parental abuse (*The Shining*). King's protagonists almost uniformly become paranormal *after* they have been traumatized. King tries to spin out other explanations for the paranormality he presents, ranging anywhere from army LSD experiments to basic human genetics. But in almost every case King's characters are traumatized first, "gifted" later.

We can see from the children we have met in this chapter, however, that the paranormal "gifts" following trauma are not really "gifts" at all. There is a sense of being gifted. But no real "gifts." Our young friend, Natasha Dimmit of "shark car" fame, for instance, began thinking a year after her accident that she was "psychic." The thirteen-year-old said, "I didn't used to believe in predicting the future, but now I do. I had a dream the other day about my new friend, Shelly, and a balcony in my old town in Russia. I can tell you what my dream means. It means my friend should not go out on balconies."

Natasha had told me months before that she had been extremely frightened one time as a preschooler when she accidentally shut herself into a refrigerator on Grandma's balcony. "I think I know why that Russian balcony of your dream makes you feel so uncomfortable," I said. "It represents the lock-up you experienced as a little kid in a refrigerator."

"No," Natasha argued. "The dream is *only* about my friend Shelly. I have warned her, 'Stay off balconies!' "

Long before Shakespeare put the words, "O call back yesterday, bid time return," into Lord Salisbury's mouth (*Richard II*, act 3, scene 2), people had given voice to the wish to turn back time after personal shocks. The wish to reorder sequences turns up in both the Orpheus and the Persephone myths. Gabriel García Márquez's brilliant novel *Chronicle of a Death Foretold* functions almost entirely as a post-traumatic "omen." Márquez repeatedly turns back time in his story so that some villagers in the tale will try to make sense of a meaningless killing. Each character in the Márquez novel tries, in retrospect, to convince the narrator that he or she knew that the young protagonist would, indeed, be murdered. Each insists that there was a turning point at which the inevitable could have been stopped. But the reader recognizes that there really was none.

There are psychological experiments that confirm how automatic, how important, how spontaneous are the retroactive adjustments of time we make. In two separate experiments on how "outcome knowledge" (what actually happens) influences college students' predictions of what *will* happen, Baruch Fishoff and his associates "slipped" false or true outcomes of little known world events to their student subjects. The subjects later were asked for their guesses as to what would happen in these world events. These students answered on the basis of the "slipped" outcome information, true or false, not on the basis of the set of facts given them. When a different group of college students who had already predicted the outcomes of an important, yet-to-be-decided world event were asked, a year later, to write down what they had actually predicted, these students wrote the actual outcomes of the event rather than duplicating their original guesses. In other words, hindsight overruled foresight. Those old, hated "I told you so's" often come from this same kind of time tampering.

We all wish to turn back time. No wonder young film audiences scream with delight when Superman, unable to get to Lois Lane in time to save her life, zooms off into space in order to make Earth spin backward. By turning back time, Superman grants us a universal wish, the wish for a second chance.

Wally Shawn, that wonderful realist of Louis Malle's film *My Dinner with André* (1981), has a solution to the universal tendency to tamper with sequences. He holds his solution in check for about an hour and a half, quietly listening to his wildly instinctive friend, André Gregory, hold forth at dinner with weird tales of wild experience. But then Wally blurts it all out, musing on whether Chinese fortune cookies can tell the truth and reliably predict the future:

> But in my conscious opinion, this [fortune] is simply something that was written in the cookie factory several years ago and in no way refers to me . . . the man who wrote it couldn't have known about me . . . if I were planning to go on a trip on an airplane, and I got a fortune cookie that said "Don't go," I mean I admit I might feel a bit nervous for about one second, but in fact I would go, because I mean that trip is going to be successful or unsuccessful based on the state of the airplane and the state of the pilot. And the cookie is in no position to know about that.

The last of the functions of time that becomes distorted by psychic trauma is "temporal perspective." For the ordinary kid temporal perspective resides in the present and future, not in the past. A child's future stretches to infinity. Everything is either "today," or it lurks ahead beyond the vanishing point. The past does not hold importance to most children. Kids will tell you about boys or girls they'll marry someday or about terrific careers that await them. That boundless future out there looks stupendous and unstoppable. And those big ideas help a child cope with the small frustrations. That is, until trauma hits.

Psychic trauma destroys a child's sense of the future. Big as the future once appeared, it disappears with trauma. Bang. The future is gone. Even when a child can't really remember his trauma, the way little Sarah Fellows couldn't remember Leroy Hillgard and his day-care pornography, the future goes out the window. Poof. "People get killed in armies and stuff," Sarah Fellows said when she was only five years old. "I won't be in an army—I don't want that. But people get shot anyway. Maybe I'll be killed instead of dying."

Tama Whittaker, a fifteen-year-old traumatized child spoke to me, too, about her sense of futurelessness. "I can't see myself at sixty," she said. "I don't think I'm going to live *that* long. Probably sixty, and that's *if* I don't die of car accidents or weariness if I have kids. The world is dangerous and weird, but otherwise OK. I hope nothing else terrible will happen. Sometimes I feel bad luck is on me." Tama's leg was crushed by a falling forklift truck when she was only two and one-half years old.

Once a seemingly impossible event happens, everything else becomes possible for the traumatized child. Do you remember Frances Carlson, for instance, the kindergartner whose father's spying friends tried to lure her out of her bedroom window? Well, at age six, Frances fretted about her mother's future as well as her own. "Mother might die of 'young age,' " Frances said, chewing on a nail. "Some people *do* die young," she went on. "Some kids get shot. Or other things." Frances no longer felt invincible or everlasting, as most nontraumatized children do. She knew that shocking things could happen at "young age."

Normally, a broad temporal perspective carries with it good defensive and coping possibilities. An untraumatized child is able to plan far into the future for a career, loving relationships, and a long life. Children come to the conclusion that patient work will bring happy rewards. Children expect good futures even when their current life's circumstances are not so good. They hope to do better in life than their parents did. For most youngsters, therefore, psychic trauma destroys an already comfortable trust in the future. Something snaps. The world turns topsy-turvy. Time goes "out of joint."

In Chowchilla, twenty-three of the twenty-five victims I interviewed four to five years after the kidnapping expressed pessimism about their personal futures. They expected shortened life spans and new disasters. Many were unable to envision marriage, raising children, or finding a career. One boy said he did not expect to have children—"in case of an emergency there will only be time for me," he said. An eleven-year-old girl thought she'd die at twelve: "Somebody will come along and shoot me," she said. One of the two Chowchilla kids who had denied to me that she had limited future expectations "announced" a year afterward on national TV that she didn't expect to live very long. When these traumatized children considered the possibility of future disaster or personal bad luck, it seemed less a question of "if" than "when."

I asked my McFarland and Porterville control kids how they saw their own futures, and five children expressed limited expectations. Two of these kids gave somewhat shortened projected life expectancies, fifty or sixty years old, and it turned out later that they were feeling temporarily depressed about their relationships with peers and school work. Their attitudes about their personal futures changed drastically by the time I reinterviewed them five months later. But three of the McFarland-Porterville control kids exhibited a relatively unmovable sense of future limitation. It turned out that each of these three kids had been traumatized. One boy, Thomas McAuley, age fourteen, stated "I don't see my future too good. I'm not sure I'm going to be around. I think I'll die by thirty-five." Another, Veronica Bentley, age nine, said she would die by fifty. Fifty was "a little old, a little young. I don't think I'll live as old as my grandmother and aunt are [seventy-five and ninety-three, respectively]. I think I'll die in the middle of my life of cancer or something." And a third child, Martin Vasquez, figured he'd die in his sixties. After that, "You're tired, I hear." Each of these three control kids, it turned out, had been psychologically overwhelmed by an accident or a life-threatening illness. A sense of a limited future, in other words, appeared to be a good indicator of childhood psychic trauma.

The Swedish filmmaker Ingmar Bergman does more upsetting cinematic tricks with "time" than does any other director I know. Of course, several great movie makers have temporarily disrupted our senses of time. Alain Resnais probably gave us the best single example of time disruption that we have in film with *Last Year in Marienbad*. But if you are looking for the most consistent tendency to destroy time over an entire career in movie making, you just can't beat Ingmar Bergman.

Bergman told a story about a traumatic incident from his early childhood (as reported by Peter Cowie, Bergman's biographer) that probably represents the beginnings of young Ingmar's tamperings with "time." Bergman was very close to his grandmother. They were "special" together. One day when his grandmother was looking after him, the boy was accidentally locked into a standing wardrobe chest. Bergman's grandmother ran about the place looking for a key, and Bergman says he experienced fury and shock beyond anything he had ever felt in his life. By the time he was released from his captivity, he had torn with his teeth through the hem of a dress that was hanging in the closet.

Ingmar Bergman gives us this same terrible sense of confinement in many of his movies. In *Hour of the Wolf* he tells this same story, much as a kindergartner might bring the tale to "Show and Tell." Through the mouth of his protagonist, Johan Borg (Max von Sydow), Bergman relates this wardrobe chest incident to his wife, saying that while locked in he felt terrified that "a little man would gnaw at [his] feet in the darkness." After his personal lock-up incident Ingmar Bergman tended to hallucinate. He also tended to be fearful. Perhaps a child less sensitive than Ingmar might not have been so overcome by a lock-up in a closet. But there is little question that Bergman did feel overwhelmed.

Ingmar Bergman experienced post-traumatic visual distortions. He spent countless childhood hours "listening to the sunshine" and watching his grandmother's Venus de Milo "move." He stared at the nursery window blinds while innumerable figures, "no special little men or animals or heads or faces but something for which no words existed . . . crept out of the curtains and moved toward the green lamp shade or to the table where the drinking water stood." In *Fanny and Alexander*, the great director puts these very same hallucinations into the eyes of his semi-autobiographical counterpart, young Alexander.

Ingmar Bergman, a probable childhood trauma sufferer, tends to destroy time in his films. It makes the viewer uncomfortable. But I think Bergman likes this. In *The Magician*, he "magics" a medieval conjurer who is under house arrest (similar, of course, to the confinement of a nursery-aged boy in a wardrobe chest) out of his confinement with a royal proclamation on July 14th, Bergman's own birthday. This is an inside joke, of course, but a "time" trick, all the same. Bergman likes to give his viewer confusing flashbacks, flash-forwards, and even projections into other people's pasts, presents, and futures. Occasionally, Bergman disorients his audience so completely that it loses the sense of reality (*Through a Glass Darkly* or *Persona*, for example). In *Persona*, the nurse (Bibi Andersson) walks into the doctor's office but at the very same time is entering her patient's room.

One of Bergman's most disturbing time tricks occurs in *Fanny and Alexander*. The trick occurs in a scene that directly evolves from Ingmar's old lock-up in the closet. In this scene, two young children have been locked into a tiny playroom by their wicked stepfather, the bishop. Their kindly Uncle Isak comes to the bishop's house, bearing a trunk. As the children lie on the floor, locked into their at-home prison, they are simultaneously carried out of the house inside of Uncle Isak's trunk—a neat destruction of all laws of time. (These laws, of course, would have meant nothing to a four year old in trouble, the real Ingmar Bergman.) Ingmar, at age four, must so urgently have wished to be let out of his captivity that he pictured himself, while locked into the chest, carried off to safety. By hallucinating —or by strongly imagining his rescue, the young Ingmar Bergman must have felt in "two places at once." This is the feeling that the director instills into his audience in *Fanny and Alexander*. By doing a scene of simultaneous confinement and escape, Ingmar Bergman may have discharged a small amount of his own traumatic anxiety. But in receiving the confused imagery, the audience leaves the theater nervous and confused.

Bergman's view of the future, as conveyed in his films, is—like the attitude of the typical victim of childhood trauma—bleak. His young knight in *The Seventh Seal* (Max von Sydow) sits on the shore of a desolate lake playing chess with Death. One knows from the beginning that the knight must lose. It is Black Plague time in Europe. But the knight and Death play on. One watches, fascinated. And the image sears into the mind. One has no sense of ultimate suspense in *The Seventh Seal*—one simply accepts tragic, untimely, unfair death. That is futurelessness—the sense of not hoping, of accepting what will come in a day's time, or a year's time, or whenever.

I love Wally Shawn on "time," so I will conclude these thoughts on time and trauma with another quote from the film *My Dinner with André*. (Yes, I am still in Bellagio—all time-adjusted and relatively unecstatic.) Shawn, the realist, has his own ideas on all this "kooky" stuff, the prescience, telepathy, and claims to psychic power that his friend, André Gregory, seems to like. Wally tells André:

> If you believe in omens, then that means that the universe—I can hardly begin to describe this—that somehow the future can send messages backward to the present. Which means that the future exists in some sense already in order to send these messages.

It should be easier to believe that time sense goes awry during and after psychic trauma than it is to believe in an already fixed future sending "messages backward to the present." At least I think so.

CHAPTER 9

Remembering Trauma

I was assaulted by an old man I didn't know. I was ten. He chased me
... he raped me. My life was kind of in danger. . . . When I was little,
nine or ten, I had repeated nightmares. It was about an old man chasing
me. . . . It scares me. I don't want to die.

Christine Young, age sixteen

W HEN MCFARLAND, CALIFORNIA, first was settled somebody named
it Rock Pile. Rock Pile would have fit right in with the occasional
Button Willow, Crows Landing, and Lemon Cove that you still
find scattered about the Central Valley. In the waning days of the last
century they changed the town's name to McFarland and invented a slogan
for it, "The heartbeat of agriculture." You read that as you drive north on
Route 99 from Los Angeles. The funny thing is, neither "Rock Pile" nor
"heartbeat" seems to fit this town. There are better rocks up north at the
Pinnacles and more impressive ranches just about anywhere else in the
Valley. McFarland is a relatively poor town. What's rich about it, its
"heartbeat," is its kids—and they have been moving in and out of this
book whenever we consider how a group of "normal," supposedly untraumatized children compares to the children of Chowchilla. The story I want
to tell now, however—something that sticks in my mind—is about a road,
the shortcut between the two towns I used as controls, McFarland and
Porterville.

There is a little road you can take from McFarland to avoid Route 99.
Frank Dyer, the principal of McFarland High School, put me onto this
pleasant shortcut one afternoon in 1981. When you do a field study every
shortcut helps. Many things in a field study take longer than you would
have thought or planned. If this little road in the foothills would pare off
as many minutes from my transit time as Frank had promised, I'd make

Porterville in time to interview a few kids before they left school. That meant I could easily finish the entire elementary school control group by late afternoon the next day and get back to San Francisco by midnight. And that sounded good, good indeed.

Frank Dyer's road, a narrow two-laner burrowing like a trench through endless lemon groves, was spectacular. It's midday scent invited a leisurely pace. But I fought the urge, flying around curves at around sixty miles an hour, the fastest I would dare. Suddenly I drew up on an old Buick. The lady in it—I think she had violet-tinged hair—was giving herself up entirely to the lemons. She was doing thirty-five at most. A solid white line warned me not to pass. That, plus a solid lineup of cars coming at me from Porterville, assured me not even to try. So I settled down to a crawl, telling myself to go ahead and enjoy my enforced stay in citrus heaven.

Backing off from the violet lady's rear, I started to study the trees. "Funny how lemon blossoms and fruit grow at the same time on the same branch. Funny, too, how patent-leather-shiny-blackish-green the leaves are —like the paint jobs they put onto the ground floors of fancy townhouses in London. Funny how they always leave one or two lemons on the—." Suddenly trouble whizzed into my rearview mirror. A huge truck. One of those monsters Stephen King writes about. Damn, he was coming up fast.

Oversized and impatient, entirely immune to lemon, the truck hissed his brakes. Cutting left to pass, he darted back to avoid that oncoming parade of cars. He tried again. No luck. Too much traffic. No shoulders. And two ladies to pass. Jiggling back and forth, the monster tailgated, hissed, honked, and tailgated once again. He was behaving like a frustrated Godzilla. I was beginning to feel a little scared. This was too much. This guy was in a crazy hurry to get to Porterville and beyond. And I was going to have to move.

Starting to watch for gaps in the oncoming traffic, I scanned the curves up ahead. I memorized the colors of oncoming cars. If I could judge a gap far up ahead and pass as fast as I could, I'd be able to make it, I figured. That is, unless there was a hidden side-road or a driveway that would feed in new cars. The mechanical monster maintained the bare two to three feet gap that he kept between us. He jiggled and hissed.

He growled just as I found my opening. Jamming my foot onto the gas pedal, I shot out. Wheeeeeee. I passed the old lady in half a second and settled into the clear at sixty miles per hour. God, was I glad to get out of there. (But where was *he*? Why wasn't *he* right on my tail?)

I glanced into the rearview mirror. A cloud of brownish dust was exploding from the road far behind me. What in the hell was that? I looked again. The lady's Buick was in the air, flying into the trees. A hill. Nothing to see. Again. *He* was coming at me in the distance. But wait, I was gaining on him, yes, I was clearing him. *He* was slowing down, no, stopping, to inspect his prey. Another curve. And another. And that was the last I ever saw of them—the violet lady and the monster that got her. But then again, that's not true. I see both of them every time I think about tailgating, or about the color, pale, pale violet, or lemons, or Godzillas, or airbrakes, or the honkings of giant trucks.

The picture I see is tiny and frames itself into a small horizontal oblong, a rearview mirror in fact. The picture belongs to a mercifully limited collection of silent tapes, of horror films playing in my small exitless theater. In this one, the images are strange—they get smaller as they retreat into the distance. An interesting piece of film work. Cheap admission, too—it plays for free. Just remind me. By the way, the tape is running right now.

Horrible experience creates permanent mental pictures. Vivid ones. Moving pictures. At Chowchilla the kids talked of their memories with such remarkable detail that they sounded "painterly" at times.

The memory of trauma is shot with higher intensity light than is ordinary memory. And the film doesn't seem to disintegrate with the usual half-life of ordinary film. Only the best lenses are used, lenses that will pick up every last detail, every line, every wrinkle, and every fleck. There is more detail picked up during traumatic events than one would expect from the naked eye under ordinary circumstances.

Something about the calm of a child's voice during one of these tellings makes the story worse—like the best tale of terror told by a restrained Vincent Price or a Boris Karloff. The calm of the thing tends to intensify the impact. Consider in this regard a school essay written seven months after the Chowchilla kidnapping by twelve-year-old Sheila Sheldon. This essay is done in simple language. Sheila employs few adjectives and adverbs. In the best Hemingway tradition, Sheila tells her story straight out, horrifies her reader, and quickly retreats. There is no attempt at drama here. No elaboration. Yet the story carries its own power to engage and to hurt. Here it is in its original, unedited state, except for the children's and the bus driver's names, which I have changed:

> It was a day in July and almost the last day in summer school. And most of the kids went swimming The fourth & third grades. After school was over we got on the bus #1 and everyone was happy. Jack got on and told everyone to settledown. So we started going and Jack let about 5 kids off, there names are Janette, Frannie and Stewart Letinnen & Tim Donnario, & Frankie Scarborough. After they got off he was going down Ave 21 and a white van was parked In the road and jack tried to pull over and a man jumped out he had a stocking over his head and told Jack go to the back of the bus and he did. There was another man that got on the bus and sat

in the front seat and had a gun pointed straight at us. Then another one started to drive down the road and turned down a slough called BRENDA SLOUGH. He told everyone to hold on to their seats. Because we were going down the slough and It was rough. Then when we got down right into the bottom half of the people had to get in the white van and the other half had to get in green van and they started to drive for 13 hours in there finally they stopped and let us out and told us to come out one at a time. Then they asked me are name and how old we were. Then we had to get in this hole and it had a bunch of matress and alot of cases of water and alot of food and bread. After a while everyone started to cry and holler. The Men said that they would be back in 24 hours but they didn't so Jack and Bob Barklay and some of the other boys started to help to dig out as they tried to and finally they got half way out and after a couple of hours we got out and we were by a rock quarry and the police came and took everyone to a place where we had ate and changed. Then we had to get on this bus and they took us home everyone was so happy to see everyonce. The End.

Psychologists break down memory into three functions—perception (or input), storage, and retrieval. Each of these functions is a fluid, "living," affair that can be influenced. For instance, a child's perception, or registration, of a story can be changed experimentally by an "inadvertent" remark (planned in advance, of course, by the experimentalist), a uniform that someone on the experimental team is wearing, or by a doll "planted" at the site of the experiment. While a child's memory, theoretically, rests in storage, it too can be influenced by psychological input. New stories, for instance, can be told, new "slips" by the experimenter can squeeze additional "data" into the remembrance, or the child can be hypnotized, altering his memory or entirely changing its emphasis. The experimentalist may influence a child's memory in the retrieval phase, also. By disbelieving a child's tale or by ignoring it altogether, the psychologist may be able to force the child to discard a memory. All of these techniques actually change what is remembered. The original input is often lost. But all of this happens, obviously, under pleasant, nontraumatic, experimental conditions.

Traumatic memory, however, functions differently from the more ordinary kinds of childhood memory—and here the experimental psychologists, as I have already explained, cannot conduct their projects. Traumatic memory incorporates the same three basic functions of memory—input, storage, and retrieval. But traumatic remembrance is far clearer, more detailed, and more long-lasting than is ordinary memory. As with matters of perception, it appears that overwhelming excitation creates a different state of thinking—in the case of memory, a clearer, more detailed picture with little chance of gradual wipeout.

I have already established with the reader, I hope, that all of the kids kidnapped at Chowchilla on July 15, 1976, clearly remembered the events of their kidnapping, whether or not they stayed in town afterward, read the newspapers, watched TV, or otherwise received memory reenforcement and suggestions from their parents, school teachers, etc. Their mental pictures remained clear whether or not they believed they had been taken by a "lady" or a "peg-legged mastermind" and whether or not they had mixed up the sequencings. These memories, some children said, were the clearest memories of their lives. There was no overlying haze.

At the four- to five-year mark, the Chowchilla kids were still offering details that only they could have remembered. There appeared to be little to no modification in the storage or in the retrieval process of what they said had happened.

Here, for instance, is a kidnapping memory told by Bob Barklay, the "children's hero," to an American television news team nine years after the event. The young "hero" was twenty-three years old and a rodeo cowboy when he made this statement. In it Bob revealed a detail of his experience that, to my knowledge, no one else at Chowchilla had mentioned to an outsider:

> Well yeah, Jack Wynne [the bus driver who was declared a hero by the press and the town officials] went through a bad deal you know—all those kids were his responsibility, and twenty-six little kids on there [Jack's bus]. He just couldn't handle it. It was too much for him. He just, he took me aside in the "hole," and he told me it looked like we were gonna have to stay down there and kick the bucket.
>
> And he was an adult, so I believed him. And then I thought, "Well if I'm gonna die down here, at least I might as well do it tryin' to get out." So in a way Jack got us out. 'Cause if he wouldna' told me that, I probably wouldna' tried to get out.

Bob's nine-year-old memory was gallant, in a way, toward Jack. It was not, as far as I could tell, self-serving. After all, the kids had consistently acknowledged Bob to be their "hero." He didn't have to prove anything. It was the part about Jack Wynne taking Bob aside and telling him they were all going to "kick the bucket" that was new to me. This detail was typical of how traumatic memory comes through. It was clear, precise, and understated. It appeared to have defied elaboration in storage or upon retrieval. It was frightening also, frightening enough, perhaps, to give the TV listener that evening a nightmare or two.

Traumatized children do not ordinarily deny the single shocking event. They may later deny a bit of the aftermath—saying, for instance, that everything was to the good. But they do not deny-away their memories. Consider the English filmmaker John Boorman, for instance. Boorman begins his written preface to the screenplay of *Hope and Glory,* his account of his own childhood during the London Blitz, with the words "How wonderful was the war." This sounds like a denial of the pain that was connected with the Blitz. But Boorman also admits to clear, persistent memories. And he admits to a need to repeatedly relate them. Boorman tells his reader that before he made the film, his daughter picked up the *Hope and Glory* screenplay and put it down after only twenty minutes' reading. She explained to the director, "I skipped all the stories I knew, which didn't leave much, did it?"

Boorman's autobiographical film shows tremendous precision of remembered detail, as does Louis Malle's personal film about his own childhood in France during World War II, *Au Revoir Les Enfants.* Louis Malle says that his film was inspired by "the most tragic memory of my childhood." Malle was attending boarding school in Fountainbleau, France, in 1944 when "a new boy," with whom Malle had made friends, was dragged off by the Gestapo. The boy was a Jew. He had been hiding at Malle's school. From the very beginning of Malle's career in film, the director says, he had wanted to make a film of this experience. As time passed, he says, "the memory became more acute." This is the difference between traumatic memory and ordinary memory. Traumatic memory stays vivid.

Let us consider one last Chowchilla memory as recorded by the NBC television news team nine years after the kidnapping in order to review once again how the remembrances of trauma tend to stand out in detail beyond all other memories. Alison Adams was ten years old when she was kidnapped. By the time she was interviewed, she was a nineteen-year-old high school dropout and the divorced mother of a three-year-old child. Alison's tendency to asthma had long since been overcome. The television news team found Alison Adams living in Chowchilla with her mother and father, trying to figure out what to do next with her life:

REPORTER: Why should the kidnappers stay in prison *now?* Why?

ALISON: Just—what they put us through, you know. Especially when we went down in the "hole." You know, we didn't know what was gonna happen. 'Cause we could hardly breathe. And you know, we coulda died down there for all I knew—because I was so scared. That's what I was scared about, you know. Dying. And never seeing my mom and dad again.

When I went to McFarland and Porterville in 1981, I checked a few of the four- to five-year follow-up findings from Chowchilla (dreams, life expectations, fears, play, and world view) against this normal control group. I asked the principals of McFarland High and Burton Elementary School to "screen" any known cases of psychic trauma from our lists. Then we selected kids at random from the student names. In other words, the large pool from which I eventually selected control kids to interview was weeded out ahead of time for trauma.

Every control child was asked the same question toward the end of his interview: "Do you remember anything terrible that ever happened to you?" What impressed me at the time, and what still impresses me today when I think about it, was the kids' answers. Here were children, screened out ahead of time for known psychic trauma, who could vividly remember terrible events from their pasts. They recalled the time "Great Grandma's house fell on her during an earthquake" (Lois Edstrom, nine); "there was a road accident near home . . . a girl got killed" (Joan Butler, fifteen); "I saw uprooted trees the morning after the last big tremor we had in the Valley. I felt if I had been walking under I would have been pinned," and "I slipped and fell [on a hike]. I slid to the bottom [of a hill]. It didn't hurt me, but a rock hit my arm. My arm was pinned under some rocks. My Dad got me undone. My arm was broken" (Darlene Proctor, age thirteen). There was considerable hidden fright out there in the world of kids. And kids *could* remember what had happened. Their memories, as a matter of fact, remained intensely alive.

The stories that the McFarland-Porterville kids told me ranged from direct, personal horrors, such as a rape, dog attack, or accidental injury, to indirect horrors—Great Grandma's collapsed house, a stranger killed out on the highway near home, or the time Dad was hurt in a car crash. The control group's answers to "Anything terrible ever happen?" were uniformly clear, tense, vivid, and fresh, whether or not the events had occurred in the child's recent past or in the far distant past. Here are three of these memories as I heard them.

From Martin Vasquez, eleven, a student at Burton Elementary School, Porterville: "One day I had a fever—yeah I did. I forget how old I was. [Martin later remembered two ages, eight and ten. One of these ages was incorrect, perhaps both.] It was when school was out for Easter vacation. . . . I was pretty scared being so sick. My Mom at the time said I might die. She was crying. She could barely say it. *That* frightened me! I kept saying 'I *can't* die at *this* age!' "

From Thomas McAuley, fourteen, a high school freshman at McFarland High: "I'm afraid I'll die in a wreck or something. My dad and sister got in a wreck two, three years ago. It was real scary. I was pretty small. I seen pictures of the wrecked truck. [Note that Thomas never actually *saw* the accident itself but was frightened nonetheless.] I seen the truck itself [after]. I seen my dad and sister at the hospital. It just happened suddenly. They phoned and told Mom. When she got to the hospital, she started crying. At first she didn't believe it."

From Josie Blake, thirteen, an eighth grader from Burton Elementary School, Porterville: "When I was little I fell and knocked out my front teeth and got a scar on my lip. . . . I was screaming when my brother was chasing me [on a family camping trip]. . . . My mom told me 'Be quiet' . . . then I fell on a barbecue pit. I was in shock. I didn't know anything. I stopped screaming and walked over to the camper. Mom had told me to be quiet before when I was being chased. I screamed really loud when it happened, and she told me to be quiet again!

"I couldn't feel anything. My mouth was like it was numb. I didn't see blood. I didn't feel holes. I could feel the roof of my mouth hanging down and I couldn't talk. . . . I was in the operating room three or four hours and in the hospital overnight. I had to stay in San Clemente two weeks. The doctor had to make sure everything was OK. . . .

"I dreamed we, my brother and me, were in the park. I wandered into a dark place. A man put me in a room and wouldn't let me out [this dream "room" probably symbolizes the emergency suite at the hospital]. My grandma took me out of the place."

"Do you know the reason your grandma rescued you in your dream?" I asked.

"I thought of Grandma when I hurt myself. I wished she could've been there."

Thirteen of twenty-five "control" kids at McFarland and Porterville produced vivid remembrances of particularly upsetting events in their pasts in response to my request to "Tell me the worst, the scariest thing you can remember." Ten of these children showed symptoms of extreme fright or psychic trauma. One additional kid of the thirteen was found to be suffering from long-standing grief related to her father's accidental death. And the two remaining kids showed single, isolated findings of psychic trauma, but they did not exhibit enough symptoms to make the "diagnosis." It appeared, therefore, that horrible memories from childhood almost always are associated with at least one post-traumatic symptom. And it also appeared that single, school-aged traumatic events are uniformly remembered with clarity and with punch.

How many of the kids at McFarland and Porterville were abused? How many of them had been repeatedly thrown against walls before they ever started kindergarten? How many had suffered incest? Or rape at the nursery school? How many had been the victims of wild satanic rites or strange festivities conducted in the name of "religion"? I did not find a single one in the twenty-five. But wait. That did not necessarily mean that none of these kids had been repeatedly harmed before they reached the age of five. What it meant—or so I thought in 1981 but didn't know for sure —was that repeated abuses, as opposed to single-blow shocks, might go far underground; that they might flee consciousness. They might be fought off completely by the defenses of "denial" and "dissociation," or they might be remembered only in spots or as fuzzy, sepia-toned memories. Perhaps memories of repeated abuses before age five could not be formed in the first place. Perhaps the child would be too immature to form a memory. What I was picking up at McFarland and Porterville, in other words, were the memories of single traumatic events from the post-kindergarten years. The karate chops. The ones most like the experience of Chowchilla. What I might be missing were the long-standing, the repeated, the very early experiences.

Is there such a thing as a false traumatic memory? What I mean is, can a child remember something that never happened at all? Or, can a child create a living memory of something that did indeed happen, but not directly to him?

I remember Stefan Zweig's book on Marie Antoinette in this context. Zweig tells how the little Dauphin of France was made by the Revolutionary prosecutors to come forward with tales of incest involving himself, his mother, the queen, and her sister, his aunt. The prosecutors, you see, needed a "legal" reason to put Marie Antoinette to death. Once the young Dauphin testified against his mother, he disappeared. Fled history. And Marie was guillotined. They say that the Dauphin died because he had always been a frail and sickly child. And maybe that's true. Maybe not. But did the young dauphin of France believe the tales he told before he died? Had his indoctrinators told him the stories so convincingly that the little boy could visualize an ordeal that never really happened? He intrigues me, that pitiful prince with his patently false tales.

Some workers in the childhood-incest field say that sexually abused kids don't lie. But I have come upon a few young bearers of false tales in my own psychiatric practice. Certainly, Viola Edwards, the petite accuser of Uncle Roger of the infamous "Dumbo's Trunk" game, had been pushed by her mother, a policeman, and a social worker to misperceive, if not to tell an outright falsehood. Yes, Viola was an exception. And yes, we must take every child who comes forward with a sex accusation very seriously, at least seriously enough to examine the child's entire body carefully, to do a thorough child psychiatric evaluation, and to study the family and/or caretakers. But I think that a very small number of young bearers of false tales will still come forward with the sensational accusation—with the powerful way of getting rid of someone or of collecting money for somebody. They did it at Salem. And they did it at the fictional school of Lillian Hellman's play *The Children's Hour*. They'll do it again.

Children make false accusations, not only for their own sakes, but for the sakes of others. Most often, they have been pushed. But sometimes it is spontaneous. Some of these young accusers come to believe their stories —like the doomed Dauphin of France, perhaps, or like our own little Viola Edwards. One child I know of had been asked by a social worker twenty-five times on tape whether her daddy had asked her to suck his "pee-pee." Twenty-five times the child said "No." But when the question was asked for the twenty-sixth time, the child said "Yes." She gave no further details. A judge stopped all paternal visitation for the next year on the basis of that twenty-sixth answer.

Once I was asked by a court in Indiana to see a girl, an eight year old named Loretta Jones. Loretta's custody was in question both in Indiana and in California because Loretta's mother had committed suicide. The child had been left in a will to the mother's first cousin in Indianapolis. Loretta had been living with her cousin's family for six months. The problem was, Loretta had a healthy father who lived in California. Nobody had told the father that his ex-wife, Belle, had killed herself. Nobody told him Loretta was living with a cousin. Joe found out accidentally.

But let me backtrack a bit. Joe Jones and his wife, Belle, had been divorced in the state of California when Loretta was two years old. Joe was then removed from contact with Loretta by California court order when she was three years old. The relationship was severed when the three-year-old Loretta accused her father of forcing oral sex upon her. The California judge, after reading the police report of an interview with Loretta, cut off all paternal contact. Joe Jones made his monthly child support payments to a post office box. He was allowed no phone calls and no visits. The child had described to the policewoman who interviewed her, "sticky, white stuff on daddy's pee-pee," and a "big, hard, dark" penis. The description was given in child language and convinced the judge.

After Joe Jones learned that Belle was dead, he petitioned the Indiana court to allow him temporary holiday visitations. The court concurred. Because of this new court order, Loretta knew Joe by the time I met her. She liked her father and was enjoying her time with his new wife, Susan. I learned that this was to be the very first child psychiatric visit that the eight-year-old Loretta Jones had ever had. She had been permanently removed from her father's custody purely on what she had told a policewoman. Once.

Loretta showed no psychiatric symptoms relating to her old sexual "trauma." She did not exhibit fear, rage, shame, or psychic numbing. She could produce no memories of sex with her father. No one had reported observing compulsive masturbation on her part or strange sexual contacts with other children. She had no bad dreams about sex or about men.

Loretta, however, had been traumatized by her mother's suicide, and she showed several symptoms related to this: persistent grief, an omen, guilt, nightmares, and poetic thoughts about a reunion with Mom.

I asked Loretta to tell me what she remembered about her visit with the California "policelady" when she was three years old. She said, "I can't remember. I do remember, though, going to the police in Indiana [when she was around seven] to get rid of Mom's boyfriend, Frank. That time," she went on, "I told the police a story about white stuff and Frank's penis. It really worked. Me and Mommy never saw Frank Mora again."

"Why did you tell that story to the police, Loretta?"

"Because," the petite child replied, hazel eyes soft and sad. "Because Mommy had a big imagination. I didn't want her to kill herself. And I always knew she might. Frank never really did any stuff to me. But I needed to take care of Mommy. So I told the stuff she told me to."

Well, that's what can happen. I think Loretta Jones was, is, a good, morally upright child. She had to make a terrible choice at age three—and again at around age seven—her mother's life versus her own relationships with "fathers." She chose Belle's life. The choice worked out fine for five years. And then Mother's drive to self-destruction demanded action anyway.

I explained the situation as I understood it to Loretta's father. He could see the child's dilemma. He said he would have made the same choice if he had been three years old. Joe Jones forgave his child. And the Indiana courts awarded Loretta's permanent custody to Joe. As far as I know, they are doing fine together. Loretta, when last I heard, was in psychotherapy in Los Angeles.

Most "false traumatic memory" has nothing at all to do with lying or with suggestion. It stems directly, instead, from what was heard and felt during a traumatic occurrence. The reader will remember, for instance, that Betsy Ferguson's visualizations of her grandmother's murder stemmed not from seeing it but from what she had heard about it and from what she later imagined such a death might feel like. The reader will also remember that Henry Hall felt his dead brother's missing occiput with his own hands and later clearly visualized his brother's horrible, half-skulled appearance. Both of these young trauma victims were telling an internal truth. They had transferred perceptual impressions from one modality (feeling or hearing) to another (seeing). Neither had fallen victim to suggestion. They simply had experienced a transfer of perceptual impressions. They had come to suffer bothersome, visual memories of what had never, originally, been seen.

One of the Harrison children, Winifred, the youngest of the tragic Harrison family group whom we have already met, illustrates this inadvertent tendency to create false visual memory. Winifred Harrison was only two years, one month, old when her five-year-old sister, Holly, was eviscerated in a freak pool accident at a kiddie pool. Winifred saw nothing. She was being carried around by her mother in the adult pool at the time that Holly sat down upon the unprotected, uncovered drain. Mrs. Harrison saw a surprised look on her son, Duane's, face. She took note of a quickly-forming crowd over at the kiddie pool. Holly, at dead center of the small pool, could not be seen. Mrs. Harrison handed Winifred to a neighbor who directly took the toddler home. Winifred was sheltered from all associated events until a couple of days later when her parents explained to her what had happened.

When little Winifred Harrison was four years old, her parents asked me to "check" her. I saw Winifred only one time at their request. Winifred had no memories of the incident. She was suffering no post-traumatic symptoms.

Then Holly Harrison died. Holly went off to a hospital in Pittsburgh, Pennsylvania, where they had started to do heroic liver and intestinal transplantations on children. Holly needed both. But she didn't make it out of surgery. The Harrisons were shocked. They had not allowed the thought of Holly's death to enter their minds. Winifred Harrison was traumatized by the news. And she began to receive nightly visits from "Holly's ghost." In my office Winifred, now an active patient, repeatedly played games involving death-trips to Pittsburgh. But also at this point, Winifred insisted for the first time that she had *seen* Holly's evisceration. She could remember it, she said.

What did Winifred's newly formed "memory" consist of? It consisted of clearly visualized elements—of Holly sitting down flatly, strangely; of Duane's mouth open wide to shout; of lengths of intestines clinging to the bottom of the pool; and of Daddy starting to pick Holly up. Winifred's story, so late in developing, completely coincided with the ones Daddy, Mommy, Duane, Cindy, and Holly had told at home. It was a composite of everyone else's memories. Winifred Harrison gathered her memories through her ears, not her eyes. She had learned her memories from family lore. The tales became visual. The resultant memory sounded as clear and as real as if it had entered her brain down the optic tracts.

The great Swiss child psychologist Jean Piaget suffered himself from false visual memories. He tells the story in his book *Play, Dreams, and Imitation in Childhood*. From the time young Jean was two until he was fifteen years old, he could remember—clearly and visually—an incident in which somebody tried to kidnap him from his pram. His nurse had chased away the would-be-abductor, and then she had taken the young boy home.

When Jean Piaget was fifteen, his nurse, long absent from the Piaget household, returned to the family to make a confession. It had been bothering her all these years. In order to garner praise from the Piaget family and to secure her position in the household, the nurse had made up the entire tale. There was no kidnapping and rescue. Piaget had heard the false story at age two. And he had strongly visualized what he heard. From age two to age fifteen, young Jean Piaget harbored an entirely false visual memory. Piaget apparently was able to drop the memory once he realized that none of it was true.

What happens to the very earliest memories of trauma? As you can probably tell, I started thinking about this after finishing my control study at McFarland and Porterville. I found myself increasingly curious about the youngest cutoff point for verbal memories of terror. The kids of Chowchilla had been ages five to fourteen at the time they were kidnapped, and every single one of them had remembered. What would have happened if they had been one, or two, or three years old?

I tried to figure out how to go about studying preschool memory of trauma in a field study. But while I was trying to figure out how to do this, I realized that there were thirty-two charts of patients traumatized below age five sitting right in my files in my San Francisco office. I had evaluated them all myself. And I had taken word-for-word notes from each child. Was there any way to check the actual events against what these very youngest children had said about the events to me?

Then I thought of something. Maybe I already had documentation of the events inside of the kids' charts. Many of the youngest kids I had seen were involved in civil lawsuits. Perhaps their parents had submitted outside documentation—photos, police reports, confessions, bystander statements, or detective records—at the time the children were brought to me. Because I routinely ask every possibly traumatized child to try and remember the worst, the scariest thing that has happened to him, I have numbers of bad childhood memories recorded in my files. Some of these memories could, therefore, be matched-up against the outside documentations, if they indeed were in my charts.

I found twenty preschool trauma charts that included the documentation I needed. This was a pitifully small group when one considers a huge scale, twentieth-century epidemiological project. But you can't do a huge project until you know exactly what you are looking for. And at this point I didn't know. My group of twenty children traumatized below age five was big enough to offer a few preliminary answers to some interesting questions. How did the youngest children remember? Visually? Behaviorally? Verbally? If a child could not remember in words, was he traumatized anyway? Were preschool verbal memories of traumatic occurrences accurate? What about behavioral memories? Did they accurately reflect the old traumas that had inspired them?

From the twenty cases I reviewed, I discovered that below the approximate age of twenty-eight to thirty-six months at the time of a trauma, a child could not remember most of a trauma in words. He might retain a small part or a vague, generalized sense of it. But before about age twenty-eight months, a child seemed not to possess the mental capacity to take in, retain, or retrieve full traumatic images in words. Of seven children in the group of twenty who were less than twenty-eight months old at the time of their traumas, only three retained any verbal memories at all. These were snatches, such as "There was grave danger at a lady, Mary Beth's house" (Sarah Fellows from age fifteen to eighteen months at the Hillgards'), or "I don't know if it's a dream or real, but I remember going into the bathroom and cleaning my face off" (Faith Goodman, age eleven, from a boating accident in which she fell face first, into an exposed inboard motor at age twenty-three months). None of these memories from below age twenty-eight months was complete.

This cutoff age for verbal retention of what happened, twenty-eight to thirty-six months at the time of the trauma, fits in well with some new, convincing research on the physiology of young children's brains. A tremendous spurt in left brain development (verbal skills reside in the left brains of right-handed people) occurs at around age three. Complete verbal memories can be established once the verbal centers are well-developed.

The second finding from my review of twenty preschoolers with documented traumatic events was the fact that behavioral memory (fears, play, reenactment, dreams) is almost universal. No matter what the age of the child when he experienced a terrible event (the youngest of my twenty cases was Gloria Rivers, newborn to six months old at the time she attended the Hillgard day-care home), the child repeatedly behaved in a fashion consonant with that event. In most instances, the children indulged in more than one kind of behavioral "memory." (Gloria Rivers piled my office pillows on top of each other as if they were human. When she thought I wasn't looking, she poked a finger into the crotch of the fanciest doll in my office.) These behaviors turned out to be the truest, most accurate indicators of what traces of memory still existed in the mind of a child exposed very early in life to a traumatic event or a series of events.

Eighteen children of the twenty youngsters in this study behaved in a fashion entirely consonant with their particular traumas. Children, much too young to have remembered anything verbal at all, demonstrated in behaviors what had happened to them. Of course, I had the advantage of having the documentation before me on my desk. Figuring out backward from a child's behavior to an *unknown* traumatic event would obviously be a far more difficult task, often an impossible one. But if a child showed no kind of behavioral memory, one might have to wonder if a traumatic event had indeed taken place—or if the event had happened directly to the child.

The two exceptions in this group of twenty children, the two youngsters who, as far as I could tell, never demonstrated a behavioral memory in the present or in the past, were explainable. The first was Winifred Harrison, who harbored the false verbal memory that I have just related. She, of course, showed no behavioral memories corresponding to the "events" because she had never actually been exposed to them. The second child, Doris Béja, was an intelligent forty-two month old, who had watched her baby brother fall several stories out of her bedroom window. Doris came to my office one year before I had recognized what I now call post-traumatic play and reenactment, two very powerful forms of behavioral memory in childhood. Because Doris Béja became my patient before I had the chance to study one group traumatized in a shared incident (Chowchilla), I did not know what I was looking for. I most likely missed Doris's behavioral memories because I could not "see."

Psychic trauma appears to leave an indelible mark in a child's mind, no matter how young he is when the trauma strikes. Perhaps traumatic occurrences are first recorded as visualizations, or even, by the youngest infants, as feeling sensations. These perceptual registrations occur long before any remembrances can be recorded in words. Perhaps what I was seeing in this group of twenty traumatized preschoolers were two different kinds of memory—one a primitive kind operational from the earliest moments of conscious life (perceptual-behavioral memory), and the other, a more developed form that does not become fully operational until some time around twenty-eight to thirty-six months (verbal memory). Perhaps traumatic events, if used as markers of very early childhood memory, might lead to a new understanding of the process of memory itself.

There was a third interesting finding from these twenty preschool trauma cases. The type of traumatic event bore a significant influence upon whether and how completely a child would be able, verbally, to remember what had happened. Short, single events were by far the best remembered. Of the thirteen children in the study at or over twenty-eight months at the time of their traumas, seven had been exposed to short, single events. These seven children could completely remember their experiences in words. And their statements were quite accurate. On the other hand, there were six kids at or over twenty-eight months who were exposed to very long or repeated ordeals lasting anywhere from eleven hours to three months. Only one of these children, Alan Bascombe, recalled his entire story. Four others retained spot memories, and one, a twenty-eight-month-old boy, forgot everything. The accuracy of those children exposed to very long or to repeated events at or after age twenty-eight months was considerably poorer than was the accuracy of those youngsters exposed to one short event at these very same ages.

Why does the nature of the traumatic event exert so much influence over whether what happened will be remembered in words? It appears that sudden, fast events completely overcome any defenses that a small child can muster. Long-standing events, on the other hand, stimulate defensive operations—denial, splitting, self-anesthesia, and dissociation. These defenses interfere with memory formation, storage, and retrieval. When the defenses are completely overrun by one sudden, unanticipated terror, brilliant, overly clear verbal memories are the result. On the other hand, when the defenses are set up in advance in order to deal with terrors the child knows to be coming, blurry, partial, or absent, verbal memories are retained. The child may even develop blanket amnesia for certain years in the past.

Let us briefly "skim over" three examples from the group of twenty—one, a child who was subjected to a quick trauma and, thus, had a full, accurate memory, and the next two, children who had endured long-standing experiences that left snatches of relatively inaccurate memory.

The first of these children is Duane Harrison. He had total recall of his sister Holly's evisceration, much as he wished he could have forgotten it. He had been forty-eight months old at the time of his trauma, well over the twenty-eight to thirty-six month cutoff point for verbal memory. He had also endured a short, single event. His memory was accurate. And it was complete.

On the other hand, Muffy Miller and Sylvester Stallings, both the victims of long-standing traumas, had inaccurate, blurry memories. Muffy's mother had died of an accidental poisoning when Muffy was twenty-seven months old. Muffy had kept watch outside her mother's locked bedroom door for two weeks while her mother lay dying. She was at the borderline age for verbal memories of childhood trauma. Her trauma had lasted for at least two weeks. It had included the long-standing complication of grieving for a dead mother.

Muffy could remember something verbal from her trauma at age eleven, "I was sitting on a floor outside a closed door," she said. This was a partial memory that stood for the whole. It was a snatch of a memory, not a complete remembrance of the events that had figured so strongly in her own life.

But Muffy Miller was also inaccurate as to the events themselves. She had misplaced the firing of her housekeeper, Ella Mae, a year after Muffy's mother died, and had put this memory into a condensed remembrance with the maternal death. This is how it sounded: I had asked the eleven year old, "What happened to Ella Mae?" "I think," she answered, "Ella Mae died before my mother. I think she left before—no, after—no, before —my mother. Wait. I think Ella Mae died. No. I think she died after [Muffy broke into nervous giggles at this point.] I think Ella Mae left after. No. No. Before my mother died."

Let me give one more example of the kind of blurry, inaccurate, fragmented memories that arise after long-standing or repeated traumatic events in early childhood. Sylvester Stallings, age three and one-half at the time of his trauma, was, along with his brother, grabbed by the arm from a park where his maternal grandmother was walking him one sunny afternoon. Sylvester's father, "Graham Stallings" I'll call him, is a Hollywod movie star. Graham grabbed Sylvester and Sylvester's younger brother, Clint, age twenty-eight months, and then took the boys on a two week, worldwide runaway, complete with agent, lawyer, public relations man, and a couple of Graham's men friends. The boys' mother hired private detectives. They pursued the two towheaded boys and the relatively large assemblage accompanying them, occasionally missing them by only a few minutes before they flew off again. The boys felt confused, overexcited, and scared on their trip. They were also ignored by the adults. They had no idea of what was happening. After two and a half weeks, Graham Stallings returned his boys home. It had been a "vacation," he said.

Gloria Stallings asked me to do a "house call" the day after the boys came home. The interval between "end of traumatic event" and "interview" was only slightly longer than it had been in Wanda Forrest's case. Both boys were overexcited. Both were flying little planes all over their playroom.

Clint Stallings could verbally remember nothing of the two week runaway when I asked him at age six about "bad things" that had ever happened to him. The series of experiences had been long-lasting and Clint had been at the borderline age for verbal remembrance.

But Sylvester Stallings was different. He had been forty-two months old when his dad had grabbed him from the park—old enough to take in and store some sort of verbal remembrance. Several months after the runaway, at Christmas time, Graham Stallings exercised his visitation rights. He would "take the boys to the East Coast to relax," he told Gloria. Graham, however, put both boys on stage, each garbed in a tiny tuxedo, for a surprise midnight appearance at Radio City Music Hall. The stage appearance was not traumatic. But it felt scary.

Sylvester Stallings emerged from both experiences confused. In Sylvester's mind the memories of the "childnapping" merged into the memories of the Christmas performance that had followed it by several months. "There was a frightening trip once," eight-year-old Sylvester told me when I saw him after several years' absence. "I went to Chicago, Switzerland, and maybe Africa. I was three then. [All of this is correct. Sylvester Stallings was telling the real story.] It was—I think, Christmas [Wrong]. I had a scary trip at Christmas time. I had a tux—yeah I did. I wore a baby tuxedo [Wrong]. I thought, I think, my mother was leaving me [Correct— Sylvester could not let his mother out of his sight after he returned home]. I took lots of planes on that trip [Correct]. People were touching me when I was walking [Wrong. Probably this is the Christmas performance]. I can remember thinking Mommy had left me [Correct]."

It appeared from my study that no child was too young to be traumatized. And no child was too young to show behavioral memories afterward. We would need bigger and better studies of psychic trauma in the youngest victims, however, before we could draw any universal conclusions.

The Belgian painter, René Magritte, was fourteen years old when his mother committed suicide. He had decided to become a painter two years before his mother killed herself. When he was twelve years old and playing among the dead leaves and broken columns of the local cemetery, René chanced upon an artist who had come from the city to paint there. The boy was impressed. He told his biographer, Suzi Gablik, that he decided on the spot to become an artist.

Young René Magritte had a profoundly depressed mother. She was subject to repeated bouts of mood disorder, some of them suicidal. There were times when Magritte's mother slept in her youngest son's room so that the lightest sleeper in the house could watch out for her. One night René's younger brother discovered that their mother had slipped away. He alerted the family. A search was undertaken, to no avail. A day or two later they found Magritte's mother in the Sambre River. Her body was laid out at the house, as was the custom. And then she was buried.

The suicide of a parent is an unusually shocking experience for a child. So is the viewing of a dead parent's body—especially if that body was submerged in water for some time. Magritte did not like to speak about his experience. He also could not face either his past or his future very well. According to the New York psychoanalyst, Milton Viederman, who interviewed Magritte's widow a few years after the painter's death, Madame Magritte said her husband "never spoke about the past or the future and would refuse to make plans for the immediate future if he could avoid doing so." Magritte, in fact, deliberately threw off his biographical chronologies and misdated some of his paintings. In other words, Magritte had his own problems with "time," a difficulty, we have already seen, that is typical of childhood trauma. Magritte also tended to reenact his trauma in behavior. He was fascinated with coffins, and one day at a coffin-maker's shop he climbed into one of the finished products and spent the entire afternoon there.

René Magritte consistently denied that his mother's death had been traumatic for him. He told his official biographer, Suzi Gablik, that he had forgotten all about it (except for the good part, the attention he had received from friends and family at the time). Magritte did not seem to want anyone to think that he had been badly affected by his memories. All of his life, probably as a result of his unwillingness to face his trauma, Magritte avoided the psychoanalysts, a group especially fascinated by his paintings. He even created a sculpture called "The Therapeutist," a mocking work that shows an analyst with an empty bird cage for a chest and no head at all.

So much, however, for Magritte's persistent avoidances of his own terrible remembrances. The event had been short and single. Magritte had been fourteen years old. It was highly unlikely he really would have forgotten.

One of Magritte's old friends, the Belgian poet Louis Scutenaire, tells the story of Madame Magritte's death as Magritte supposedly told it to him. From Scutenaire's account, one begins to catch some of the horror that must have infiltrated the Magritte household at the time of the tragedy. And one realizes that Magritte, indeed, must have harbored a memory.

> She shared the room with her youngest son who, waking to find himself
> alone in the middle of the night, roused the rest of the family. They
> searched the house in vain; then, noticing foot prints outside the front
> door and on the sidewalk, they followed them as far as the bridge over the
> Sambre, the river which ran through the town [Chatelet]. The mother of
> the painter had thrown herself into the water and, when they recovered the
> body, they found her nightgown wrapped around her face. It was never
> known whether she had covered her eyes with it so as not to see the death
> she had chosen, or whether she had been veiled in that way by the swirling
> currents.

How do we know that Magritte was indeed affected by his mother's suicide? Because in his paintings he offers us visual memories from his experience. Again and again and again. We call Magritte a surrealist and accept all of his weird art pieces as part of the surrealistic movement-at-large. Many of them are. But if one looks at the body of work that

Magritte completed through his entire lifetime, much of it has to do with specific memories of his mother's suicide and memories of her body—the river, the nightgown, the coffin, and the face (probably ugly, swollen, and mutilated by its contact with the river—rocks, crosscurrents, eels, fish, and all).

René Magritte was not made creative by his mother's suicide in the Sambre River. He was already going to be a painter. And he was going to be good. What his mother's suicide did to Magritte was the same thing that Poe's mother's young, tragic death did to him. It set the theme for a life's work in art.

Let us consider Scutenaire's tale of the nightgown. Madame Magritte was found with her gown wrapped about her face. René Magritte paints human faces wrapped in white fabric—he does so in at least two paintings from 1928 (don't forget he mixed up his chronologies), *The Heart of the Matter* and *The Lovers*. In this way Magritte behaviorally reproduced the horrible adolescent memory he told to Scutenaire.

Magritte gives us a direct view of what may have struck him with the most force as an impressionable adolescent. His painting *The Rape*, done in 1945, shows a woman's face with breasts for eyes, navel for nose, and genitals for mouth. It is a horrible looking thing—too gruesomely close to a fourteen-year-old boy's shocked impression of the exposed trunk of his mother's naked body for comfort.

Magritte frequently does coffins. One often finds a woman laid out (in *The Threatened Assassin* [1926–1927], *The Reckless Sleeper* [1927], *A Night's Museum* [1927]). His painting *David's "Madame Recamier"* (1967) shows an empty coffin partly sitting, partly lying. The coffin sits in the identical position and on the same couch in which the French painter, David, had posed his beautiful model Madame Recamier the century before. Death hits all beautiful women, Magritte proclaims. But he proclaims it shockingly, as was once done to him by a beautiful woman. (Magritte's mother, as shown in the old photos, was indeed beautiful.)

Magritte invokes his old terrible memories of rivers and of bridges in his paintings. There are endless vistas of water. These vistas are often quite menacing and sometimes sad. In one of his well-known paintings, *Home-sickness*, created during Belgium's occupation by the Nazis (1941), Magritte shows the Belgian lion sitting near a forlorn bird-man who is leaning over a bridge contemplating the river, perhaps thinking of suicide. The painting serves as a reminder of the terrible stress for any Belgian during the war, and it also serves as a reminder of Magritte's own personal trauma. No matter what he said about it, René Magritte could not stop seeing his mother's suicide inside his mind's "eye."

Magritte's visual memories become harder for an audience to take, scarier, when he depicts his mother's body. His "fish women," as metaphorically close to bodies fished from a river as one can get, take on various forms, most of them ugly. Magritte gives us, for instance, a sleeping, perhaps dead, mermaid reclining on a couch in *The Forbidden Universe* (1943). But worse, much worse, he draws the head of a fish onto the naked hips and legs of a human female in *Le Chants de Maldrodor* (1948). Worst of all, he gives us the drowned cadaver of a fish-headed woman washed ashore in *Collective Invention* (1953). Here we see the fully visualized memory of an ancient, personal horror as painted on canvas by a great artist. The body of *Collective Invention* has been recovered late. The state of this painted body makes one feel almost certain that it took at least a couple of days before the unfortunate Madame Magritte was recovered from the river she had chosen for her death. The bloated cadaver strikes the viewer with the same impact that the clear, brilliant memories of a child-witness to murder strike the listener.

Magritte's "trademark," what the average museum goer remembers of him most, is the painting without a face. Magritte uses bowler hats, apples, clouds—anything at all that he can dream up—to hide the human face. One can follow this trend in Magritte from the very beginnings of his forays into surrealism to the end of his career (*Familiar Object* [1927–1928], *The Idea* [1966], *The Pilgrim* [1966], and *The King's Museum* [1966]). In other words, René Magritte, over a forty-year period, provided us with a parade of faceless people. Rather than depict his mother's ruined face, a horrible image that probably lingered on in Magritte's memory, the painter preferred to give his audience no faces at all.

Throughout his career, René Magritte conveyed the tone of trauma. Because his style of painting is very smooth, very realistic, everything on a Magritte canvas looks perfect. One is shocked, then, at the content. A perfectly painted lady is standing among some perfectly painted black birds in *Pleasure* (1928); but the lady just happens to be gorging herself on a live bird. Disgusting. Horrible. Her perfect little teeth smile with tight pleasure. What Magritte does here, as he so often does in his pictures, is to establish the emotional tone of trauma. He remembers his own trauma—behaviorally, at least. He then hands it to his viewer. A horror, sudden and unexpected, is injected into the most serene of landscapes, the most perfectly drawn and realistic of settings. The juxtaposition of real and horrible tends to jar the onlooker. Inside the viewer's mind, a small aliquot of psychic trauma sneaks in. The trauma lasts for just an instant. But the viewer may be sorry that he stopped to look. One cannot get rid of the Magrittes simply by leaving the museum.

CHAPTER 10

School Work and Fantasy Work

I can't see why you think Jackie is still affected by the kidnapping. I can't see it. She is getting great grades this year. Her attitude is real good, and she's made it into the top group of kids, you know, the leaders of Middle School.

>*Judy Johnson, mother of Johnny and Jackie*

A T AGE FIVE, HOLLY HARRISON suffered an unfixable disaster at a kiddie pool. We have already looked at its aftereffects from the points of view of Winifred, Holly's little sister, and Duane, Holly's closest friend, confidante, and brother. But it is time now to tell Holly's story from my own point of view—from the viewpoint of the child psychiatrist.

Holly came into my hands a year after her accident and a year before she died. She was in first grade. She took a little teasing from her six-year-old peers for the jaundice—"Greenie," they called her. And, once in a while, a kid mistook her fluid-filled belly for chubbiness, and so she got called "Fatty" a couple of times. But Holly Harrison kept on going to school. She liked it. And she got terrific grades. She'd arrive in the morning in Mom's car, and get picked up when it was over. True, she'd miss a few days for going to the hospital now and then—to open up a blocked intravenous feeding tube or to start an entirely new channel for her feedings. Once they tried to hook up her rectal "stump" to the six inches or so of small intestine that she still had left, but it didn't work, and Holly had to accept her "ostomy bags" as permanent. Other than that, however, Holly kept going to school.

Holly did a bit of homework, too. It was kind of easy for her. Once in a while Holly would miss an assignment because her nighttime "on line" intravenous feedings had taken too long or because the private-duty nurse had talked too much (she was quite a talker, that one particular nurse—Mildred). But if you looked at the whole of it, you'd have to say that Holly Harrison "creamed" school. She died completely caught up in every subject. Academically she was at least a year ahead of herself.

By the time Holly underwent her final, fatal surgery—that ill-fated gut and liver transplant in Pittsburgh—she could read just about anything on the third-grade shelves. She had read *Charlotte's Web* to Duane and Winifred, and I wondered if Charlotte's fictional death forced Holly to think about her own. I mean, Holly never did speak about death to me, so I don't know exactly what she thought. But once she said to her mother just before they tried to hook her intestines back together, "Mommy, I don't want to die." And as they were wheeling Holly into surgery, Margaret Harrison had run after her promising, "I won't let you die." Margaret had meant it. That's one reason that the Harrison family was so shocked when, despite Margaret's promise, Holly died five months after the pledge had been made.

But I was talking about Holly's terrific reading. Her math was every bit as good. She could do all her "adds," her "subtracts," and she even knew some of her "multiplies," the easy ones like the fives and the tens. She was working on the twos when she died.

Holly was funny, too. She made up jokes, plays on words, and crazy pantomimes. She and Duane invented a secret language. They'd talk their Chinese-sounding nonsense for hours. And Holly would tease. As a matter of fact, she'd tease the living dickens out of Daddy and Duane, though of course she never thought to tease Mommy. Mommy was from England. England was too proper for heavy-duty teasing.

When Holly was feeling good, she liked to organize great costumed games that included her little sister and brother as Knights of the Round Table to her King Arthur. Holly's big sister, Cindy, would join the little kids once in a while, understanding in advance, of course, that she would have to surrender all powers of seniority. Holly always was boss, always leader. They say she was like that before she ever got hurt in that swimming pool. But they also say that the trait became exaggerated afterward. It was all those private-duty nurses, they said. The nurses were trained to take orders. They worked with Holly at night when everybody else in the family was asleep. Holly told them what to do. So Holly just figured she was Boss. And nobody disputed the fact.

Freud defined mental health as the ability "to love and to work." Others afterward thought that one might add "to play" to this short list. How would one translate this list to children? "To love" would translate for children into commitment to family, empathy toward others, psychological intimacy with one or two peers, flexibility regarding the day-to-day problems that occur among kids, and a general sense of give and take, of enjoyment of sensuality, and of cuddliness. Holly had the ability to love, even though she was both eviscerated and psychologically terrified. She did love.

"To work," when one speaks of kids, has to do primarily with school. When a child is asked his occupation he says "student." That is a child's work. Several researchers in the field of children's mental health, and particularly those studying coping skills of vulnerable children, have used school grades and test scores as primary sources of "objective evidence" as to how children fare under adversity. Well, if you looked at Holly's school grades, all those outstanding marks, you'd have to say she was an "invulnerable child," immune to all outside forces buffeting her life. Of course, "to work" includes other things besides school—doing family chores, earning money at the lemonade stand, and practicing your scales at the piano, for instance. And Holly couldn't do much of that kind of thing because she was sick. But when she was up to it, Holly persevered. She was a worker. She knew how to work.

Holly Harrison also met that extra, added qualification for childhood mental health, "to play." She was one of the world's best "players." That's why Holly's brother, Duane, could have kicked himself a thousand times over for not feeling like it when Holly had asked him "Do you want to play?" just before she was eviscerated. It would have been fun to play with Holly. When Duane Harrison refused, Holly removed the loose cover from the kiddie pool and sat down all by herself. She was curious. She loved to play. Every small kid in the neighborhood knew you could remove that funny, squarish plate that fit over a pipe in the kiddie pool. You could stick little pebbles into the pipe and they'd go swirling down to a place nobody could see. Everybody at the pool had been trying that. Holly began to pretend that the pipe in the drain had a personality. "What if I sat on the pipe and let the pipe suck me?" That's playing! Holly Harrison knew how to play—and she was even playing just a day before she died.

So a psychically traumatized little girl could work, could love, and could play. Hard. Well. Completely. She fulfilled the traditional criteria for mental health. And she fulfilled the criterion that had been added later. Yet I say Holly was mentally affected by her trauma. And I'll prove it shortly. My answer is that the criteria for good mental functioning apply better to problems with internally generated psychiatric disorders than they do to problems that develop after terrible external events. When a child is traumatized, something more discrete and more specific happens than a general loss of capacity for love and work. An ever-present, ever-draining abscess forms. The child goes on living an ordinary life. But if something touches the traumatic "abscess," the child hurts.

Holly was a wonderful little girl. We never had to deal in her therapy with the Freudian qualities of mental health. Holly, instead, showed that an "abscess" had formed inside of her during the traumatic events one hot afternoon at her neighborhood pool. The "abscess" was a long-standing sense of helplessness. Yes, Holly spent many therapy hours with me. I was trying to help her erase the recurrent nightmares, the bad habits, the occasional reenactment, and the ongoing fears. I suspected from the first time I met her that Holly was going to die. But I felt that Holly, like the incurable cancer patient, deserved some relief from her pain. And trauma *does* create pain.

The psychiatric literature on adults has established that the work productivity of some traumatized adults is poor. A small number of persons traumatized as adults cannot work at all, whether or not they are involved in ongoing lawsuits or about to collect a pension or disability payments. In this regard, one must note that the Vietnam War has extracted a very large, late cost from the American taxpayer—the cost of supporting some fully grown adults, former soldiers, who no longer work.

One reason traumatized adults tend to lose their work effectiveness, or even, perhaps, their total ability to work, is their tendency to deny the memories of trauma and then to experience interruptive flashbacks. The respected California psychoanalytic researcher Mardi Horowitz has shown that those adults who are particularly prone to massive denial after trauma are also plagued by repeated, interruptive flashbacks. The denial seems to bring on the flashbacks. And the flashbacks bring on profound irritability, insomnia, and trouble concentrating, which interferes with work. Children, on the other hand, do not tend to suddenly interrupt themselves with flashbacks. Even when children deny some awful event, they appear to daydream about it in an easy, leisurely way. Children, therefore, are able ordinarily to concentrate in the aftermath of trauma. And they are able to work.

At the four- to five-year mark of my Chowchilla study, I found that, of twenty-five children in the study, only four were having any significant trouble at school. Two of the girls, Ellen Mendosa and Sandra Sturgis, had stopped learning on an academic basis during the year that followed the kidnapping. They had been unable to think and to concentrate. But they managed to cut their losses there. Ellen stayed behind eight months or so after that. She lost no further ground. Sandra had caught up completely by the time I met her for the first time in Visalia in 1980. In other words, an acute trauma could create acute academic problems. But learning quickly would return to normal.

Elizabeth Vane's school difficulty stemmed from an entirely different source. This Chowchilla girl felt afraid of school buses after the kidnapping. Elizabeth hid from her school bus for the entire year following the abduction. Once Mrs. Vane realized what was happening, she would drive over to the bus stop and find Elizabeth in the bushes, on a stranger's front stoop, or down the road from the bus stop—anywhere, in other words, but on the bus. Elizabeth missed so much school the year after the kidnapping that she failed. But it was not a matter of knowing or learning—it was a matter of feeling afraid.

Alison Adams, the fourth "school problem" I encountered at Chowchilla, like Elizabeth Vane, failed to do well for nonacademic reasons. Alison had fought with her mother the morning of the kidnapping. She and her cousins had agreed to skip school. Alison reenacted her rage after she returned. She took a habitually feisty, snippy approach to teachers, especially to the females. And one doesn't get good grades when one displays such bad manners. So Alison Adams did poorly because she was angry. Alison dropped out altogether when she turned fifteen.

The vast majority of kidnapped Chowchilla children went through school without a blip on their records. They were a bright bunch. Their parents had put them into summer school in the first place as a way to keep them busy and challenged. Celeste Sheldon went right on getting her straight As. Rachel Mendosa cheered, played in the school band, and performed on the varsity girls' basketball team all within the same year. Johnny Johnson kept on writing his brilliant essays. And everybody, even Elizabeth Vane, eventually got used to the school buses, because they *had* to ride them. As a matter of fact, if you used the Chowchilla report cards to decide if these young kidnap victims had been harmed by their experience, you would come up with a very easy, but very wrong, conclusion.

A few years ago David Kinzie, Richard Angell, and William Sack, psychiatrists at the Oregon Health Sciences University, organized a team of schoolteachers, psychologists, and doctors to interview and test fifty children who had recently immigrated to Portland from Cambodia. Among other measures that they studied were the refugee children's school grades and school comportment. Both were consistently good. These Cambodian kids were remarkably industrious students, no matter how repeatedly traumatized or how depressed they were. Many had been cutoff from school for years while they were incarcerated in the Pol Pot regime's concentration camps. Once they reached America, however, they bounced right back at school. The healthiest part of these youngsters' lives was school. Yes, Asian societies traditionally produce hard-working children. But the Chowchilla kids were Caucasian, Hispanic, and American Indian, not Asian, and they, too, tended to work hard in their classrooms. One can therefore safely conclude, not only from my study but from the studies of others, that psychic trauma does not usually affect school performance, at least in the long run. (The traumas meted out within families, sex abuse and physical abuse, may eventually turn out to be exceptions to this general rule. But we will need more studies before we know this for sure.)

As for the ability to love—well, I used to go out to Chowchilla on Saturday mornings. My problem in making appointments with kids was finding a time that they could see me, a time that they weren't off playing with a friend, having pizza with the group, or doing a little shopping with a pal who lived in Merced. The Chowchilla kids had friends. And they were busy. They passed Freud's two-pronged test, "to love" and "to work," with brilliant marks.

The solid, cognitive kind of mental "work" that goes into good school performance, of course, is not the same as the wispy work of fantasy.

Holly Harrison, for instance, good student that she was, figured all by herself that her wicked drain pipe was a "He." Holly had spent some of the first part of her ill-fated summer at the pool testing "Him." Several kids had showed Holly late that spring that you could move aside the squarish steel plate covering the kiddie pool drain—the plate wasn't anchored down. And then you could watch the drain pipe "eat." Small stones, for instance, would go down the pipe's stomach in a spectacular way. They'd swirl about a bit and then plunge directly down. Down, down they'd go into that place deep inside of Him that nobody could see. Big rocks, on the other hand, would absolutely refuse to budge. He couldn't catch them. Larger things, lighter things, like people's toy boats, seemed as if they might go down His gullet. They'd swish around, start to spin, and then float right back up to the surface, somehow evading His voracious appetite at the very last minute. But your body—that's what was interesting—what would he want to do with *that*? He was a people eater, you could tell. If you put your foot right over His mouth, for example, He'd pull on it hard. You could withstand Him. But He'd pull. If you tried to feed Him your finger, however, He wouldn't even bother with it. The pool monster wasn't interested in playing "Hansel and Gretel" games. He wanted a whole foot, not some skinny, no-good finger.

The time that Holly Harrison first sat down over her pipe monster's mouth—that horrible day in August—*that* was the first time she ever tried that particular experiment. And the wicked pipe swallowed Holly's entire gut. Holly could remember the terrifying suction. A year later she told me "I was sitting there like a table. And I was trying to get off. But HE was pulling me soooooooo hard."

Holly Harrison had embellished her fatal drain pipe with fantasy. She had done considerable fantasy work upon her drain pipe before He, monster that He was, ever created a real disaster for her. You see, at the time Holly Harrison was pulled down, down, down into the swirling bottom of her pipe-monster's belly, she was dreaming up oedipal fantasies. She was four years, eleven months, old. Afterward, her phase-specific fantasies stuck with her.

Holly was rushed to the hospital. The doctors had to remove Holly's large and small intestines—they were ruined in the pool. The surgeons inserted a drain, a tube that would release the fluids building up after surgery. But Holly hated her tube. The surgeons, she figured, had put a "snake" into her. Ed Harrison, Holly's father, told me, "She kept saying [in the hospital], 'I don't want the snake in my tummy which keeps biting me.' It was *her* idea, that snake." Ed went on to elaborate, "The drainage tube was put in under general anesthesia. When Holly woke up and saw it, she hated having it there. She had never been afraid of snakes before, although she had said 'yucky' at a snake once." Holly's swimming pool monster apparently had spawned a "child" or a "clone." He had left a new monster inside of Holly Harrison.

What we were seeing here in Holly's thoughts was an elaboration of traumatic imagery with phase-specific fantasy. A trauma need not stand simply for what it was—a threat to life and to ongoing connections with others. It could also be elaborated with preexisting, internally derived, unconscious developmental conflict. Holly was almost five years old when she was traumatized. She was exactly the right age to feel concerned about snakes, monsters, and dinosaurs. She was actively engaged in a developmental phase in which she felt curious and jealous about the adult mysteries—sex, love, romance, and, perhaps, even death. And her curiosity and jealousy were already resting upon a drain pipe. Holly's "pipe" was serving as a symbol inside her oedipal fantasies.

When Holly Harrison was eviscerated, she elaborated the trauma with symbols already active inside her mind. This is not to say that Holly's traumatic experience had lost the quality of an externally derived "abscess." It is just to say that Holly had injected some phase-specific metaphor, some symbolism, into the abscess, making it bigger and more complicated. Holly Harrison knew exactly what her trauma had been. Her memory was intact. But her memory had been elaborated with the typical fantasies from ages four or five. The drain pipe of Holly's swimming pool, her oedipal monster, was lurking at the bottom of this child's most horrible moment of life.

Holly Harrison started pretending to *be* her monster. Every day, Mommy started finding foreign objects in Holly's colostomy bag. Although the dying little girl had no appetite for food, she had developed a new craving. Pebbles. And so every morning Margaret Harrison found little round stones in Holly's bag. She, like her pipe-monster, had developed the habit of eating rocks.

If you're going to do fantasy work with monsters, you may as well create a witch or two. The first time I met little Holly Harrison she already had a witch symbol in place. Holly had just been speaking about her male monster, the drain pipe, when she added, "There have been more things more frightening. At night when I lie there, a witch would come by my window and push it through. I think that every night. She'd steal my toys. She would take my feeding tube away and put it in her broom. I had this [the witch idea] before the accident."

Margaret Harrison, who was sitting in on our session, interrupted—"Holly never talked about a witch before the accident." The five year old was demonstrating that she had apparently skewed time here, misplacing a fantasy that had come after the trauma into the preceding, or warning, position.

"Later, in the hospital," Holly went on, correcting herself briefly, "I thought of witches. My daydreams made it up. But now I think it [the witch daydream] happened before, and the witch made it [the terrible accident in the kiddie pool] happen."

In her little story about a witch, Holly showed that she was continuing to elaborate her trauma with developmentally derived fantasy. Busy as the cognitive functions of her mind had been at school and in the hospitals, Holly still had enough fantasy functioning left to put an oedipal twist to a fixed reality. Because she was five and six years old in the aftermath of her trauma, Holly had found an oedipal meaning to her accident. She came to blame her accident upon a pipe-monster and a witch.

Holly's monster and witch were, at bottom, five-year-old impressions of Ed and Margaret Harrison. The witch would lurk near Holly's bed hoping to steal Holly's snake. The snake monster—though originally feared for his biting and pulling—was urgently needed by Holly by the time she turned six years old. Her mind invested the snake with realistic functions, the life-saving functions of her intravenous feeding tubes. And Holly even came to identify with Him. Holly's traumatic mental representations of her evisceration, thus, were imbued with oedipal symbolism from the first. The meanings of her symbols changed as the snake changed in meaning from a feared object to a needed one. But the "trauma" was the same, no matter what new stage-related or reality-related variations were applied.

Preschool children are not shy about showing internally derived, fantasized, developmental concerns. Until the feelings connected with the oedipal stage become sensed as naughty, most kids are quite open in stating wishes originating from within. Infants openly demand to be fed, and they openly suck on their hands, feet, fingers, and pacifiers in order to cater to their internalized "oral" drives. Toddlers are internally immersed in fantasies about "who controls whom?" They use restaurants, sidewalks, bathrooms, dentists' offices, and supermarkets to stage their grand operas on the theme "who is boss?" There is nothing private about bathroom battles with toddlers except for those quiet moments during naptime when two year olds engineer their "accidents." This stage, the "anal" stage, carries open enough and obnoxious enough fantasy to have earned for itself the nickname "the terrible two's." When youngsters reach three or so, they outgrow the need to indulge in battles for control and enter into the "phallic" period. During this time girls try to stand up to urinate, various parts of the body are valued to the extreme, everybody screams at the sight of blood, and competition is the main business at hand. Children build towers to the point of collapse for lack of structural steel during the phallic phase. Everybody has more and better miniature cars or more and better stuffed animals than does anybody else—at least that's what most of them say. Everybody races something. Faster. Faster. Zooooom. Varrhoooom.

Following the phallic period, the oedipal phase, which we have just observed in the case of Holly Harrison, kicks in. "Latency" follows. And then there is "adolescence." But let us stop for a few examples of how phase-derived fantasy occasionally effects the meaning of a young child's trauma.

Elaboration of traumatic imagery with oral symbols is difficult to demonstrate. If a child has been sexually abused before age one, for instance, the child tends to play the type of "sex" to which he was exposed, not an oral stage elaboration. Furthermore, there is no verbal memory at age one to which oral elaborations might easily adhere. I have observed one instance of oral elaboration of trauma in fantasy, however. Even though the traumatic incident, an airplane crash, occurred when little Nicky Gregory was already twenty-eight months old and, therefore, well past the most intense period of his orality, Nicky did tie-in a lingering oral idea with his traumatic imagery. I asked the thirty-five month old what had happened to his Mickey Mouse suitcase, a going-away present from his Aunt Mimi just before he took off on the ill-fated flight. Nicky answered, "The airplane swallowed my suitcase. It vomited my suitcase all over the sky."

Nicky Gregory had also inserted anal and phallic phase fantasies into his remembered experience. Nicky's anal symbols were probably the most active ones in his mind because his plane crash had occurred when he was twenty-eight months old, the height of the anal period. Nicky still could remember seven months later just how it had happened—the reality of it. He made an airplane of his hands and dropped them to the floor. "It went like this," he said. "It felt like this." And he dropped his hands again, the way a runaway elevator drops from the top floor of a skyscraper. Straight down. His mom nodded that the boy was right. She had been in the airplane crash, too. But Nicky now added his anal elaborations. "Crazy pilots," he said to me after finishing his elevator-like demonstration. "They were crazy pilots." [These Brand X pilots, in other words, were willful toddlers.] "I'm going back to my house on [Brand Y] Airlines. They have a signal on [Brand Y] for flushing. And that's good." [Nicky, here, was declaring Brand Y a good anal-stage company with lights that signal washroom vacancies and good flushing toilets.] They *want* to be cuckoo at [Brand X]." [Terrible two year olds, these Brand X pilots.]

By the time he reached age thirty-five months, Nicky Gregory had entered the phallic stage of development. He came to my office already competitive and wild about monsters. He picked up a small Brand Z plane from my toy cabinet and started buzzing it about my desk, coughing, choking, and sputtering it down to a crash. He then looked back to my toy Brand X, the same type of plane in which he had crashed seven months before. "*I'm* riding Godzuki," he said. "That's a little, but a very good monster. *You*," he pointed at me, "*You* ride the bad Godzilla!" The child looked over at my Brand X plane once again. I took it up in my hand. He pitted his good, little plane, his Godzuki, against my bad one, my Godzilla. Plane crashes, you see, could be regarded as phallic competitions—that is, if you had already reached the age of three. Nicky demonstrated that fantasies from the ongoing phases of development influenced how a trauma was experienced. Even when a developmental phase followed a trauma, that new phase might exert considerable influence.

The oedipal phase consumes years five and six, give or take a year or two. We have already seen how Holly Harrison's oedipal phase fantasies colored her thinking about her swimming pool accident. During the first elementary school years, childhood emotional development ordinarily puts the oedipal problems aside and progresses into "latency." The child's resolution of his "romance" with his parents ushers in a long period characterized by concern with what is right and what is wrong and attention to order and detail. A child appears free to learn. He has a conscience. This phase is called the "latency period" because sex, according to the early Freudians who named the phase, was not an important issue for school-aged youngsters. (Sex *is* an important issue, many of today's developmental experts say.) Rules and organizations are the commanding force behind latency. They are the reason that playground battles are waged. They are the reason that treehouse clubs collapse. The phase of "latency" rests upon law and order, albeit childhood law and order.

Cindy Harrison, the oldest of the four Harrison children, was sailing through her latency phase when she witnessed the horrible scene in the neighborhood kiddie pool we have already reviewed several times. Cindy elaborated her trauma with seven-year-old, latency-specific symbols. She needed to reconstruct some order from the chaos, some rules from the anarchy. And so, Cindy elaborated her horrifying experience with "strings."

Cindy Harrison saw something like "strings" emerging from under Holly's bathing suit at the time of Holly's evisceration. Whereas most of us conceptualize intestines as tubes, Cindy Harrison thought of them as ropes and twine. This latency-stage fantasy came to Cindy Harrison because she wanted more than anything at that time of her life to keep things tidy. Cindy had seen the traumatic event correctly. She later told it correctly. But she had added "strings" to her fantasies because she was traveling through the latency period when her trauma struck. Cindy Harrison began collecting ribbon, rope, twine, string, yarn, and thread after the accident. Tying tiny knots into the ends of the bits she collected, she began rolling a ball. By the time I met her a year after the accident, Cindy had a giant ball on her bedroom floor. Whenever she waited in my waiting room for her monthly appointment, Cindy Harrison would be spinning a web of yarn suspended by three small twigs or doing a cat's cradle, that yarn game that usually requires two players. This child, because of her immersion in a trauma-related fantasy that had combined with latency-stage symbolism, was becoming a modern-day personification of Arachne, the Greek maiden who tried to out-weave the goddess Athena, herself. An actual traumatic sighting, a string of intestines, had condensed with a fantasy of strings as organizers.

Charlotte Brent was about fifty-four years old when she told me an adolescent fantasy that she had appended to her mental representations of the traumas she had experienced at age two or three on the beaches of San Francisco. Adolescent fantasy often includes sex, rebellions at parents, and brave independence. Charlotte told me her adolescent fantasy only once. Although I tried to bring up the subject again on a couple of occasions, Charlotte insisted that she no longer could remember. Charlotte obviously did not wish to discuss her fantasies any further. But the "story," a developmental elaboration of her trauma, went something like this: A strange family kidnaps Charlotte from Ocean Beach. They hold her in their own palatial home, refusing to let her go to school or out on dates because they don't want her to escape. (This reflects Charlotte's adolescent wish to join a new family and to escape the pressures she felt at school. It also directly repeats the trauma, the loss of control experienced at age two or three on the beach.) The new family pays Charlotte special attention. They give her beautiful clothes. They make sure her hair is done "just right," the way other girls' hair is done. (These are normal adolescent wishes, but rather than having Charlotte seek these things out for herself, the family does this work for Charlotte. This part of the fantasy reflects Charlotte's avoidant awe of her teenaged peers and her disappointment at her own parents, who seemed incapable of helping her.) The fantasized parents talk a great deal with Charlotte. But they also insist that she have sex with them. Both the woman and the man insist upon Charlotte's sexual participation. (This is a direct repetition of the girl's preschool trauma, most likely involving, as we have postulated from Charlotte's dreams, adults of both sexes.) Although the teenaged Charlotte finds these sex acts distasteful, she no longer feels as terrible as she did on the beach (this is Charlotte's adolescent wish to recover from her trauma—a compensatory fantasy.) Most of the sex is oral (a direct repetition of the traumatic experience).

Charlotte Brent consciously hated the sex acts that she constructed within her teenaged imagination. She told me so. But she must also have unconsciously found something stimulating inside of these fantasies. Sometimes she would touch herself intimately as she thought these thoughts during her adolescence. The very straight-laced Charlotte began to feel that she must be very depraved. She would rise above her sex drives, she decided. Charlotte Brent, therefore, made a vow in her midteens. She would be celibate. And Charlotte Brent kept her vow.

We have considered up to now the elaborations of traumatic thinking that come from phase-specific fantasy. But there is a second kind of post-traumatic fantasy, "compensatory fantasy," which springs directly from the idea of the trauma itself. Compensatory fantasies come and go. But they, too, affect how a child thinks and acts after a terrible experience.

Let us look at a few examples from Chowchilla. "Revenge" was the most popular compensatory fantasy I encountered the first year after the kidnapping. The children's hero, Bob Barklay, told me that he wished to "put hinges and a padlock on that metal plate [over the 'hole']. I would put the kidnappers back in there where we were. They'd have as much food and water as we had." Leslie Grigson, when she was seven, wished for a revenge that would be quicker and more certain than the "hole." "I think he [Fred Woods] should get executed," she told me. "Maybe a firing squad. Or a gas chamber." Benji Banks, age six, wished for a very personal revenge. "I still hate them [the kidnappers]," he said. "I double hate. I mean I twiple hate 'em. After Sunday it'll be a few days before I get this cast off. [Benji had broken his leg.] Then I'm going to kick 'em in the mouth." Susan Hunter, at five, simply wanted to "starve them to death." Susan, in the meantime, was rapidly gaining weight.

Some Chowchilla kids wished to be heroes after the kidnapping. Their fantasies reflected this wish. Even the real heroes, Bob Barklay and Carl Murillo, wished they could have been more effective. Bob told his mother he wanted to show the kidnappers a thing or two by winning the world rodeo championship. Carl told everybody in his New Mexico school that he had a twin brother living back in California, Bob. The two of them, he said, shared many great adventures. Carl had joined himself in a fantasied twinship with his cohero, Bob Barklay. Carl's real brother, Louis, age eight, wanted me to demonstrate to him how to use guns. He, too, had decided to be a hero—at least in fantasy. Perhaps I would be willing to show Louis how to find the jail where they kept the kidnappers, he suggested. Then, he said, he'd go there and "hit them with a papaya."

Fantasies of revenge almost merged in content with the fantasies of heroism that were stimulated by the kidnapping. Johnny Johnson, age eleven, decided never to let himself become overweight again. Once he returned home, his body must be kept perfectly ready for any required act of heroism. Terrie Thornton even began thinking that she had been heroic all along. "I believed we'd be able to get out of the hole," she wanted me to know. "If they set their mind to it, anybody can do anything."

A couple of Chowchilla kids came out of the traumatic experience harboring angry fantasies at their parents. In their daydreams, they had displaced their rage from the kidnappers to those nearer at hand. Benji Banks, for instance, thought that his parents would fix up his bedroom "when I die." Benji wasn't kidding. He saw himself dying in a few months—his future perspective was drastically foreshortened. In his imagination, Benji Banks saw his parents rejoicing over his death. Even Mandy VanderStyne, a seven-year-old child who was intensely devoted to her parents, accused them of hoping that she would disappear back into the "hole."

But the children of Chowchilla also imagined that they could be safe forever within their families. Timmy Donnario, age five, the boy who descended from the bus just as it was captured, thought his mother was "magic" because she had arranged a few days before the kidnapping to have him let off first, not last, from the bus. Timmy followed his mother everywhere after the kidnapping. She was "good luck," he thought. Mandy VanderStyne began believing, like Timmy, that within the magic confines of her large family, she could remain safe. She said at various times to her mother, "I'll never get married," and "I'll live with Mom for the rest of my life." Mandy told her mother, "I will marry a rich guy, build you a house to live in, and get you to baby-sit." She even told her mother she'd give her "a penny" for all that baby-sitting.

Occasionally a traumatized child will go much further in his imagination than revenge, heroism, or magic. Taking-in or letting-out the mental imagery of a weakened self or a dead friend's persona sets up a wilder, weirder kind of fantasy. Solomon Wilson, the seventeen-year-old car-accident victim, for instance, imagined that his dead buddy, Joe, had taken over Solomon's thinking and Solomon's younger brother's soul. I have recently heard that a number of adults who suffer from "multiple personality disorder" claim to be the personal recipients of other individual's reincarnations. Many child and adult psychiatrists today state that multiple personality is generated by the experience of long-standing child abuse. The type of compensatory fantasy reported in this condition, therefore, is completely in line with the fantasies that other childhood trauma victims, like Solomon Wilson, tell.

Of course, there must be sources other than childhood psychic trauma for all the "exorcists," the channelings, and the Shirley MacLaine-style experiences that we so often hear about from friends or read about on the front pages of the tabloids while waiting in the checkout lines at the supermarket. But compensatory post-traumatic fantasies are probably important sources for many of these stories. Realistic thinking occasionally stretches close to the breaking point after a childhood trauma. But society seems to accept this. Some of us thrive on it.

As for the more usual compensatory fantasies—the ideas of revenge, or of power, or of staying at home for safety's sake—these ideas tend to set the tone for young lives. Susan Hunter gained weight. She would allow no one ever to starve her again. Johnny Johnson lost weight in order to put on muscle and to be a "hero." Mandy VanderStyne stayed at home, as close to her family as she could get. She planned to stay in Chowchilla forever. And Benji Banks picked on the younger kids. "I double—twiple hate," he had said of the kidnappers. And now he was taking it out on the objects of his displacement, small children. Bob Barklay dedicated himself to practicing the rope tricks, the bronco riding, and the calf wrestling that he would need for his future as the "Rodeo Champion of the World."

Before we leave the subject of post-traumatic compensatory fantasy, it might be interesting to look at just one case in blown-up detail. Alan Bascombe, our little kidnapped friend from the south, told me one of the spookiest tales of compensatory fantasy that I have heard. Alan visited my office five years after he had been kidnapped for ransom, and he demonstrated that in his imagination he had extruded the imagery of his trauma. He had "split off" the hurt part, the bad part, from the good. Here's how Alan's fantasies sounded—I had been asking Alan whether he had pretended anything after he came home from his kidnapping. "No," he answered, "I don't think so." But then he sat up straight and considered my question again.

"Wait," he said, drawing his chair toward mine. "Oh yeah, I did pretend something. A long time ago—I guess I was five—I had a fake person I made up. I would say to myself, he would die someday. And my person *did* die. And he had a funeral.

"I called my fake person 'Olive.' I named him for a jar of stuffed green olives I saw on the table. I made him up a couple of years ago when I was five, and I still have him in my mind. Olive never speaks. [Recall that Alan had been silent during much of his abduction. So Alan's 'Olive' was behaving as Alan, himself, had behaved. Olive *was* Alan, at least part of him.]

"I pretend Olive is dead. I look up at the sky now and I see his face. Olive was just my age. He had black hair, a light blue face, and yellow eyes. [Olive's coloration was an approximate photographic negative of Alan's own. Olive must have been the mental negative to Alan himself.] I made him up because I picked up a rotten olive. I picked up my doll—a boy doll—and I said 'You're rotten, too.' Then I saw Olive. He looked like my doll, but my doll didn't have a blue face and yellow eyes." [Olive, Alan Bascombe's fantasied alter-ego, must have been born while Alan was mental associating himself with the idea of "rottenness." Alan's alter-ego was rotten. All frailties, in Alan Bascombe's eyes, were rotten.]

"So how did Olive happen to die?" I asked, encouraging the boy to go on.

"It happened when I was six. On my birthday, Olive died. He was going outside, and he had a heart attack. [You see, it was not safe for Olive to leave his house. Alan knew from his own experience how unsafe it could be to leave a house.] I called the hospital. And they said they were all filled up. Then I didn't know *what* to do. Then Olive just died." [Note the traumatic way in which Olive died. Everybody, including Alan, had lost control of the situation.]

"What happened then?"

"I pretended I had a coffin. I put Olive in. Then I pretended my mom called the funeral service, and the funeral was the next day."

"Was that the end of Olive?" I asked, thinking that the child had, at least in fantasy, put an absolute end to this sick, helpless side of himself.

"No," said Alan. "Olive is in space now. I see his face at night time. He is floating around his coffin. [This was a hallucination.] Now E.T. [Stephen Spielberg's film creation] is on top of him with his little finger glowing. [Alan had incorporated a recent movie into his post-traumatic fantasies. More material could be added, apparently, at any point.] They're just floating up there."

"How does that make you feel?"

"It doesn't bother me. It's not comforting either. It just makes me sad 'cause Olive's not back."

Well, that was the story of "Olive." Alan Bascombe, through the manufacture of "Olive," had enabled himself to go to school, to get all As, to comport himself perfectly at home, to have friends all over the place, and to never, never get into trouble. By "splitting" himself off—the rotten, traumatized kid away from the competent school-aged boy—Alan Bascombe was able to maintain the appearance of perfect mental health. He loved and he worked perfectly. And he could play.

But there was a price to be paid for all this fantasied "splitting." "Alan," the good self, had to maintain perfection—perfect table manners, perfect school manners, and perfect diplomacy with peers. Alan was too good to be true. As a matter of fact, the boy felt he must take responsibility for what was happening in the world at large. After all, if one has extruded all weakness, all helplessness, one has to be totally strong and totally responsible. Listen:

"How does Olive work for you now that he's dead. I mean, do you think that by having Olive's ghost around, you benefit?" I asked.

"I feel," Alan answered, "Olive keeps me safe. I don't expect another disaster—except another kidnapping—and I'd use my fire escape if somebody tried it. I have an escape route. I think I can predict another kidnapping. I just guessed there'd be another kidnapping *soon* and there *was*. He [the kidnapper and murderer of a three year old in the same city where Alan lived] got his idea off *me* [Alan's kidnapping]. I think I *caused* that kidnapping. I think I can predict other things too."

"Give me some examples, Alan."

"Like, Hawaii will have a volcano. There's going to be an earthquake somewhere in California. [These are cheap predictions. Everybody knows that Hawaii is built upon active volcanos and that California sits upon active earthquake faults. But can you imagine Alan's guilt when such events occurred? Alan was taking responsibility, it seemed, for far too much.] Like my friend Troy. He *will* grow up. [Was there ever a question that Troy would grow up? Nontraumatized children would not tend to wonder *if* a Troy would live to grow up.] Troy wants to be a rock star, but he won't. He will be a psychiatrist like his father. [Another cheap prediction.] I think I will cause it to happen by thinking it. Now I think I am magic. Ever since I was kidnapped."

I spent some time explaining to young Alan Bascombe that he had created "Olive" in fantasy. I pointed out that he had split off the weak, the traumatized part of himself from the rest. It was too hard, I thought, to demand all that "goodness," all that perfection, from the "Alan" side of himself. He was "Olive," too, and he should try to live with the hurt part as well as with the healthy. Alan, always pleasant, always perfectly mannered, listened. But he said very little.

Alan's compensatory fantasy had led him to a "doppelgänger," to "Olive." Alan's doppelgänger, "a ghostly counterpart or companion of the person; especially a ghostly double of a live person that haunts him through life and is usually visible only to himself" *(Webster's Third New International Dictionary),* had arisen out of the post-traumatic defense, "splitting." Alan Bascombe's fantasy had extruded the sick and had kept in the healthy. The boy's tale was quite like Henry James's ghost story "The Jolly Corner." In this tale, a late middle-aged man, the narrator, returns to New York from England (England was James's residence all of his adult life, but New York was where he grew up). In New York, the narrator meets the ghost of himself as he would have been had he stayed all of his life in America. He is a wretched "person," this ghost. The split-off part of James's protagonist, the part that had remained in America, had grown up isolated, angry, and ugly. The protagonist of "The Jolly Corner," in other words, had "split" himself in fantasy the same way that Alan Bascombe had split himself. In both James's fictional story and in Alan's real one, neither protagonist could recognize that his ghostly double *was* himself—the weak part, the extruded part.

A child's perceptions and thinking are affected by overwhelming external events. Thinking cannot be isolated, however, from feeling and from behavior, the other two "structures" I have outlined in this book. Childhood post-traumatic fantasy does not always stay fantasy. It may impel action. It may inspire dangerous or damaging action, in fact.

Remember Holly Harrison's "witch"? Well, something happened the Christmas before Holly died. At the time, Holly was doing well physically but we noticed that she was acting sad and quiet. Moody. Holly didn't seem to laugh very much. And that was strange for Holly. The pediatrician thought that Holly might be disappointed that her intestines were not yet reconnected. But Holly told me that wasn't it. She was used to her colostomy. "Was it death?" I wondered to myself. No, that did not seem to be on Holly's mind. "Being teased?" No. "What then?"

I asked Holly why she was becoming so gloomy. "Mildred, my nurse, slaps me," Holly replied. "She hits me a lot, and it hurts."

"Really?" I asked. I couldn't believe this. We all knew that Nurse Mildred talked far too much. She could be "a pain" with all that mindless chatter. But she seemed to like Holly. And she was a well-trained professional.

"Show me a bruise," I asked. Holly showed me three.

Margaret Harrison, listening in on our session, was appalled. She said, "I must report Mildred to the child abuse people, and to the Nurses' Association. But I'm not sure this is true, Holly. Is this the truth?"

I phoned Holly's pediatrician as Margaret and Holly sat in the room with me. "Is Holly spontaneously bruising?" I asked. "Yes," he said. "It's from the malfunctioning of her liver."

"Holly," I asked. "What is Mildred really doing that is upsetting you?"

"She's mean. She hurts me."

There was no question about it—Mildred was going to have to go. Holly was demanding this, and we had to give Holly every benefit of the doubt. Neither Margaret Harrison, nor I, nor the pediatrician really thought that Nurse Mildred was abusing Holly. The child was bruising all by herself. I believed that Nurse Mildred was being designated as Holly's "witch" of the moment. Holly needed her mother and me much too much to fashion either of us, in fantasy, as a frightening female avenger. A nurse, Holly already knew, could be replaced. She had seen enough of them come and go. Holly Harrison's oedipal "witch" fantasy, resting on Nurse Mildred now, demanded action. The child was doing whatever she could do to dismiss the "witch."

The Harrisons hired a new nurse. Mildred went back to her agency with good recommendations and, of course, with no complaints of child abuse. Holly instantly snapped out of her quiet, sad mood. And she never mentioned witches again. Not for the rest of her life.

As for Alan Bascombe—well, I have some follow-up about him too. It's about "Olive," as a matter of fact. Not too long ago the American Board of Psychiatry and Neurology conducted their oral exams in the same gracious southern city where the Bascombes lived. I help examine for the boards, so I was there. My psychiatric friend who had initially arranged for me to evaluate Alan told the Bascombes that I would be coming to town. And they insisted upon taking my friend, his wife, and me to the best restaurant in town. It was a marvelous evening—superb food, the greatest of wines, good conversation, and a warm sense of friendliness all around the table.

Toward the end of the evening, Janet Bascombe asked me, "Would you like to speak on the phone to Alan tonight? He's thirteen now—kind of a mischief maker and a cut-up—but you'd love him, I think. It's funny," she went on, "he gets Bs now. Not all the As he used to get. And his manners aren't perfect. But we like Alan much better. He's great fun—a super kid."

Indeed I did want to talk to Alan. When I reached him at the end of the evening, he said he'd been waiting up for my call. The boy was incredibly open on the phone, almost as if five years had not intervened between his one visit to me and this one phone call.

"That trip I made to San Francisco helped me a lot," Alan said. "I felt much better after."

We chatted a little bit about this and that. Finally I had to ask the question. "Whatever happened to 'Olive'?" I inquired, sounding as casual as I could.

"I gave him up. I did it the day after I came home from San Francisco," Alan said. "Olive's gone. And he's not been back since."

CHAPTER 11

Repeated Dreams

I had a dream about the kidnapping just a couple of weeks ago. It wasn't the same situation—you know—as on the bus. But it was a bunch of people. We were in a house and this guy had us. And I took a couple of kids and I put them out this window when the kidnapper wasn't looking. And then when I seen him walk around the corner I took off running. Now, the only thing I can remember—the kidnapper guy was chasing me. And he almost catched me. And I got away. And I got somebody to help me. And we were taking him to the police. We drove around a while and we ended up at that guy's house again. The guy who was supposed to be helping me—like, he really was helping *him* [the kidnapper]. And the dream was pretty, um, it was really real.

Bob Barklay, age twenty-three,
from an NBC-TV News interview
in 1985

I SPENT NINE YEARS at the University of Michigan. I came, a college kid. I left, a child psychiatrist. While in Ann Arbor I met a few professors who profoundly influenced me. The most obvious one is Selma Fraiberg, the author of *The Magic Years*. Selma was a social worker and a child psychoanalyst who taught at Michigan. She liked me. And I read what she wrote, thought about what she had to say, admired, and liked her, too. We stayed friends until she died.

Selma allowed me, while I was in training, to bring a brown bag lunch to the Children's Psychiatric Hospital every Tuesday—or was it Wednesday?—and observe the proceedings of her research group. I loved it. They were studying the Piagetian development milestones in blind babies, and it was the first time that I realized research could be fun.

But what I want to tell here is not a research story about Selma but a story about Selma the teacher. I tell it because Selma Fraiberg opened up the world of psychic trauma to me, and I don't even think that she herself was that interested in the psychology of the external or that she ever realized she had helped introduce me to "my" subject. It happened this way: There was a brilliant young faculty member at Children's Psychiatric Hospital, a fellow named Jack McDermott, who now runs the psychiatry programs at the University of Hawaii and is the editor of the *Journal of the American Academy of Child and Adolescent Psychiatry*. Jack was chosen to present the "Continuous Case Conference" of 1965, and the child he was presenting was an eleven-year-old Central American boy who had been running the streets of his capital city by night, drinking, getting into fights, stealing, and, occasionally, trading sex for money. Trouble was— the boy was rich and he came from a highly visible, political family. His behavior and the family standards didn't hang together. The family, when they discovered what was going on, shipped the boy off to North America —to become a resident patient at what was then one of the three or four top child psychiatric programs in the country.

Jack McDermott came week after week into our Continuous Case Conference with the most complete, the most detailed notes you could imagine. Everything that the boy had said and every nuance of how Jack had responded was put to paper. You see, we were learning intensive psychotherapy at Jack's and Selma's hands. Selma Fraiberg would make probing and insightful comments. How to proceed and how not to proceed were discussed with great care. Jack would try out Selma's suggestions. And the next week we would hear all about it. In this way we could learn week by week how we were supposed to conduct psychiatric treatments of the "talking" kind. The Continuous Case Conference was, in its own way, a psychiatric soap opera. "Tune in next week and you'll find out what happens in the treatment of a Central American street boy whose father just happens to be minister of finance."

Well, week after week the boy told Jack his dreams. They were violent. Sexual. Awful. The dreams told stories of menaces coming up from behind, from dark alleyways and in doorways. The boy's nightmares promised the most terrible kinds of surprise attacks, the kinds of action you cover your eyes not to see at the movies.

One day Selma stopped Jack in the midst of describing a dream "analysis." "The boy's dreams," she said, "are all essentially the same. Did you notice? Each nightmare tells the same story although there are all kinds of elaborations." She glanced about the room. "You all know what that means," she said. And she paused.

We must have looked quite blank. I certainly didn't know what repeated dreams meant. I hadn't had any myself. And no patient of mine had ever mentioned them.

Selma said after a while, "Something exactly like these dreams must have actually happened in our young patient's life. Dreams, when they are repeated, are not likely to be the usual, more internalized product. Instead, they repeat terrifying experiences that derive from actual, outside events."

"You mean if you have many repeated dreams it might reflect one, single outside event, Mrs. Fraiberg?" somebody in our group stuck his neck out. Most of us were afraid to say much at Continuous Case Conference.

"Yes, good question," Selma said. She almost always said "good," even if the question was rhetorical or she was about to flay somebody alive with her response. "In this case I would guess there is only one traumatic event in our patient's history. But that is only a guess. Jack," she turned back to Jack McDermott to ask, "the boy has not told you any old traumatic exposures yet, has he?"

"No," said Jack.

"Go back and get his story," instructed Selma. "There is traumatic anxiety behind all those repetitions, I am sure. Trauma demands repetition. And Jack," she smiled her Mona Lisa smile, the most mysterious smile I have ever seen on a living human being. "The boy's trauma will also explain his repetitive behaviors in the back alleyways of his city. You will see."

I don't know why I was so excited, but I was. This was new. I loved the idea of guessing what had happened to someone entirely from a repeated dream. It intrigued me. It was an easy solution to a complex mind teaser —like doing a single move in a chess game and wrapping up a sure check-mate, like reading carefully for the one real hint that Agatha Christie would throw at you between pages three and ten, checking out her list of characters, guessing the murderer, looking at the third from the last page, and, if you were correct, dropping the whole book then and there. Selma Fraiberg had just neatly dissected away the mystery from a certain type of nightmare. And I loved it. The slippable knot. Magic. Pig Latin of a sort.

The next week Jack McDermott came to Continuous Case Conference with the boy's "story." The young fellow had been anally raped. His attacker had been a gardener on the family estate. The boy could clearly remember it. The experience at age eight or nine had set up an unquench-able thirst in the lad for taking risks on nighttime city streets. He had never connected the event with his behavior. The boy didn't realize it, but his dreams and actions all told exactly the same story. They simply repeated his old, indigestible horror, a rape in a garden.

From the time he spewed out his whole account to Jack, the young fellow began, remarkably, to improve. And he didn't need too much more treatment after that. His behaviors on the hospital ward changed dramati-cally and his attitude became workable. Within a couple of months Jack began making discharge plans for the boy, and one day a Central American employee of the young fellow's family came up to Ann Arbor to fetch him. We had to find another patient and another presenter for Continuous Case Conference. As a matter of fact, Continuous Case Conference at Children's Psychiatric Hospital was never the same after that. At least, that's how I felt about it.

That one day has lasted in my memory. I had learned something of value from Selma and from Jack. And better than that, I had been touched by psychiatric excitement. I would read Freud on "repetition" and on "trauma." And I would check out what the psychoanalytic scholars writing between, during, and just after the two World Wars had to say. I would read Kardiner, Waelder, and Fenichel. And I would see what my favorite oldtime child psychiatrist, David Levy, thought. I'd find out as much as I could. Because this "trauma" stuff was interesting. Really interesting.

Psychic trauma sets up four kinds of repeated dreams: exact repetitions, modified repetitions, deeply disguised dreams, and terror dreams that cannot be remembered upon awakening. All of these dreams leave the dreamer with an uncomfortable, nervous feeling. This lingering discomfort follows the dream because dreaming a repeated dream does not discharge all of the tension stirred up by a trauma. So little tension is dissipated from the act of dreaming that one may dream trauma-related dreams from childhood or adolescence for many years of one's life. Charlotte Brent did. And so did the writer William Manchester.

The simplest post-traumatic nightmare, the exact repetition, replays blow-by-blow part of the traumatic event or an idea from the event. If you were kidnapped at Chowchilla, for instance, you'd dream that the men were coming onto your bus, or that you were in a "hole," or that you were bouncing around somewhere in the dark. You might also dream an idea— that someone was coming to throw you into the ocean, for instance. (Louis Murillo immediately thought the kidnappers wanted to drown him. He had been afraid of the water before he was kidnapped. And so he dreamed his trauma-inspired thought again and again.)

It is rather amazing, but traumatized children do not usually recognize that they are dreaming their old traumas, even though they dream the sort of exact repetitions that I am describing. Parents do not always recognize these dreams as representing old frights either. Tina Goldfine, for example, the British-born wife of a Maine Medical Center child psychiatrist, remembers an exactly repeated dream of her own that nobody in her family was able to understand for years. Nor, for that matter, did Tina understand the dream herself until she turned ten. Evacuated at age two from London because of the Blitz, little Tina Curle had moved in, for safety's sake, with her uncle, the composer Ralph (pronounced by the family, "Rafe") Vaughan Williams. They lived in a house in Surrey, a place that lay directly on the German flight path over Great Britain. At about age four, Tina began to dream a repeated nightmare. She was out in a garden and a burning plane was falling on top of her. She clearly remembered the scene by day. And she dreamed it vividly at night. Little Tina Curle eventually asked her mother if a plane had ever fallen on her, and Tina's mother had answered, "No. Of course not, dear. You're not injured, are you? You're not burned." But Tina kept dreaming her dreams despite her mother's repeated reassurances. The dreams were always the same. A plane burned up in a garden. It would fall out of the sky. It would seem to fall on her. The dreams were horrible. And Tina's daytime visualizations were the same.

Finally, when Tina was about ten years old and still dreaming, she asked her mother, "Did a German plane ever crash into Uncle Rafe's garden while we lived at his house?" "No," said Mother, "not in his garden. The plane crashed into a field next to Uncle Rafe's house." Mother had been given the "right" question at last. A plane had not fallen *onto* the toddler, although that had been the trauma-inspired idea that was repeated in Tina's dreams. A plane had, instead, fallen *close* to Tina into a field just outside of Uncle Rafe's garden. Tina had perceived it as crashing closer than it actually had. Tina's fright had been a real fright, and all those nightmares had evolved from a horrible reality. But nobody could solve Tina's nightmare for her until she asked exactly the "right" question. When Tina received her answer, her exactly repeated dreams became understandable to her. The nightmares began to come along less frequently. Tina Goldfine has no Blitz nightmares now, she says. "They stopped when I was about eleven."

Most repeated dreams eventually become modified through new elaborations. They no longer stay "exact." New life circumstances add to the dreams, as do new internal wishes. The modified dream carries a traumatic nucleus with a changeable orbit. If you were sleeping one night on your couch, for instance, as Sammy Smith did the night he came home from his school bus ordeal, you might dream, as Sammy did, that the kidnappers grabbed you from your couch. Or if you went camping, as Sammy Smith did four years after he was kidnapped, the kidnappers might take you in your sleep right out of your tent, sleeping bag and all. You might also add a healthy age-appropriate fear of monsters to your dream. Seven-year-old Leslie Grigson, for instance, dreamed she was "in an alligator 'hole' and the alligator bit me." Leslie's hole was the same hole as was used during the kidnapping. But her kidnappers had metamorphosed into a single, snapping monster. You might finish your post-traumatic dream satisfactorily by "putting the kidnapper in jail" yourself. Five-year-old Mary Vane did that one night. Or you could worry yourself and simultaneously discharge some anger over a fight with Dad in a post-traumatic dream. Johnny Johnson watched his father "hung in a sack by the kidnappers." The kidnappers were still there. But Johnny Johnson's dad had joined them.

The central horror of a post-traumatic dream, no matter how elaborate it becomes, stays the same. The Chowchilla kidnapping victim, Sheila Sheldon, eleven, for instance, had been afraid in the "hole" that she would smother. She dreamed the year after the kidnapping that she and seven friends, along with Jack Wynne, the bus driver, had been buried by the three kidnappers in tiny, individual tents. Sheila's girlfriend smothered to death at the end of Sheila's dream. The dream modification spared Sheila herself from her own worst dread generated by the kidnapping, the dread of smothering. But the dream was horrifying nonetheless. It carried as its central core Sheila's worst trauma-inspired fear.

Occasionally, as the years go by, a repeated dream will take on enough deeply disguised symbolism, wish gratification, and modification with recent content that it no longer seems, at first glance, to be a repeated or a traumatic dream at all. Under careful scrutiny, however, such a deeply disguised dream will often reveal its origins as traumatic. One good way to understand these heavily camouflaged dreams is by listening to the child's thoughts in "association" to the dream. Another way is to plug in what you already know about the child's experience to the dream symbolism and see if it works. Here are a couple of examples—one from Chowchilla and another from a child's terrible accident at age two and one-half with a forklift truck. The first heavily disguised dream could be explained by the child's one-sentence association to her own dream. The second dream could be understood by knowing in advance what the child's trauma was and finding the place that the trauma played within the dream.

In 1977 I asked seven-year-old Leslie Grigson to tell me a dream that had nothing at all to do with the Chowchilla kidnapping. The little blond laughed and said, "I dreamed I ate ice cream at Disneyland." The smile fled the child's face at once. "We didn't get to eat ice cream at Disneyland," Leslie said. She looked grim.

Dream associations, thoughts that come before or after telling a dream, are the keys to its meaning. The kidnapped children of Chowchilla had been taken to Disneyland in August 1976 as guests of the Orange County Lions Club. The children had had a great time. But Hal Warrenberg, the man who had been assigned to squire Leslie Grigson about Disneyland, promised the young girl he would keep in touch; yet he never wrote or called afterward. The small child felt abandoned. It reminded her of a tragedy in her life a year before the kidnapping—her natural father, divorced for years from Leslie's mother, had, at the mother's urging, given up his parental rights. Leslie's name had been changed officially to Grigson. Three events, therefore, stood condensed into Leslie's one-sentence dream association—"We didn't get to eat ice cream at Disneyland"—Leslie's two abandonments by father figures and her kidnapping. The dream, basically a wish fulfillment dream with ice cream symbolizing Leslie's temporarily regained "fathers," carried traumatic anxiety along with it, too. After all, the children of Chowchilla would not have been visiting Disneyland in August 1976 had they not been through a terrifying kidnapping. The kidnapping, therefore, lay at the bottom of Leslie's "ice cream." This deeply disguised, heavily symbolic dream, supposedly having nothing at all to do with the kidnapping, had, in other words, very much to do with it.

The second example of deeply disguised, post-traumatic dreaming comes from Tama Whittaker, age fifteen. Tama was the victim at age two and a half of an accident in a forklift truck. Tama's brother, a teenager, had offered his girlfriend and his little sister a ride around the factory where his father served as plant manager. The teenager, who knew nothing about forklift trucks, drove so fast that the toddler had screamed "Slow down." The boy shouted back, "Shut up, stupid." The boy then lost control of the machine. Tama Whittaker fell off, the truck fell over sideways, and the little girl's leg was crushed underneath. Following several operations, Tama's surgeons finally amputated her leg when she was nine years old. I met Tama Whittaker at age fifteen, and I asked her to tell me a dream that had nothing at all to do with her accident.

She first answered that she had had a number of repeated dreams of the accident from the time she was thirty-four months old until she was six. What was clearest in Tama's dream and in her waking memories of the incident was a repetition of her brother's "Shut up, stupid." But Tama's dreams had finally, spontaneously, stopped. Tama then blushed and told me a recent dream that, she believed, had nothing at all to do with forklift trucks:

"My boyfriend proposes marriage," Tama said. "We walk along a beach to an eighteenth-century house. Characters from the movie *The Shining* are there, waiting to axe me. I go over to the beach with my boyfriend. Giant crabs are there, ready to attack."

Tama's dream at age fifteen included a number of wishes and two moments of horror. The wishes—to be with her boyfriend, to be proposed to, and to wander through a beautiful eighteenth-century house—were internally derived, age-appropriate, adolescent wishes. They were the material of many an ordinary teenaged fantasy. And of many a romance novel.

The first moment of horror in Tama Whittaker's dream, however, comes after her three wishes have been expressed and fulfilled. A scene from the film *The Shining* in which the psychotic Jack Nicholson chases his wife and child with an axe is replayed, only this time the menace is directed at Tama. Children often dream a scene or two from scary movies. But Tama Whittaker, of course, was different. She actually *had* been "axed." Her leg had been surgically removed. For her, *The Shining* had been incorporated into a horrible, real memory. Stanley Kubrick's movie was not just any old horror film for Tama Whittaker. It was a personal reminder.

The final dream scene in Tama's nightmare, of course, the one that actually forces the young girl awake, is its horrible ending. Giant crabs pursue her down a beach. This scene, a moment of absolute panic, represents the original traumatic moment for Tama—the moment she fell from the forklift truck and the forklift truck, in turn, fell over her. What looks more like a forklift truck, after all, than an oversized, shiny, bright orange, Alaska king crab?

Why would a traumatized child need to dream the very same thing night after night? Or even dream it once a month, or in clusters of dreams every seven years or so? Freud says that what lies behind this tendency to repeated dreaming is a kind of anxiety unique to psychic trauma, "traumatic anxiety." This horrible feeling, different from the much more common anticipatory anxiety called "signal anxiety," is not dissipated by a single dream or a nightmare. A single dream easily works off "signal anxiety" because it gratifies the naughty, internal wishes that lie behind this kind of anxiety. But ordinary dreams are not equipped to dissipate traumatic anxiety, the anxiety of the external. The anxiety stirred up by trauma is far too massive, far too intense, to be handled by one or two ordinary nightmares. Dreams, the ordinary coping devices for warding off internal emotional conflict, do not "work" after massive horror, terror, and disgrace. Dreams simply are too weak a mental mechanism to handle this kind of intensity. The psyche will use its ordinary, old coping devices, dreams, but it cannot successfully work off a trauma this way. The mechanism overworks. The dreams repeat and repeat. In many instances the mechanism fails to burn out on its own, however. The traumatized dreamer may be granted a month's rest or even a year's respite. But sooner or later the posttraumatic dream will come back. Traumatic anxiety apparently does not spontaneously dissipate during one's lifetime. Once this anxiety has been set into motion, it may recur with new life stresses, especially those that carry echoes of the old helplessness and loss.

Consider the example of the well-known American biographer and contemporary historian William Manchester, for instance. Manchester published the nonfiction book *Good-bye Darkness* in 1979, about thirty-five years after he had served as a marine in the Pacific Theater of World

War II. Manchester had been an adolescent at the time of the war. He had lied about his age in order to enlist. Manchester fought the Japanese in a few fierce Pacific island battles. Then he needed to tell his story. He waited to write his book, however, just as John Boorman and Louis Malle had waited to do their autobiographic films. Manchester says he developed a repeated World War II dream shortly after his friend, President John F. Kennedy, was assassinated. The dream was stimulated by the sudden, unexpected stress of a national and personal tragedy. It was a dream of a young marine, tired, scared, and angry, climbing a hill. The marine was William Manchester himself as a teenager. Manchester says he experienced this dream frequently at the time he was writing his account of World War II in the Pacific—he had already gone through thirteen or fourteen years of post-traumatic dreaming, in other words. He begins *Good-bye Darkness* with one version of this repeated dream. He then goes on to show how the dream reflects some horrible realities connected with a hill over which his platoon had fought the Japanese.

Manchester says that his repeated dream impelled him in the 1970s to revisit the major Pacific island battlefields. The dream, he says, also made him write his book about these battlefields. Yet, I would venture to guess that the dream, Manchester's travels to the Pacific islands, and the act of writing itself, each a kind of personal, post-traumatic repetition, would not have completely dissipated William Manchester's anxiety. The feelings stirred up by scary battles from the teen years would not necessarily disappear with ease. Time helps. But we know from examples like Alfred Hitchcock that time does not cure everything. If we dared to ask William Manchester today whether he still occasionally dreams his repeated dream, his answer might well be "yes."

Charlotte Brent, our familiar old friend from the San Francisco ocean front, like William Manchester, dreamed of places she had frequented many years before. Like Manchester, too, Charlotte dreamed over a long span of years. Charlotte tended to dream in spurts, as Manchester must have dreamed. But Charlotte's dreams were of civilian terrors—of forced sex on the beaches of her own home town. Charlotte's nightmares came at times of significant stress (just as Manchester's dreams began when his friend, the president, was killed). Charlotte dreamed when her mother died, when her father became ill with the last illness of his life, when she started thinking about retirement, and when she met the only boyfriend of her life, Jim. Each time a significant stress occurred in "Charlie's" life, she would mentally return in sleep to those old ocean beaches of San Francisco. Her nightmares were always the same—of the beaches and of the human menaces that lurked behind the dunes. But the precipitating stresses were different each time.

Childhood trauma sets horrible images, once and for all, into the mind's circuitry. These horrid pictures will "run" by day, unconsciously impelling silent musings, fantasies, physical discomforts, actions, and play. But the pictures will also "run" by night (in the R- and the X-rated versions), propelling the kind of dreams that, as Macbeth says, "murder sleep."

When I interviewed my control group from McFarland High School and Burton Elementary School, I was particularly interested in checking out a few new findings from the Chowchilla study—the sense of personal future-lessness, concerns about impending world disaster, post-traumatic play, and repeated dreams. I wondered before seeing the McFarland and Porter-ville kids whether one could predict "trauma" in normal populations simply by using these findings. (As it turned out, they were pretty good indicators of the possibility of trauma.)

One attractive, redheaded girl from McFarland High, Christine Perkins, showed how a repeated dream plus a foreshortened future perspective could just about nail down the diagnosis of post-traumatic stress disorder, even though our diagnostic manuals, at present, require much, much more. Christine had had a dream, she told me. But first she wanted to talk about the inevitability of disaster. The presence of these two phenomena made it almost certain that what Christine mentioned last—the traumatic event—would have had to be there. This is how our talk went:

"Do you have any idea about disasters happening in the future, Christine?"

"I feel sure things will happen. Things have happened to me. I'd rather not talk about it."

"Do you ever have the same dream again and again?"

"When I was little—nine or ten—I had repeated nightmares. It was about an old man chasing me. I'd wake up in the middle of the night."

"Did that ever really happen?"

"That actually happened at ten. [Note Christine's time-skew here. She says her dreams started at "nine or ten" but the terrible event I was to hear about within another minute or two actually took place at age ten. This difficulty with placement of events, time-skew, forces Christine to conclude that her dreams may be predictive.] My life was kind of in danger. I don't know . . . the world's future scares me. I'm afraid of war—the draft—the economy's falling apart. I kind of ignore it. I'm almost positive, though, something bad is going to happen."

"What *did* happen, Christine?"

"I was assaulted sexually by an old man [a stranger]. He chased me . . . he raped me."

Not everybody who is traumatized will dream nightmares that can be remembered. First of all, you have to be old enough at the time of your trauma to dream and to recall the dream. Second, you have to absorb the traumatic events and realize their implications, and third, you have to have words for your feelings—words to apply to the dream experience.

If you were very young, an infant or a toddler, at the time you were traumatized, for instance, you might not be old enough or mature enough to register or to remember your dreams. If you employed a large amount of self-anesthesia or emotional numbing in order to handle a long-standing series of horrors, you might experience only unremembered terror dreams. And if you were a particularly nonverbal older child when you were traumatized, you might call out in your sleep, say things, sleep walk, or sit up in terror in your bed; but you might also tend to forget by morning what you had dreamed.

I found in my own study of twenty children who had suffered documented psychic traumas before they turned age five that only eight of them showed any evidence of dreaming. Four youngsters over age thirty-four months at the time of their traumas had been able to remember the content of their dreams. But four others who had been over age twenty months at the time of their traumas suffered sleep interruptions as their only sign of dreaming. The majority of the twenty traumatized preschoolers, twelve of them, exhibited no evidence whatsoever that they had had nightmares. It thus appeared that it would take a certain cognitive and emotional maturity at the time of a trauma in order to dream "repeated nightmares" and then to remember them. It also takes a single event rather than a multiplicity of events in order to dream a clearly remembered post-traumatic dream at this very early stage of life.

Abused youngsters, because of their almost uniform attempts to keep their abuses secret, tend to dream many unremembered terror dreams. These children are afraid to sleep alone in their rooms and they hate the dark. Sometimes they have a "bad feeling" that they have dreamed. But they cannot remember anything of the dream experience. Occasionally a parent will hear such a youngster call out "Help" or "Leave me alone." But even if the parent asks the child about it the next day, the child cannot recall the content of the dream. It appears that long-standing abuses encourage nonverbal qualities in children. And nonverbal qualities, in turn, encourage unremembered terror dreams.

The dream pattern of unremembered terror dreams—fears at bedtime, sleep interruptions, sleep-talk, occasional sleep-walking, and/or a failure to remember dreams by morning—is not specific to child abuse or even to psychic trauma. But it is common enough to the traumatic situations of early childhood, especially the chronic, repeated, long-standing ones, that persistent patterns like these in children must be investigated. Abused kids ordinarily are not good "talkers." This factor, in addition to the massive denials so frequently seen in these cases, accounts for a preponderance in these children of unremembered dreams. We will see at the end of this chapter that Virginia Woolf, an unusually verbal person, was an important exception to this "rule." She dreamed a terror dream related to her long-standing trauma, a dream that she remembered all of her life. Most children who live with long-standing terrors, however, learn to shut their mouths and to put away their pens. They dream their dreams in silence.

Many people in America cannot talk well about their emotions. Most of these individuals never were traumatized—it's just that stoic, American, Gary Cooper way to be. The Chowchilla children, like any other children in America, started out life either verbal or nonverbal about their emotions. These were personality style issues, not psychic trauma issues. I ranked the children of Chowchilla after the kidnapping for verbal abilities and found seven kids who were relatively nonverbal about emotions from the beginning. Six of these seven experienced only unremembered terror dreams the year after the kidnapping. Occasionally one of the seven nonverbal children would scream out, "No, no" or "Leave us be!" from sleep. And occasionally one would walk about the house at night, glazed eyes giving away the child's nonwaking state. These six nonverbal dreamers could not remember anything of their dreams by morning. The nonverbal youngsters of Chowchilla, in other words, tended to dream unremembered terror dreams only. Even though they had been traumatized once, their nonverbal natures encouraged the kinds of dreams that could not be retained by morning. Their families knew, though, that their sleep patterns were unusual. They didn't dare tell the child, however. "Telling," they thought, "would only make things worse." You see they, too, were not very verbal.

One child I met not too long ago had a father who did notice what she was doing in sleep and who did tell her what he saw. The child was surprised, indeed, to hear what he had to say. Manuel Montoya, a chef at one of San Francisco's Mission District Mexican restaurants, had been trying for months to "teach" his seven-year-old daughter how to sleep. Debbie used to know how to sleep, Manuel told me, but she had "forgotten." Manuel Montoya did not know what might be propelling young Debbie's nighttime behaviors. Despite the fact that Manuel had been teaching Debbie how to sleep for about a year, it took a visit from two attorneys and an evaluation at my psychiatric office before anybody really knew why little Debbie Montoya no longer understood how to sleep. But I am telescoping my tale here and I want you to meet Debbie yourself. This child illustrates two kinds of post-traumatic dreaming; the unremembered terror dream that I have just finished explaining and the modified repetition, the type of dream that Selma Fraiberg demonstrated so long ago to our Continuous Case Conference at Michigan. Debbie Montoya also illustrates that the particular body posturing and behaviors employed during "bad" sleep often mean something. Debbie, in fact, tells one of the most upsetting tales one might ever hear from the mouth of a child.

Debbie Montoya's English is perfect, but you can hear a Spanish lilt to the cadences. She has black eyes, blindingly lustrous hair, and the kind of skin you wish you could reach out and stroke. Debbie is frightened. It seems that something happened at school last year. She is a second grader now. And she is a good student. Debbie never talked about what had happened in first grade. She felt too scared. (Scared as she was, she had learned her numbers, how to print, and how to read. She demonstrates the point I made in the previous chapter that traumatized kids rarely do poorly in school.) The terrors that had been visited upon Debbie Montoya the previous year had been chronic, repeated, and secretive. They had been meted out by Mrs. Georgiana Trask, Debbie's first-grade teacher.

Manuel Montoya had known something was wrong almost from the start. "I thought Debbie didn't know how to sleep anymore. How to breathe. You'd touch her at night," Manuel told me, "and she'd stand up. She stood up in bed. With open eyes. In bed. She looked weird. Like a zombie. One day she walked with open eyes in her sleep. She fell. It was scary."

Sometimes Debbie would "choke" in her sleep. She would tell her father that she had been dreaming "that a woman wanted to choke her." Manuel Montoya recalled that Debbie would make choking sounds and open her mouth wide, "like she really *was* being choked. I took a picture of her like that once," Manuel told me. "I showed Debbie the picture and she didn't believe it." At this point Manuel Montoya had to stop talking for a while. "I don't feel so good about this," he said to me, blowing his nose hard into a Kleenex.

Well the upshot was—until the two lawyers came to the Montoya house from the school district—that Manuel Montoya tried to "teach" his little Debbie how to sleep and how to breathe. "I spent hours with her trying to get her to control her sleep," said he. "That whole year we worked on it. Sleeping, breathing, sleeping, breathing. I thought she didn't know anymore how to sleep."

The two lawyers from school said that they were investigating a possible problem in Debbie's first-grade class. Mrs. Trask, the teacher, had been suspended by the district pending a full investigation. A number of children had mentioned Debbie Montoya's name to the lady and the man who had come to visit them from the school system legal department. The kids remembered that Debbie Montoya had had a scary time with Mrs. Trask. They had seen it. And they had been scared themselves by what they saw.

Debbie Montoya refused to come into my room alone. "Ladies are scarier than men," she said. She brought her dad in with her. I guess Debbie felt a little safer with a chaperone present. And I think it helped Manuel Montoya to hear what his daughter had to say. Debbie had a tale or two to tell about Mrs. Trask, and so I'll give you a few of the stories in Debbie's own words and then demonstrate what I think Debbie's sleep and dream problems meant.

"Mrs. Trask wanted our principal to get pajamas for the first-grade kids," Debbie began. "And he did [I think it was Mrs. Trask who actually bought the pajamas herself]. She'd go to the bathroom with somebody [a kid] and say, 'Take off all your clothes and put these [pajamas] on.' Nobody wanted to. But you'd have to. She was forcing me to put pajamas on. Once it happened because I was giving something to a friend, a toy my friend had lended to me."

That old, borrowed toy got Debbie to thinking about a special toy duck she had once brought to school from home. "Mrs. Trask would take things away and try to break them," Debbie said. "She took a hard plastic toy away from me—a duck from my house. She tried stepping on it to break it. Then Mrs. Trask got a hammer, but the duck wouldn't break. So she got an axe. But it wouldn't break."

Let me interject here one of Debbie Montoya's nightmares. Debbie dreamed "a woman with an axe tried to cut my head." She had dreamed it repeatedly. This was one of the dreams Debbie had told her father when he asked if she was dreaming. Can you believe it? A first-grade teacher wielding an axe in class? One of my child-psychiatrist friends, Joe Green, of Madison, Wisconsin, told me he thought Stephen King's novel *Misery* was one of the most terrifying things he has ever read. But King wrote *Misery* about a female fan trying to axe a full-grown male writer. How much more terrifying would a first-grade teacher be, wielding an axe before a class of six and seven year olds? Debbie's dream was a modified playback dream. The axe and the woman were the same as reality. Debbie's head was substituting for the plastic duck.

When her axe couldn't destroy Debbie Montoya's little plastic duck, Mrs. Trask told her first graders, "I'll take the plastic duck home to burn it. Or give it to my pet dog and he'll eat it." "I never saw my duck again," whispered seven-year-old Debbie in my office. "Mrs. Trask didn't ever tell me nothing about it after that." She didn't have to. A dog like Mrs. Trask's dog was enough to stop any further conversation.

But we had opened a new Pandora's box with Mrs. Trask's dog. "Mrs. Trask would say to us, 'I'll bring my dog to school and he'll eat Jonah Andrews up so Jonah won't be showing, anymore.'" Mrs. Trask apparently didn't like the fact that Jonah Andrews seemed unable to close his mouth. Jonah was a mouth-breather. "Mrs. Trask would say, 'I'll take Jonah to the zoo,'" Debbie recalled. "She'd get boxes, and then said she would put Jonah in and take him out to the zoo so the lions could eat him. Once the second-grade teacher walked in and saw Jonah in a box. But Mrs. Trask told her 'I'm giving Jonah a lesson,' and so Miss Yamato left."

Debbie would awaken nights, mouth wide open, gasping for breath. Her father had thought she had forgotten how to breathe. However, Debbie Montoya *was* Jonah Andrews by night, taking in air through her mouth and feeling confined to a box. She physically identified with the miserable little Jonah, although she could not remember the content of these dreams by the time she woke up. "No man is an island," the poet John Donne had said many years ago. "Ask not for whom the bell tolls, It tolls for thee." Debbie Montoya would not have understood Donne at the age of six. But John Donne understood Debbie. She *was* Jonah Andrews in her sleep. She was entirely able to identify with a miserable, fellow human being. Debbie Montoya was no "island."

"I remember," Debbie went on, "the first time Mrs. Trask saw Jonah with his mouth open. She tried to sew it shut with a needle and thread. Jonah told us it didn't hurt too much. She just sewed up his loose skin. But it looked scary to me. And at school we would say, 'We won't go to school tomorrow'—and some people wouldn't go. But most of us would be there the next day. Or we'd say 'We'll pull Mrs. Trask away from Jonah.' But we didn't help Jonah. [They couldn't.] Jonah told me once Mrs. Trask said she'd cut his penis off. Jonah stayed home from school the next day. It didn't happen."

Debbie Montoya felt unable to help Jonah Andrews combat Mrs. Trask's threats. "She told us her dog eats meat," Debbie said, "*children* meat. She said 'I sliced up some kids who were mean to me, and some kids who didn't care for me. And I gave the slices to the dog.' We talked about it later out on the playground. We thought Mrs. Trask would go to jail for *that*. [But she didn't go to jail.]

"Once Mrs. Trask got angry because I was handing Hazel a toy I brought from home. She took me in the bathroom and she put my head in the toilet. I pushed up away from the water and I hurt my back. She was holding the flusher with one hand and my head in the other. Mrs. Trask said she'd flush me down. But I didn't believe her. I couldn't fit into that little hole—I didn't think so."

Now it was possible to tell why Debbie Montoya sat upright so often in sleep—stiff, eyes wide open, trying to struggle upward, coughing, and choking. Although this little girl had no memory of it by morning, she was reliving the time her head was forced into the toilet bowl. Debbie was dreaming it but couldn't find words for the experience upon awakening. Her physical responses—the coughing, choking, and struggling to an upright position—were all that one could see of her forgotten dreams. The dreams repeated a minute or so of terror in a school lavatory. Debbie's body, in sleep, mimicked her old terror.

'I know more," Debbie went on. I wanted to say "Stop already! I've heard enough!" But, of course, I let the poor kid continue. "I seen *everything*. Mrs. Trask hasn't gone away yet. She watches my house. She knows what I'm doing. She said she would always watch us. I didn't believe it when she said it. But I'm not so sure now. I dreamed," she went on, "we went somewhere in a big city. It was a field trip. [To the zoo?] Mrs. Trask said 'wait here' and she left. [Debbie was reliving in this dream the old threat to feed first graders to the lions.] Then she went to her house and saw her father dead. I knew Mrs. Trask was sad. Her father had a heart attack while we were in first grade. He had died in the middle of the year. He was taking pills. In my dream, he died from the pills. Really, Mrs. Trask didn't ever come back to school when her father died. . . . But I think she is still around. Around school. And around my house. And I think she killed her father."

Now Debbie Montoya told another dream that corresponded to these thoughts. "I dreamed a couple days ago that Mrs. Trask had an axe," Debbie said. "She came to our house. She killed my cousins, my auntie, and my friend Julio. And then my mom and dad and my two brothers came, and we ran away. I don't remember more dreams right now, but I have lots of dreams about Mrs. Trask. I wake up scared. Every other night it happens, even now," said the second grader. Debbie was telling me these things a full year after her last contact with her psychotic first-grade teacher. But perhaps Debbie would stay in first grade for the rest of her life —at least in her dreams.

"I feel Mrs. Trask in my room," Debbie concluded. "Night or day. In the closet. I'm afraid to look in my closet. Mrs. Trask once said to us, 'I look through your windows at night. And I don't see no one brushing their teeth.' I didn't believe my teacher when she said it, but I wasn't sure. Like the time at the toilet. Like when she said she'd flush me down. I didn't believe her but I wasn't sure. Anyway, I didn't tell my parents what Mrs. Trask was doing in school because I thought she might see me talking to my parents in my house."

Well, that's about that. Debbie Montoya still expects to see Mrs. Trask peeking through her bedroom window. She still is afraid to talk. She still "sees" her teacher out on the streets and inside of TV programs—"Nell," for instance, on the show *Give Me a Break*. "Nell is a bad person," Debbie says. "She scolds her boy and tries to hit him with a hammer. I think now that Mrs. Trask doesn't teach in our school anymore. They have put dark makeup all over her and her new job is to be 'Nell' on TV."

Mrs. Trask has managed to infiltrate Debbie Montoya's future. "I won't get married," the little girl told me. "Because if I married, I'd have babies. And I can't take care of them. I'm afraid it's too hard to take care of children. I've been afraid since I turned seven." Debbie also feels mortified, ashamed, about what happened to her in first grade. "I am ashamed," she said, "for what Mrs. Trask had done to the kids and me. I don't want people to know what happened." Debbie looked at me with those huge, black eyes of hers. "It makes me feel smaller than a person," she said.

The dreams, though the main thing that Manuel Montoya noticed before the two lawyers from school came to his house, were just part of Debbie's story. But the dreams were the one sign that in Debbie's case could have allowed Manuel to recognize her trauma before the "lady and the man" from the school system stopped by to talk. Debbie dreamed modified playback dreams of her terrible realities at school and of the thoughts that had accompanied them. But worse for Debbie, more frequent, and so very obvious to Manuel Montoya, were the child's unremembered terror dreams, dreams that caused the little girl at times to choke by night on her own internalized toilet water. Nose closed, mouth opened, she could even become Jonah Andrews in sleep, sewn up lips, mutilated penis, and all. Eyes wide open, fast asleep, Debbie stared unseeing at the ghost of Mrs. Trask, a ghost that could loose the lions of the zoo or the dogs of hell at you. Eyes straining into the distance, Debbie Montoya looked blindly by night into her own closet and onto her own TV screen for a madwoman who would never, never go away. The eyes of the mind stay fully awake during sleep. In those eyes, the Mrs. Trasks of this world teach far more than first grade.

There will be, by the way, a civil lawsuit on behalf of Debbie Montoya and some of her classmates. Mrs. Trask is presently teaching elementary school in a public school district to the south of San Francisco. Nobody I have asked knows how this came about.

Some traumatized children die in their own dreams. This dying surprised me the first time I heard about it at Chowchilla. Over the five-year period that I worked with the Chowchilla kids, fourteen of these children eventually experienced nightmares in which they themselves died. The kids told me two kinds of dreamed deaths—those in which they kept watching their dead bodies after they had "died" and those in which the entire dream blacked out after they had "died."

Personal death dreams were something new. Psychiatrists had inferred in the past that you could not let yourself die in sleep. Yet more than half of the Chowchilla children had died in their dreams and were unable to accept the reassurance that they would stay alive. These children tended to believe that the next traumatic episode might strike at any moment. And their death dreams, they thought, were predictive.

Rumors about death dreams stirred the gossip channels at Chowchilla. "If you dream you die, *do* you die?" Mary and Elizabeth Vane asked me. These kids had been talking about their dreams with friends and with each other, you could tell. They were expecting to die.

Freud once said that the unconscious does not believe its own death— "in the unconscious every one of us is convinced of his own immortality," he had written. Yet here in Chowchilla was the "unconscious," that mental element that stages dreams in the first place, conjuring up death after death, night after night. Post-traumatic dreaming was proving an exception to Freud.

I looked at my McFarland-Porterville control group to see how prevalent death dreams were in this "normal" population of children. I asked each kid about life attitudes, dreams, repeated play or behaviors, and traumatic events. Eight kids at McFarland and Porterville said that they had died in their dreams. Two of these death dreams defied explanation. The dreamers seemed to have been untouched by trauma and their dreams were "accidents," perhaps, of dreaming. But six of these "normal" kids were dreaming their own deaths on the basis of two kinds of past losses of control— fainting or psychic trauma. If a child had experienced delirium, fainting, seizures, or head injury before, he might dream "death" because these experiences had felt like death. After all, the child had suddenly been deprived of consciousness, an experience very close, I would imagine, to death itself (and, by the way, a loss-of-control experience close to, but not quite the same as, psychic trauma). If the child had been psychically traumatized, he could dream of his own "death," too, because of the loss of control inherent to trauma. Often the traumatized child accepts the possibility—no, the probability—that he will die during and after a traumatic event. Once he is traumatized he can believe in his own death.

The death dream and the waking sense of a limited future both reflect old losses of childhood invincibility. This kind of loss follows directly from trauma. Even when a disaster happens to someone else, a child may suddenly, intimately, become "acquainted" with his own mortality. Once such knowledge is acquired, a child can allow himself to die both in imagination and in dreams.

Let us "listen" to a few Porterville-McFarland control group youngsters as they tell their death dreams.

From Veronica Bentley, nine: "Sometimes I have the same dream—you dream something and then it happens. [This child is saying here that she believes that dreams predict.] Once I died in a dream. I was six or seven when I had it. I was twenty in the dream. I was driving. A man crashed into me. He took me to the hospital and I died in the hospital. It felt weird. The dream just blacked out. . . . I actually went to the hospital when I was about eight years old. I had pneumonia. They stuck a needle in my hand. I was in a car accident at seven. I was in a truck. Somebody hit us. A man. He didn't hit us that hard. I wasn't hurt. But it scared me a lot." Note how two frights, the hospital and the accident, are condensed into one horror in this dream. "Condensation" is a classical dream mechanism.

From Martin Vasquez, eleven: "I died in two Mayan dreams I had. There was a girl and guys in a place where they picked someone they wanted to sacrifice. Two girls fought to the death. Then a girl picked *me*. She was about to hit me but I moved. And then they held me down and went 'Whap!' Then I was dead. They had a funeral and stuff. Just before the funeral started, my alarm went off. I saw my face [in the dream]. I was floating-like. I was eleven when that happened. . . .

"I was home, three, four days [a while ago] with a fever. I slept three days and woke the fourth feeling terrible. The doctor said my temperature was 108 degrees."

From Thomas McAuley, fourteen: "I've had a few dreams where I died. I was hanging from a cliff and I fell and I hit bottom and I died. Everything went black. I believe the dream would predict.

"I don't make plans. . . . I'm afraid I'll die in a wreck or something. . . . For two, three years after my father and sister's accident I crashed and wrecked cars inside the house. When I was outside I played basketball. I have dreams of wrecks. Repeated ones. Maybe ten. In the dreams I sometimes die. The dream just blanks out. Just like that. . . . The world will die out, I guess, probably before the year 2000. It just seems. Everybody says. Not *my* church. Probably by an earthquake."

From Dorothea Blake, fifteen: "I had two dreams where I died. One was from when I was fourteen. It was weird. I died because I was getting sick —a fever. I *was* really sick. I *had* a fever. [This is how current life circumstances interject themselves into dreams.] I see myself in a coffin. My family is there. It's like laying there still alive and imagining how everyone else is feeling. And then the dream ends.

"At fifteen a girl I know from Taft High got in a volleyball accident and messed up her knee and couldn't play anymore. I dreamed it happened to me. And I couldn't walk. I dreamed somebody shot me then—I don't know who, I don't know where. I just died. That was weird. That's it."

The girl thought for a couple of seconds when I asked her whether she had ever been frightened in the past or whether she had ever fainted.

"I've fainted before when I was small, seven or eight. From the heat—the sun. It was hot. I was in craft activities for the summer. That was *very* frightening. I didn't know how I got home. . . . I'm afraid of dying. It was weird. I suddenly asked the teacher if I could get a drink of water. It was a blackout—no dream, no nothing. I woke up and I started crying. I was home laying on the couch."

The dreams this girl gives appear to represent deeply disguised replays of an experience with heat prostration—of standing up in crafts class, losing knee stability, and then fainting dead away. The second dream also appears to be related to a recent traumatic occurrence to someone else—a girl who had "messed up her knee" at volleyball. Both fearful events, the direct one (fainting from heat) and the vicarious one (having a knee all "messed up") are condensed in the second dream this girl tells.

The world believes in dream prediction. Almost a hundred years after Freud, we seem to think that dreams represent messages from fate, from a predetermined destiny lying entirely outside of ourselves. The great writers don't help much in this regard. Shakespeare has Julius Caesar's wife fall upon the emperor the day he was about to visit the Senate (to be killed), saying "Please don't go, Julius," (I paraphrase Calpurnia here). "I've had a dream that your statue is bleeding in a number of places and the senators are bathing in your blood." John Irving, in his *World According to Garp,* plants several dream predictions and omens that seem to choke out other options as to how life proceeds. When Charles Dickens's old miser Scrooge has his dream-visions of Tiny Tim's death, most readers do not cry out in disbelief. Instead, they shed real tears for the boy's "obviously" absent future. We know that Scrooge's dream will come true. We are accustomed, from so much exposure, to the idea of dream prediction. Martin Luther King, Jr., created such a sense of certainty, of timelessness, in his two most memorable, most prophetic, most visionary, and most dreamlike speeches, "I have a dream," and "I have been to the mountain," that these orations are often shown on television as King's presentiment of his own imminent demise.

There is considerable psychological truth to the idea of dream prediction, but it is an internal truth, not an external one. Our deep inner drives impel us to action—certainly to future action. By giving our drives expression in dreams, Freud tells us, we do reveal something of our personal futures. But these futures are internally derived destinies, not prefixed fates awaiting us outside of ourselves.

I am not in a position to comment on prophets, psychics, fortune tellers, and dream predictors. But some traumatized people *do* claim to have these powers. And I can comment on trauma. We have already seen several examples of dream prediction in this book. In childhood trauma, paranormal "powers" develop after, not before, the overwhelming events. By virtue of time-skew and repetitive dreaming, traumatized children come to think that they are psychic. One wonders how many professional psychics have had traumatic occurrences in their own pasts. Did psychic trauma establish the sense of "power"? It would be fun to study psychics and fortune tellers. But I doubt that they would allow it.

Virginia Woolf, the great writer, had a post-traumatic dream of her own in childhood that she needed to tell two years before she committed suicide. Virginia was a sexually abused child. When she was five or six years old, in fact, Virginia's teenaged half-brother, Gerald Duckworth, used her as a sexual object, most likely, repeatedly. When she reached adolescence, she was sexually abused by a second half-brother, George Duckworth. In other words, there were two periods in Virginia's youth in which she was abused, and there were two abusers. This is how Virginia Woolf describes the first of her early sexual traumas in her "Sketch of the Past," written at age fifty-seven, two years before she waded out into the River Ouse, pockets weighted down with stones. (Virginia Woolf probably suffered from manic-depressive disease, or, as we would call it today, "bipolar disorder." In other words, she simultaneously suffered from two psychiatric conditions—severe mood swings on a biological basis and psychic trauma on an environmental basis.)

> There was a slab outside the dining room for standing dishes upon. Once when I was very small Gerald Duckworth lifted me onto this, and as I sat there he began to explore my body. I can remember the feel of his hand going under my clothes; going firmly and steadily lower and lower. I remember how I hoped he would stop; how I stiffened and wriggled as his hand approached my private parts. But it did not stop. His hand explored my private parts, too. I remember resenting, disliking it—what is a word for so dumb and mixed a feeling? It must have been strong, since I recall it.

Yes, Virginia had words for her repeated abuses, something that the repeatedly abused child often lacks. "My natural love for beauty was checked by some ancestral dread. Yet this did not prevent me from feeling ecstasies and raptures spontaneously and intensely and without any shame or the least sense of guilt, so long as they were disconnected with my own body."

Virginia Woolf obviously had trained her sex organs into anesthesia.

This was the same type of physical numbing we have already observed in young Frederick Waters, the boy who endured numerous physical abuses at the hands of his stepfather. But we are primarily interested in dreams here, and in this context we need to understand Woolf's "mirror" symbol. The mirror represented Virginia Woolf's ongoing traumas in her mind. The mirror probably witnessed her incest with her half-brother. And it later stood in mute witness to the death of Virginia's mother, Julia Stephen. Let us hear what the grown-up Virginia Woolf, compelled to write almost every minute that she was free and functional, says about these mirrors:

> There was a small looking-glass in the hall at Talland House [Virginia's childhood home]. It had, I remember, a ledge with a brush on it. By standing on tiptoe I could see my face in the glass. When I was six or seven perhaps, I got into the habit of looking at my face in the glass. But I only did this if I was sure I was alone. I was ashamed of it. A strong feeling of guilt seemed naturally attached to it. . . . At any rate, the looking-glass shame has lasted all of my life, long after the tomboy phase was over. I cannot now powder my nose in public. Everything to do with dress—to be fitted, to come into a room wearing a new dress—still frightens me; at least makes me shy, self-conscious, uncomfortable.

Childhood trauma victims feel ashamed. Victims of sexual abuse feel doubly ashamed because they have to live both with the feelings of being less-than-human and the feelings of being sexually soiled. By her own account, little Virginia Stephen was "soiled" for the first time on a ledge in the hallway outside her dining room. There was a mirror at hand, she says. Virginia may have seen some reflection of her own sexual abuse in the mirror, in fact. She knew afterward that she was "dirty." And she had trouble looking at her own reflection from that time on.

Virginia Stephen had a dream when she was still quite young. She always remembered it.

> Let me add a dream; for it may refer to the incident of the looking-glass. [Woolf mentally associates her looking glass to the dream, an almost sure sign that the two are closely connected.] I dreamed I was looking in a glass when a horrible face—the face of an animal—suddenly showed over my shoulder. I cannot be sure if this was a dream, or if it happened. Was I looking in the glass one day when something in the background moved, and seemed to be alive? I cannot be sure. But I have always remembered the other face in the glass, whether it was a dream or a fact, and that it frightened me.

Woolf's dream, as she tells it, sounds single, not repeated. But this early childhood nightmare lingered in Virginia's mind until the end of her life.

This is significant. The memory of the dream stayed vivid. Virginia Woolf, in fact, was not perfectly sure if the dream was real or imagined. This clarity of remembrance suggests that the dream was post-traumatic. The mirror of the dream, I think, overlooked the original trauma, the attack on the six-year-old Virginia by Gerald Duckworth. Who was the beast of the dream? It must have been Virginia Woolf's abuser, himself. Virginia tended to describe Gerald or his brother George in beast-like terms. George had, Woolf says, "the curls of a God, and the ears of a fawn," but, she goes on, "unmistakably the eyes of a pig." Gerald is described in letters and diary entries as a pig, or later in life, as a slovenly, disgusting alligator.

Virginia Woolf spontaneously dissociated in the manner of the other repeatedly abused children. She experienced "derealization," a strange alteration in the perception of her surroundings, in the presence of her own reflection in a mirror or in water:

> There was the moment of the puddle in the path; when for no reason I could discover, everything suddenly became unreal; I was suspended; I could not step across the puddle; [my old high school teacher, the ancient Miss B., told the girls in our English class never to step across a puddle. "Boys stand there," she said, "and wait for a view up your skirt"]. . . . But it was not over, for that night in the bath the dumb horror came over me. Again I had that hopeless sadness; that collapse I have described before; as if I was passive under some sledge-hammer blow; exposed to a whole avalanche of meaning that had heaped itself up and discharged itself onto me, unprotected, with nothing to ward it off, so that I huddled up at my end of the bath, motionless. I could not explain it; I said nothing even to Nessa [Virginia's sister, Vanessa Stephen] sponging herself at the other end.

Experiences with her original "animal-monster in the mirror," Gerald Duckworth, must have repeatedly forced Virginia Woolf into a detached mode. From the age of six on, Virginia took in all of the details, but she numbed herself emotionally. Mirrors, in particular, served as instant signals for Virginia to "space-out." Here is the story of Virginia Stephen's mother's death as told by Virginia—and as seen with a mirror in attendance (Virginia was thirteen years old when Julia Stephen suddenly died):

> We were taken into the bedroom. I think candles were burning; and I think the sun was coming in. *At any rate I remember the long looking glass* [my emphasis]; with the drawers on either side; and the washstand; and the great bed on which my mother lay. I remember very clearly how even as I was taken to the bedside I noticed that one nurse was sobbing and a desire to laugh came over me, and I said to myself as I have often done at moments of crisis since, "I feel nothing whatsoever." Then I

stooped and kissed my mother's face. It was still warm. She [had] only died a moment before.

Virginia's dreamed "monster" made an appearance the day after Julia Stephen died. Virginia does not connect the old monster-in-the-mirror she had dreamed in her kindergarten days with the "man" she hallucinated at age thirteen. But I do. Virginia Stephen was led back, probably the day after her mother died, to Julia Stephen's bedroom by her older half-sister Stella Duckworth. This was to be the last time that Virginia would ever kiss her mother. The child felt the coldness of her mother's skin and was horrified. When her older sister came to her bedroom later:

> She said to me, "Forgive me. I saw you were afraid." Stella had noticed that I had started. When Stella asked me to forgive her for having given me that shock, I cried—we had been crying on and off that day—and said, "When I see Mother, *I see a man sitting with her.*" [My emphasis. Virginia was apparently visually hallucinating, something we already know that traumatized children do.] Stella looked at me as if I had frightened her. Did I say that in order to attract attention to myself? Or was it true? I cannot be sure, for certainly I had a great wish to draw attention to myself. But certainly it was true that when she said: "Forgive me," and thus made me visualize my mother, I seemed to see a man sitting bent on the edge of the bed.

A male monster, an abusing older stepbrother, lurked in the background of Virginia Woolf's worst moments of childhood. Her dreamed monster in the mirror served as the symbol for all of this. Virginia Woolf, I think, suffered the kind of repeated, long-standing childhood trauma that stimulates a numbing of the body and a deadening of the emotions. Many of the characters in her novels are emotionally deadened, as she was. It is difficult for some people to respond emotionally to the fiction of Virginia Woolf. This, in my view, is not due to the effects of Woolf's manic-depressive condition. It is, instead, due to the nature of her childhood trauma. She had emotionally benumbed herself. She dissociated and derealized. And her stories, therefore, suffer from psychic numbing and dissociation, too.

Traumatic dreams are contagious, not only in literature but in life. Leslie Grigson's little sister Marjorie, in fact, reported her first dream at age three —and it was a vicarious "caught" nightmare. Marjorie Grigson, upset by stories of her older, kidnapped sister's ordeal in the "hole," awoke screaming one night. It was difficult—no, well-nigh impossible—to console this toddler. "I in a 'hole.' In a 'hole,' " she finally was able to say.

Not every repetitive dream is contagious or post-traumatic. Two "common theme" dreams bother almost every child, whether or not the child was ever traumatized. Dreams of falling happen to almost everybody. So do dreams of being chased by huge animals. Carl Sagan points out that these common-theme dreams reflect the menaces common to ancient man —falling out of trees during sleep, for instance, or being chased by wild animals. Such dreams, if Sagan is right, would have to be transmitted into new generations of children by genetic "memory." And, as yet, I don't think anyone has proved *that*. But perhaps these dreams reflect everyone's deepest fears during infancy. Almost every infant is instinctively afraid of falling and of looming objects.

Sometimes a traumatic dream will incorporate one of these common-theme dream "plots." But if the dream is post-traumatic, it will end differently. A kid from Chowchilla, for instance, dreamed he was falling. But he landed—plop—dead—at the end. A dog-bite victim dreamed she was being chased down the street by an already dead animal. But he caught her and killed her before she was able to wake up.

By the way, Tina Curle Goldstein, who dreamed of a German plane crashing into Uncle Rafe's garden, belongs on her maternal side to the family of Virginia Woolf. "Everybody in my family knows," Tina says, "that the Duckworth boys used to abuse Virginia. It's been the talk of the family for years."

PART III

The Behaviors of Childhood Psychic Trauma

CHAPTER 12

Post-traumatic Play

The cars are going on the people. [She zooms the hoods of two racing cars toward some finger puppets.] They're pointing their pointy parts onto the people. The people are scared. A pointy part will come on their tummies, in their mouths, and on their—[she points to her skirt]. My tummy hurts. I don't want to play anymore.

Lauren Philpot, age three and one half

M Y CONSULTING ROOM SITS on the twenty-fifth floor of the largest medical office building in the world. The building, along with a few bigger, newer ones, overlooks Union Square, the heart of San Francisco. But our suite—I share it with my husband, who is an allergist —sits high on the opposite side of the building. From its oversized windows my office takes in the Bay, Telegraph Hill, the downtown waterfront, and Alcatraz. As a matter of fact, if you wanted to spy twenty-four hours a day from my office, you could count every military vessel stationed from Alameda to Mare Island to the Oakland Naval Yard, every vessel, that is, that moves through the narrows of the Golden Gate.

Ada Louise Huxtable, the *New York Times* architecture critic, once wrote that our medical building, "The 450 Sutter Building," is a Mayan Art Deco "classic." The exterior of the building and its two-story ground-floor lobby are loaded with ornate, 1930s Mayan motifs. Fierce-looking Mayan monsters climb the corners of the place and come inside to menace those who wait in the lobby to ride the elevators upstairs to their doctors' offices. But nobody seems to complain, not even the children who visit the building. The monsters are so Art Deco that they have lost the ability to inspire much terror. Beyond the lobby, the Mayans cease to inspire anything whatsoever except for a gloomy conference room on the third floor called "The Mayan Room."

Some doctors and dentists who work at 450 Sutter have stamped personal imprimatures to their suites. A few have set up English, club-like places complete with dark walls, hunting prints, and antiques. A few have created something grass-clothy and very "fifties." One or two are working amid the new, hi-tech Milanese styles. And a number prefer pure "California ranch" all the way. The majority of medical offices, however, are undone, though clean, hodgepodges of examining tables, X-ray viewing boxes, file cabinets, and loose charts—huge pilings of equipment and records with little space for the poor patients who, over the years, have nicknamed our building "450 Suffer."

None of the doctors and dentists on the twenty-fifth floor pipe canned music into their offices, thank heaven. They used to play a steady stream of the stuff on the office elevators, but luckily the electrical connections must have shorted-out. Or else somebody complained. (George Szell, the late conductor of the Cleveland Symphony, once said that the most painful part of going to the dentist was the Muzak.) So after a crowded, slow, but mercifully unmusical ride up to the twenty-fifth floor, you amble all the way down a medical-looking corridor, and at the end, you find our suite.

The place is bright and kind of eclectic. The walls are painted white, and in San Francisco white manages to stay white for quite a while. Ab and I share the waiting room. We sometimes find the children from both practices crayoning together at a low, glass-topped table for which I needle-pointed a top long ago that shows Donald Duck, Daisy Duck, Huey, Dewey, and Louie strutting their stuff. My consulting room is white with various blues on the windows, chairs, and couch. The couch is strictly for sitting, not for lying and free associating—that is, unless you're tired enough to curl-up fully into its short, two-seated frame. On one wall sits a unit of teak shelves and cabinets, crammed with books, pottery, prints, sculpture, and more books. There is a little built-in desk for kids, and some closed cupboards down below. With an easy sideways swipe, the closed cupboard doors shove aside and, "Presto," the toys appear. Toys, you see, are the stethoscopes and the "pills" of child psychiatric practice.

Child psychiatrists use fairly standardized toys. Almost everybody has a doll family. I have a little rubber one with a china dog and cat. I've found a grandma and grandpa finger puppet, so we can get three generations into the same game. There are also a few aunts and uncles, or cousins, or friends, if you would prefer. And some *Star Wars* characters. As it turns out, the puppets and the dolls in my office can be anything a child wants them to be.

Almost everybody in child psychiatry keeps a doll house. Mine is a two-room wooden model I found in Italy. It folds into a neat little box. Almost everybody has some blocks. Mine are clear and brightly colored plastic.

And almost everyone has a car or two. I keep fifty miniature cars inside of a snap-top box. A fold-up roadway inside of the little built-in desk serves as a course for the cars to race on. When they snap open the box of cars, kids "go crazy" over the collection neatly laid out on the trays inside— they're so bright, shiny, and "cool" looking. I like them, too. But I don't play with my cars when the kids are not there. Honest. Watching them, commenting upon them, sharing them with my small patients—that's enough.

There are a few toys in my office of which, I think, some other child psychiatrists might not approve. I have a miniature army of men, tanks, jeeps, and cannons, for instance. The guns can fire matchsticks several feet across the room. I figure that an aggressive, stormy child or even a chronically inhibited one could better work things out with an army inside of my office than out on the streets or in the schoolyard. This means providing military toys despite my very real concerns about war. On the other hand, a number of child psychiatrists have recently bought anatomically correct dolls for their offices, and I have not done so. I've explained why already —they're just too suggestive. I also don't keep clay in my office, although a number of my colleagues do. A replaced rug made me feel sorry about my original intention to set up the "compleat" child-psychiatric office. I decided to make do with basins of water, needleless syringes, and lots of paper towels for those youngsters who must, as part of their treatment, make a mess.

On my own desk across from the wall of shelves, I keep a collection that proclaims my psychiatric practice as one for the not-too-disordered, or as Mel Brooks puts it in his film *High Anxiety,* for the "very, very, very nervous." I keep an assortment of rocks, shells, fossils, and small boxes that would sorely tempt the psychotic child, that is, if I routinely saw such children. Most of my desk-top treasures are found, not bought. For instance, a rhomboidal piece of marble came from a hike that Ab and I took along the roadbed between Eze and Monaco. An eleven-year-old boy brought me an arrowhead—a very crude one—from a Santo Domingo beach. A girl, who long ago must have passed elegantly into womanhood, brought in a translucent chunk of something shot full with sand and chalk. She had picked it up on Treasure Island, and we never could figure what it was—glass or quartz. Nor can any kid who has inspected it since.

When a child really wants to play something imaginative in my office, I've noticed, the youngster may ignore those sliding teak doors on the cupboards in the wall unit behind my desk and take up my rocks, shells, and boxes instead. "It's a child," says four-year-old Helen Symes, pointing to the black, Santo Domingo arrowhead. "They're putting him into a van. Now he's going to a bad place." From the ages of two to three Helen

Symes was taken in a van or a car, we think, to a house in San Francisco where satanic practices were forced upon small groups of preschoolers. "We'll put in more children," she says as she forces several small rocks into an applewood box sitting on my desk. "They're all scared," she says, with a scared look on her face.

Making sure I look down into the box, not up at Helen, I comment blandly, "Scary things seem to happen at that house."

"I don't want to play anymore," the little girl stops everything and begins to rearrange my stones, shells, and boxes. It is still a "dangerous" thing for me to say much about Helen's game. She will give me the "sign" later, perhaps. But I must let her play without intervening for a while. And I must watch her carefully.

I do love my toys. I have two Madame Alexander dolls that are so beautiful they're almost irresistible. But the little girls who like to play with them can play them hard, as far as I'm concerned. It's OK. When a doll is ruined, even a little, I can buy another. So my little friends comb my dolls' hair and take off and put on their dresses, and check their underpants, all in the spirit of good play. I don't think that I could do what I do unless I really liked to play. Inside the child psychiatrist, after all, there must be a child.

I discovered "post-traumatic play" for the first time at Chowchilla. I "saw it" in the very first child I met there, little Leslie Grigson, age seven. After I realized that Leslie's play was different, special—a definable variant of ordinary child's play—I went back into the psychiatric literature searching for something like this play in the old studies. Anna Freud and Dorothy Burlingham, in their *War and Children*, had written of a little London boy, Bertie, a bombing victim, who for months bombed his bed with paper airplanes. But Freud and Burlingham had not defined Bertie's play as special. They did not consider the monotonous nature of Bertie's play a specific residue from the bombing he had experienced. Gaynor Lacey, who, long after the war, studied the child survivors of a terrible mining disaster at Aberfan, Wales, described this unusual kind of child's play, too. But he did not set it apart. As early as 1942, David Levy had described a grimly repetitive type of play in American children who had undergone surgical procedures. But Levy, like the other great figures of his time, did not designate this play as anything specific to trauma.

The everyday play of childhood, however, is free and easy. It is bubbly and light-spirited; whereas the play that follows from trauma is grim and monotonous. A few "games" will evolve in an ordinary child when he needs to master an upcoming step in life, to gratify an inner wish, to deal with an uncomfortable fear, or to cope with the aftereffects of an unpleasant event. The child will move away from himself in ordinary play—he will be a bear, Superman, the doctor. The further the child moves away from himself, the more successful his play will be in helping him to achieve mastery.

If you were a girl and dressed up, for instance, in "wedding dresses" in order to get married at age four, you would only need to do so three, four, or five times. The play marriage would gratify a wish to grow up, a wish to experience grown-up love and to have babies. The play handles worries about how it feels to be in love and to get older. Because marriage is not a serious problem for the ordinary kid at age four, the youngster does not mind changing roles in this kind of play. One day the child may be "minister," marrying another four year old to her baby brother. Another day she may be "bridesmaid" to an entirely imaginary couple. At long last, she may be "Bride." And then it's over. At least, for a while. Or the game may change significantly. For instance, "Bride" can become "Honeymoon" and then convert to "Travel Agency," complete with price lists and bus tickets. The game is flexible, but more important—the game is equipped to master anxiety. It ends when the anxiety ends.

But play does not stop easily when it is traumatically inspired. And it may not change much over time. As opposed to ordinary child's play, post-traumatic play is obsessively repeated. It is grim. Furthermore, it requires a certain set of conditions in order to proceed—a certain place, a certain assortment of dolls, certain playmates, or a certain routine. It may go on for years. It repeats parts of the trauma. It occasionally includes a defense or two or a feeble attempt at a happy ending, but post-traumatic play is able to do very little to relieve anxiety. It can be dangerous, too. The problem is—post-traumatic play may create more terror than was consciously there when the game started. And if it does dissipate some terror, this monotonous play does it so slowly that it might take more than a lifetime before the play would completely dissipate all the anxiety stirred-up by the trauma.

Let us look at an example. Helen Symes, just four years old, was a post-traumatic player who liked a game something akin to "Bride." Like many other youngsters of her age, Helen wanted to be "Bride." But she refused to adjust to others' desires to be "Bride," too. Once, Helen's mother walked into the child's room at an unexpected moment and she found her little girl lying on the floor, spread-eagled, with a sharp toy poised at the opening to her vagina. Helen's two small coplayers were watching her, pop-eyed. Growing-up games for Helen did not mean what growing-up games mean to the ordinary child. Helen Symes had been sexually attacked by adults connected with her nursery school. They had subjected her to satanic rites, to long afternoons of being tied up, spread-eagled, and stuck. Helen had said nothing about these events to any adult who could have helped her. But much later, after an entire schoolful of youngsters began playing the weirdest, the most monotonous kinds of sexual games, a few parents caught on. And a few children, not Helen, began to tell their stories. A few told their dreams.

Pretend is the most dramatic thing in a normal child's repertoire. Pretend functions as a kind of scenario making, an improvisation deeply buried in metaphor. The playing child may never realize that his protagonist is really himself. Lost entirely within the metaphor of play, the ordinary, nontraumatized child will work things out. He does not have to know in his play that he is the hero of his game. As A. A. Milne notes in his poem "Nursery Chairs," little Christopher Robin has no trouble *being* an explorer, a lion, or a captain while he plays on his nursery chairs. The only time Christopher has any trouble playing is when he tries to pretend he is himself, just a little boy.

The Christopher Robin that Milne portrays in his poem has not been traumatized. After experiencing a trauma a child becomes stuck having to play himself in his play. He cannot easily be an explorer, lion, or captain. At bottom, he finds little chance to disguise his trauma with metaphor. The traumatized child, after all, has trouble identifying fully with the villains or the victims who were connected with his trauma. And if he tries to attach metaphor to the real events that happened to him, the camouflage will easily break down, revealing the true traumatic material behind it. The game cannot veer far from the actual situation that inspired it. A three-year-old incest victim, for instance, may disguise her stepfather's penis as the hood of a car. But, within seconds, her metaphor erodes. "I have a tummy ache," the little girl says. Her play must stop. The metaphor is too close to the actual facts. The child cannot move away from her trauma far enough to afford herself the relief she expects from play.

Trauma, in other words, is not particularly translatable to metaphor. It remains literal. A post-traumatic game does not fully satisfy the player. The game becomes grim, monotonous, and overly specific. It is hard to know whether the process of playing post-traumatically is so slow in mastering anxiety that the child would have to play for years before much relief would come—or whether the play actually creates new terror on top of what was there in the first place.

But let's get back to Leslie Grigson and my first "opportunity" to focus on post-traumatic play. Mrs. Grigson had approached me the first day that I came to Chowchilla, December 16, 1976, to say that Leslie and her toddler-aged sister, Margie, were playing a "weird game" on the kitchen table. Mrs. Grigson didn't know what to do about it. Leslie's game had started a month or two after the kidnapping—she called it "Busdriver." In "Busdriver," two chairs were placed by Leslie onto the kitchen table. Leslie and Margie climbed up and took seats four feet above the kitchen floor. Dangerous, yes. Leslie always sat up front, and Margie, her wobbly sister, sat at the back. "I'm worried about the game," Mrs. Grigson said to me at my first Chowchilla parents' meeting. "It looks scary to me. Margie might fall off. She's not all that steady on her feet yet. And the girls keep playing the same thing two, maybe three times a week."

When I met Leslie Grigson for her first interview in January 1977, I asked about her game. But the angelic-looking brunette seemed not to want to say much about it. She treated her game as a secret. "We just go somewhere and I call off stops," she finally, reluctantly said. "Marjorie is the passenger, but I pretend there are other kids too."

"Sounds like the kidnapping," I commented blandly.

"Oh, no. I drive a *safe* bus. No one on my bus ever gets kidnapped," her eyes flashed blue at me.

After a bit of questioning, I was able to get Leslie to reveal the names that she had been calling off from her perch on top of the kitchen table. They belonged to the kidnapped children of Chowchilla. Leslie's "pretend" was literal, in other words. It was not metaphoric. All that Leslie was doing in her so-called "pretend" was trying to "undo" a real experience.

I interpreted the game to Leslie and told Mrs. Grigson how to explain its meaning the next time she saw Leslie playing. Mrs. Grigson made a couple of attempts to do this. But both of us ran up against the same resistance. Clear as Leslie's play seemed to us, the child could not see how her "Busdriver" game related in any way to her school-bus kidnapping. Nor could she "hear" about it. By March 1977, we decided to ban "Busdriver" outright. It was simply too dangerous a game.

Looking across an entire group helped me realize that monotonous, literal play was rampant at Chowchilla. Amazingly, the children did not realize they were playing out the kidnapping. After that, I asked many questions about play. I learned that about twenty-five children were playing "Kidnap Tag" on the Chowchilla Middle School playground. Only one of the players, Janice Bennett, had been kidnapped. Janice was "It." But two dozen or so interchangeable buddies of Janice's were playing the tagging roles of "kidnappers." They shrieked, squealed, and looked so "weird" that, after about a month of watching it, one of the teachers banished the game. Learning about Janice Bennett's game taught me another important fact about post-traumatic play. It was highly contagious. One did not have to be traumatized to join in.

In 1950, a Frenchman named Boyer wrote a book entitled *Forbidden Games*. Shortly afterward the book became a French film of the same name, directed by René Clément. Boyer must have been watching carefully during those horrible years of World War II. What he fictionalized in his book, and what Clément so graphically showed in his movie, was post-traumatic play. *Forbidden Games* tells the story of a little French refugee girl who is escaping the Germans with her parents. They flee with a long line of French refugees, a line extending out to the horizon. A single plane spots the refugees and strafes their column, fatally wounding the little girl's parents. The group buries its dead at the side of the road. It continues on with its, by now, shocked and devastated little child. The girl breaks away from the column as it reaches a nearby village, and she quickly is taken in by a family there. The family consists of two parents and a boy a bit younger than the little girl.

Now the little girl begins her post-traumatic play. She finds a dead mouse. Placing it in a tiny box, she goes outside to bury it. She finds a dead bug and a spider. Both are buried near the original spot. The play is monotonous and literal. It recreates the roadside burial of the little girl's parents. The little girl discovers that she is having trouble finding enough dead things lying about to bury as many as she wishes. So she begins to kill small animals—say, a bird and a rabbit. She has turned her game to reenacting the killing of her parents as well as their burials.

The boy of the family discovers the refugee child at her play. He joins in. Soon the boy and girl have organized a fairly large graveyard filled with the already dead animals that they have found and the animals that they have killed.

They must have a cross for their cemetery, the little girl now decides. She requests that her younger friend climb to the top of the local church steeple and pry off the cross. He does it. But in so doing, the young boy falls from the church roof to his death. Nobody sees this except for the little girl. After all, forbidden games, post-traumatic child's play, require secrecy.

The next day the search begins. No one can find the little boy. Someone finally notices that the cross has come off the village church steeple. "What is it doing stuck in the ground over there?" "And why is the earth so freshly dug up over here?" Well yes, of course, they find the boy's body buried in the children's secret cemetery. And that is where both book and film end.

Boyer and Clément, French observers of World War II, had put to fictional form a "new" psychiatric phenomenon. The novelist and the film-maker were accurately depicting a secret, dangerous, monotonous, ghoulish, unconsciously connected kind of routine that follows from childhood trauma. These two Frenchmen had it right. Eighteen children of the twenty-five youngsters I interviewed at Chowchilla played post-traumatic games sometime during the five-year period that I studied them. They played "Kidnap Tag," "Busdriver," "Punch-the-Couch," "Closet Jumping," and "Kidnapper," among other things. They wrote kidnapping "books" and made up television scripts. Their play was as contagious as the Plague.

Years ago when I was a house officer in psychiatry at the University of Michigan, there were three "Christs" living fifteen miles away at Ypsilanti State Hospital. We rotated out there as residents. How could a "Christ" get along inside the very same state hospital where two other "Christs" were also living? These men seemed to manage it. In fact, they attended group therapy together for a while. The state hospital grounds, acres and acres, were probably large enough for the three Christs to avoid one another much of the time. And the Christs' fellow patients, six thousand of them, would have allotted a satisfactory number of "believers" for each Christ, that is, if he needed believers. The three Jesuses had different styles. Each "did" Christ his own way.

So it was, too, with the post-traumatic play that I found at Chowchilla. Even though twenty-six children were exposed to the identical events, each of the eighteen youngsters who eventually played post-traumatically enacted the kidnapping in a unique way. What represented the most terrifying nucleus of the incident for one child was a relatively negligible event for the next. Therefore, no two post-traumatic games could be identical, just as no three psychotic Christs could ever play-out the identical role of Jesus. Mental illness and, even more important, personalities are unique. No matter how literal a post-traumatic repetition seems to be, the psyche will enter in and make the repetition special to the individual.

I thought I might present the "The Three Barbies of Chowchilla" in this spirit. Three little girls who endured the identical situation on a school bus felt impelled to play "Barbie." But each child, as she played, expressed her individual anguish, a personal and individual kind of dread. And, thus, each "Barbie" of Chowchilla represented a different aspect of childhood horror. Each "Barbie," as did each "Christ" of Ypsilanti State Hospital, put forward a different face.

First of all, there was Leslie Grigson's Barbie. We know Leslie. She was the kid who played "Busdriver" until Mrs. Grigson and I banned it. Leslie was the first child I saw in 1980 for the follow-up interviews. I asked the eleven year old whether she still was playing "Busdriver." "Oh no," she said. "I don't even think about that game anymore." So our ban had held.

Did Leslie play other kinds of pretend things? "Baseball," she answered, "stuff like that." Then she thought for a moment. "And, I guess, I do my Barbies sometimes."

"What do your Barbies do?" I asked, passing over baseball as too standardized a game for much improvisation.

"Nothing."

"No. Really. I'm interested in your Barbies," I urged Leslie on.

"They don't do anything. They just go somewhere. Then they come back." The girl shrugged her shoulders nonchalantly.

"Try to explain it, Leslie," I requested, probably with an edge to my voice. The girl was evading me. Her game sounded secret.

"I put my Barbies into a Barbie mobile home that I have at home. I load up all her clothes, her accessories, and all that stuff into the trailer. Then I have Barbie go someplace. Then she comes back. That's all!"

"You mean," I asked, "that Barbie doesn't do anything once she gets to the place where she is going?"

"No. She doesn't *have* to do anything. The whole idea is getting her there. Then back. That's the whole thing. That's all."

Leslie Grigson had gone on playing "Busdriver," alright. She had never stopped. The only difference between her "Busdriver" game of 1976–1977 and her "Traveling Barbies" of 1979–1980 was that Leslie's new game was played in miniaturized form, and thus, it was far safer. No big chairs had to perch on top of kitchen tables with wobbly, live toddlers in them. Now we were simply dealing with plastic, with Barbie, with America's sweetheart. But Leslie's two games were thematically identical. Somebody was taken away on a bus, a mobile home, or a what-have-you. Then, that somebody was returned safely. It always ended safely. But the safe ending didn't solve anything much for Leslie Grigson. The game required another repetition, and another, and yet another, because the real story conjured up too much horror to be released. The Chowchilla bus ride of July 15, 1976, had been unsafe, unsafe, unsafe. And dark-haired, blue-eyed Leslie Grigson knew that for a fact.

The second variation on a "Barbie" theme was played out in 1977 by little Mary Vane. Mary was about to enter kindergarten when she was kidnapped. For Mary, being buried alive in a "hole" was the ultimate horror. Mary Vane thought during her burial that she would never see Mommy again. She had trouble breathing. Thoughts of strangling and of abandonment devastated the small child. Mary's post-traumatic play centered upon her burial in the "hole." She used her Barbie to act it out. Mary confided to me with a hand cupped over my ear, "There is a cement place at my grandma's which is like a hole. I put clothes in it and my Barbie dolls. I pretend they're stuck in there."

Mary Vane, at age five, was burying her Barbies. Alive. Yet she was entirely unable to see any relationship between "Burying Barbie" and her own feeling of suffocation in the "hole." The longer I tried to help Mary see this relationship, the less she was willing to admit that she had ever played "Burying Barbies." By the time I met Mary again at the age of nine, however, she was almost addicted to suffocating her dolls—that is, when she wasn't playing a dangerous variant of "Kidnap Tag" with her kidnapped sister and their cousin, Ryan. Mary had moved in 1978 to Kansas and then had moved back to California. Obviously, Grandma's cement hole would not have stayed functional for "Burying Barbies" once Mary moved out of town. But this deterrent to a perfect, literal repetition had not stopped young Mary Vane. "Barbie strangles a lot in the back seat of my car now," the nine year old told me. "She dies a lot. I wish this didn't have to happen to Barbie, but it does." Mary's play was a little too close to René Clément's *Forbidden Games* for comfort. I, too, wished that Mary's Barbie did not have to die. I hoped Mary's family would get her some psychiatric treatment. But, despite my repeated recommendations to them, Mary's parents continued to believe that the child would "grow out of it."

The third Barbie that I heard about in the aftermath of the Chowchilla kidnapping was a Barbie who "lived" in Visalia, California. She belonged to Sandra Sturgis, age twelve. What had bothered young Sandra Sturgis most during her kidnapping four years previously was the unspeakable filth and the loss of dignity that had gone with the experience. Sandra recalled a horrible sense of disgust because somebody's sweat had run down her arm. During the eleven-hour van ride, she had felt somebody else's urine trickling down her leg. When Sandra Sturgis finally did have the chance to go to the bathroom in the "hole," the fastidious child would not, could not let go. "It smelt too bad in there," she said.

Sandra Sturgis returned home in July 1976 from her two traumatic days away, wanting "more than anything else to take a bath. . . . That's all she wanted," said her father, Paul Sturgis. "She's never gone to a bathroom in a gas station since," Wilma Sturgis added. "She says they all smell too bad." For the several months that followed the kidnapping, Sandra Sturgis took two baths a day. The child admitted she had rarely felt "clean." Even after she moved to Visalia, Sandra Sturgis bathed far too much. But Paul and Wilma Sturgis thought they understood. Sandra had always been a neat girl, a clean girl, a well-organized girl. She was just a bit "more so" now. I understood it a different way, however: Sandra was compulsively acting upon an ugly sense of dirtiness and shame stimulated by the kidnapping. She had been a symptom-free, but obsessive-compulsive, child to start with. She was obsessively-compulsively symptomatic now. She felt dirty.

I asked Sandra what, if anything, she had been pretending over the past four years. "I play something called 'Barbie at the Spa,' " she told me. She said it quietly, so quietly that her parents, hovering nearby, may not have heard her. "I wash my Barbies at the 'spa.' I play almost every day. Sometimes I play two or three times in a day." "Are your Barbies OK after all that washing?" "I had to throw one Barbie out. She was ruined," whispered Sandra.

"Barbie at the Spa" was Sandra's secret. A dirty secret, I think. Sandra's preexisting psychology, her perfectionism, and cleanliness, had shaped the unique nature of her own post-traumatic experience. And Sandra's experience had shaped her play. Sandra's "Barbie" game was unique to Sandra. Barbie was being scrubbed to death.

Does playing post-traumatic games make a kid more creative? It may. Nobody knows this for sure. Nothing has been proven. One thing trauma does do, however, is to extend the number of years that a child has for playing. Whereas the ordinary, untraumatized child probably plays "pretend" from about age two and one-half until twelve, the traumatized child may play "pretend" over a longer time. For instance, two little babies, a boy and a girl, traumatized at ages seven months and fifteen months, respectively, *played*. They indulged in a "game" together at an age where mutual play would not have been expected for a couple more years. These two babies had been satanic cult victims. A babysitter had written a confession to the infants' mothers. Both infants, it seems, had been squatted upon, urinated upon, and defecated upon by adults with whom the babysitter had joined in satanic rites. Sasha's penis had been cut with a ritual knife. I saw the cut. It was straight and clean.

How did these two infants play out their trauma? Kathryn, the fifteen month old, took to sitting on Sasha's head at home whenever she had the chance. She sat on his head again and again. And the little infant boy let her do so. Silently. Without protest. Is that play? I don't know what to call it. Is it creative? Not particularly. But the activity had begun at an extraordinarily early age for shared activity. And it was compulsively repeated—ritualistic in nature, almost. I guess one would have to consider it post-traumatic behavioral repetition of some sort. Probably "play."

Traumatized children seem to be granted more room in their lives for "pretend" than are ordinary children. And their play may be so important to them that these youngsters turn away from the lures of the television set and electronic gear in order to pretend. The post-traumatic "game," therefore, may actually expand a child's creative experience. And in this sense, trauma may promote a greater amount of artistic endeavor than does plain, ordinary child life.

Most post-traumatic play, however, is barely creative. And the themes remain quite narrow. Only geniuses seem able to make something of this kind of narrow repetition. The themes of trauma—man's helplessness, the world's randomness, and ugly, unexpected death—are difficult ones for a person to express in art.

Bob Barklay of Chowchilla played a particularly boring, repetitive game. The children's "hero" took to "digging." "Every night Bob [age fifteen] takes the cushions off the couch," Mrs. Barklay said a year after the kidnapping, "and he punches the cushions until he's worn out. We have barbells, but he wasn't using them. It was superaggressive, and Bob looked very intense. He pounded the cushions so hard that he tripped the circuit breakers on the other side. I feel better with him gone for the summer." Bob's "game," in other words, had lasted two hours a night for two weeks. It occurred just before the kidnapping's first anniversary came up on the calendar, and it ended because Mrs. Barklay took away Bob's opportunity by sending him off to relatives in Wyoming. The boy's play had been mindless, boring, and dull. It may have looked dangerous, too—although tripping the circuit breakers in a house trailer probably does no harm. The boy's digging, something that had truly been heroic for the group-at-large, had been traumatic for the boy himself. Bob needed to repeat this aspect of his trauma—again, again, and again.

Post-traumatic play is so literal that if you spot it, you may be able to guess the trauma with few other clues. In other words, by hearing about the play and by knowing little else about the child, you can postulate a certain traumatic event.

Jack Fountain, fourteen, for instance, was a cheerful, powerfully built high school football player in the McFarland High School control group. Jack told me that he had played the same game for two years between the ages of ten and twelve. "I built houses of cards all the time and then I let them fall. That was my main game for about two years." One could postulate from Jack's play that either he had fallen or something had fallen on him. Two years of "houses of cards" with the object of watching them fall sounded unusual and post-traumatic.

Had Jack Fountain fallen himself? He said he felt afraid of earthquakes. When I asked him to guess about the future of the world, Jack said, "an earthquake may happen. I'm scared of those. Something will fall on me. And I don't know what my chances would be." One could now guess that, rather than falling himself, Jack Fountain had experienced something falling *on* him.

Did Jack have repeated dreams? "Yes," the boy said. "I had one dream over and over, but I forget it." The fact of the repeated dream confirmed psychic trauma in Jack, although at this point no substantial clues had emerged from the dream content. Did Jack ever do anything strange that he couldn't understand? I was looking here for behavioral reenactment, the subject of the chapter to follow. "Yes," said Jack. "Sometimes I yell when I'm not mad. I've done it a lot. . . . I'm not good at telling this but I'm also afraid of strange noises in the dark. Somebody banged on my wall at night when I was twelve. Just once. My brother didn't believe me. But I was sooooooooo scared."

Jack Fountain, by his various statements about his behaviors and fears, was confirming that something heavy had indeed fallen on him. His repeated play, watching houses of cards fall, his fears of earthquakes, his panic at a sudden noise in the dark, and his habit of yelling over nothing pointed to this particular kind of event. Had something cracked into this young football player's head—making a deafening sound, causing him to scream out, and making everything go dark? Jack Fountain finally told his story when I asked the last question of the control interview, "Did anything terrible ever happen to you?"

"I got my head cracked open," he said. "It was in third grade. My dad made a ladder. I pulled it, and it fell on me. My skull was fractured. I wasn't unconscious. I was in the hospital two days or so. I was delirious. I had no dreams of it. I was pretty confused. I remember the ladder falling. *That* was scary. I always dream of ladders and boards falling on me. That was the dream I was telling you about that I had at thirteen! That was it!"

Post-traumatic play is probably the best clue one ever gets to the nature of a childhood trauma—that is, if one doesn't get to see the traumatic event itself. This play, when it comes, is absolutely literal. It may reflect a child's compensatory wishes, too. But it will recreate the child's trauma the way a theatrical production recreates a certain mood or a history book recreates a specific happening.

Brent Burns, a four-year-old traumatized youngster who was very large for his age, came closer to putting on a theatrical "play" production for me than has any other child who ever demonstrated his trauma in my office. I wished Brent's post-traumatic play could have been preserved on television or audiotape, but I will try to reproduce it from my notes. Brent, another of the Hillgard day-care pornography "child stars" (I saw six of them eventually), had been three months old when he entered the Hillgard program and twenty-four months old when he left. The reason Mr. and Mrs. Burns pulled young Brent out was that by the time Brent left the Hillgard home, he had lost his speech. He stayed mute for a few more months, it turned out. The Burnses learned two and a half years after removing Brent from the Hillgards' care that Brent was sexually molested there. No photographs of Brent had remained in Leroy Hillgard's files, but several other abused children, whose photographs were there, could remember a boy named Brent who had danced and posed naked along with them. Brent's loss of speech confirmed, in retrospect, that something awful had happened to him. But would his play show anything two years later?

As might have been guessed from Brent's silence between the ages of eighteen months and two years, the four-year-old Brent did not want to talk much during his first two psychiatric sessions. He hinted that he would play later, so I invited him to come back a third time. Brent Burns came through this third time, as he had promised.

He ambled in, slid open the sliding cupboard doors on the opposite side of the room from my desk, and pulled out every one of those beautiful, shiny, miniature cars I keep in the snap-top box.

"They're going to the hotel," he said of the "guys" in the cars. "They like it. They're going in. They like the doors and the movies."

"They get to watch movies?" I asked, purposely taking the opposite tack from Brent's very likely traumatic exposure.

"No, stupid," Brent corrected me. "They *make* movies. A man, the person who does the movies—he is going to take the children's pictures. I don't know what they do. They take pictures with their clothes off. They like to."

One might have thought—from how verbal this play "production" had quickly become—that Brent Burns could remember his terrible experiences at the Hillgards' day-care home in words. After all, here he was saying that there was a hotel where people made pornographic movies of children. Regardless of his talk, however, Brent Burns remembered nothing of his experience. He had answered "No" when I asked him if anything terrible had ever happened to him.

"The children fight and play around," he went on with my cars. "They sometimes take their pictures, too, without clothes. [We now knew for sure that it had been children who were being exhibited naked, not just adults.] They like each other. The grown-ups at the hotel are Gumdrop Mommy and Gumdrop Daddy. [Interestingly, Brent accurately remembered here an aspect of Mary Beth and Leroy Hillgards' life-style. They were well-known for keeping gumdrops about the house.] I don't know the children's names. But they all have gumdrops."

Wondering if Brent remembered anything about other babysitters and day-care programs he had experienced, I asked if he could recall any people like "Gumdrop Mommy" and "Gumdrop Daddy.' "I can't remember," Brent said. I asked him if he knew the name of his current babysitter. He knew it. I then asked if he could go backward from there. Brent stopped at age three. His pale eyes went blank. He could remember no further back.

"They're still making movies," the boy plunged back into his play. He took up a car carrier and loaded it with tiny automobiles. "The children are still at the hotel. They're not tired of it. They're all naked. Gumdrop Grandma and Gumdrop Grandpa are taking their pictures." [Brent had now put the correct ages to Leroy and Mary Beth Hillgard.]

"Are we playing about *your* Grandma and Grandpa, Brent?" I asked. I would rather suggest opposites to a child than oversuggest.

"I have a Grandma and Grandpa," Brent replied. "They live by Jimmy. But they don't take my picture naked."

The four year old began to look aroused. Something was sexually exciting him. He flushed pink and breathed in short, quick heaves. Brent's play was probably coming very close to what had actually happened. The boy had switched to first-person singular without even seeming to notice. "They don't take *my* picture naked," he had said. Back to his play, Brent blurted out, "They're doing this! Pictures! They get excited! [There was a high likelihood that Brent's penis was now erect beneath the corduroy trousers] There. [He sighed a long sigh.] Their penis unties—looses off—it comes off their bodies. [This was a toddler's eye view of erection and detumescence, a point of view first established for him under sexually traumatic circumstances. Before Brent had reached the age of two, he had concluded that you could lose your penis following high excitement. The boy turned to a fuscia-colored sports car and lifted up the hood.] This thing on your car goes up and down. See. [Brent was practicing at erection and detumescence. This time he was using the metaphor of an automobile hood.] See. [He demonstrated the up and down action.] When the children stop playing, fussing, and taking pictures, their penis gets very softer. When does this part of your sports car come all the way off?"

In this boy's mind, any excitement as high as what he had experienced at the Hillgards' hands was punishable by castration. Brent commented, "They go looking around the hotel for the guy's penis."

Brent Burns appeared ready now to finish his "theater" of the day. I noted by my clock that it was indeed time to stop. I would be able to reconstruct what young Brent must have experienced at the Hillgard Day Care Center, and I would be able to testify for the boy in court. In my view, no child could make up a game like this who had not gone through the literal horrors that the game represented. Brent Burns's play was specific to his own experience. There wasn't much "fun" to it—very, very few of the champagne bubbles that one sniffs around the play of a nontraumatized child. There was excitement in Brent Burns's play, yes. But this excitement was laced with terror. It was not "fun" to think that penises come off and get lost.

Once in a while, a young child does become sexually aroused in my blue and white office above the Bay. When a child becomes aroused, the child comes close to losing all control. He or she spirals quickly toward wildness, screaming, and hysteria. The stomach or the head hurts. It is not a pleasant thing to watch. While Brent Burns was aroused, he babbled about genital loss and the loss of control. This loss of control had originally frightened Brent into becoming mute before the age of two. Loss of control was now impelling Brent to play "Hotel." As he put all my little cars back into their places in the snap-top box, Brent Burns made an offhand comment to me. "You know," he said, "that guy on the truck is real quiet now that he has played."

The big lad silently snapped on the lid to the snap-top box and put it back onto my shelf. "He has stopped talking," he mumbled, still responding to his imaginary "naked guy on the truck." Brent silently slipped out of my blue and white office into the arms of his waiting mother. He had recreated not only his trauma, but the speechless state that had followed.

Early in 1987 I saw Rob Reiner's film *Stand By Me*. What showed first and most obviously about this film was its passage-into-adolescence theme. The movie is a very American, very charming, and very accurate portrayal of what it means to be a twelve-year-old boy at the brink of manhood. The moviegoer sees and enjoys four boys' overblown sense of "macho," their need to break off babyish ties with family, their intense concern about their own genital apparatus, their deep distrust of all adults, and their dawning realization of abstractions such as "intimacy" and "hypocrisy." The prepubertal dialogue in the film is striking. Although I am "a girl" and never heard any of my twelve-year-old friends term one another "wet ends" or throw out invective such as "suck my fat one," the preadolescent in me still understands. The children of *Stand By Me* are speaking the language of American childhood.

This passage-into-adolescence theme may be what you, as a reader, wish to think about when a film, as accurately evocative of preadolescent childhood as this one is, comes along. However, there was something else in *Stand By Me* to which I will devote the conclusion of this chapter—and that is its mood of terror. Terror strikes the viewer of this film, I think, from the very beginning. A full grown man sits in a pickup truck reading his newspaper. His best friend from childhood, Chris Chambers, has been killed trying to break up a knife fight in a fast-food restaurant. How suddently, how unexpectedly, does a life end. How horrifying.

But we have little time to reflect. We immediately meet the four boys from the truck-owner's past. First, there is Teddy Duchamp, whose psychotic father, a war veteran, has burned up the boy's ear and rendered Teddy partially deaf. Teddy is an abused child. A second boy, Vern Tessio, turns out to be fat, a little stupid, money obsessed, and besieged at home by a frighteningly delinquent older brother. The third boy, the leader of the small gang, Chris Chambers, the dead-man-to-be as we already know, has a dad who drinks himself stuporous but often comes home invigorated enough to beat the boy silly. And fourth, we meet Gordon Lachance, an author-to-be, the narrator. Gordon, too, it seems is living a nightmare. His older brother, Dennis, has been killed a few months ago in an auto accident. Gordon is the "invisible man" at home. His parents are the benumbed survivors of a personal disaster. The young lads we have met, therefore, are four extremely stressed youngsters—two sure-fire psychic trauma victims and two youngsters suffering the possible effects of horrible, ongoing, external events. Although we already know that in my small-town control study of twenty-five ordinary young kids, I found ten psychically traumatized or severely frightened youngsters, even I felt surprised to count four of four in this movie. This, indeed, was a horrifying number. The film would be no ordinary "passage into adolescence," I began to feel.

One settles into the movie, however, and begins feeling the plain, ordinary feelings of a journey into adolescence when—close to the middle—a scene develops that is so scary, so monstrous, so unexpected, that it reproduces the feeling of childhood trauma right then and there. I remember saying to myself during this scene, "Whoever wrote this movie is playing post-traumatic games with me." My mind suddenly found channels other than the movie with which to occupy itself. I found myself entering into an old game I occasionally play by myself—one might call it a variant of "Detective."

"The writer of this film," I said to myself, "obviously is a man because boy life is so accurately portrayed. He has been writing most of his life because the boy in this film is actively writing at age twelve and he already knows that he *will* be a writer. The author actually saw a dead, mutilated child in his own childhood. I believe that this must have occurred in reality because the writer has set up such a strange goal for this journey-into-adolescence trek along the tracks—the goal of finding and viewing a dead, mutilated boy. And the author of this story has been traumatized by a train. It happened when he was young—some time in the 1950s because this is the era so carefully portrayed on film, complete with striped, collared shirts, early rock tunes, hot-rod cars, and several presently extinct species of comic book. Brilliant," I said to myself, "but is this true? I'll look it up tomorrow."

We stayed on for the credits. The writer of the novella from which *Stand By Me* was taken, a story called "The Body" (in *Different Seasons*), is Stephen King. Stephen King is the most widely read, widely watched, widely interviewed, and widely followed writer of horror fiction alive today. By sensing the terror in *Stand By Me*, I had run into the master of terror himself.

The next day I visited my favorite bookstore and checked out Stephen King. It took only one look to determine that my playful "Detective," often wrong by the way, had been quite right the night before. I found the following autobiographical quote in King's own nonfiction account of the recent history of horror writing, *Danse Macabre*, and I later found a duplicate in Douglas Winter's book on Stephen King. I have added a small point about the loss of bladder control that I found later—from *Bare Bones*, Underwood and Miller's collection of Stephen King interviews:

> The event occurred when I was barely four, so perhaps I can be excused for remembering [my mother's] story of it but not the actual event.
>
> According to Mom, I had gone off to play at a neighbor's house—a house that was near a railroad line. About an hour after I left I came back (she said), as white as a ghost. I would not speak for the rest of that day; I would not tell her why I'd not waited to be picked up or phoned that I wanted to come home; I would not tell her why my chum's mom hadn't walked me back but had allowed me to come alone. [In a 1983 interview, King says, "I peed in my pants" before coming home that day.]
>
> It turned out that the kid I had been playing with had been run over by a freight train while playing on or crossing the tracks (years later, my mother told me that they had picked up the pieces in a wicker basket). My Mom never knew if I had been near him when it happened, or if it had occurred before I even arrived, or if I had wandered away after it happened. Perhaps she had her own ideas on the subject. But as I've said, I have no memory of the incident at all; only of having been told about it some years after the fact.

Stand By Me apparently was a kind of post-traumatic play from a man who had experienced a trauma at age four. Much more happens in a lifetime than just one trauma. I must caution myself about this point as well as cautioning you. We will only pick up glimmers of an early trauma —not the whole picture—in an author's life and creations. But the literal, specific scene of boys running from a train had indeed been what I thought it was—an example of post-traumatic play from the writer, Stephen King.

Despite his penchant for granting interviews, making appearances at horror and supernatural conferences, and writing short, semisarcastic autobiographical sketches, Stepken King appears to be a private kind of person. He lives in Bangor, Maine, with his wife, Tabitha, and three kids, behind a gate that features two huge bats on gateposts that loom over a spider web entrance. We have been given the skeleton of King's life but not the fleshed-out version. His dad left one ordinary day when King was two.

The elder Mr. King said he was going out to buy cigarettes and he never returned. Stephen King has no idea today if his father is alive or dead. He never supported the family. There was no contact after age two except for Stephen's discovery at around age twelve of a pile of science-fiction paperbacks that his dad had left in Aunt Ethelyn's attic. This, of course, must in part have settled young King into the choice of writing as a career and even helped to set his course toward fantasy fiction. But Stephen King was actually writing horror stories from the time that he was seven years old. His first work was a tale of a run-amok dinosaur that eventually turned tail after a whiff of some belts and boots. You see, old dinosaurs were"allergic" to leather, according to the seven-year-old Stephen.

Stephen King's mother is consistently praised by the author as a woman who worked herself to the raw skin at menial jobs in order to support Stephen and his adopted brother, David, who was two years older. Any possible criticism of King's mother is only implied, not stated by King. The trio, mother and two boys, drifted from place to place in New England and the Midwest until Stephen reached the age of eleven and the family settled in Durham, Maine, with Mrs. King's aging parents. King's mother was a deeply religious Methodist. She insisted that the family attend church two or three times a week. Stephen's mother used the stories of the Bible to get her points across to her sons. She also confined the boys in an outhouse when they acted up, insisting that they pray while locked inside. Whether King's mother still lives for him as the Bible spouting horror-of-a-mother depicted in *Carrie* is a point only for speculation. King never spoke of any such analogy in print or in interviews. But he does say that you can't beat the Bible as horror literature. And we will see in a moment that he must have been mightily impressed, indeed, by the ancient tales of horror that his mother told him.

It appears to me, although we know only the barebone outlines of Stephen King's life, that the train trauma and the loss of his father are probably the two major external forces behind the character of the writer. Stephen suffered the fearful symptoms of psychic trauma as a child—bugs, monsters, fires, explosions, storms, and the dark terrified him—and he is still a fearful man—bugs, elevators, planes ("I hate surrendering control of my life," he says), the dark, and choking (his mother died of cancer and that night, "practically the same minute actually [my] son had a terrible choking fit in bed at home") *still* terrify him. As a boy, Stephen King was a semiloner, fat, unathletic, unhappy, and fascinated with the supernatural. He collected a secret scrapbook on the exploits of the mass murderer Charles Starkweather. The Holocaust occupied his mind, too.

Stephen King may have repeatedly played something analogous to "trains" post-traumatically during his latency years. He says that he liked to play a game by himself about Sodom and Gomorrah, ever-mindful of how Lot's wife had turned back to look at the twin cities and turned to salt. "I used to pretend," he says, "I was one of these guys running away [from Sodom and Gomorrah] and could hear the city burning behind me and the screams from the bolts of fire coming down from heaven—I could feel my head go 'Boooooom!' Scared the shit out of me." This sounds very much like the type of activity one might expect from a child who, spending some time with a chum at a railway track, ran away from a quickly advancing train, not looking back until it was too late. "Boooooom!" King's stated response to his own game—feeling more scared than he felt before starting to play—is typical of what happens to children who play post-traumatically. We have already seen that post-traumatic play does little to relieve the kind of anxiety stirred up by trauma.

As a boy, King began writing because he needed to. His stories flowed at their best when, he says, they were "unconsciously" done. Stephen King consistently wrote of horror and the supernatural. A sufferer—always— of terrible dreams and insomnia, he conveyed his nightmares to people through his writing. And as his writing became more adept, King was able to substitute writing for that old, monstrous Sodom and Gomorrah game that he had played. King's writing, in and of itself, became his post-trau- matic play. As a character says in his novel *It*, "He sold nightmares to others—that was his trade." King, like other childhood trauma victims, has never seemed to believe in his own personal future. Convinced until age twenty that "I'd never live to reach twenty," he now frets that one of his children will die in childhood. As for his own future, he says, "I go day by day." His life goal is "to try and stay alive," or, put in King's more strident, metaphoric tone, "we know that sooner or later we're all going to be eating worms, whether its fifty years or sixty. It might be tomorrow. It might happen today."

Stephen King had a second chance to write a new, phony autobiography when, between 1977 and 1982, as a successful novelist, he wrote a series of novels under the pseudonym Richard Bachman. (King needed to write the books under the phony name because he tended to write more than his publishers would allow him to publish.) The Bachman "biography," like much of King's other writings, turned out to be playfully post-traumatic. Bachman was supposedly an isolate living alone with his wife on a New Hampshire farm. He had spent several years at sea before settling down, similar to what King's mother had told him of his father, a man who supposedly had wandered about the world having love affairs and adopt- ing various aliases—Spansky, Pollock, and finally King. Richard Bachman, the pseudowriter, had had a brain tumor removed successfully with very delicate surgery. That sounds traumatic. But he had also experienced a permanent, absolutely uncorrectable disaster. Bachman's only child, a son, crashed through a closed well cover, fell in, and drowned. So Richard Bachman, Stephen King's phony self, also suffered from psychic trauma.

King majored in English at the University of Maine, where he met and married his wife. He says that he used several kinds of abusive substances during his college years. He drank and still drinks prodigious amounts of beer ("Two quarts a day," he has said). He popped and still pops dozens of headache pills. (Do you recall that his head would go "Boooooom!" in his Sodom and Gomorrah game? There is a good chance that the headache started with the train trauma. In other words, the headaches may have been a kind of psychophysiologic reenactment.) King has told an interviewer that he took about sixty psychedelic "trips" in college. But he says he uses no street drugs now and he has had no bad trips or lasting residuals from his old forays into psychedelics. One might speculate that all that drug use in college was King's way to reestablish control over the previously uncontrollable. In small doses.

King taught high school in Maine for a short while in order to support his young family after he graduated from college. By his mid-twenties, *Carrie*, his first novel, was doing well and had been sold as a movie. His success from that time on was a matter of spiraling fame and fortune.

From this brief summary, I think it is likely that Stephen King still suffers from the effects of a traumatic event in his childhood. He says he experiences nightmares, fears, headaches, and insomnia. He demonstrates a sense of futurelessness. He appears to employ very active denial. But King has never seen a psychiatrist or a psychoanalyst, as far as I can tell. He has stated that he is afraid psychoanalysis kills creativity. He uses Ray Bradbury as one example of an author whose writing was better when he was "totally-apparently-fucked up" than it has been since he was treated and became, according to King, "very boring." King says he cannot remember his trauma from about age four. But, as we have already seen in this book, that age is slightly old for total amnesia on the basis of developmental immaturity. King's characters in fiction have slippable, "on again, off again" amnesias, by the way. We can see examples of this in *It* and *Pet Sematary*. One wonders if this partial memory of King's fictional protagonists is closer to the author's actual life experience than is his autobiographical claim to total amnesia. Stephen King says he believes he could write, if he wanted, nonhorror fiction. But he does not. And he has not. His writing is devoted to one emotion—terror. And it is this narrowing of theme that helps to define his art as a traumatic product.

Now that we have come to an end of this very brief look at Stephen King's life, I wish to point out one additional post-traumatic and semiautobiographical note from the movie *Stand By Me*, the film that first set me onto King. Did the young King actually view the body in the basket that day at the railroad tracks, or did he see it solely in his mind's eye? I would guess the latter from King's latency-age Sodom and Gomorrah game in which the object was to run away from a cataclysm without looking back. But we cannot tell for sure what of "The Body" the author did or didn't see from his statements or from his film. There is no question, however, that corpses preoccupy King, and that the idea or the actual viewing of that four-year-old body bothered him indeed. In his novella "The Body," from which Rob Reiner took his movie, King spends several pages describing the dead boy's body, complete with ants, maggots, a beetle, some ugly swellings, some bad smells, and a hail storm to attack the youthful cadaver at the railroad tracks.

Rob Reiner does not go for any "gross outs," on the other hand, in *Stand By Me*. A film director is able to correct for the overly zealous writer who is "playing" with his audience. Reiner showed his "body" in two segments lasting about two seconds each. The director had nothing to prove with his young cadaver. He went for the PG rating, not for the audience's "shit-in-the-pants level." (This, by the way, is not how I talk. It is how Stephen King talks.) No matter how bland and likable Reiner makes it, however, we were seeing in this film Stephen King's four-year-old visualization, his remembered or imagined "body." This visualization, the remnant of King's trauma, still has the power to send a shiver up the collective spine of the audience. Stephen King, it seems, is a post-traumatic player.

But let us consider at this juncture exactly how Stephen King post-traumatically plays with his reader. First, he literally repeats his four-year-old trauma, almost endlessly in fact. He needs to. And we somehow need to watch. He gives us literal trains. And he gives us their analogues— mechanical monsters.

King's trains, for instance, kill the twelve-year-old boy whose remains are the subject of "The Body." They kill Frank Dodd's father in *The Dead Zone*, smashing his body between two flatcars. King's werewolf tears up a train switchman in *The Cycle of the Werewolf*. (In the movie *Silver Bullet*, made from the werewolf stories, the switchman's severed head sits on a train embankment while trains whiz by. The head is a "part," perhaps, later to be brought home in a 1950s wicker basket.) In *Christine*, King uses his train at the opening of a climactic chapter. He quotes from a Mark Dinning rock song, "That fateful night the car was stalled, Upon the railroad track, I pulled you out and you were safe, But you went running back." Here, the writer finds in another person's lyric the perfect complaint of a four-year-old witness to a terrible accident. We can just about picture the four-year-old Stevie complaining to his dead chum that he doesn't understand why the boy stayed on the tracks. Whether or not Stephen

King could verbally remember what had happened, the Mark Dinning song literally tells his tale. Trains whiz by in the night in several King stories. They whistle in the backgrounds. They help to set King's tone of terror.

But King's ancient trains become even more interesting when translated by the writer into their mechanical analogues, devices that can smash or grind up human beings "at will." The more I read the works of Stephen King, in fact, the more I realize that his mechanical monsters are, by far, his most appealing characters. King's machines have more personality than do his humans. They have malicious souls—gamey, foxy ways about them. They like surprises. And they share few values with humans—they have no morality, no wishes for money or success, no patriotism, no hope. These are *power* machines. And the human beings that they meet look like flies in their paths.

King gives us several killer automobiles (one starts out Bachman's *Thinner*). A murderous taxi-truck collision sets up the plot for *The Dead Zone*. We find an unrelenting, devilish pickup in "Uncle Otto's Truck." But King's machines do not necessarily need legs, wheels, or other propelling mechanisms to do their damage. Toy soldiers wipe out a Mafia killer in "Battleground." Exploding oil tanks blow up much of the civilization that wasn't wiped out already by a plague in *The Stand*. A malicious ironing machine goes after people in "The Mangler," King's short story that expresses the same theme Nathaniel Hawthorne had outlined to himself a hundred years before. The only difference I can find between the two men's plots about a killer industrial machine is that whereas Hawthorne's people come to the machine, King's machine comes to the people. In order to be like King's ancient train, the machine, whether or not it has legs, must be the one to move.

King makes mechanical monsters primary to his plots. An exploding furnace destroys the Overlook Hotel in *The Shining* (1977). Stanley Kubrick, who made a film from the novel, vetoed King's screenplay and eliminated the explosion of the hotel. In an interview after the movie was made, King expressed dissatisfaction with Kubrick's interpretation. He didn't like the director's emphasis on the people who had lived in the Overlook Hotel. "The hotel was not evil," King said, "because those people [the bad ones in the hotel's history] had been there, but those people went there because the place was evil." One can see here that it is the nonhuman, not the human, element that intrigues Stephen King most.

Stephen King cannot escape his "trains" even when he sets up a plot that centers upon an animalistic horror—a vampire, a devil, or a chimera, for instance. In order to "properly" terrify his reader, King unconsciously reaches back to the train metaphor. King's monster of *The Stand*, Flagg, a kind of devil, has a black visage, beacon eyes, and can run faster than cars.

When Flagg unmasks himself to a woman, she sees "the searchlight of his face bear down upon her in the gloom." When a crowd sees Flagg unmasked, an instant before they are all vaporized in a nuclear explosion, he is "something monstrous . . . something slumped and hunched almost without shape—something with enormous yellow eyes." For King, I think, the devil looks like a locomotive.

The train metaphor also permeates the climax of *It*. When Bill, the hero, spots "It," a chimera in its true form, "It was perhaps fifteen feet high and as black as a moonless night. Each of its legs was as thick as a muscle-builder's thigh. Its eyes were bright, malevolent rubies" and "Its belly bulged grotesquely, almost dragging on the floor as It moved." When Bill at last glimpsed the "shape behind the shape," he saw "lights, saw an endless crawling hairy thing which was made of light and nothing else, orange light, dead light that mocked life." This sounds like a child's-eye view of an old, lumbering, Maine freight train, orange refrigerator cars and all.

One cannot escape the train in King. A monster rushes forward at "express train speed" in *It*. A dying person with terminal breathing problems in *The Stand* says, "Listen to me, I sound like a fuckin freight train goin up a hill." King's "Woman's Credo" begins, "Thank you, Men, for the railroads" (*The Stand*). A jilted girl curses her negligent lover in *The Stand*. "I hope you fall in front of some fuckin subway train!" she shouts after him. A pregnant woman is decapitated in a freak taxi-truck accident at the emergency entrance to a New York City hospital ("The Breathing Method" in *Different Seasons*). As her mouth puckers in the gutter where her severed head has landed, the pregnant woman's body on the sidewalk makes the huff-and-puff sounds and gestures of a train. The body delivers a normal infant—all because the woman had been taught in her Lamaze classes to "breathe like a locomotive." This, of course, *is* King's "Breathing Method." Its train-like origins are horrifying.

Why do we put up with the post-traumatic play of writers and pay our good money to receive yet another terrifying exposure at the movies? Because there is something to post-traumatic play that fascinates everybody, something that leaves a lasting impression. Traumatic anxiety is special. A piece of us recognizes this specialness. And so we wait in long lines to catch a glimpse of the Carries, the Cujos, and the Christines. A traumatized Stephen King can pull in a bigger audience today than can a non-traumatized Flaubert. Or a Shakespeare. I was once a speaker on a program on childhood trauma at Einstein Medical Center in Philadelphia, along with the novelist and Nobel Peace Prize winner Elie Wiesel. In passing, Wiesel complained to me, "All my teenaged son reads these days is Stephen King." His eyes drifted heavenward in a silent plea. But I have also read a few of Wiesel's books. What he went through as a teenager in the Holocaust is repeated in various forms in his novels. Much of Wiesel's artistic product, in other words, like Stephen King's, is a product of post-traumatic play. The traumatized four year old at the railroad tracks and the traumatized teenaged Holocaust survivor share a number of things in common.

It is spring now—a hot San Francisco spring day—and Ab and I walk Ocean Beach from Irving Street to Seal Rock. Near the place where Charlotte Brent's parents used to do their tattooing and where "Charlie" herself used to play all alone, I spot a Hispanic-looking little girl sitting on the berm with her Barbie. The girl is burying Barbie naked. Not up to the chin or even up to the nose, but past the eyes, past the hair—she is burying Barbie alive. "What's the name of your game?" I ask, looking the child straight in the eyes, but smiling. "No name," the girl says, shrugging me off. "What happens?" I ask, knowing this to be my last question. "Nothing," she says. The little girl's secret holds. But during the few seconds that we chat, the little girl keeps her hand casually over Barbie's nose, her mouth, and her face. She is killing Barbie as we talk. And I am supposed not to notice.

When Ab and I drive down to Southern California, we sometimes pass the Mattel factory in central Los Angeles. Over the place is a huge sign, "Home of Barbie and Ken." I wonder how all those designers, testers, marketers, sales reps, and executives would take it if they knew what really happens to their pleasant plastic product—how she is washed to death, strangled, bussed off on useless trips, and buried alive. True, most of those millions of Barbie dolls are probably dressed up, taken to their proms, and eventually trashed in the spring cleaning. But a few Barbies are subject to horrors. Maybe not even a few. Maybe many. I know—we know—of four of them right now.

I watch for the little girl on my way back up the beach to Irving Street. She—and Barbie—are gone.

CHAPTER 13

Post-traumatic Reenactment

I still work extremely hard getting strong. I do "man's work" at the plant—"gorilla work." We're the gorillas of the bunch.

Johnny Johnson, age fourteen

I wonder if I can turn invisible. I know I can. I try to do it here. I do it all the time on my planet. You're just going to have to believe me. My friends believe it.

Jamie Knight, age nine

A T THE UNIVERSITY OF MICHIGAN, where I did my fellowship in child psychiatry, we taught groups of eight medical students two mornings a week for twelve weeks. The students examined a child and the child's family—a different case every week—under the supervision of the child psychiatric fellow and a teacher from the medical school. The medical students were being trained to diagnose a child's emotional condition and to formulate a basis for the youngster's disorder. If all went well, every medical student graduating from the University of Michigan at that time could claim to have evaluated and understood twelve unique situations involving both a young child and his family. It was a good program.

Each week after the evaluations were completed, the fellows were supposed to teach some basic principles of child psychiatry to the medical students—first, the unconscious as it applied to children's behavior and family dynamics, then Freudian and Piagetian developmental schemes, and then a beginning exposure to a few psychiatric conditions special to childhood—autism, elective mutism, school phobia, and anorexia, for instance.

During the two years I trained in child psychiatry at the University of

Michigan four student groups came under my supervision. And three of them did quite well. But it is the fourth group that I remember most vividly. As a matter of fact, they were the most negative group of young men that I have ever met.

The first week after we evaluated a child and family, I started, as usual, to talk about the idea of "the unconscious." The family we were seeing that day was a good illustration. They had been frantic when their two-year-old son developed asthma. He had required a couple of emergency hospitalizations. Now, ten years later, they were overprotecting him, giving him automatic "cuts" from his junior high school gym classes and keeping him out of school whenever he complained of anything, from an itch to a stitch in the side. The kid was being teased and tormented by his peers. He hated to leave his family, preferring his mother's company to that of his twelve-year-old classmates. Everyone in the child's family unconsciously was harking back to that old asthma, a condition that, by now, had almost completely resolved.

When our group met alone after the family had left the clinic, one of the students brought up the obvious unconscious motivations in this case. The teaching session was going just about as expected. But then a second student entered our discussion and argued pointedly with the first about whether there actually was an "unconscious" mind. And somebody else joined in on the negative side. I intervened, quoting a little Freud in defense of the unconscious. But two more students jumped onto the "con" side of the argument, insisting that "Everything going on in the mind is known. Nothing exists outside of consciousness."

It was an unusual argument for the mid–twentieth century. And I was concerned. By the next week we'd move on to child development, and perhaps the medical students would read their assignments so that we'd be on firmer ground. I came back for Round Two ready to move ahead.

But my medical students returned to our conference room seemingly firm in the resolve that the unconscious meant absolutely nothing to child psychiatry. My staff supervisor and I made the diagnosis by ourselves that week, and the eight students in the teaching group did not begin to understand what we were trying to do. Behind closed doors they fought me about whether anything unknown could underlie an emotional problem. The students had read their books by now, but they still did not believe.

By the third week I went to see a young faculty member, Mel Reinhart, who had previously been a teacher of mine. I asked Mel why I could not get through to this group. "There is a leader," Mel said. "Find the leader." "I haven't been aware of anyone arguing more than the others," I pointed out. "The leader will show himself," Mel said. "Sometimes a leader is very quiet," he went on. "But leaders have strong, unconscious reasons for leading. The leader's motivation will force action out of the group. Once they act, the leader will signal some sort of approval."

I watched my group. They kept arguing. They couldn't accept the oedipal stage of development. They didn't believe that guilt could propel human behavior. They couldn't agree that "No" might represent an emotional milestone. The group was slow. We hadn't even mentioned Piaget yet. And these eight, smart, young men had already entirely "missed" the four cases we had evaluated.

But I had located the group leader. He was the quietest one in the lot. He sat every week at the opposite end of the conference table from me. He nodded, barely nodded, whenever somebody argued. And the other seven students seemed to watch him, waiting for that barely discernible nod.

I went back to Mel Reinhart. It was week five. "Mel," I said. "I've found the leader. I'm sure I have spotted the right person. But he never speaks. He won't give me an opening. I see how, but I can't understand why, he maintains such a hold over the group. I can't seem to break it."

"You will find a way," Mel answered, as close to the style of Buddha as a psychiatrist can come. I left, frustrated.

Weeks six, seven, eight, nine, ten, and eleven passed—too quickly because nobody learned much and I couldn't flush out the leader. But the weeks passed slowly, too, because the useless fighting inside of the group was beginning to bore me. It all centered on unknown motivations, on the unconscious. And it all vectored back to Victor Martin, the very quiet, thick-set, blondish, greyish-eyed group leader who sat across the table from me, nodding at his peers and averting my eyes.

Over breakfast the morning of our last session I turned on radio station WJR in Detroit and heard a shocking piece of news. A distinguished surgeon who worked at the county hospital a couple of towns away had been murdered early that morning. Somebody had waited for him (perhaps all night), stuck a handgun onto the closed window of his car, and shot. The killer had not yet been apprehended, but the police suspected a disgruntled patient. The doctor's files were being checked for clues. Perhaps, tragic as the circumstances were, this news would be my "way," as Mel Reinhart had put it, to flush out the leader. The conscious and unconscious reasons for hating a doctor enough to shoot him should be of interest to this group. After all, they would be physicians themselves within the year.

I began our session with a statement about the killing. What did they think, I asked the group. They looked blank, having collectively wiped out the unconscious as a motivating force for anything in the world of people. But the "leader" spoke. It was the first time I had noticed more than a phrase emerging from his lips.

"How do you know it wasn't an accident?" he asked me.

"They say on the radio that the gun was aimed directly at the surgeon's head."

"Maybe the guy who killed him was playing around and his finger slipped," the grey eyes looked greenish.

"The shot was point blank."

"I think his finger slipped. He didn't want to do it. He wasn't planning to kill anyone. Whoever it was—he was just playing around. He had no reasons."

"That's ridiculous," one of the seven others broke in. "I heard the news myself this morning. Some creep carrying a thirty-eight waited for that surgeon to come out of the hospital and to get into his car. Then he shot him point blank."

"You don't know anything about it," the group leader began to rise from his chair, face reddening now. "I've had an experience with this. A finger can slip."

"What do you mean?" I asked, suddenly feeling a bit breathless. "What *is* your experience?"

The student, standing now, face pink, eyes green, and chest moving in quick rhythm, looked into space. "My finger slipped on a trigger once. I was six. My brother was four. I was playing with my dad's gun in the garage. It went off. My brother died."

The group looked shocked. No one spoke.

"But I never meant to do it," he went on. "I didn't want something bad to happen to my brother. We played a lot. Our mother liked us both. It was an accident. Nothing more to it. A slip of the finger. A slip." Suddenly aware of us, our leader began to sit down, a helium-depleted balloon settling back to earth.

I said something like "There, there now," although not quite those words, just the idea. Victor Martin trembled in his chair. So that was what had made the "unconscious" a dangerous concept for him. That was what had made our group unconsciously consider the unconscious a dangerous idea, too. This young fellow, about to be a doctor, had been warding off his own fear, a fear of learning some unknown, unconscious motivation for a deadly act he had committed as a first grader. And, in this process, he was forcing his costudents away from learning. He was continuing to behave as if he could not afford to know what lay behind his six-year-old actions. And our group, unconsciously, was behaving as if each participant could not afford to know, either.

Well, at this point, the group started talking about the unconscious. They ignored their muscular leader, who by now, deprived of all charisma, did not "exist" for them. They went back to cases two, five, and seven—cases that they had seen during our twelve frustrating weeks together. They thought that the unconscious may have been at work inside that pubertal kid who had developed ulcerative colitis the week his mother left him. And maybe, also, there was unconscious activity in those parents of the mentally retarded kid who had felt guilty for giving birth so late in life—maybe they were blaming themselves without realizing it, and that had kept them from having the boy assessed before this. But we had only one hour left of our entire twelve weeks together. It was far too late to learn much child psychiatry.

At the end of our session Victor Martin stayed on for a couple of minutes. "Do I need to see a psychiatrist?" he asked me.

"Yes," I said.

"Will you find somebody?"

"Yes."

I gave Victor the names of two good psychiatrists in Ann Arbor. I hope he went to one of them. But I never found out if he did.

Victor Martin, untreated, would not be able to perform well as a physician. Victor Martin, untreated, would tend to be blind, deaf, and dumb to the hidden motivations of his patients. As if he himself were threatened every time he came up against a patient's unconscious, Victor Martin would easily miss alcoholism, AIDS, and the other silently invasive diseases. He would certainly miss the secrets, the conflicts, and the naughty wishes that impel so much human behavior. Victor Martin had exposed eight onlookers to his post-traumatic "behavioral reenactment." And they, in turn, had "caught" his behavior.

Traumatized children repeat in actions. Whereas adults who are shocked or severely stressed tend to talk about it, dream, or to visualize, children take far more action. They certainly take more dramatic action. And they repeat. After traumatic experiences, children appear to have two behavioral options, to play or to reenact. And sometimes the boundary between these two behaviors is indistinct. Children, however, will define their post-traumatic play as "fun," even when it looks grim and joyless to the outsider. And they will describe their behavioral reenactments as "how I acted" or "something weird I did," or even "how I am as a person." Since children do tend to make the distinction, "fun," between play and reenactment, I will separate the two behaviors with this qualifier. It is an entirely practical distinction, "fun." But perhaps this is the only distinction that can be made.

Behavioral reenactments, if repeated frequently enough, tend to create personality changes in the child. Donald Taylor, a twelve-year-old boy from San José, exemplifies this point. Donald wished to hide. He therefore repeatedly reenacted the wish not to be around. Donald had been run over on a sidewalk in front of his house by his next door neighbor's car. By the time I met him eight months after his accident, Donald had changed from a quiet, but relatively enthusiastic and flexible fellow to a morose, stand-offish, rigid human being. Donald's wish to hide, in other words, was being unconsciously repeated enough to make the boy adopt the lifestyle of a twelve-year-old recluse.

But I am getting ahead of my tale. Let us go back to the beginning. The story starts during the spring, toward the end of Donald Taylor's fifth-grade year. Mr. and Mrs. Taylor had decided that May to accede to their son's long-standing request for a skateboard. They bought him the fanciest kind available, the kind with the movable wheels and the broad foot-stand. Donald's mother, of course, gave him a set of safety rules as she handed over the hard-earned skateboard. "Use it *only* on the sidewalk," she told the boy a couple of times.

The following morning Donald Taylor carefully tried out his skate-board. On the sidewalk, of course. Donald was hit as he rode down his block. Mr. Prindge, the Taylors' neighbor, fresh from an early Saturday morning argument with Mrs. Prindge, backed out furiously from his garage and ran the boy down. Sensing that he had hit something, Mr. Prindge put his car into "Drive" and charged forward. The boy miraculously was spared serious injury despite being hit by the car twice. There were tire abrasions on Donald's belly, yes. But the automobile had entirely missed Donald's vital organs. After an afternoon in the emergency room, Donald Taylor was released.

But Donald Taylor was not "alright" following his release. He began to withdraw. Not wanting to be seen and attacked again, Donald stayed home after school. The discarded skateboard sat in a hall closet. The discarded baseball mitt languished in a corner of the boy's bedroom. Donald Taylor had decided unconsciously to "get out of the way." He was reenacting a wish—to avoid any ugly surprise.

Teachers began commenting to Mrs. Taylor that Donald rarely spoke anymore in class. Teased because a child had spread the rumor that Donald's penis had been smashed in the car accident (Donald worried about this very same thing), Donald stopped playing sports. Just at the age when boys all over California are becoming crazed over tackle football, Donald Taylor refused to get into the games. His athletic friends began abandoning him. Donald took to his home computer after school, and his television set played for hours. He found a few unathletic boys to phone or to invite over. And at school, he developed two tag games that he offered as alternatives to the football that most boys were playing. The first was called "Scrotal Tag" and was exactly that. The second was called "Minstrel Tag" (an obvious misnomer), in which "It" was declared to be a girl having her period. You see, Donald had been very impressed with how close Mr. Prindge's car had come to destroying his penis. His avoidant behaviors were reenactments of the wish to have ducked a menacing automobile. His play was a repetition of the same trauma; but it reflected a fear instead of a wish, the fear of castration. Donald was playing post-traumatic games and he was reenacting. The reenactment was the bigger of the two problems.

Donald Taylor's parents brought the boy to my office after they had watched his behavior for eight months. This was a different Donald than the one they had known before. The Taylors were afraid that Donald might "freeze" this way. What kind of adult would he become?

We decided to try a combination of behavioral modification and psychiatric interpretation to stop Donald's withdrawal. The Taylors could not bring Donald to see me very often from San José, a city more than an hour's drive away. First, I suggested that we insist that Donald participate either in a sport or a school activity. He signed up for the school play, but he skipped the early rehearsals. One of his parents eventually had to accompany him to practice. Donald performed well at great expense to everybody else. But by spring Donald started to feel more confident and signed up for the baseball team. The boy showed his ambivalence about "coming out," however, by refusing to field the ball when it came at him. We found a high school boy to throw and catch with him on Saturdays. Eventually the Little League coach moved Donald into the infield. The young fellow was doing much better. Our behavioral modification approach apparently was working.

In my office, I worked with Donald on the trauma-inspired fears that had demanded his continual, ongoing reenactments of the wish to escape. We talked of castration, of death, and of lost pride. Donald began to understand. And as he understood, his actions became less predictable, more flexible, and quite a bit more ordinary. During times of stress, however, Donald would revert to his solitary lifestyle. It took about two years of once-in-a-while therapy to return Donald Taylor's behaviors close to his previous ones.

Donald came back to me quite recently as a late seventh grader, asking about what to do when the ninth graders shoved him aside to get onto the school bus. His immediate urge—to retreat—he knew, was wrong. Donald was having trouble, however, picking an alternative. The change toward normal was clearly apparent by the next time Donald returned. Donald told me he had challenged a ninth grader with a "Get the hell back where you belong," and the kid had retreated. Donald felt pleased with his rediscovered nerve.

Most personality shifts that follow from childhood psychic trauma are problematic. These changes occur because children need unconsciously to repeat trauma-related thoughts, wishes, and behaviors. When the repetitive actions come frequently enough to amount to "personality traits," the child's parents will often notice a change for the worse. The child will seem quieter—or bossier—or meaner—or more babyish—or more like a clown. Nineteen of the kidnapped children of Chowchilla exhibited these kinds of shifts in personality by the fourth year after their kidnapping. Most of the shifts could be traced back to a trauma-related thought, a wish, or a fear.

Personality takes a more extreme deviation when the trauma is long-standing or frequently repeated. Instead of the relatively subtle personality rearrangements that a child will make after a single event, the reenactments of long-standing or repeated traumas pour out of the child so thickly, so frequently, that they amount to massive distortions of character. Repetitions of such behaviors as self-anesthesia and dissociation, and of such primitive defenses as splitting and identification with the aggressor, lead to large-scale personality problems. These problems affect not only the child himself, but often the community as well. The distinction between the kinds of character changes one gets after single traumas versus what one sees after multiple or long-standing traumas is usually, but not always, clear. Certainly, Donald Taylor might have become seriously character-disordered had he been allowed to remain in full retreat for another year or so, and Victor Martin, if left untreated, was not going to be a good doctor. But some of the character problems one sees after long-standing childhood ordeals are so extreme and represent such problems for society that they make the personality shifts from the single shock look insipid in contrast.

Let me exemplify this point with the unfortunate little Joe Hillgard, the grandson of Leroy and Mary Beth. Joe's mom, although she herself had been sexually abused as a teenager by her father, Leroy Hillgard, had assumed that both her mother and father together could take reasonably good care of her child in their day-care program. Joe was a boy—so what could Leroy want with him? Joe Hillgard's mother went back to work a couple of weeks after he was born. Joe stayed with Leroy and Mary Beth at their home. He stayed, in fact, for three years. And we know the rest of the story—Leroy was arrested by U.S. Customs agents for trying to ship child pornographic materials out of the country. He eventually went to prison. Pornographic pictures of Joe—thrusting an erect penis at the camera, dancing naked, being sodomized by an erect, adult penis, crying, laughing, screaming—these photos were picked up in Leroy Hillgard's files. I saw the pictures. They were terrible. Joe Hillgard had been raised to be the "star" of Leroy Hillgard's child pornography "studio."

I met Joe only once. His attorney needed my opinion about how much damage had been done. Joe's personality was "hail fellow well met," the type of problematic character one so often sees in young, repeatedly abused children. The boy had no idea who I was, yet he immediately smiled and let me in on secrets that the ordinary person would tell only to the most intimate of confidantes. He danced his dirty little dances for me even though I never asked to see them. He scratched his anus freely. When I asked him, following an intense bout of scratching and poking, if his "butt" hurt, he responded, "I won't call the police on you for saying bad words."

Joe Hillgard did his "bumps and grinds" about my office at several different times during our session together. He broke several toys. "This is a broken jeep," he would say. He then would try as hard as he could to break the big, expensive jeep. Joe loved armies, he told me. And he was looking forward to the killings he might do in the future once he was inducted into the Marine Corps. Joe Hillgard had been abused for three long years. He had been abused very young. And I think—although one can't be entirely sure—he had been abused almost daily. He made the Donald Taylors, the Tania Bankses, and the Sheila Sheldons—in other words, the kids who had been traumatized only once—look like saints. "What does your gun do?" Joe asked me. "Does it shoot real people? I want to shoot bad guys. Robbers. Bad guys push you down. They make you bleed." Joe Hillgard had suffered from a bleeding anus for years. He now wished to turn the tables. This wish was leading a bandwagon of personality shifts in this young, very angry boy.

The anger one picks up from the long-standing child abuse victim is extreme. The withdrawals one sees are extreme, too. The flights into invisibility can be frequent and a little out of control. And the tendencies to repeat the specifics of the sex attacks or of the physical brutalities may become almost unstoppable.

Not every repeatedly traumatized child will develop a problem of character. But when a chronically abused kid does develop one, it is usually quite big. It is usually based upon a series of behavioral reenactments from the original group of traumas. Wishes, feelings, past behaviors, fears—all of these can be put to use by the traumatized child. If the child reenacts often enough, his developing character will be affected. Bet on it. This is the best single reason why any child discovered to have been repeatedly abused should seek professional help—even years after the abuses are over. Once the discovery is made, the child—or the adult—should consider psychotherapy in order to break down the maladaptive character structures that were initially erected to cover the trauma.

Occasionally a traumatized child will reenact with his body. The significance of these physiologic reenactments does not usually reach consciousness. The repeated bodily sensations mimic the physical sensations that originally were connected with the trauma. Or they mimic wishes originally connected with the trauma. Self-anesthesia is a good example of this. Once a child has been sexually abused the child may automatically go "numb." The "answer" of just how numb the child will feel does not usually arrive until the child has reached full maturity and is active sexually. Sexual numbing certainly is a reason for a course of psychotherapy at the time of onset of sexual activity. (Emotional numbing is a reason for starting therapy whenever it appears.) Numbing, however, is not the only way sexual reenactments go. Some sexually abused children, like Joe Hillgard, feel almost constantly overexcited and overstimulated. Others become conscious of pain whenever the issue of "sex" comes up. Others, through some miraculous sparing from repetitions of this type, stay sexually responsive and "normal."

Children who originally felt funny feelings in the pits of their stomachs during traumatic events often come to feel these same funny feelings when new stresses arise. I call this return of trauma-related feelings "psychophysiologic reenactment." Those children who originally felt chills dashing up their spines during an event tend to continue to get them at odd moments. Johnny Johnson of Chowchilla felt chills from time to time. As a matter of fact, a chill went up Johnny's spine when he first spotted his captors coming onto the school bus.

One boy I evaluated had been belted into his seat during a frightening automobile accident. He immediately felt a "pinch" in his abdomen as the crash took place. The pinch probably came from the seat belt pushing into the boy's skin. Within a few weeks of the accident the boy developed abdominal cramping and diarrhea. It lasted for two years. No physical cause could be agreed upon by the various doctors who were consulted. The dysfunction of this boy's intestinal tract, his pains in other words, were the result of involuntary bodily overactivity. The overactivity, in turn, was probably based upon unconscious psychological repetitions of the trauma.

Bodily systems controlled by voluntary musculature can also be affected by psychophysiologic reenactment. Frances Carlson, for instance, the girl whose father tried to kidnap her from a friend's house, wet her pants at the time he tried to carry her away. Afterward, when a male stranger unexpectedly walked into Frances's classroom—or another time when a male stranger entered an ice rink where Frances was skating—the child wet herself. Frances did not make any conscious connection between her first, trauma-related bout of wetting and the later bouts. But these were psychophysiologic reenactments. A man who surprised Frances served as an instant signal for the young girl's bladder to empty. Even though the bladder is controlled after age two or three by voluntary sphincters, these muscles were responding to unconscious, trauma-inspired signals.

The children of Chowchilla provided the best group data I have regarding the phenomenon of psychophysiologic reenactment (although there were problems in verifying the data because I did not have access to the children's medical records.) Four years after the kidnapping, five of the Chowchilla children were experiencing ongoing bladder problems without any corresponding physical disease. These bladder difficulties included urgency to get to the bathroom, urinary withholding at school, and urinary incontinence. Each of the bladder problems, of course, mimicked the children's original urinary dilemmas in the vans.

Two Chowchilla youngsters who had gained a large amount of weight the first year after the kidnapping remained significantly overweight four years afterward. Reasonings like "nobody will ever starve me again" had receded from consciousness. But the physiologic messages of hunger had remained at work. Five of the Chowchilla kids experienced stomach aches whenever they were anxious. This hadn't happened before the kidnapping. Terrie Thornton remembered that one of the kidnappers had slammed his gun butt into her stomach when he wanted her to stop dismounting the bus. This original trauma-induced stomach ache, in other words, had set up hundreds more to follow.

As far as I could tell, Elizabeth Vane inadvertently chose the most extreme sort of psychophysiologic reenactment available to a Chowchilla child after the 1976 kidnapping. She stopped growing. Elizabeth, at age nine, had been of smallish but not dramatically "off" size. And her sister Mary had seemed just about right for a five year old. But by the time she reached age fourteen, something remarkable had happened to Elizabeth Vane. Sammy Smith warned me of this before I recontacted the girl in the fall of 1980. "Elizabeth is very small now. I saw her this summer at the swimming pool," he had told me, "and she's real tiny." When I met Elizabeth, she appeared to have frozen in size about where she had been at nine. By the age of fourteen, Elizabeth stood well under five feet tall—in fact, during our interview, she said she was four feet, eight inches tall (and she looked smaller than that). Elizabeth was developing breasts and a few pubertal pimples. Yet she seemed entirely to have missed the preadolescent growth spurt. I had no access to Elizabeth's pediatric records and could not tell how small she had been when she was born or how small she had been as she developed. I had had an impression of a petite child when Elizabeth was nine, but it had not been striking. Elizabeth looked almost dwarfish now.

Do you remember the little boy in Günter Grass's *The Tin Drum?* The fictional boy had been ordinary sized until he fell down the stairs (a shocking surprise) and decided not to grow any more. We do not have to depend upon literary examples, however, when it comes to post-traumatic growth stoppages. "Failure to thrive" is a well-known pediatric condition in which youngsters, largely those who are abused or neglected at home, shut off their hypothalamic and pituitary hormones and stop growing. This condition corresponds in many ways to the dilemma of the little boy in *The Tin Drum* and to the dilemma of Elizabeth Vane. "Failure to thrive" is not caused by conscious decisions to stop growing. The pituitary shuts down automatically. "Failure to thrive" children grow like magic beanstalks in anyone's but their parents' care. At the hospital, they grow. In good foster homes, they grow. At home, they stop. Elizabeth Vane had developed something like a "failure to thrive" syndrome after her kidnapping at Chowchilla. I considered it a psychophysiologic reenactment, a massive one. But I would not be able to prove it because I had no access to a complete set of Elizabeth's pediatric records, nor did I have heights and weights of the rest of the family.

Mutism (Brent Burns from the Hillgard day-care program), paralysis (Rachel Mendosa of Chowchilla felt unable to move at times), "frogs in the throat" (a woman victim of a department store strip search developed a recurring "lump" in her throat relating to her initial inability to call out for help), numbness in sex (the banker whose father had abused her all through her childhood could not "feel" intercourse), and nighttime sensations of weight pressing on the chest (the original "nightmare," a common post-traumatic complaint), are often traced back to traumatic incidents. It may turn out that certain cultural groups, particularly those that frown upon talking about feelings, experience more psychophysiologic reenactments than do other groups. Some of the great successes at Lourdes and of the American faith healers may derive from the amenability of psychophysiologic reenactment to strong suggestion. No matter how "mental" the origins of post-traumatic psychophysiologic reenactment may be, however, the pains and bodily sensations that the victim feels are absolutely real. The link between body and mind remains unconscious to the victim. The body responds to the trauma. And the mind—the unconscious mind, that is—drives this response.

Single behavioral reenactments take very dramatic forms. This kind of incident is what you usually hear about when you ask a childhood trauma victim, "Have you done anything weird?" Single behavioral reenactments also become the focus of parental complaint. At Chowchilla, the parents tended to miss the underlying reason for their children's single behavioral reenactments. They overlooked the trauma. But they did not overlook the behaviors themselves.

Leslie Grigson's runaway serves as a good example of the single behavioral reenactment. The story will feel a bit familiar because of its linkage to Leslie's games "Busdriver" and "Traveling Barbies." Leslie did her very weird, single "thing" when she was ten years old. She left home for a night. Running away isn't all that weird—it's just the way in which Leslie ran that was so unusual. Mrs. Grigson figured for a short while that Leslie had been kidnapped, as a matter of fact. But let's listen to Leslie herself in 1980 as she talks about what happened:

"It was probably February 1979, on a school day. In the middle of the night I packed up my stuff—my clothes and goodies—bubble bath, statues (Jesus, the Blessed Virgin, and Sacred Heart), and earrings. I had been mad at Mom at other times. But this time I was extra mad. Mom had made me stay up soooooooo late to do loads of clothes. I hadn't done 'em in the day. It was 1:30 in the night. I decided to run. I almost wrote Mom a note. But I didn't.

"I put a glow-in-the-dark rosary around my neck. And I took some blankets. I wanted to get to my aunt J.R.'s house in L.A.

"A man picked me up by the railroad tracks. [This is the Southern Pacific Railway line that runs north-south through the Valley. Southern Pacific is one of the busiest railroads in the United States.] I dropped everything I was carrying. The man scared me. But he was a redheaded guy who looked like my dad [the reader will recall that Leslie's father had signed off his parental rights to Leslie the year before the kidnapping. Leslie missed her dad. But she was employing extremely bad judgment in searching for his look-alike in the middle of the night at the railroad tracks.] Three people stopped to pick me up at the tracks—there was a camper, and I noticed somebody inside who didn't look like he'd be nice, and there was a green car with some Mexican boys and I said 'No way!' and then the man. He picked me up going camping. He took me home [to his house] and re-packed my stuff. He gave me enough money to go to J.R.'s house.

"I bought a bus ticket, called J.R. at L.A., and she was there. Whew! The operator gave me her number."

Leslie's behavior had been extremely risky. She had gone somewhere "safely," as it turned out. And she had returned home "safely." But she had gone off in the middle of the night, solo and hitchhiking, in order to get where she was going. She had walked the Southern Pacific tracks without a clue as to the train schedules. She had stopped to talk to three groups of male strangers, and had eventually gone to a male stranger's apartment. She had accepted money. And then she had traveled alone on a bus to Los

Angeles, not knowing exactly where she was going or whether or not her aunt would be there.

"Sounds a little like the kidnapping," I commented casually.

"No, no. The kidnapping was—*they* were taking me," Leslie waved me off. "This was —that *I* was going."

I could have said "Sounds like 'Busdriver' " or "Sounds like 'Traveling Barbies.' " No matter what I did say, however, Leslie would have said "No way." The child was unable to see a link between her traumatic experience and her behavior. The connection was burrowed deep in Leslie's unconscious.

Leslie's adventure, a single behavioral reenactment, was far more dangerous and far less miniaturized than had been any of her games on the same kidnapping theme. One could see what a fine distinction separated post-traumatic reenactment from post-traumatic play. One could also see that reenactment is occasionally very dangerous.

Celeste Sheldon was nine years old and a bit oedipal when she was kidnapped at Chowchilla. Celeste and her older sister, Sheila, had stood arguing with their mother at the front door the morning of the kidnapping. Mrs. Sheldon had pushed them both out of the house. Sheila had stayed angry after that. She repeatedly reenacted her anger, making irritable cracks at everybody including her teachers. It became an irritating personality trait. But Celeste, still oedipally competitive with her mother at the time of the kidnapping, did something else. She immediately misperceived one of the kidnappers to be a "lady." She ducked down in the school bus while she was captured. "I didn't want the lady to see me," Celeste said. Celeste was not aware of it, but she had affixed the mental representation of her "avenging" Mom onto her mental representation of the trauma.

When Celeste Sheldon returned home from her kidnapping she described "the lady" as "five feet, two inches tall with straight, darkish blond hair down to her shoulders, and pretty." If the FBI had put out an "all points bulletin" on this person, they would have arrested Celeste's mother, Samantha Sheldon. The child's description fit her perfectly.

Celeste Sheldon remained convinced that her "lady," indeed, existed. She described the lady four years after the kidnapping—just as freshly and as vividly as she had described her upon her return home in 1976. But Celeste Sheldon also developed a single-style reenactment. This behavioral reenactment coincided exactly with what the child had thought on the school bus—"I didn't want the lady to see me."

Celeste hid or ducked whenever a familiar female showed up in an unexpected place. Her girlfriend turned up once, for instance, at Red's Market. Celeste dove under a counter. Her school teacher strolled by the First Baptist Church just as Celeste was walking down the street from the opposite direction. The child dove into the bushes. Once, four years after the kidnapping, a junior high school teacher alluded to the plight of the Iranian hostages and surprised Celeste by asking the class, "What would *you* do with a gun pointed at *you*?" Celeste ducked in her seat. She had no idea what had impelled her action. Her thought, "I didn't want the lady to see me," evaded her conscious understanding every time it impelled a behavior. But it was actively in operation.

Probably the most dramatic of all single reenactments after the Chowchilla kidnapping was an episode in the life of Bob Barklay, the children's hero. One Sunday afternoon eighteen months after the kidnapping, the adult Barklays noticed a car parked on the road edging their property. The hood of the strange car was up. "Go see what's going on, Bob," one of the Barklays suggested. The fifteen-year-old boy banged the door and went outside. A few minutes later shouts and screams in an Oriental language broke the calm of the afternoon. Cookie and Hal Barklay ran out. A tourist from Japan had stopped his rented automobile outside the Barklay's property. It had been overheating. The tourist had lifted his hood in order to check the radiator. Just then Bob had come charging out of his house. He shot the tourist with his BB gun. It hurt. Stung the man badly. The tourist was both confused and outraged. What was wrong with this boy? These country people must be crazy.

We know what was wrong with Bob Barklay. The Chowchilla kidnapping had started, as far as Bob was concerned, with a van "in trouble" at the side of the road. As Bob's school bus had slowed down to pass the van, three masked men had jumped onto his bus. Eighteen months after that, Bob spotted another vehicle seemingly in trouble at the side of the road. The start signal for a kidnapping popped off in Bob's mind. The kidnapping was to take place at Bob's own house. Everybody, his parents, his sister, and himself, were in danger.

Bob came out shooting. Nobody was going to kidnap him again. If Bob had to be a hero, he'd be a hero fast, not after hours of mental anguish. So Bob Barklay shot first and thought later. That's what I mean by a single behavioral reenactment. It's dangerous. Crazy. But it makes perfect sense when you think about it.

I have told many tales of post-traumatic behavioral reenactment in other chapters of this book. When the middle-aged Charlotte Brent put her boyfriend's penis into her mouth, she was behaviorally reenacting an ancient abuse. When little Belinda Peck hid under her parents' dining room chairs, she was reenacting a terrible experience that originally took place under a department store display table. When Gloria Rivers piled my office pillows one on top of another, she was reenacting the smothering sensation that a baby of six months experiences as an adult poses for pornographic pictures on top of her. The pillows seemed to be waiting there, holding as they smothered a baby, until, the self-timer on some ancient camera clicked off in little Gloria Rivers's mind.

Each of the traumatized artists whom we have followed in this book exhibited behavioral or psychophysiologic post-traumatic reenactments in their lifetimes. According to Peter Cowie, Ingmar Bergman's biographer, the adult Bergman, a childhood lock-up victim, locked himself into projectionists' booths during the openings of his early theater productions. At times he would lock himself into his bathroom, even after company had come to call. Bergman's friend, the actor Stig Olin, said that Bergman would stay locked in the bathroom for such long spells that Olin wondered "if he was alive, dead, or just sulking."

Edgar Allan Poe indulged in a number of actions that most likely were inspired by his trauma at age two years, ten months, at Elizabeth Poe's deathbed. Poe unconsciously aimed throughout his life to witness deaths similar to that of his mother. He married the frail, tubercular, thirteen-year-old Virginia Clemm, for instance, and then watched her fade into death. He insisted upon tending to his tubercular, older brother, William, until he died. Edgar Allan Poe probably aimed unconsciously at such a death for himself. He eventually achieved it, alone, alcoholic, and stuporous in a Baltimore flophouse. He couldn't die of TB—he must have been immune to it. So he died of substance abuse, the closest he could come to a tubercular death.

Although Poe's life history demonstrates how multiple reenactments can establish the tone and outcome of a life, he also engaged in what I think were single behavioral reenactments from time to time. Maria Bonaparte tells us in her psychobiography of Poe that at West Point, where he, as a young man, made a brief, unsuccessful try at military life, Poe enlisted a colleague to throw a bleeding gander into a roomful of cadets. He was somehow able to convince the cadets that they had just seen the axed-off head of one of their professors.

Edith Wharton and Virginia Woolf both experienced post-traumatic reenactments of the psychophysiologic kind. Wharton, according to her biographer R. W. B. Lewis, suffered much of her young adult life with something diagnosed as "neurasthenia." The condition was eventually treated psychiatrically and it improved. Wharton's symptoms were "an occult, and un-get-at-able nausea," terrible fatigue requiring six or seven rests a day, weight loss, headache, and an inability to make decisions. These symptoms are quite similar to those of typhoid fever. Wharton may have been unconsciously recreating her trauma from age eight. Virginia Woolf, on the other hand, apparently suffered no reenactive pain. She experienced a lifetime of sexual numbing and emotional anesthesia. Quentin Bell, Woolf's biographer and a member of the Stephen family, tends to minimize the importance of Gerald and George Duckworth's sexual abuses of Virginia. He suggests that the writer's frigidity was inherent to her character, an innate trait, perhaps, or an inherited one. There is, however, nothing innate or inherited about incest. It is an environmental problem. We know today that incest is often handled by the child with emotional numbing, physical erasure, and mental escape. These were Virginia Woolf's psychophysiologic reenactments. And they stayed with her for life.

I think that Stephen King behaviorally reenacts just as some of his traumatized, creative predecessors did before him. His audience loves the reenactments, too, it seems. King appears to enjoy teasing and torturing his fans. He, himself, acted in an American Express TV ad, complete with a sliding bookcase and swinging sconces. He also took a lead part in the film *Creepshow*, and the small part of a graveyard minister in *Pet Sematary*. His Jordie Verill character in *Creepshow* is overtaken by a green growth from outer space. King wrote the film. He must have wanted his audience to see him destroyed this way.

Stephen King has scared his own kids with what I think is a behavioral reenactment. He says in Underwood and Miller's book of interviews and lectures, "I'm not above instilling certain fears in my children, if it will help me to get my own way sometimes. For instance, my kids wanted to sit in the third row whenever we went to the movies and although it didn't bother them I'd spend three hours with these giant people looming over me like an avalanche. So I finally told them we couldn't do this anymore and they said, 'Why not?" and I told them that the screen was a hole and they could fall into the movie and they'd never be able to get out. They looked at me in this uneasy way and said, 'Naah, that's not true,' but I said, 'Sure it is. See those people in the background? You don't think they can pay that many people to be in the movie? Those are people that fell in and can't get out.' So they didn't want to sit in the front row anymore. I solved the problem."

I have mentioned some of René Magritte's probable reenactments earlier in this book. He botched up his chronologies. He misdated his paintings. Once, Magritte spent an entire afternoon at the coffin-maker's shop inside a coffin. But Magritte looks like a reenactment "amateur" when you compare him to the master of all post-traumatic reenactor-artists, Alfred Hitchcock. Hitch's "pranks," his famous "practical jokes," appear for the most part to be post-traumatic behavioral reenactments. He must have needed to repeat a double-crossing, a traumatic event at the local police station. From the time he was six years old, Hitch felt tempted to double-cross and to lock up anybody he knew. The tables *had* to be turned.

When Alfred Hitchcock was an early teenager, for instance, he and another boy led a young student from their parochial school into the school basement. The two older boys took off the boy's trousers and tied him to the school boiler. After making some ominous, scratching sounds, Hitchcock and his friend ran away and the boy found himself terror-struck as a series of explosions sounded from the region of his underpants. Hitchcock, unbeknownst to the boy, had pinned live firecrackers to the young fellow's briefs. The Reverend Robert Goold lived to tell his tale to Hitchcock's biographer Donald Spoto. Goold claimed never to have seen a movie made by Alfred Hitchcock. One need not wonder why.

Throughout his career, Hitch loved to confine his actors to small, impossible spaces—spaces reminiscent of jail cells. He once gave a party for the forty person cast and crew of *The Farmer's Wife*. He scheduled it, unbeknownst to them, in the smallest room of a West End restaurant. He then hired forty aspiring actors to serve as waiters, instructing each of them to serve as rudely as possible. Once he sent the famous actor Gerald du Maurier a dressing room gift—a horse.

One of Hitchcock's worst confinement pranks, almost certainly a reenactment of his own kindergarten-aged term in jail, occurred when a propman accepted Hitchcock's bet of a full week's salary if he would allow himself to be chained for an entire night to a camera. Before he left the set for the night, Hitch fed the man a glass of brandy laced with a laxative. One can imagine the rest.

Hitchcock repeatedly chose themes of confinement, helplessness, and humiliation for his behavioral repetitions of his five-year-old trauma. Once, the actress Elsie Randolph asked the director to disallow cigarettes on his set. Hitchcock contrived that she play her "scene" in a telephone booth. Once inside, the actress found herself shut in amidst great billows of smoke. She left the set, sick and scared. Hitchcock's teenaged daughter, Pat, asked her father one night if she might take a ride on the ferris wheel that commanded the carnival scene for *Strangers on a Train,* a film in which Pat was playing a significant role. When Pat reached the top, Hitchcock ordered the ferris wheel stopped and all the lights on the set put out. With the area totally dark, Hitchcock left to direct another scene. Pat was hysterical with fear. Her father left her stuck up there, it turned out, for more than an hour.

Alfred Hitchcock recognized an uneasy tension between the film stars Madeleine Carroll and Robert Donat the first day they were introduced on the set of Hitchcock's *The Thirty-nine Steps*. They had never met before. Hitch handcuffed them together that first day for the handcuff scene. He conveniently lost the key and did not let them escape one another until the end of the day.

I am sure that the careful reader of film biography will find other practical jokes of Alfred Hitchcock's that don't fit my "trauma" hypothesis—the time he served all-blue food at a dinner party for Gertrude Lawrence, or the time he invited a famous actor to a supposed costume party, only to have everyone else there elegantly decked out in black tie. But there is a theme to the majority of Hitchcock's pranks, and that is the theme of confinement. This theme was established by a five-year-old boy's trauma, the trauma of confinement in a jail cell. What has been considered the director's ultimate practical joke, his gravestone inscription that supposedly says, "This is what happens to naughty boys," puts Hitchcock directly back into his kindergarten-aged fix. Poor guy. His body would stay confined for eternity. He would be forced to go on reenacting his trauma. Forever. (There is an odd "afterword" to the Alfred Hitchcock gravestone story. I wished to photograph the stone because it represented such a striking example of an artist's—how shall I say this?—"after-life reenactment." I asked the Hitchcock estate where the director's grave was located. The answer came a few days later, indirectly from Pat Hitchcock. Her father was cremated, Pat said. There is no stone. The graveyard story I had heard a couple of years before in Boston appeared to have been a rumor. It was one of those mass-held stories that shows us that we all reenact a little, inadvertently of course, in response to another man's trauma.)

There are four key repetitions that occur in childhood psychic trauma. I have repeated three of them in the last three chapters—dreams, play, and reenactment. The fourth, repeated visualization, came up earlier as we considered post-traumatic perceptions and memory. The current American diagnostic manual divides the symptoms and signs of psychic trauma into three categories: repetition, avoidance, and hyperalertness. Of these three categories, repetition is the clearest, the best indicator of childhood psychic trauma. As Selma Fraiberg put it so long ago, "Literal repetition often means trauma." In children, and in the untreated children who turn out to be troubled adults, these monotonous, literal, specific repetitions—the dreams, play, reenactments, and visualizations—are the surest cues we get to childhood trauma.

Are post-traumatic behavioral reenactments contagious? Indeed they are. Celeste Sheldon impelled Jackie Johnson to hide the day their teacher asked how it felt to be an Iranian hostage. The girls glanced at each other. Both ducked down in their seats. How did Jackie Johnson, not the same under-the-counter-ducker or into-the-bushes-jumper that Celeste Sheldon was, know to hide, too? She must have felt it across the room.

But each of these girls was a kidnap victim. What about nontraumatized kids? These kids "catch" post-traumatic reenactments, too. Seven medical students "caught" Victor Martin's "denial," didn't they? And a few boys on a sixth grade playground "caught" Donald Taylor's "Scrotal" and "Minstrel" tag. Helen Symes induced a number of four-year-old classmates to touch and to smell their own vaginas. And Jamie Knight induced four or five friends to believe in invisibility.

But let us leave reenactive contagion with a couple of the artists whose childhood traumas we have already considered. Stephen King loves the fact that his fears and his behaviors are catchy. He watches for his audience's contagious responses, which he sees as a sure sign of success. He is quoted by Underwood and Miller as saying, for instance, "So if somebody wakes up screaming because of what I wrote, I'm delighted. If he merely tosses his cookies, it's still a victory but on a lesser scale. I suppose the ultimate triumph would be to have somebody drop dead of a heart attack. I'd say 'Gee, that's a shame,' and I'd mean it, but part of me would be thinking, Jesus, that really *worked!*" King even acknowledges that three real-life murders have been connected with his work. (There has been a *Carrie* murder, a murder committed by a woman who was carrying *Salem's Lot,* and a cult murder in which "REDRUM," an inverted word taken from *The Shining,* was written on the wall.) "Maybe there is a copycat syndrome at work here," King says of his audience's response, "like the Tylenol poisonings."

Alfred Hitchcock, in the same sense as Stephen King, always showed intense interest in how an audience or a friend would respond to his behavioral reenactments. He seemed to have wanted people to "catch" his own terror. How, for instance, did the very proper Madeleine Carroll meet her own bathroom needs with the actor Robert Donat handcuffed to her arm? Hitchcock asked some very personal questions about the two of them the next day. He needed to know.

A well-known child psychiatrist from the state of Maine, Diane Schetky, approached the podium a couple years of ago following a talk I had just given about the effects of Hitchcock's boyhood trauma. "You know," Diane said, "that story you told about how Madeleine Carroll and Robert Donat were handcuffed together for a day—well, that was absolutely true. I used to hear it over dinner at home."

"What do you mean, Diane?" I asked, not quite sure what she was talking about.

"Oh," she chuckled. "Madeleine Carroll was my stepmother. That prank of Hitchcock's really *did* affect her. She talked about it to us."

"Telling," you see, is also a repetition that sometimes follows from shocking external events. Hitchcock had traumatized Madeleine Carroll, at least a little. He had scuffed her, nicked her, with his own boyhood lock-up. She needed to tell the story afterward. Probably more than once.

PART IV

Treatment and Contagion of Childhood Psychic Trauma

CHAPTER 14

Treatment

"How are the kids now five years later?"
"All right. After all, two of the girls is married."
Jack Wynne, Chowchilla school-bus
driver, on television news (July 1981)

I N JUNE 1981 the graduating psychiatric residents at the University of
California, San Francisco, gave a dance. I teach at UCSF, so I try to go
to the graduation parties whenever I can. This was one of the nicer
ones. Usually there is food—no dancing. This time there were both. At
about ten o'clock, a graduating psychiatrist came over to where I was
standing and asked what I thought about the Chowchilla kid who had
been killed. "What?" I asked. "Who?" "What happened?" My head felt
strange.

"I don't know how it happened," the young man replied. "But it was a
girl. 'Johnson,' 'Jackson,' something like that. I heard the news on my car
radio on the way up here. It was an industrial accident, I think."

I could not stay. How could anybody have fun on such a night? It
appeared that Jackie Johnson must have met with a freak accident. But the
story did not hold together well. Jackie was the kind of girl who went
shopping most Saturdays at the big shopping malls in Merced or Modesto.
She was a junior high school cheerleader who led a quiet, somewhat sedate
life. What I knew of Jackie did not link up well with "industrial accidents."
Johnny, her brother, was a different matter. He took his chances. Johnny
had missed the opportunity to be a hero during the Chowchilla kidnapping. Afterward, he prepared to be a hero for the "next time." Johnny, like
the best of the piano virtuosos, had committed himself to a lifetime of
practice. We turned on the radio and did not have to wait long.

The graduating psychiatrist had most of it right. He had remembered the Johnson family name correctly. He had recalled the industrial accident. He had, in fact, missed only the sex and first name of the victim. It was Johnny Johnson, not Jackie. Johnny Johnson. The radio reporter said that Johnny, age fifteen, had been killed at his father's plant when a truck hoist broke. The boy was crushed between a wall and some crates that he had been unloading. It was Johnny, all right. Johnny Johnson was dead. I went to bed and battled against sleep.

Johnny Johnson was eleven years old when he was kidnapped. A very smart kid who liked to take the part of the comedian before the events of July 1976, Johnny functioned the same way everybody else did during the kidnapping, except for a sarcastic "Who, me?" when the kidnappers ordered him to the back of the bus and a "Now they'll have to smell them, not me," when the kidnappers took away his shoes. When the bigger boys decided to dig their way out of the "hole," Johnny was not asked to take part in the decision. Johnny Johnson, of course, volunteered when he saw what was going on in the cubicle above him. But down in the "hole," somebody told him "No"—he was too weak and too fat. That "No" wounded Johnny. The reasons given to him wounded him, too. He was weak. He was fat.

Carl Murillo dug, and he was almost a year younger than Johnny. The older, chubbier boy stayed down below in the "hole" removing dirt. Johnny grumbled in silence to himself. During his mindless labors Johnny thought back to the film *Dirty Harry*. Johnny had seen *Dirty Harry* years before with his dad. Johnny's father had interrupted a climactic scene in which a school bus full of kids is held hostage by a murderer in order to ask, "What would *you* do if that happened to you?" Johnny could not put that question inspired by *Dirty Harry* out of his mind. As he pushed away the dirt and stones, he thought back. He could have saved his friends quickly, effectively, Johnny figured. If only he had answered his dad. He could have turned out thinner. Stronger. He would have been ready. Ready to be a hero.

When I first met Johnny in the winter of 1977, he was determined to build up and to toughen his body. He spent his leisure time chopping wood and lifting weights. He had sent for a Charles Atlas course that winter, he told me. And he had used his own money. But then, in a fit of dismay, he had burned the whole thing up. Charles Atlas was recommending fourteen, not twelve, as the age to begin serious muscle-building. Johnny Johnson could not wait for Charles Atlas to catch up with him. He *had* to get started now.

By the summer of 1977, Johnny Johnson looked leaner and harder. He had been busy pounding in fence posts about his parents' property. Did Johnny need extra psychiatric treatment to stop him from this single-minded quest for heroism? He was showing a personality change. In 1977 Johnny Johnson appeared not to need any special psychotherapy for this. He had been traumatized but he appeared no worse off than anybody else at Chowchilla. Nineteen kids were exhibiting some shift of personality style, and Johnny's change seemed only a bit more exaggerated.

By the time I next met Johnny Johnson, in the spring of 1980, his personality shift was far more obvious. Johnny had entered adolescence by then, and adolescence seemed to have fixed the character change into place. The boy was wearing a "Class Clown" T-shirt the first day that I saw him in 1980. His quips, however, were falling far too fast and furious to allow for Jack Benny timing. Although Johnny knew that he was smart, he told me he was spending most of his time irrigating, feeding cattle, and preparing for next fall's high school football team. When he wasn't exercising his muscles, he was exercising his comic powers. In fact, he had written a funny story, "Gnaws," a takeoff on *Jaws,* that told about a town held captive by a giant beaver. The trauma-related theme stood at the center of Johnny Johnson's spoof. It was clear that he was valiantly trying to rise above his trauma with lots of laughs and with sheer muscle power. Johnny Johnson had joked a couple of times during the kidnapping and now he felt impelled to joke most of the time. He had missed his chance at heroism. Now he was practicing for heroics whenever he could. The trauma was still very much alive in Johnny Johnson's life. But he did not realize it. Nor did his parents.

Over the summer of 1979, the Johnson family inherited some money and Johnny's father bought a plumbing supply company. In 1980, Johnny started high school and took a job at his father's place. The boy prided himself at how strong he was becoming. "I still work extremely hard getting strong," he told me that fall. "I do a man's work at the plant—'gorilla work.' We're the 'gorillas' of the bunch!"

I tried to get Johnny Johnson to understand that his overdetermined choices of brawn over brain, of funny over serious, might not eventually work out well for him. Despite the fact that he was extremely bright, Johnny's grades were starting to fall. Johnny, like the other Chowchilla kids, however, saw his future as a nebulous thing. He lived "one day at a time." He could not see the point of studying. In an essay on his life's purpose, Johnny wrote, "I started out in this world to give my parents something to do. Without me, they would have sat around and played Scrabble. In the future, my purpose, as far as I can see, is unknown." I never was able to convince Johnny Johnson to carefully reconsider his style of behavior. He liked the way he had become. And so did his parents. Johnny clowned about me, as a matter of fact, just two weeks before he died. A reporter from the *Fresno Bee* had asked him if he experienced any lingering fears now that five years had elapsed since the kidnapping. "No," Johnny had quipped. "Just fear of psychiatrists."

The Chowchilla kidnapping turned Johnny Johnson star-struck. He followed the lives of heroes from that time on. He had worshipped Bob Barklay, the children's hero, and he closely checked what they said on the back pages of the Central Valley sports sections about Bob's rodeo career. If I ever had a question about how Bob was doing, I could count upon Johnny Johnson for the answer. "He's number seven in the 'Juniors,'" he'd say. And I could be sure that Johnny's information was correct. In fact, Johnny Johnson, in his quest for "stars," even phoned Steven Stayner, the Central Valley boy who had been kidnapped and held by Kenneth Parnell, a pederast, for seven years. Johnny had called the boy shortly after Steven rescued a newly kidnapped five year old and led both of them to safety. "I stammered like he was a movie star," Johnny told me. It was clear that Johnny Johnson loved any kind of heroics. He achingly waited for a chance at heroism. He wanted another chance.

Johnny's wish to be a hero turned out to be his fatal flaw. He fell in with the "gorillas," the men who loaded and unloaded the heavy plumbing equipment that came and went from his father's plant. Johnny was killed when a truck hoist broke as he was unloading heavy crates. More than a ton of plumbing supplies lashed back at the boy, crushing him against a wall. Whether a full grown man would have better known how to position himself or how to otherwise avoid such a catastrophe remains a haunting question. I doubt, however, that Johnny Johnson, at age fifteen, would have been on that loading platform at all, if not for his obsession with heroics.

Johnny Johnson died a hero. Radio broadcasts, television news, and papers all over California reported his death. They treated his passing in the same way that they treat the passing of a minor movie star or a retired sports figure. Johnny received the proper notice for a hero. But he did not know it.

After the Chowchilla kidnapping, Johnny Johnson was unable to stop feeling he had missed his golden chance. When he died he was simply doing his "gorilla work." As far as he was concerned, this was only "preparation," not real heroism. I miss Johnny. And I remember him well. I wish he had undergone some intensive psychiatric treatment, not just the brief work we did together. But then, who knows? The same thing might have happened anyway.

How do you decide which traumatized child needs treatment? Johnny Johnson's death taught me an important lesson—major personality shifts that come about as a result of childhood trauma require intensive treatment. This "rule" takes in, of course, almost all abused, mistreated, and sexually misused kids. Almost every one of them shows personality changes of the angry, fearful, borderline, or benumbed types. And these changes are extensive indeed.

Of course, there is a "rub." Many children who have been the victims of chronic, repeated, long-standing abuses become wards of their counties and states. They live in foster homes and in small institutions. Many of these children have no means whatsoever to pay for treatment. Worse yet, even when their doctors cost "nothing" directly to them or their families, these youngsters usually have no one to transport them to their doctors' offices or to make sure that they take themselves there. These very children, the ones researchers have found prone to abuse others later in their lives and even, in certain instances, to become hard-core delinquents or murderers, are the very ones for whom it is often impossible to arrange psychotherapy.

More fortunate children, however, also occasionally suffer the character problems so typical of the long-standing abuses. The Hillgard day-care victims' certainly fit into this category, as did the youngsters, like Helen Symes, who were exposed to satanism at their nursery schools. I testified in court for Leroy Hillgard's child pornography "stars" in order to enable them to collect enough compensation to undergo the amount of psychotherapy that they needed. I suggested they be enabled to have one course of psychotherapy immediately, one course at whatever time they became sexually active, and one course whenever they started raising children of their own. (It could be postulated that each of these stages of life represented a potential time for the dormant trauma to reawaken.) But most people cannot afford all of this treatment, especially when no civil lawsuits have been filed on their behalf. If a parent could pick one thing to "buy," however, for the child who has suffered long-standing or repeated abuses, one good complete course of psychotherapy would be the thing. The chances that a child will develop disordered personality traits are too high to put off this kind of purchase. And if one could afford nothing at all for the child, then the clinics, especially those connected with university departments of psychiatry or psychology or with major training hospitals, offer adequate treatment for children at sliding-scale rates.

But what of the single-shock traumas that do not, in most instances, seem to affect a child's personality so profoundly? Johnny Johnson's personality changes—in retrospect—demanded attention. But in most circumstances a parent of a single-blow psychic trauma victim would have to watch for other symptoms. Is the child having terrible nightmares? Trouble sleeping? Does he play something repeatedly, grimly, monotonously? Is he fearful? Are the fears trauma-specific, the kind that the Chowchilla kids experienced? What about the child's attitudes about the future? If one knows the child well, one can ask a number of questions and observe the child's behavior on different occasions. Has the child done something unexplainable or weird? Reenactments, of course, are often the most troublesome and dangerous symptoms of childhood trauma. Has the child developed a sense of the supernatural? What are the subjects of his essays, stories, journal entries, and poems? What does he fantasize about? What does he draw?

A parent is better off *not* counting up the symptoms and then making a "go—no-go" decision regarding whether to seek psychotherapy for the child. The decision should be made on the basis of the degree of symptom intensity rather than number of symptoms. Children will show fears at certain developmental stages. Sometimes there are quite a few fears. But are these fears particularly intense? Do they interfere with something important? Every child pretends. Is the pretend strange, rigid, too intense? Is it morbid? Repeated? Dangerous? Every child frets about the future. Is the youngster overly pessimistic? Has this pessimism existed for some time without changing?

General physicians, emergency-room doctors, and pediatricians can help parents make decisions about whether and when to consult the child psychiatrist. General doctors, however, have not yet become well enough informed about the signs, symptoms, and findings of childhood psychic trauma to be counted upon across the board for reasoned opinions. Advising the reader to consult with his physician about a potentially traumatized child will probably be a good piece of advice ten years from now, but it is not timely now. In the future, good family doctors and pediatricians will know how to spot childhood psychic trauma. It is an increasingly important issue. Over the next several years, however, it may be necessary to start first with an evaluation at the child psychiatric office. A child psychiatrist will employ three or four visits to take a history from the parents, to examine and to play with the child, and to go over the findings with the child and family. This should be sufficient time to decide if trauma is present, if the trauma needs treatment, and what kind of treatment would be the best. In the evaluation process, questions are asked and answers given. In treatment, on the other hand, both doctor and family pursue the goal of relieving symptoms and helping the traumatic memories scar-over with as little residual as possible.

The brief treatments I gave to the kidnapped Chowchilla children in 1977 and 1980 turned out to have done very little, either good or bad, for the youngsters. I was primarily studying the children, not treating them. We talked and I explained, made a few suggestions, and interpreted. I also worked with the kidnapped children's parents. But I did not know fully what was happening in the kids' minds at the times that I saw them. I had to correlate the group results after each phase of the study was completed. I knew much less about how to treat childhood trauma at the time that I saw the kids than I knew later—when I saw the results. Because of the Chowchilla studies, *other* traumatized kids would get a better break in treatment. Unfortunately, the Chowchilla children would not.

I know now—though I did not know it then—that it might have been better to bring a boxful of toys to Chowchilla "interviews." It might have been better to draw and to play, if the children would have allowed it. I should have come on stronger about the character changes I saw in the kids. And I should have tried harder to enlist every single parent in the treatment process. My main point would have remained what it was then, however. The Chowchilla interviews were set primarily as research probes. This was the first point I made to the parents when I came to town, and it remained the major point behind everything I eventually did there.

It became apparent from the Chowchilla studies that the longer you waited after a traumatic event, the less interested the traumatized child and his family would be in obtaining treatment. Even the five months that had intervened between the kidnapping and my first visit to Chowchilla may have been too long. The children were regrouping, trying to look normal. Walls of suppression were being erected by youngsters and by their families. Even the community was building walls. These walls were almost too high to climb and too thick to penetrate by the time I returned to town three and one-half years after the first leg of the study was finished.

I will give but one example of this walling-up here, but there are many other examples earlier in the book. When I arranged to return to Chowchilla for the four- to five-year follow-up project, I negotiated with the Rosenberg Foundation to support the Chowchilla studies once again. The foundation suggested that the Alview-Dairyland school system administer the grant, as it had done for the 1976–1977 project. The Alview-Dairyland School District school board, however, refused. "The kids have been through enough," they said. "Better to leave them alone." And so my follow-up project had to be done without any help from the schools. I had to administer the study myself. No wonder by 1980–1981 we had to sit on hard park benches in warm or cold weather. The schools had decided to stay out of the study.

Defenses go up very fast after trauma strikes. People do not wish to think of themselves as abnormal, hurt, or changed. Parents discover that their children's grades, for the most part, are holding steady. They find quickly, too, that their friends and relatives do not want to "drag it all up again." Families that were "normal" before a trauma do not wish to see themselves as changed afterward. It's not fair, they feel. And they are right —it's not fair. It does not seem right to put a "normal" child into treatment, parents often conclude. But this is probably quite wrong. Children's lives, "normal" or "abnormal," may organize around a trauma.

After I left Chowchilla, I learned that young lives were continuing to arrange themselves around the school bus kidnapping. Parents phoned me to say so. And, once in a while, a kid phoned. Even a neighbor or a grandparent called me a time or two. Reporters and television news producers let me know what was happening in Chowchilla. A doctor phoned once. And much of what they told me intimated tragedy.

Two of the Chowchilla girls had married by the summer of 1981, at the ages of fifteen and sixteen. A third girl married a couple years later, several states away, when she reached fifteen. These girls' mothers or sisters had not quit high school in order to marry. The girls themselves appeared to have lost the ability to pursue a lifelong goal or to become committed to a series of life-enhancing projects. Their sense of futurelessness had taken material form.

Age fifteen appeared to be an especially difficult time in the lives of several of the kidnapped children of Chowchilla. At that age, Leslie Grigson went to a public agency and made a serious accusation of her family. The police became involved. Leslie was sent off to live in foster care. Leslie's mother phoned me a few times about it. Nobody proved anything one way or the other, as far as I know, although the Grigsons and the district attorney fought it out for more than a year. But Leslie had, at last, played her "Traveling Barbies," or "Traveling Leslie," for real. She had left home and had landed safely elsewhere. "Safely"—that had been Leslie's objective from the very beginning. After a month or two, Leslie Grigson begged her parents to let her come home. But her parents could do nothing about it. The situation was well beyond their control.

Life goes on, and things other than childhood trauma certainly contribute. Benji Banks went off to an institution for juveniles, a reporter told me. The charges against him did not seem directly to relate to his kidnapping at Chowchilla. But I could follow the Chowchilla kidnapping like a fine metallic thread through the fabric of many of these developing, young lives. "Futurelessness" lay at the center of what happened. One boy told me that he wanted to live his life in isolation in the mountains—so that people would never harm him again. He said he'd like to be a computer engineer somewhere high in the Sierras, an unlikely possibility unless telephone and computer costs became cheaper. Another kid said she wanted to be a professional photographer. But she had become too passive and too distrusting of the future in the course of the kidnapping to save enough money to buy a good camera or to take a photography class. Besides that, the girl wished never to leave town because "the world" felt too unsafe. Her chances as a photographer were seriously limited, young as she still was.

After a while, Bob Barklay stopped paying his entry fees for the rodeos in which he rode. With a pack of bill collectors and rodeo "enforcers" on his back, Bob drifted into a marginal existence on the run. As he jumped from state to state two steps ahead of his pursuers, Bob, like many of his peers on that ill-fated school bus, began living the futureless life. Bob was forever escaping from the "bad guys." He continuously reenacted. It appeared that—although Johnny Johnson did not understand this—heroes are not immune themselves to trauma. They are victims first, heroes second.

It is a very sad ending to a very long story. But the story, of course, is not yet over. The Chowchilla children are just now reaching adulthood. Some of what I have just reported were the last gasps of the teenaged years, never easy even in the most "normal" of circumstances. A number of the Chowchilla victims have not yet settled into their more stable late twenties. Several children, like Terrie Thornton, Mandy VanderStyne, and Billy Estes, seemed to be going about their ordinary late-childhood business without too much trouble, at least from what I last heard. I would like to do a fifteen-year or a twenty-year follow-up of the Chowchilla kids, if I could. It would be much more obvious by then how their lives were actually shaping up. Everybody seemed to be finishing their business with me, however, the last time that I spoke with them. I could not tell if these children, grown up, would open up once again. My guess is that they wouldn't. The walls seemed too thick to penetrate after I left Chowchilla. But I will try. I will know much more about treatment the next time that I contact these kidnapped "children." And they will know more, too. All of them will be adults by then. Except, of course, for poor Johnny Johnson.

Years ago, long before I saw the kidnapped kids of Chowchilla, I analyzed the findings on thirteen medical-legal cases of childhood trauma in which I had participated as an expert witness for either plaintiff or defense. I particularly wanted to understand what really happens to the money that children collect as a result of civil suits regarding their "traumas." After all, you go to court as a psychiatrist and ask that a child be given a certain amount of "damages," money to correct for the emotional harm caused by somebody else. And very often in cases involving children, that emotional harm amounts to some kind of psychic trauma. So I became curious about how, after I had informed the court that a child would need a certain amount of money to pay for the medical treatment of his terrible experience, the child actually used the money. Between 1966 and 1975, the dates of injury to the thirteen children whose court cases I followed, treatment for psychic trauma was not as sophisticated as it is today. But there were several good options for relatively long and intensive treatments.

Of the thirteen kids in my series of court cases, I learned that five had received some treatment before their trials took place. Three of these children received adequate and complete courses of psychotherapy before they went to court. Two others, because of financial constraints in the families or reluctance of the attorneys or doctors to allow treatment until the legal issues were settled, received only brief help before their trials. No real good was accomplished, as far as I could tell, in these two instances. One child of the two had seen a social worker a couple of times, stopped seeing her, and then tried to commit suicide. The second had checked into a mental hospital for two weeks, but did not see a psychiatrist from that time on.

I was able to follow-up what eventually happened in the seven plaintiffs' cases in which I had testified (the six "defense" cases could not be followed-up because I supposedly was on the "opposition" side). Once the seven child-plaintiffs for whom I had testified had been granted their money through the court system, the funds went into trust for the children, available upon parental request for treatment. Two of the children, it turned out, won such small awards that after they had paid off their attorneys' fees there was nothing left for psychiatric treatment. These two children did not seek free or low-cost psychiatric help afterward, although —as I have already explained—that has long been available through university clinics and training hospitals. A third girl (Caroline Cramer) stayed in therapy with me for a few weeks after I testified at her trial; then she disappeared with barely a whisper. I noticed that Caroline was missing appointments and then, suddenly, she slipped entirely off my schedule. Caroline's treatment was almost complete by the time that her case came to trial. I would not have thought of ending the therapy, however, the way it eventually did end—without a good-bye.

In three of the seven plaintiffs' cases that I followed-up, the childrens' money stayed untouched in trust. There were no plans to use the funds for treatment, the children's parents told me when I phoned. There would be no treatment, in fact, unless these children—as adults—wanted the treatment. The last of the seven plaintiffs, a boy who had endured a gas explosion, eventually used all of the money he collected to buy a hardware store. The boy was a grown man by the time I caught up with his mother in Iowa. Although the boy had experienced no physical injury in the sidewalk gas explosion that had sent him flying across the street, he had become fearful and "changed" after that. "He's still crazy as hell," his mother said over the phone. Her boy had been traumatized, we both agreed. "But at least," the boy's mother went on, "he's got his own business now."

From my little survey I could tell that families who put their traumatized children into treatment *before* the child's court case was settled ran the risk of receiving inadequate therapy. They, however, might obtain a completely adequate course of treatment for their child. On the other hand, families that waited until after the court case was finished tended not to put the youngster into psychotherapy at all. If a parent waited so long that a traumatized child became an adult, the child was more likely to "buy a hardware store" than to see a psychiatrist. Time, as we have already seen, means a great deal when it comes to the treatment of trauma. The longer time goes by, the less likely are the chances for obtaining a complete course of therapy.

Putting off treatment for trauma is about the worst thing one can do. Trauma does not ordinarily get "better" by itself. It burrows down further and further under the child's defenses and coping strategies. Suppression, displacement, overgeneralization, identification with the aggressor, splitting, passive-into-active, undoing, and self-anesthesia take over. The trauma may actually come to "look" better after all these coping and defense mechanisms go into operation. But the trauma will continue to affect the child's character, dreams, feelings about sex, trust, and attitudes about the future. Count on that. If the child is a genius, his trauma may come to be incorporated into a parade of thematically linked works. But if the trauma had been effectively treated, the genius probably would have produced a more universal, more versatile kind of art.

Charlotte Brent's parents never found out what had happened to their wild little toddler as she roamed the ocean beaches of San Francisco. But suppose they had? Suppose the police had arrested a sex "ring" of carney people, of beach bums, and of Coast Guard enlisted men. Suppose Charlotte had been around age seven when they discovered it—four or five years beyond her trauma. Suppose somebody in the sex ring had talked. And suppose that person had remembered Charlotte Brent's name. Suppose Mr. and Mrs. Brent had found out everything that had happened to their cute, sweet, little Charlotte. What do you think would have happened then? Well, Mr. and Mrs. Brent probably would have looked Charlotte over. She had turned shy, that was for certain. And she wasn't wild in the way that she had been when she ran the ocean beaches by herself at age three. But that was good, wasn't it? And she was doing well in school. So that sex stuff hadn't gotten to her there. And she was not masturbating. She was a very private person, a modest person. She was a good girl. Shy. Just a little too shy. Too scared of people. But, hell—Charlotte was going to be OK. It was her little brother who was the "problem." *He* always was trying to get his own way. *He* was the one running wild down at the ocean now.

I do not think that Mr. and Mrs. Brent would have obtained treatment for Charlotte even if they had known everything that had happened to her. Four years' delay would have been far too long. They would have opted to watch and wait.

I had the chance to meet old Mr. Brent shortly before he died. Charlotte was in the hospital to have a breast biopsy (everything turned out OK), and Mr. Brent stopped me on my way out of Charlotte's room and on his way in. "Oh, *you* are the doctor Charlotte goes to," he said. "I hope you can help her. She's been such a shy person. She lives at home with me. I don't know why she's so shy. She relies on me. I'm afraid of how it will be for her after I'm gone. She's dependent. But she is a good girl. Steady as they come. Dang shame she never married. But that's the luck of the draw, I guess. Charlotte never was very lucky. That's her problem. Luck. I wish she'd marry. It would help me to leave this world if she was married. I'm worried about her. I don't know how she's going to do without me around anymore."

At the time I met Mr. Brent, he was eighty-eight or eighty-nine years old. He was suffering from the cancer of the prostate that would kill him within three or four months. Charlotte had remained a complete mystery to him. He never understood that her celibacy was not "luck"—that it had been a clear, premeditated plan of Charlotte's from early childhood on. Charlotte had vowed not to have sex. She was fully able to take care of herself and she worked hard and earned good money. She was hungry for human companionship, but she was not overly dependent. Charlotte lived at home with her father so that she could be sheltered from men her own age—and from the women, like the small-breasted woman on the beach, who might laugh at her. Charlotte was as steady as they come. But she was a childhood trauma victim all the same. And she would be doomed forever to the effects of that trauma.

Whenever psychic trauma becomes apparent, parents should arrange quickly for their child's psychiatric treatment. As soon as a parent knows for sure about a trauma, he or she is well advised to take the traumatized child to the child psychiatrist. Even if a child is discovered, many years after the fact, to have undergone a terrible series of events, the child should be evaluated and, most likely, treated. I know an excellent psychiatrist in another state who did not realize until he reached adulthood that he had been gang-raped by a group of older children when he was a young preschooler. He recovered the memory gradually in two ways: the incident began coming back to him in the form of picture memories as he drove back and forth from a juvenile delinquent institution where he consulted, and he was able to find the place where the trauma had occurred by going back to the town of his birth and following his visual and positional memories to a shack that corresponded to the terrible pictures he had begun seeing in his mind. This psychiatrist told me that he decided to go into therapy with a colleague of his. A year later, he told me he was "much relieved." In other words, though the long delay had made his therapy much more difficult, psychiatric treatment still remained the option of choice.

How does a child psychiatrist treat childhood psychic trauma today? Several choices are available and many of these depend upon the training and preferences of the psychiatrist. First, to get them quickly out of the way, we must consider prescription medications. Tranquilizers are not particularly helpful for the traumatic anxiety of childhood, but they may be able to steady adult family members who need shoring-up at the time of a disaster. When a child first returns to school following a terrible episode, some minor tranquilization (with benzodiazepines, such as Ativan or Xanax) may help the youngster get through his anxiety. But in general, this approach is not particularly effective and can only be used short term.

The beta-blocking agents (such as Inderal), drugs that serve to stop uncomfortable heart palpitation, sweating, and shaky knees, can be effective in certain instances of trauma. A recent study of eleven children found that these agents helped children through the day with their trauma-related anxieties. The study, however, was only preliminary and not "double blinded." One dose of beta-blockers given in advance, however, may eventually be found to help traumatized children get through situations that are expected to be anxiety-provoking. The child dog-bite victim might be able to walk down a sidewalk patrolled by dogs and the little girl might be able to pass the town park where she was raped if they took a medication like Inderal a half hour before embarking upon the journey. It takes about fifteen to forty minutes for a beta-blocking agent to work. So a child must know in advance that a traumatic reminder will be coming. Children need only to "walk the gauntlet" enough times to decondition their fear. And since children's schedules are fairly fixed, a deconditioning program may be aided and anticipated with the help of beta-blocking agents.

Antidepressants, especially the tricyclic compound imipramine (Tofranil), are useful if psychic trauma is compounded by unending grief or chronic depression. Imipramine seems to work, too, in panic or phobic states, although its mechanism for this, as yet, has not been worked out. It is obvious, however, that imipramine itself is not equipped to treat the entire psychic trauma syndrome. As a matter of fact, none of the medications that I have mentioned will do so.

Clonidine (Catapres), an adrenergic agonist, has been found helpful in some cases of adult trauma, especially those connected with long-standing grief or the hardships of war. As yet, to my knowledge, it has not been tried on traumatized children. However, this medication has been used for several years for children with Tourette's Syndrome, an entirely different kind of psychiatric condition. It is likely that clonidine will eventually appear as a treatment option for childhood psychic trauma. But, again, I do not think that the medication will be able to do the whole job.

Far more promising ways than pharmacologic agents have emerged over the past several years with which to treat psychic trauma in children. Group psychotherapy, for instance, can be very helpful. Mini–marathon sessions may be quickly organized for groups of mixed ages who have very recently endured the identical event. If you take an entire group of early trauma victims and treat them together for several hours at the hands of an outstanding professional, one traumatized person's clear remembrance may help defeat another person's denial. One person's post-traumatic play may demonstrate to another what his own secret play means. One poem about the catastrophe may encourage another poem. Or a song. Group efforts, if led by knowledgeable, well-trained, mental-health professionals, can afford quick and early relief for trauma. One may conduct a couple of two- or three-hour sessions in the immediate wake of a traumatic event, and that may be enough treatment for a significant number of those who were involved in the disaster.

Schools are natural settings for group work with traumatized children, especially those who were touched by trauma in a school connected or a nationally connected way. When a youngster dies over summer vacation, for instance, or when a classmate commits suicide, school groups may aid children indirectly exposed to the events to express their emotions and hear the emotions expressed by their peers. Training in group therapy for selected school teachers and counselors, I think, would be an important facet of teacher preparation for work with potential trauma. Group therapy in the schools holds considerable promise as a preventive mode for handling large groups of children who have undergone similar terrors. It may also represent a starting point for the stabilization of traumatized children in their homes. It is also an important means of identifying those children who eventually will require individual psychotherapy for their traumas.

After the San Francisco earthquake of 1989, I combined the mini-marathon idea with the idea of training professionals for group work in schools. I ran mini-marathon groups for professionals who planned to organize large-scale treatments for children. By helping some of the professionals who themselves had endured the frights of the "Great Quake of '89" into expressing their feelings, sharing their symptoms, and placing the event into a larger context, I trained them, I hope, to do the same for children.

If a certain traumatic event involves a whole family—for instance, the family was held hostage or endured an accident together—then family therapy may be the preferred treatment. A few problems may arise, however, when a family approach is used in childhood trauma. Young children tend to retire and to feel bored while their parents or older siblings take the floor in a group session. Youngsters may not tell their fantasies and secrets in the family context. Art work, poetry, and psychodrama have recently been added to family and group-therapy approaches, and these particular techniques may aid families or groups to express more inner feelings in this kind of setting than otherwise would have come out. But most likely, some individual sessions for the traumatized child will have to supplement group sessions when an entire family or a school group has been severely frightened by an external event. The direct victim's outlook on the trauma will tend to be individual enough that he or she must occasionally be heard alone.

Two situations involving a whole family probably should not be treated by family therapy—sexual and physical child abuse. Abused children need freely to express their rage, and most children find this hard to do in the presence of an abuser. Children are better off talking alone about their abuse with a therapist than they are talking in family groups. Abusers tend not to be able to admit to others what they have done. Their spouses have a similar problem with denial. If one were to try a family group approach to incest and abuse, most sessions would come down to "Did it really happen?" and "Who really did it?"

In newly discovered, relatively mild, physical child abuse, a conjoint treatment of the adult couple while the child remains living with the family may work. When such a treatment plan is used, the child must receive individual psychotherapy and be "safeguarded." Safeguards, such as frequent pediatric examinations, random, unscheduled home visits from public-health nurses, and checks of the child by school personnel, are mandatory. The child should be taken away permanently if the abuse continues under these safeguards or if the child is seriously abused later following the removal of safeguards. But the potential benefit of preventing a breakup between child and parent probably outweighs the potential for reabuse of the child when relatively mild child abuse is discovered early in the course of the problem. Of course, there are many exceptions to this treatment plan, and each case must be appraised for its unique set of circumstances and psychologies.

In cases of incest, the marital or "significant other" couple must work toward correcting their friendship and their sexual relationship. Either by becoming closer and by making sure that the child is safeguarded, or by ending the adult relationship altogether and continuing to safeguard the child, the parents *must* protect the child. Chaperones are useful when the child pays an overnight visit with a previously incestuous, divorced parent. Grandparents, aunts, and uncles can be used as chaperones as long as they know about the situation and primarily watch out for the interests of the child, not the adult. Children usually need their parents, even when a sexual or a physical abuse has been committed upon them. It is important to determine if the child, indeed, was psychically traumatized by the set of events. Then it is important to provide individual psychiatric treatment for the child—and to take the child from the family if the safeguards fail.

Behavioral therapy offers a different kind of relief for traumatized children. One way of conducting behavioral therapy consists of list making and progressive exposures. The child, with the therapist's help, makes a list of feared items from least-feared to most-feared. The youngster then systematically approaches these fears in order. Using relaxation techniques (and even beta-blocking agents and/or tranquilizers), he attempts to meet each fear on the list. After the child successfully faces a fear a few times, he goes on to the next fear on the list.

Behavioral therapy techniques may be applied as emergency measures shortly after terrible events take place. For instance, a child who was attacked by a dog must first overcome the fear of going back to school or of venturing outside his house before reestablishing a normal life routine. These fears can usually, quickly, be mastered through behavioral modification techniques. Behavioral therapy, like medication, probably does not overcome the entire childhood trauma syndrome, though, because fears are not the only symptoms nor the most important symptoms of childhood psychic trauma. Some recent work on behavioral techniques in psychic trauma, however, has demonstrated that post-traumatic dreams may also be overcome by behavioral techniques. The psychologist Patricia Garfield suggests that by willing themselves to face and to overcome dreamed "monsters" during light sleep, traumatized children can force corrections to the endings of their nightmares. She notes that children may be able to fall back asleep and to redream the entire nightmare a second time, with a better ending. At best, however, behavioral modification techniques, when applied to post-traumatic dreaming or to fears, provide relief only to selected symptoms. They do not attack the entire syndrome. For this reason, I would consider behavioral therapy an excellent adjunct, but not a substitute for the individual psychodynamic (psychoanalytic-derived) psychotherapy.

We are already aware that children who expect repeated abuses tend to separate themselves from these attacks as they happen, creating spontaneous self-hypnosis and massive denial. The ease of hypnotizability of these children—created as part of the disease process—becomes both the problem (slipping back and forth between different states of consciousness or different personality styles) and its means of correction (therapeutic hypnosis). The hypnotic trance therapies are being applied today to children who have suffered from multiple abuses. Visualization aids the traumatized child in remembering and in verbalizing. Even without going into trance states, the young trauma victim may achieve considerable relief through using visualization alone, followed by some kind of talking treatment.

One wonders, of course, whether hypnosis is an entirely unclouded choice when it comes to children. Youngsters are suggestible and their identities are moldable and movable. The power of the hypnotist over the traumatized child must be repeatedly reviewed by the hypnotherapist in his or her own mind. The "new" hypnotherapy techniques, however, encourage more self-will than did the deep-trance states and posthypnotic "suggestion " techniques that used to be employed.

Children show a healthy tendency to cope with external difficulties and inner feelings through play. As we already know, this play becomes monotonous, long-lasting, and, at times, dangerous after a traumatic event. Post-traumatic play, however pathological it is, can be effectively used therapeutically. It is, in fact, the most potent way to effect internal changes in young, traumatized children. Play therapy gives the traumatized child the opportunity to work through his problems without necessarily "seeing" that problem as his own—it belongs to the "princess" or the "dinosaur" or the "Godzilla" or the "star ship," not to him. A therapist can doodle with a traumatized child (Winnecott's "Squiggle Game") or join into play with a fleet of little cars. If the child has experienced a trauma, this experience will eventually play itself out in the therapist's office.

Back in the late 1930s, David Levy, one of the pioneers of American child psychiatry, created a kind of treatment for young, externally frightened children that he called "abreactive therapy." It is a play-therapy technique that allows a recently frightened youngster to play hard, dirty, and rough. The child is allowed to pound boards, squeeze clay, or paint huge messes with squishy pigments. No interpretations are offered by the therapist. This technique apparently works well with very young, externally stressed children. It may also help children who do not yet speak the language of their adopted land. The idea is to let traumatized children play-out their feelings in a safe, professional atmosphere.

Levy also described a second type of play therapy, in which the child psychiatrist prearranges the kind of toys he presents to the child. The psychiatrist brings to the office a few toys that represent the particular external situation that the youngster has found fearful. Without any direct interpretation by the therapist *to* the child, the youngster is allowed to play-out his anxieties with these particular toys.

Other therapists have followed Levy's lead regarding prearranged play for traumatized children. But they have added spoken "interpretations" to the scenario. The psychoanalyst Stanley Shapiro, for instance, provided red paint, paper towels, and a baby doll to a young preschooler who had recently witnessed her mother's delivery of a stillborn baby in an upstairs hallway. George MacLean just "happened to have" a toy tiger in his packet of toys when a young lad, attacked by a leopard, came to visit. Ted Gaensbauer provided a collection of toy dogs for a preschooler who had been attacked by a dog. Each of these psychiatrists interpreted the child's posttraumatic distress within the metaphor of the child's play. And each child improved without hearing directly about himself.

Melanie Klein, Robert Waelder, and Anna Freud each helped separately to "invent" the classic, currently used, psychoanalytic play-therapy technique that includes direct psychoanalytic interpretation to the child. In classic psychoanalytic play therapy the child does indeed hear about himself. Each of the great inventors of child play therapy linked the child's play with the child's own feelings, thereby going well past the metaphor of play. Selma Fraiberg and Erik Erikson, innovators in child analysis, expanded upon these techniques. In regard to childhood psychic trauma, however, they employed their newly developed play-therapy techniques for diagnosis, not for treatment. With the exception of David Levy, the pioneers did not develop techniques that would directly apply to psychic trauma. Erik Erikson described and interpreted the behavior of a child who had been building pretend coffins for years after witnessing the aftermath of a death in the family. But instead of recommending interpretive play therapy for this child, Erikson suggested a nursery school and some work with the child's parents. Anna Freud and Dorothy Burlingham's "Bertie" bombed his bed with his paper airplanes for six months during the London Blitz. They let him play until the play stopped on its own. It seemed that the pioneers of child psychoanalysis preferred not to provide interpretations to their young patients if the play derived from external events rather than from internal conflict. Trauma, in other words, seemed less amenable to psychoanalytic play interpretation than neurosis.

As time went on, however, child psychiatrists and psychoanalysts found that direct, personal interpretation of post-traumatic play *could* be used after a child had been traumatized. One did not have to fear acknowledging the child's helplessness to him. Most children traumatized over the age

of three would be able to remember all or significant parts of their traumatic events. Young trauma victims, it turned out, would respond easily
to a "you" remark as they played. This interpretive linkage did not seem
to surprise traumatized children, nor did it seem to set them backward in
their treatment. This connection between "play" and "you" was quite
close to consciousness in most traumatized children's minds. A direct interpretation would serve to confirm to the child something that he already
was feeling. Most children would consider such a direct interpretation a
reassurance.

The problem remained, however, once an interpretation was made, what
to do next in the therapy. A post-traumatic game might go on endlessly in
psychodynamic therapy, even though several interpretations or clarifica-
tions had been offered. It appeared that the psychiatrist would have to help
the child to detach himself from the compulsive repetitions by enunciating
the child's feelings and then, somehow, by placing these feelings into context. The terror, helplessness, rage, sadness, shame, and excitement had to
be named and applied by both child and child therapist to the pieces of old
experience that the child was playing. The child might become overexcited
or very anxious during this naming and applying process. But this emotional response would afford release and relief. Then the child would have
to be led to some understanding of how this experience might fit in with
the rest of his life and with the lives of others.

Today's child psychiatrist often shows the child the connections between
his repetitive play and his traumatic experience. The psychiatrist works
with the youngster's dreams, fantasies, and behaviors alongside the play,
showing the child what other previous or contemporary internal conflicts
may have been worked into the traumatic mental representations. The
present-day child psychiatrist also shows the child what omens, reasons,
turning points, misperceptions, and time-skews the child has affixed to his
mental representations of the disaster in order to compensate for his original sense of helplessness. Defenses that the child employs, such as overgeneralizations and displacements, are often pointed out, especially when
they affect "transference" (the child's feelings about the therapist). The
child's relationships at home and behaviors at school are explored and
interpreted. New coping possibilities may also be demonstrated to the child
during play. New endings may be added. The modern child psychiatrist,
thus, attempts to integrate the trauma into a longer view of the child's life.
The psychiatrist weaves rehabilitation and reward into the youngster's
play. The child hopefully learns that although he was helpless in one particular situation, he will have other options in the future to avoid helplessness. He will also learn, one hopes, that others, at other times and in other
places, have also been helpless. The traumatized child is not alone.

An entire treatment through play can be engineered by a child psychiatrist without ever stepping away from the metaphor of the "game." Over-interpretation may be more confusing and wasteful than play without much direct interpretation. On the other hand, when applicable, any of the direct interpretive techniques that I have mentioned can be successful after childhood trauma.

More sophisticated modes of play may be employed today in therapy with traumatized adolescents. As I have noted previously, traumatized youngsters indulge in play at older ages than do nontraumatized youngsters. Therefore, multicolored magic markers, air-brush techniques, and computer graphics can be used to induce teenaged trauma victims to "play" in the therapeutic setting. Audio or video recorders, poetry, and dramatic scenarios may also aid the older, and perhaps otherwise reluctant, traumatized adolescent to explore his inner life. These probing, expressive techniques are often the techniques of choice in the intensive treatment of psychic trauma, whether the trauma is treated in groups, families, or individually. Imaginative, play-like activities help break down previously rigid defense patterns.

Talking therapies, with or without play, also work in childhood trauma. Talking, in fact, is a powerful technique. If there are enough weeks or months to follow ideas through with a child, the talking therapies will help a child to abreact, to accept the world's randomness, and to develop more flexible, more self-enhancing coping skills. Concerns with the randomness of events, the sense of helplessness, the distrust in the future, and the ongoing distortion of perceptual and cognitive functions often respond to "talking it out" with a therapist.

If the psychiatrist couches his or her interpretations in metaphor, in the language of jokes, in childhood "tales," or in dramatic "scenarios," the traumatized child may achieve considerable relief. The metaphor hits the child on two levels—on the "story" level and on his own, more internal level. Highly visualized language, after all, is probably the real language of psychic trauma. Trauma is perceived in pictures. It is rerun later on visual "tapes." Metaphoric or descriptive language, therefore, is an excellent route of access to trauma.

The biggest, hardest job for the child psychiatrist, of course, is to turn around post-traumatic character change and reenactment. The traumatized youngster must be made to feel uncomfortable with the character readjustments that he has made. "Pranks" and "games" must become uncomfortable. In order to accomplish this turnaround, the family must align with the psychiatrist on the side of more flexible, developmentally appropriate behaviors. Reenactments must be seen as problems. They must be referred back by the family, or even the foster family or institution, to the psychiatrist for future "talks" with the child. The child needs to question his habitual modes of response, and then to change them. He needs to take renewed chances with assertiveness in order to take renewed control of his world. If a family or an institution and a psychiatrist work "in sync" on the traumatized child's character, the child's personality will most likely move eventually in a healthier direction. Fixing these character realignments following traumatic maladjustments is probably the most significant contribution a child psychiatrist can make to the traumatized child's future. Reenactment feeds into character; character does not change after trauma unless an end is put to reenactment.

For the traumatized child, new problems will come up with new phases of development. Adolescence, in particular, reawakens old conflicts concerning compromised autonomy. A parent might consider bringing the previously treated traumatized child back to the psychiatrist once the child has entered a developmental sequence that has an important meaning related to the trauma (for instance, the physically abused preschooler might come back for a brief course of treatment once he makes the high school football team). One wonders how many traumatized children and/or their parents would consider returning to treatment, however, once they have achieved relief. Most traumatized people, as we have already seen, try almost beyond anything else to put the experience behind them.

What can parents do to prevent psychic trauma in their offspring? First, they can learn about babysitters and day-care operations by carefully checking references, by asking state agencies about previous investigations and/or convictions, and, most important of all, by carefully interviewing the principals before allowing their children to stay with them. Random drop-in visits by parents are an excellent way to make sure everything is alright at day care. Any child-care or home babysitting person that frowns on parental visits is to be avoided. And if a random visit reveals something unusual to a suspecting parent, he must visit again. Soon.

We have already seen that the implied admonition to parents from the World War II literature—"stay calm"—does not work. No parent should be asked to aim for this. To ask calmness of terrified adults is to ask the impossible. However, we must ask that parents listen and talk to their children after a traumatic event has occurred. And parents should also check for the signs of trauma if a known, terrifying incident has already taken place.

Parents who have been traumatized at the same time as have their children should consider the option of assigning others, rather than themselves, to talk with their traumatized children—either other family members, family friends, or a mental-health professional. Parents who have been frightened by an outside event frequently hate to admit that they need help—after all, they were "normal" and did not seek counseling before it happened. If parents are able to make an admission of their own vulnerability, however, the kids will benefit. It is particularly helpful to bring in friends at the time one marital partner dies in a sudden, shocking way, or after a flood, tornado, or hurricane takes up most of a parent's time and energy. Friends need to come over and hear-out the children. Rather than talking, friends must listen. Then, and only then, should a friend respond. Immediate reassurance somehow conveys to a child, "I don't want to hear this." It is amazing to note, parenthetically, at how young an age traumatized children seem to refuse to be reassured by calming words or false promises.

Some parents, if not severely shocked themselves by a traumatic incident, may listen to their children at home and respond with helpful comments. The psychoanalyst Erna Furman, in fact, suggests a technique she calls "filial therapy," in which the analyst offers therapeutic interpretations to the parent that the parent takes home and gives to the child. Filial therapy relies on the fact that a parent is often able to find a more appropriate moment at home to offer interpretations of behavior than can the therapist in a weekly or biweekly visit.

I have already noted that a family, all traumatized in the same way, may benefit from immediate group sessions together. Most child psychiatrists are equipped to conduct such sessions.

The most important preventive function a parent can fulfill after a shocking event or series of events is to watch his or her children with open eyes and to consciously avoid denial. Traumatic events frequently happen outside of parents' sight. But the symptoms and signs afterward *will* be exposed to parental view. We have reviewed these symptoms and signs throughout the book. If a child is playing monotonously, is changing in behavior, is exhibiting new, specific fears, is dreaming terrible, repeated dreams, or is making comments about something unusual, perhaps even supernatural, the child should be taken by the parents to a child psychiatrist for evaluation.

Communities occasionally take a preventative role against trauma. In San Francisco, for instance, school children are routinely put through earthquake drills at random times during the year. Local television shows instruct three and four year olds about ducking under tables and standing in doorways. When the autumn earthquake struck in 1989, numbers of parents noted how calmly their youngsters headed for the nearest relatively safe place. Drilling and TV instructions may have warded off many cases of childhood trauma. Of course, this does not prevent everything that evolves from a mass disaster, but it certainly does get through to a number of small children.

Sometimes the new therapies for trauma sound unusual. A therapist *has* to improvise—we presently have few "rules." And even when we get more "rules," some of these will eventually yield to exceptions. Marcella Stone, for instance, the twenty-four-month-old girl we already know from her pointed questions about "time," needed exceptional treatment. Because of an unusual disease with which she was born, the blond, blue-eyed girl had developed gangrene of both feet. Her feet were amputated, but Marcella's parents were unable to tell her. Her father brought her to me. While Marcella's four-year-old brother waited in the waiting room (he saw me once, too, about his fears), I saw Marcella and her father for four visits together. She lay on my floor except for part of her last session. Her parents sat on the couch. First, I had to tell Marcella that her feet had been "taken off" by the surgeons. She knew it and was not surprised. She had noticed. Then I thought of having Mr. Stone send for a tape of a widely shown television commercial made by DuPont that showed a huge, black basketball player playing the sport on two new, artificial legs. DuPont sent the Stones their ad, and Marcella watched it a hundred times or more. She called it "her" tape. Watching Bill Demby play basketball on his "resilient, flexible" limbs helped Marcella immeasurably. At age two, Marcella was able to put her trauma into some kind of larger context through this ad. It was an unusual new twist to "psychotherapy."

Marcella Stone asked her parents some odd questions about "garbage" between sessions three and four, and her dad told me about it. He was shocked, however, when I spoke to the twenty-four month old about a fear I thought she had developed. I said I thought she was afraid her feet had been thrown into the hospital garbage can. The child brightened up at once. She agreed. Yes, that was what she thought. She considered this an unspeakable topic, but she had worried all the same. We discussed together how doctors sometimes kept the most interesting feet in bottles. I said that because she was so young and her sickness had been so unusual, I thought the doctors must have made microscope slides of her feet and then put the rest in a big bottle. The child liked that. It was better than the hospital garbage. Before her last session at my office Marcella was fitted with her new artificial feet. She insisted on having the appliance makers put on red shoes. She was reestablishing her controls once again. Mr. and Mrs. Stone would much have preferred beige or brown, they told me in a phone call. They did not want to focus attention upon their child's disability. But they understood. Mr. Stone had been watching Marcella and me work together. The last time I saw her, Marcella Stone stood up and walked. Her smile—and her red shoes—lit up the room.

What if an adult recognizes the signs and symptoms of psychic trauma in himself? He will probably benefit from psychotherapy, even though the trauma lies far in the past. Although Charlotte Brent neither remembered her whole trauma nor took back her childhood pledge to stay a virgin, she did become more outgoing, more sociable, and more in charge of her own future through psychiatric treatment. Though she never stopped worrying about disasters, our work together did help her plunge ahead and buy a house near the beach, develop a close relationship with two cousins, and begin traveling about on her own. I think that psychotherapy helped Charlotte to achieve these things. And I think Charlotte would agree.

The media holds tremendous power when it comes to trauma. Television can create mass hysteria around events or stem the tide of hysteria immediately. News broadcasters uncover a number of upsetting local and national events every day; yet very little of the media's efforts have gone, thus far, into furthering an audience's understanding or its calm. If the media regularly would put the events of the day, for instance, into child language, youngsters might better digest and think through what has happened in the outside world and, in a sense, toughen themselves to future disappointments and shocks. Although there is no obvious marketing advantage to daily child-centered news programming, some public service TV channels or radio stations could perform a boon to youngsters by providing it. This type of programming should center on the same issues, such as an airplane crash or terrible earthquake, that the adult news programs cover. Kids know about these horrors, anyway. What kids need is a good, meaningful discussion by experts who are employing simple language. And they need an opportunity to hear a reasonable discussion by other children.

Obviously, news coverage must be careful, thoughtful, and mindful of the risks when it comes to the contagion and hysteria that occasionally infect children around issues such as schoolyard shoot-outs and adolescent suicides. But the opportunity to air such information for children, given enough time for adequate explanation and discussion, should aid youngsters in facing their futures and dealing with the contemporary world. Child psychiatrists, over the past few years, have become far more adept at "facing" the public on television. Some of them would be excellent adjuncts to this kind of news coverage for children.

The media has already proven it can help provide frontline treatment for victims and witnesses after disasters. Following the terrifying 1971 San Fernando Valley earthquake outside of Los Angeles, a social agency broadcasted on a local radio talk show. The very afternoon of the earthquake, social workers from the agency urged adults and children to phone in their questions and comments. The agency workers answered the questions and discussed the feelings that had been expressed. Although the agency did not provide much follow-up counseling, their immediate response to a community emergency served an urgent, and in some instances a desperate, need. A national call-in show geared toward children's questions about a disaster, such as the January 1989 Stockton, California, playground shootings, would be a natural extension of this idea. Call-in shows, in fact, were employed with seemingly helpful results after the October 1989 San Francisco earthquake.

Movies and fictional TV shows may promote traumatic symptoms among populations of children. Single traumatic symptoms that are transmitted, even though they do not comprise the whole symptom complex, do pose a serious problem. If the symptom includes a dangerous behavior, the number of childhood deaths will actually go up. In an adolescent suicide study done in New York state by Gould and Shaffer, for instance, a significant rise in New York suicides appeared to have occurred in the teenaged population after three of four broadcasts that depicted fictional, teenaged suicides were shown. The fourth broadcast, which was accompanied by a short preshow and postshow debriefing, did not lead to a significant rise in the suicide rate. In other words, the producers of the fourth show had put on a nonfiction discussion of teen suicide as part of their televised presentation. This preventive attempt apparently *did* accomplish some actual prevention in New York state. The same type of prevention might be considered when news of disasters is given on the airways.

Many more research studies must be done before we will understand clearly what promotes and what prevents single-symptom contagion among the masses. I am confident that the question is interesting enough to inspire some good research in the future. But in the meantime, the media must become more aware of the problem of post-traumatic symptom transmission. Television and radio producers must make whatever efforts they can to prevent the spread of emotionally disordered behaviors among the young.

Treatment does not always conform to the neat outlines of "group," "family," "individual psychodynamic play," "individual psychodynamic talking," "behavioral," "hypnotic," "medication," and "media" treatments that I have offered in this chapter. Much good treatment represents a combined program—some medication, some talking, and some play, or some other workable sort of mix. It is almost impossible for a psychiatrist to treat a child without providing some access to parents, guardians, or institutional directors who participate in the child's life. Parents need the reassurance of visiting the child psychiatrist. They need to know what the psychiatrist is doing, to know how the child is faring in treatment, and to know what specific plans for the child they must put into operation themselves. Once the psychiatrist is out of the picture, the family has to take over. Much of the therapeutic process consists of preparing for that time.

The "team" approach is the best approach to any child-psychiatric problem. Parents and psychiatrists must "team" together to provide the best possible treatment program for the child.

In the case of childhood trauma, a child psychiatrist must often improvise. As I hope I have already emphasized, we are just at the beginning of understanding what to do for traumatized youngsters. Marcella Stone's treatment was a plunge into the dark. But it worked. Sometimes I find myself in my white and blue office high above the Bay totally at a loss for the "key" to a certain child. I feel alone with the child's trauma, and I must grope for my own solutions. Trauma is usually quite open in the child's mind (except for incest and abuse, of course). But the solutions remain secret. There is usually a way, however, although it may not be the conventional or the already known one.

Sometimes the way to approach a traumatized child lies in a simple explanation. Frederick Waters heard that his self-anesthesia was endangering him. He snapped out of it. Alan Bascombe heard that Olive really represented his own weaker side. He got the point. And Olive disappeared. That isn't exactly the way ordinary psychodynamic psychotherapy goes. It may take many months or years. But if a traumatized child is really ready to *hear* something, the treatment, psychoanalytically derived as it is, may take only an hour or two. Even though the therapy of childhood trauma is often modeled upon psychoanalytic principles, the treatment will work out quite differently.

Most traumatized children need more than an "explanation." These children want to be able to protect themselves in the future. They need to learn actually, really, how to do so. And so I show them. I teach many of them to tape a quarter to the inside sole of each shoe. Thus, they always have the money to use public phones. I teach them to dial the operator to get the police, and to call home collect. We practice with my phone. Traumatized children feel better about this. Why? Melanie Klein, I think, might laugh if she were to see us dialing and redialing. We are not attacking any personal underpinnings here, nor are we dissecting any internal developmental fantasies. We are attacking, instead, the external environment. But that is what trauma is all about—the external environment. Frances Carlson felt much better, once she knew how to make a phone call. She stopped wetting her pants whenever strange men walked into her classroom. Frances came to feel she could protect herself if Daddy ever tried to steal her again. She felt sure she could watch the street signs and city names and know how to call home. She no longer had to think that her father was Japanese. He, like anybody else, could be reported by phone. He, like anybody else, could be traced and picked up later.

One time I had to play "murder" in my office to show a little girl that she had been powerless to stop her grandmother from being killed. Why did I want the little girl to know she had been powerless? Because I had to break her guilt, her omens, and her terrible sense of responsibility. The little girl was Betsy Ferguson, who you know from an earlier spot in this book. Betsy had been staying with Grandma for a few months because Mommy couldn't get her boyfriend, Frank Bolt, to move out of the house. Mommy and her boyfriend had been happy together for almost a year until Mommy found out that Frank was "wanted" in a few states for armed robbery and assault with a deadly weapon. Perhaps, in fact, he had committed a murder or two. Mommy moved Betsy over to Grandma's house for safety's sake and told them both to watch out. Frank Bolt, she told them, was a menace.

One morning Betsy woke up to a loud knock at Grandma's apartment door. "My God," Grandma rushed into Betsy's room. "It's Frank Bolt. Maybe he wants to do us harm. Maybe he wants to steal my car. What should we do?" Knock. Knock. The racket continued. "Call the police, Betsy!" Grandma said. And then she rushed out to answer the door.

"But I don't know how to," the tall, slender child protested. Grandma, however, was gone. Out of earshot. She was opening her front door. Frank was coming in. Grandma was offering him breakfast. She was calling Betsy to "wake up." "Come, dear. It's time for school now," she said.

Frank insisted on driving Betsy Ferguson to school in Grandma's car. That seemed dangerous, somehow, to Betsy. Grandma insisted on coming along. Betsy had not called the police from Grandma's back bedroom. She did not know how. She went to school, forgot about the little "emergency," came home, and felt surprised to find Grandma's apartment locked. A neighbor heard Betsy's persistent knocking and phoned the police. The police found Grandma inside her apartment—strangled to death on the kitchen floor. Frank Bolt and Grandma's car were gone. Grandma lay dead under a blanket.

Eventually the state police chased down Frank Bolt. When he saw that he was trapped, he shot himself in the temple. It was all over.

But Betsy Ferguson was traumatized. She repeatedly saw Frank Bolt by night. She pictured Grandma's murder by day. She was haunted with pictures. But worst of all, she was haunted with guilt. She should have called the police. She was a bad child. She should have stopped Grandma's murder before it happened.

I think Anna Freud would have turned a little pale the day I first tried what eventually worked with Betsy. The treatment—a "murder" game I invented—was not at all "standard" or "psychoanalytic." But Betsy and I needed to play. I pretended I was "Grandma" and Betsy played "Betsy." We pretended there was a knock on my door. We repeated the actual dialogue that had ensued. First, we left Betsy cowering in her room and I played an ineffective "Grandma." We let the thing happen. But then I played a more effective "Grandma." Betsy and I barricaded my door. I showed her how to put a chair-top under the knob. We added some more chairs. We asked my secretary, Ellen Creese, to come in. Ellen was unable to get into the room. She buzzed me, "I can't get in." Betsy heard Ellen's voice. She realized that Frank could have been stopped—at least for a while.

Betsy began to realize that Grandma panicked on the morning of the killing. Grandma could have called the police herself. She could have bought time with delays—with a barricade, for instance. Because Grandma had panicked, she had asked her grandchild to do the work. The killing was not Betsy's fault. It wasn't Grandma's fault, either. It was Frank Bolt's fault—plain and simple. Betsy Ferguson had had nothing to do with it. The attempts Grandma had made to protect them had been ineffective.

Our "murder" game did not entirely do the trick. Betsy and I also had to question Mommy's choice of friends. We had to wonder about Mommy's judgment. We had to learn about carrying quarters in shoes and about phoning the police. We practiced. Betsy actually called the police a couple of times from my office.

My treatment of Betsy Ferguson, something improvised and not at all "by the book," appeared to work. I had proved to Betsy that she had not been responsible for the incidents that had led to her trauma. I had proved to her she had been ignorant. I had shown her that all of us are helpless sometimes. But I had also shown her that as we grow up, we learn things that potentially protect us. Betsy Ferguson was greatly relieved by the context into which I had put her trauma. She "decided" it would be safe to grow up. She lives with her father now, and I don't hear from her. But I am confident that our "murder" game, as unconventional as it was, helped Betsy through her trauma. The game was played early—just a few weeks to a few months after the murder took place. The earliness of the game and my professional willingness to improvise were what probably worked for Betsy Ferguson. I was surprised. And so would have been my dear friend and teacher Selma Fraiberg. We need to write a new book on the psychoanalytically derived treatment of psychic trauma. But at least we have part of a chapter now.

CHAPTER 15

Close Encounters of the Traumatic Kind

My thirty-five-year-old son told me recently that he has had nightmares in which the Gestapo come up his stairs. You realize what this means? My son was born and raised in America. But he dreams *my* nightmare, *my* life.

A German-born psychoanalyst and a
survivor of a concentration camp (1988)

C HOWCHILLA HAS CHANGED in the years since I left. A nice-looking dress shop sprang up on Robertson Boulevard. The cream of tartar factory closed, but a new roofing plant opened. The Chevy agency changed hands. Some pretty, two-story colonial houses appeared at the edge of town. They enclosed the town park where I used to see the kidnapped kids. The fence forces you to enter only from the Robertson Boulevard side. I felt like writing a letter to the town fathers when I saw that fence a few months ago. Isn't there on old western song that goes "Don't Fence Me In"? Somehow the Chowchilla town fathers were abandoning an ancestral position on fences. The big square green had lost its open, old California feeling. I will bet that a drug problem forced them to do it. But then who knows? I rarely talk to anybody from Chowchilla these days, and when I do, we talk about their lives, not the town park.

Chowchilla has resloganed itself in the years since I left. Instead of "Honest Injun', There's a heap of good living here," the oversized billboard on Route 99 now reads, "Gateway to Prosperity—Agri-Business, Industry, Recreation." There is no question that the new sign looks more dignified. It displays three classical columns, one for each of the town's three virtues. But I will miss the little cartoon Indian who announced the

311

turnoff back in the old days. Somehow the dancing brave bestowed a livelier welcome.

The Mexican restaurant where Mrs. Donnario, Timmy's mom, used to work is closed now. I guess Pedro cooked so well at his tiny "Mexican Food and Pizza" place that the townsfolk abandoned the bigger spot downtown. Pedro has expanded in recent years so that his adobe took on more the airs of a restaurant than the barrio hangout it used to conjure up in my mind. Too bad. I liked Pedro's the way it was.

But this makes me think about Mrs. Donnario again. She was nice. And sort of old-worldly. Once in a while she brought coffee over to the park from her big Mexican restaurant. She could walk in then off the side street near the back entrance to her place. There was no fence. My coffee always came hot with cream. Mrs. Donnario, a good waitress, could remember "cream, no sugar" even if she heard it only once. And she never let me pay for my coffee. Her husband, probably quite a few years older, used to like to tell me stories about the old Portuguese migrations into the California Central Valley. He'd drop by at the town park, too, especially when he saw that I was waiting for somebody who hadn't shown up yet. Timmy, their boy, wasn't kidnapped. But Mr. and Mrs. Donnario worried about him. You see, Timmy had had a close call.

Timmy Donnario had been riding on the ill-fated school bus. Twenty-six of Timmy's schoolmates did not leave the bus for an additional twenty-eight hours or so. Timmy's bus stop was only a minute's drive from the place where the kidnappers were waiting. The boy had hopped off the bus, walked home, and failed to realize until an hour or two later that he had narrowly escaped something terrible. I was curious about little Timmy Donnario. I mean, how would it feel four years after a traumatic event to have missed the event altogether? Would you be traumatized anyway? Scared? Relieved? Envious? All of these?

Timmy Donnario was only five years old at the time. It was ironic. He had been designated the last child, not the first, to get off the summer school bus all season. His house was close to the school. But Jack Wynne had developed the habit of bringing Timmy back on his way home. Perhaps Jack liked Timmy Donnario's company. He was a nice kid.

Mr. and Mrs. Donnario liked Timmy's company, too. If Mrs. Donnario had not been quite so shy, she would have asked earlier. But she eventually did ask. Could Jack please drop Tim off first, not last? Jack Wynne complied at once. After all, there were only three more school days left to the season.

Timmy closed the door to his house and headed to the kitchen for a cookie. His dad was at home. They said "Hi." Then Timmy slung his damp bathing suit and towel over a bathroom hook, and settled in for the cookie and a little TV. A couple of programs later, somebody rang the doorbell. Timmy went to the door. It was a stranger. "Are you Timothy Donnario?" the person said. "You were on the school bus a little while ago. Right? Did you see anything unusual? Did the motor on the bus sound alright? Was Mr. Wynne OK? Did he act funny? Smell like he'd been drinking? Were the kids OK? Acting funny?—"

Timmy's father came to the door. "What's wrong?" he asked.

"A bus load of summer-school kids is missing. Nobody's come home. Nobody's called. Timmy was *on* that bus. He may know something."

Mr. Donnario let the man in. The man asked a number of questions. Timmy felt befuddled. Everything had seemed OK to him. (And indeed it had been OK. The kidnappers' roadblock had been out of sight from the place where Timmy Donnario had left the bus.)

Clouds gathered above Chowchilla. More men came to the Donnario house. Mom came home, thank God. More questions. More men. Timmy had seen so many strangers by this time—in the kitchen, in the halls, in the living room—that he felt confused and afraid. The men seemed to want something from him. They seemed frustrated and even a little angry. Timmy's friends were gone. It was starting to rain. The men's questions were impossible. Was he dumb, or what? A bolt of lightning ripped the air. Whew! Thunder. Geez—men, go home. More thunder. I want to go to bed. "No, you can't sleep now, son—this is important." Lightning. Thunder. I don't like this. I want to go to sleep. Thrummm. I don't feel good. Bang, thrummm. I don't like this.

Timothy Donnario finally fell asleep on his mother's bed. It was two or three in the morning. The men had gone to their cars, offices, radios, whatever. They looked angry. They were angry. The boy fell asleep. But he did not sleep well. His friends were missing. It was raining outside. He was scared—a little scared for himself but more scared for them.

Four years after the kidnapping, nine-year-old Timmy Donnario told his mother he felt very eager to meet me. There had been four other kids let off the bus—the Lentinnen children, three of them, who had since moved up to a dairy farm someplace near Turlock ("near the other Finns," the Chowchilla parents told me) and a boy named Scarborough, who had also moved some time ago ("It was back East," people thought.) Little Timmy Donnario was the only one left in Chowchilla—the only traceable child who had been on the bus but had been let off in time to escape the ordeal. So I was very eager to meet with Timothy. How would a "close encounter" with a traumatic event strike the ordinary kid?

When I "examined" him, Timmy exhibited some of the signs and symptoms of psychic trauma. He had the fears. As a matter of fact, four years after his inadvertent escape from the kidnapping, Timmy Donnario was terrified of rain storms. "In my mind," Timmy told me, "lightning and thunder is sort of like kidnapping."

Timmy felt afraid of Fred Woods and the Schoenfeld brothers. He thought it was possible they had already escaped from San Quentin. "Don't you check the newspapers?" I asked. "It would say in the papers if the kidnappers escaped." But Timmy avoided the newspapers. "I don't like hearing what's in the news," he said. Timothy Donnario believed that if the kidnappers ever escaped or got out on parole, they'd come after him. After all, they had missed him once. They would want him *this* time. So Timmy avoided all newspapers. It was better not to know.

The boy had sweet eyes. He told me he had dreamed several dreams in which he had died. His eyes widened a little. "Does this mean I *will* die?" he said. I told Timmy Donnario that death dreams come from a past experience, not from an already arranged future. The boy looked at me, surprised and a little confused. "I've had no terrible past experience," he said.

Indeed, Timothy had gone through no terrible past experience. But he had had a close encounter. What was possible for the directly traumatized kidnap victim was now also possible for Timmy. He was capable of dreaming a dream of his own death. His ideas about what might be happening to his friends on the lost school bus had planted those seeds. And his bad experience with the investigators that night had germinated them. Timmy Donnario had been powerless to help the men who were investigating the children's disappearance. That had made him feel a little dead—useless, helpless, and absent. The kindergarten-aged lad, in other words, had felt the sensations of psychic trauma on the night of July 15–16, 1976. Much of what he felt had been for *others*. These were vicarious fears. But some of what he felt was direct. Timothy had realized that human beings could lose control of their lives, that they could be weak, ineffective, and "gone." He now knew something he didn't need to know. The world could slip out of control.

Timmy told me he had been playing "Cops and Robbers" and "Batman" over the four years that had elapsed since the kidnapping. His games were devoted to rescuing hostages and victims. Timmy Donnario had had no idea—until we talked—that his play reflected his "close encounter of the kidnapping kind." He simply knew he had been playing the same sort of thing for four years. Timmy's game represented an attempt to become an effective rescuer. In his game he had become the only rescuer, the magic rescuer. In reality, he couldn't help anybody.

Mrs. Donnario told me that Timmy's behaviors toward her and toward others had changed after the kidnapping. "He used to be friendly toward outsiders," she said. "Now he isn't. He used to give himself more independence. Now he doesn't. He clings. He treats me," she went on, "like I'm good luck. He always wants to sleep with me. And he follows me all around the house."

In young Timothy Donnario's mind, his mother was more special than the ordinary mother. She needed to be followed, he felt. It would also be a good idea to sleep with her. She had special gifts. Timmy, in other words, although he had left the bus and slept perfectly safely on the night of July 15–16, 1976, showed several of the effects of psychic trauma. He feared, and he played post-traumatic games. He avoided bad news and strangers. His personality had changed. And his behavior with his mother had regressed—it was too young, too babyish. Timmy was a vicarious victim. And he was a direct victim in a small way, too.

Timothy Donnario, however, showed in two ways that he had been spared the full sting of the traumatic event at Chowchilla. First of all, he never showed the negative, pessimistic outlook toward the future that twenty-three of the twenty-five kidnapped school children showed. This probably was so because Timmy had never felt as frightened, as helpless, and as sure of his own death as the actual victims had felt. Timmy Donnario never shaved his personal future down to just "today." "I will live to be an old man," he told me the first time we met. "Maybe eighty-three. I will get married. I'll live in Chowchilla when I'm grown up—I like how small it is, and my parents are here."

"What will you be when you grow up?" I asked.

"A lawyer," Timmy said. "I don't know what lawyers do, but I'd like to see what they do. I want to go to college seven long years. You *have* to, if you want to be a lawyer!"

That brings me to the second difference between Timmy Donnario and the twenty-five direct victims whom I had interviewed. After just a couple of talks at the town park, Timmy Donnario appeared to have recovered almost completely from his symptoms. His repeated dreams were much better—not so scary and almost gone. Timmy's post-traumatic games, "Batman" and "Cowboys," had disappeared once and for all. And most important, the boy was leaving his mother alone. He went out more with his friends. He slept in his own room. In fact, over the summer and fall of 1980 there were a few big thunderstorms in the Valley, and although Timmy told me he had felt uneasy about them, he did not need to visit his parents' room as the thunder roared outside. Mr. and Mrs. Donnario could claim their bedroom to themselves at last. No wonder they liked to bring me coffee. Timmy's brief psychotherapy had really worked.

"I will live to be an old man," Timmy Donnario had told me. I am curious if Timmy is still considering being a lawyer or whether he has become committed to some other career that will be useful and "long." He must be in college now—or just about on his way.

McFarland and Porterville, like Chowchilla, changed after my control studies were completed. Porterville grew so much that the distant farms and housing tracts that were served by the "rural" Burton Elementary School back in 1981 no longer were distant or rural in any way—they had become the town itself. They built a new high school "out there"—Monache High, it's called. Sounds Indian. And a couple of good restaurants appeared downtown that I did not spot years before when I raced into town off that lemon-lined shortcut with visions of purple-haired ladies and killer trucks rattling through my head.

McFarland is another story. They're having ongoing troubles with childhood cancer. The newspapers are saying that more kids are getting leukemia, Hodgkin's Disease, and other such horrors at McFarland than would have been expected from the national averages. People wonder if there are toxic substances hidden in the groundwater. Nobody knows what toxic substances these might be, where they are, and who, of those raised as children in McFarland, is actually suffering from cancer today. But the news from McFarland is not at all good. I am terribly sorry about this. I liked the kids I met at McFarland. They're adults now—all of them. I wonder if they left town when they grew up. Most of them had wanted to.

You may recall that ten of the twenty-five "normal" kids at McFarland and Porterville showed the effects of extreme fright or psychic trauma when I interviewed them in 1981. They exhibited clusters of post-traumatic findings. That was, as far as I could tell, a surprisingly high prevalence rate of trauma and external fright (although nobody I know of has yet checked out the childhood prevalence rate of trauma across the United States for comparison's sake). But there was a related finding at McFarland and Porterville, too, one that intrigued me. Five of these twenty-five control kids appeared to be responding to something like the Timmy Donnario experience—to an indirect brush with something that had been shocking or traumatic to someone else. These five had been vicariously frightened by an external stimulus that had not directly fallen upon them.

Joan Butler, a fifteen year old from McFarland, for example, told me she experienced fears—of strangers, of being alone, of bad weather, and of accidents. And she was not very secure about her future either—"I've always wondered if I'd have an accident and get killed." In checking with Joan about her own life, she told me that three years earlier a girl on a motorcycle had stopped by her house to ask for directions. It was pouring outside. A few minutes later the girl, back on her motorcycle, was killed in a collision with a truck. Even though Joan Butler told me that the accident had bothered her "only for a couple of days," three years later she felt afraid of strangers, of being alone, of bad weather, and of accidents. Each of these fears related to one particular motorcycle accident, an accident that Joan had not seen herself. Joan Butler's "trauma," in other words, was vicarious—one not experienced first hand. She did not see the wreck. She did not see the body. But after learning what had happened, Joan had identified with the victim. She had lost a sense of magical protection that she carried with ease before. Because Joan Butler had seen somebody first-hand who then had died, she no longer could feel safe.

Here's another instance of vicarious trauma from the McFarland-Porter-ville control group. I find this example particularly interesting because it made clear that there is no requirement that a child be in the vicinity of an event to develop post-traumatic findings. Lois Edstrom was nine years old. When I asked about fears, Lois said she hated earthquakes. She also thought that bad things could happen in her future. Lois remembered that a couple years previously her great-grandmother's house had collapsed during an earthquake in the Valley. Grandma, in her house at the time, had broken her nose. Miraculously, that was Grandma's only injury. And Lois did not see anything, not Grandma's bandaged nose, not the collapsed house, none of it. But Lois *did* see the picture in her "mind's eye." And the event, vicariously experienced as it was, had made its mark. "I imagine I'll live to about eighty," Lois told me when I asked about her personal future. "But [her voice trailed off and she sighed] sometimes I imagine a disaster would happen. I'm a little afraid of earthquakes. Sometimes I'm afraid of war. Sometimes I think I will be killed. But [she paused] I don't plan on it."

All right. So you don't have to be hurt by a traumatic incident in order to experience some of it. You don't even have to be there at all. So why isn't everybody traumatized? Why isn't everybody psychologically hurt? Maybe we are. Maybe we all are a little hurt. Maybe the hurt, when it is "little," simply becomes part of our developing psychologies—not part of a psychiatric syndrome or a disorder. Perhaps trauma plays the same sort of role in our mental development as the Oedipus complex does. For most, it is an experience that leaves its mark. For some it is the beginning of a disorder.

Traumatic events can reach children without drawing much "blood." These minor "traumas" may evolve from (1) small, direct exposures to traumatic events, (2) small, indirect exposures to traumatic events occurring to others, (3) direct exposures to the post-traumatic symptoms of others, and (4) indirect exposures to post-traumatic symptoms carried by those who, themselves, were unexposed. Although the third and fourth ways are probably the most common and most contagious types of exposure to trauma, little Timmy Donnario of Chowchilla experienced a mixture of the first two types. He was exposed directly to the investigators, the thunderstorms, and the bus—but he was also vicariously traumatized by imagining how his school friends must be feeling during the period of time that they were gone. He was traumatized by imagining what *could* be happening. He did not keep in touch with his kidnapped summer-school peers later, when the kidnapping was over. So Timmy Donnario probably was spared the contagious effect of their symptoms—unless (and we do not know this) he was exposed to the symptoms of someone who was *not* a victim.

As we grow up, most of us fall far short of experiencing the entire syndrome of childhood psychic "trauma." But as we are exposed either directly or indirectly to traumatic events and to the symptoms of others we experience a kind of toughening process. And we may pick up symptoms ourselves. We do not develop the whole syndrome, mind you. Just a few findings. And these findings may indicate changes in our developing psychologies.

A structured diagnostic interview, the DIS, is being tried upon large samples of adults in order to predict how much and what kind of mental disorders affect the population at large. Epidemiologists using the DIS have come up with two interesting percentages in regard to post-traumatic symptoms in the adult population. In one study, 8 percent, and in another 15–16 percent, of the general population admitted to some post-traumatic symptoms. There were not enough symptoms in most cases to make the full diagnosis of post-traumatic stress disorder. But there were enough solitary or coupled post-traumatic findings in these "healthy" adult populations to have caused some concern. The criteria for childhood trauma I have outlined in this book are somewhat different from the criteria in the DIS, which was set up based upon studies of adult trauma. It is not possible to tell whether the solitary and coupled findings of psychic trauma in the adult population studies reflect small brushes with trauma in adult life, small brushes with trauma in childhood, or larger traumatic syndromes from childhood that had, in part, resolved.

My guess is that traumatic exposures occur as part of almost any developing child's experience. Most children do not end up traumatized. They carry instead one or two psychological scars or symptoms from the exposure.

Rumor and lore among kids may enter into these statistics on traumatic symptoms in normal adults. Minor, but significant, post-traumatic symptomatology may be picked up through gossip and rumor. If a child was truly traumatized, the child would take his symptoms to the group. The group would then talk or play. And some of the group would come to believe. Some would actually suffer a symptom or two. "If you dream you die, will you die?"—that was a big question at Chowchilla. "I knew a girl who dreamed there would be a kidnapping and there *was* one." Leslie Grigson had heard about this predictive dream from her seven-year-old group at Chowchilla. The dream indeed had been dreamed. But the timing of the dream story was off. The dream had been told after, not before, the kidnapping. I knew it. Alison Adams, age ten, had told me this particular dream. She had not mentioned it to anyone before the kidnapping. Alison had dreamed twice that young men had entered her school cafeteria and had taken the children away. Alison thought her dream had come just *before* the kidnapping. She thought it was predictive. But because of its "modified playback" nature I could feel almost certain it had been dreamed *after*. After all, Alison had told it after, not before. The recipient of the dream rumor, however, Leslie Grigson, had been unable to trace how the story had started. She simply believed it, regardless of the source. Alison Adams's time-skew, a post-traumatic perceptual distortion, had become incorporated into group folklore—and perhaps into separate individual psychologies as well.

Once, a mother came to my office to ask about an observation she had made as she served "yard duty" at her daughter's public school. About seven third-grade girls had been playing the same thing every day for a month or so during their morning recess period. Their game looked grim and monotonous to this mother. The girls chased each other about the playground and seemed terribly frightened about being tagged. They played until they were exhausted. Terrible howlings, cacklings, and screechings emanated from their small throats. Mrs. Mattsson, the mother who sought my help, was worried not only on behalf of the school—she was worried on her own behalf, too. Hilary Mattsson, her daughter, was playing this wild game every school day.

We carefully went over Hilary's history. Nothing terrible had ever happened to her. We looked at the child's internal psychological development. No untoward signs had ever come up. I asked Mrs. Mattsson what she knew of the other girls in the group. "One," she said, "was raped on Baker's Beach by a stranger. But I don't think that the other girls know about it. She's a good friend of Hilary's, so Shelby Smith may actually have told Hilary about it—but that was a long time ago—maybe eighteen months or so."

I asked to see Hilary, and Mrs. Mattsson brought her in. The game had been going on for more than a year, Hilary told me. It was called "Rabbit and Wolf." Nobody knew, Hilary said, who had started the game. But it was very scary. Each girl player was a "rabbit." A terrible, mean wolf, an invisible male ghost-wolf, chased everybody. Nobody on the playground would play the part of "wolf" because this wolf was simply too bad, too awful. The game went on until every girl was "taken" by the wolf. Sometimes the game did not end at all. Sometimes the suspense continued until the next day's recess.

When I asked her about it, Hilary remembered her friend Shelby's story. I postulated to Hilary that the invisible wolf she feared so much had been the man who had raped Shelby at Baker's Beach. Shelby must have invented the game, I guessed—or one of the girls who knew about Shelby's rape and was scared herself. It was *Shelby* who needed to work out her fears and her helplessness. And maybe a girl or two who knew about it might need some help, too. Hilary Mattsson looked relieved when she spoke of her own responses to Shelby's rape. Mrs. Mattsson took her home, and Hilary has not needed to return.

I wonder about "Rabbit and Wolf," though. Did the game develop a life of its own? Does it still bring witch-like cackles from new generations of little girls who have no idea today why they giggle and screech so violently? Is it institutionalized on only one San Francisco elementary school playground? Or has it spread?

I remember one game that had started at Chowchilla and came eventually to affect an entirely new generation of children. Sheila Sheldon had been twelve years old when she was kidnapped. After she came home she threatened her five-year-old sister repeatedly in a playful, but sadistic fashion. Sheila, as you may recall, had left her mother at the front door on the morning of the kidnapping with the parting shot—"You're the meanest Mommy in the world." Later, Sheila needed to play out the idea. She jumped from closets, leaping at her five-year-old sister and screaming "Mommy's going to cut my ears off." The five year old, unkidnapped and seemingly untraumatized by the events that had occurred while her sisters, Sheila and Celeste, were missing, was traumatized—a little—by Sheila's closet-jumping game. She shrieked in terror at Sheila. And Sheila continued her jumping. "It got so bad," Mrs. Sheldon told me, "I could not let the two girls out of my sight."

Four years later, I came to the Sheldon house for my first follow-up visit with the girls. Sheila, age sixteen, had decided to avoid me entirely that first day. She was "out" and couldn't be found. Celeste had developed a terrible stomach ache the day before I came, and lay, curled up in fetal position beneath a pile of blankets, on the living room couch. Celeste, I think, "didn't want the lady to see [her]." She was hiding.

Mr. Sheldon invited me into the kitchen for coffee. Perhaps I would see neither Celeste nor Sheila that day. I sat back and relaxed. Suddenly, two little preschool-aged girls dove into the room—one, a new little Sheldon I had not met in 1977, and the other, her friend.

"Are you the worry doctor?" the petite, "new" little Sheldon asked.

"Yes."

"Then please—" and the second little girl, the friend, added her own "please" to this, too—"do something about the way my big sister teases us."

"Which big sister?" I asked, aware that one was buried in blankets on the living room couch, one was "out," and another, a tallish, nine year old, had just entered the room.

"*Her*," said the new little Sheldon, pointing at the nine year old. This child was five at the time of the kidnapping. I had met her once then. Boy, had she grown!

"What does she do that you want me to stop?" I asked my two tiny petitioners.

"She jumps out of closets and says Mommy's going to bite our ear off."

This was amazing. Here was a game that had moved down one generation in the three years that I was gone from town. It had infected two new, untraumatized kids. Sheila Sheldon, the original player, could have "cared less" about Mommy cutting ears off by the time her sister and her sister's friend complained to me. Sheila was sixteen and beyond the range of most post-traumatic play, except for the play of the most creative kind, the Magritte, Hitchcock, or Poe kind. At age sixteen, it would be well beneath Sheila Sheldon's dignity to jump from closets. The game had moved, perfectly intact, into a new generation of children, children who had not been kidnapped at all. These children, in fact, had not even been weaned from breast or bottle at the time of the Chowchilla kidnapping. Now they were being exposed to that very same trauma—indirectly, through the symptoms of others. Even these "others" were not themselves direct victims.

Post-traumatic games often pass from one generation to the next. One wonders if the old "traumatic anxiety" stays permanently affixed to such games. Sometimes one gets a hint of an answer. Take "Ring Around the Rosie," for instance. The "rosie" is the lesion of the Black Plagues. "A pocket full of posies" are flowers for the dead and amulets carried to ward off the Plague. "Ashes, ashes" represent the charred remnants of burning bodies—there was no time to bury so many so quickly, and so bodies were burned in medieval alleyways. "We all fall down" means just that—we die. "Ring Around the Rosie" is a Black Plague ditty, in other words. It still "plays" in the twentieth-century nursery school. The players are at least twenty generations removed from the traumatized originators.

Does anyone still feel the anxiety? Yes. My daughter, Julia, felt it when she was four years old. She had been refusing to play "Ring Around the Rosie" at preschool, and I had asked her about it. "That game makes me feel funny," Julia said. "I don't like it." "Funny," I think, meant nervous, apprehensive, terrified, horror-struck, or something like that in Julia's four-year-old vocabulary. Julia had picked up the traumatic feelings that were still attached to an old childhood verse of the Middle Ages. Even though it was four or five hundred years removed from its origins, the verse still carried a highly emotional message. Although I thought Julia's refusal to join in "Ring Around the Rosie" a little strange when it was occurring, I realized thirteen years later at Chowchilla what Julia had experienced. She, like my two little four-year-old petitioners in the Sheldon house, had "caught" a fear that was a transmitted symptom from somebody else's trauma.

Here's a much more modern post-traumatic game, and it appears to have caught on at the playground, too. Alison Lurie quotes it from an English schoolyard in her novel *Foreign Affairs*. An American child psychiatrist told me recently that she jumped rope to this ditty just a few years ago on a Midwest American playground. It goes:

> Polly at the railway,
> Picking up stones,
> Along comes a train,
> And breaks Polly's bones.
> "Oh," said Polly, "That's not fair,"
> "Oh," said the engine driver, "I don't care."
> How many bones did Polly break?
> One, two, three, four . . .

The rhyme obviously stems from a trauma—a trauma far more meaningful to modern schoolchildren than are the horrors of the Black Death. Children immediately recognize the terror connected with the more modern "Polly" ditty, and a few potential jumpers probably refuse to join in at all. But many more will jump to the thought of Polly's bones because the rhyme sounds so "delicious." A little traumatic thrill may actually feel pleasureful. After all, the jumper has successfully avoided all those broken bones herself—all those scary engine drivers, all that fear. Why not enjoy one's health? "One, two, three, four . . . " Jump. Jump. Jump.

I promised earlier in this book to tell about a haunted house that became haunted as a result of a childhood psychic trauma. The story, again, shows how traumatic symptoms are imparted to the general population of children. A couple of Junes ago, the chief of child psychiatry at a large north-eastern medical center invited me to spend the day with his child psychiatry fellows and to attend their graduation banquet that evening. In the morning, the child fellows presented a case to me and asked me to interview— behind a one-way mirror—the little girl whom they had presented. They put the two of us into a small room, and then we were supposed to talk as they watched.

There was a little trick to this, I soon discovered. The little girl did not *want* to talk. As a matter of fact, she had hardly talked at all to her doctor, one of the child fellows, for the several months that they had been working together.

A year before, the little girl had been out on a drive with her aunt and uncle, an older sister, Hyacinth, and two cousins. They were riding along a Berkshire Mountain route when, suddenly, a huge boulder toppled off an adjacent hillside onto the roof of their car. The little girl's older sister and one of her cousins were killed. The little girl, her other cousin, and her aunt and uncle emerged untouched.

The little girl and I sat before our all-too-exposed mirror (Virginia Woolf would have absolutely hated it) and the child all-but-refused to talk to me. She told me she had nothing to say about the accident—"I don't want to talk about it." And she would say nothing about fears, play, or weird behaviors—"I don't want to talk about that." She indicated that dreams and the future were out—"I don't want to talk about it." And she didn't much want to discuss school or friends either.

But then I hit upon a topic that apparently did not turn her off. "Does your sister ever come to you now?" I asked. The child fellows must have thought me mad. But the little girl immediately brightened up. She understood.

"Oh yes, she does," the little girl smiled her first smile of the day. "Almost every night."

"How does she look?"

"Good," the little girl said. "She looks just like she used to before she got killed."

"And what does she wear?" I asked.

"All kinds of different outfits. Pink ones. Orange. Once she wore a purple and green one."

"Does she look solid?"

"Yes."

"What does she say?"

"Nothing. That's a little scary—I mean, what she's going to do. But— like—I'm glad to see my sister anyway."

So that was that. The little girl had demonstrated something new to the child fellows. Her ghost was fully fleshed and colorful, in the mode of

Bergman's *Fanny and Alexander* ghosts or the ghosts of Stephen King's *It*. We said good-bye, and I was pleased as I emerged from behind the one-way mirror that I had been able to converse with this very reluctant, very quiet little girl.

But I had not heard the whole of it yet. A child fellow who had been working with the little girl's family spoke up after the little girl had left. Over the Memorial Day weekend, he said, the child's family and several other families in their suburban neighborhood had put on a block party. A friend of the older sister had come over to the house for the first time since the tragedy. The little girl had "entertained" her sister's friend in her bedroom.

That night the friend's mother phoned the little girl's mother. "I am sorry," she said, "but Linda won't be able to visit your house anymore. Your house is *haunted*."

We don't know exactly what happened in this instance, but it is not difficult to guess. Our little girl must have told Linda that her sister, Hyacinth, Linda's best friend, had been "visiting." The little patient might have shown her the very spot that her sister frequented in her green and purple clothes. Linda might have "seen" her best friend, too. A trauma was being indirectly transmitted to a nontraumatized but susceptible child. The friend was susceptible because she had already experienced the traumatic event vicariously and directly. She must have imagined how it would feel to die crushed by a boulder. She, in addition, had lost her best friend in a shocking, sudden way. The misperceptions conveyed to her in "ghost" form immediately took hold. Within a couple of hours the untraumatized little girl had told her mother about the ghost. Her mother, in turn, with a full, adult vocabulary at hand, designated the house as "haunted." Within days, the entire neighborhood would know that a new, "haunted" house had been born. Peculiar, I thought. Our little patient's sister had been killed in a car, not at a house. The car had been struck at least a hundred miles away from the coastal city where the bereaved family lived. But this fact did not seem to make any difference. A haunted house would be designated at the place where the post-traumatic symptoms resided, not at the place where the traumatic event occurred. Hauntings rested with people, not with houses. Within days everybody at the block party would know about the neighborhood's new "haunted house." By next Halloween, who knows how many other neighborhoods would know?

On January 28, 1986, the *Challenger* space shuttle blew up. My daughter phoned the office to tell me. It was 8:45 in the morning. Julia was sniffing away a few tears. She had seen *Challenger* explode on TV. It had unnerved her.

I think it is already obvious that I am interested in knowing how a traumatic event, safely experienced from a distance, impacts the normal child. The *Challenger* space shuttle disaster presented a unique way to gather some new data on how normal youngsters integrate a shocking event into their psychologies. Children all over America cared about the *Challenger*. They especially cared about the first school teacher who was to go into space, Christa McAuliffe. Most children could not have felt indifferent to what had happened. NASA had prepared them for weeks to receive the "lessons" they were to be given from the *Challenger* as it orbited the earth. Children could not have felt entirely indifferent to the first school teacher in space who was already telling them from the earth to "reach for the stars."

There was an interesting time differential when the *Challenger* blew up, an East Coast versus West Coast difference. Children on the East Coast were on, or close to, their lunch hours. They were actively watching school television sets at 11:45 A.M. Every television monitor available to the schools would have been going. But many school kids on the West Coast were initially "blinded" from the event. They were riding their school buses. These West Coast children heard about the disaster when they arrived at their schools. They saw replays later—almost all of them. But, at first, the shock was heard, not seen. (I had come to an ironic full circle, moving from a school bus at Chowchilla that had taken part in a disaster, to school buses all around rural California, Oregon, and Washington that had, perhaps, shielded kids from the full impact of a disaster.) The *Challenger* explosion was first experienced by children away from their parents. This initial separation from mothers and fathers allowed for an absence of the good or bad influences that immediate family responses may bring to bear during the first moments of shock. There was nothing unusual about those children in either part of the country who were watching or hearing about the disaster. They were "normal" kids in "normal" schools. The *Challenger* tragedy presented the kind of study, in other words, that I often think in advance about doing. (No, I do not go about "doing" disasters. They, unfortunately, keep on happening.) I could compare East versus West Coast kids and perhaps find out if and how unexpected, untoward world events would seep into their psychologies.

I decided to interview eight year olds and fifteen year olds on the East Coast and the West Coast of America. I chose these two ages because they were so typical of the latency and midadolescent stages. I chose Concord, New Hampshire, because it was Christa McAuliffe's hometown, and every child at school would have been paying attention to the TV monitors there. Christa had taught at Concord High School, but she had been gone for a year before the ill-fated space mission while she trained in Houston. If I interviewed third graders and tenth graders who did not know Christa

McAuliffe personally, I would be studying a group of normal school kids who cared a great deal about what had happened on the *Challenger* voyage, but who cared mainly from a distance.

As I said earlier in this chapter, my old California control-group town for the Chowchilla study, Porterville, had grown a great deal in the years that had followed my study at Burton Elementary School. By the time the *Challenger* space shuttle disaster occurred, Porterville had grown almost to the size of Concord. Concord had a population of 30,000. Porterville had grown to 28,000. Porterville served as a market town and sat at the base of the Sierras. Concord, New Hampshire, served as a market town and sat at the base of the White Mountains. Porterville had a 25 percent nonwhite population in its schools, as opposed to Concord's 1 percent. But there was no town I knew in the West Coast time zone that could match Concord's ethnic mix. One had to be realistic. Porterville, also, was not a state capitol, but that was another of those things that one hopes to match in the field, and often cannot.

I phoned somebody who knew somebody else who phoned one more person. (It turned out that the entire "chain" was three phone calls long.) Within two days of the disaster I had reached John Reinhart, Ph.D., the director of psychology for the Concord schools. John was interested in helping me set up the project, and, indeed, he put our logistics smoothly into place. Within another couple of days, both the Concord and Porterville school systems had approved the study. By the end of one week I had received a "quick" Officer's Discretionary Grant from Robert Haggerty, M.D., a distinguished pediatrician who directs the William T. Grant Foundation of New York. This grant would enable me to get the project started. And then, all I had to do—and that took some doing—was to close the office for a month, obtain "human subjects" approval from the University of California, San Francisco, and write a "structured interview" that was largely based upon the findings for childhood psychic trauma that had come from the Chowchilla studies. A structured interview is the kind of interview that is set up in advance. Everybody gets exactly the same questions. Everybody gets the same wording. Everybody gets the same stimuli, in other words. What the researcher loses in childhood spontaneity and completeness is compensated, perhaps, by the potential reliability and validity of the group data. It was a different kind of study for me, and that, aside from all the other factors, made it interesting.

We chose kids at random from the enrollment lists of the Concord and Porterville schools. In Concord I met the mother of two school-aged children who had volunteered after the space shuttle disaster to help the school district in any way she could. This woman, SuzAnne Metayer, became the technical assistant to my project. We did the study twice—once five to seven weeks after the shuttle disaster, and once again in March, 1987, thirteen to fourteen months after the disaster. The Grant Foundation provided me with a second, larger grant with which to complete the work.

I interviewed 149 kids. The main study groups consisted of 30 eight year olds in Concord, 30 eight year olds in Porterville, and 30 fifteen year olds in each of the two towns. That made 120 kids. There were eleven additional kids who had traveled from Concord to Cape Canaveral and had watched the explosion "live" from the viewing stands. These children had known Christa McAuliffe or her children personally, and they were a more directly involved group. Nineteen additional youngsters were interviewed at Concord in 1987 only. These children represented an "internal control group"—a group selected at random and interviewed in order to see if the 1986 interviews had changed anything in those children who had been interviewed at that time.

So what did the *Challenger* study show? Well, I can only give a general guess now—a clinical impression rather than a full delivery of all the data. My impression has to do only with the 120 kids in the main study group. (The statistics on the entire study are not yet ready—that will take a bit more time and some additional manpower.) My clinical impression from the study is that ordinary school kids are affected by extraordinary events. The *Challenger* explosion, even though the event was remote, did leave some psychological marks upon the young witnesses. As long as a kid cared, he ran the risk of developing one or two isolated post-traumatic findings. It did not seem to matter crucially if the "insult" was initially visual or auditory—if the event was shocking enough and important enough to the child, it would make its mark.

By five to seven weeks following the spacecraft explosion, most of the children on both sides of the country had developed a new fear or exaggerated an old one—fear of airplanes, of explosions, of space exploration, or of death and dying. These fears were more common in eight year olds than they were in the fifteen year olds, although about half of the adolescents had developed new fears or had exaggerated old ones after the disaster. Many of the specific fears landed inside of the children's own worlds rather than floating about entirely in "space." They had come from the shuttle explosion—you could tell from the content and their timing. Yet many of these fears had to do with house-heater explosions, scary hot-water tanks, and out-of-control cars. The children's minds had brought the disastrous event closer to home, in other words. The *Challenger* disaster reminded children of other disasters in their lives. A month after the explosion, several youngsters dwelled upon deaths in their own families and the times that other things had gone wrong. The kids also told me about scary movies, milk carton kids, and local killings and kidnappings. It seemed that external events of all kinds had been integrated into the children's mental representations of the space shuttle explosion.

More children on the East Coast, in both age groups, reported repeated dreams than did children in the West Coast group. The East Coast youngsters had taken in something, both surprising and shocking, to visualize. They could dream. Some of these dreams had to do with Christa McAuliffe and "space," but many also had to do with dead grandparents and other past shocks in the child's life. The East Coast children also tended to play more games related to the space shuttle explosion than did the West Coast children. They played space, and they drew pictures, composed poems, and wrote letters to their friends. If they were older, the children might make lengthy entries into their journals or do an essay or a poem. It appeared, therefore, that two of the classic repetitive symptoms of childhood trauma, dreams and play, were stimulated more by viewing a disaster than by hearing about it.

On the other hand, it appeared that nearly everybody visualized the disaster, whether it entered by the eyes or the ears. Even when delayed tapes were seen in actuality or when mental pictures of the explosion were put together from photos or imaginings, the visual traces stayed alive afterward in the children's minds. Visualization appeared to be the most common sign of shock and surprise in both large samples of kids of both age groups following the *Challenger* explosion.

There was little evidence of behavioral reenactment at either Concord or Porterville. Of course, I was asking the kids themselves about reenactment, and these changes in personality or in behaviors are better picked up by third parties. But my guess is that behavioral reenactment is usually reserved for closer-at-hand, more direct trauma. When reenactment does occur as a response to distant shock, of course, it presents an enormous problem. One adolescent suicide in response to a news report of an adolescent suicide is one suicide too many.

Large numbers of children in both parts of the country who had been exposed to seeing or hearing about the *Challenger* accident reported fantasy as a response. More than half of the kids on both coasts imagined, pretended, and daydreamed their way through the aftermath. Many identified with how it felt to die—to blow up, to be torn apart. They "blew up" as they sat in their classrooms or lay in their beds. Many imagined happier endings—Christa and her colleagues landing on a desert island, or even finding some safe haven in space. A few kids tried to redesign the shuttle—to mentally engineer their way out of the disaster. And a few tried to picture how it feels for a child to lose his parents. They vicariously grieved in their daydreams.

Magical shields of invincibility partly broke down in about one-third of the East Coast group and one-quarter of the West Coast group. No longer did these youngsters take life for granted. These kids said things such as "I'm trying to live each day as if it might be the last." The *Challenger* space shuttle disaster had inspired this kind of thinking. Not all of these rethinking efforts were "bad." A number of kids were working harder at school and were thinking more seriously about their contributions to the world. A number of children, for instance, told me they were thinking more of others and getting to their chores more quickly now that they had realized that they might not live forever. A significant number also admired school teachers more after the explosion than they had previously. Teachers had feelings, too, they said.

By thirteen to fourteen months after the *Challenger* disaster, many of the post-traumatic symptoms in the children and adolescents had disappeared. Had they gone underground or were they truly gone? There were still some dreams a year after the explosion and still some instances of space-related play. Lingering fears remained on both sides of the country —of planes, of the family car, of space, and of fire. But there were far fewer fears at the one-year mark than there had been at five to seven weeks. And there were far fewer dreams or instances of post-traumatic play. "Scars" apparently were forming. The partly traumatic process was resolving.

One remarkable finding at thirteen to fourteen months, however, indicated that virtually every child on both coasts of America was affected by this external event. Almost every single kid could tell me exactly where he or she had been standing or sitting at the time he or she saw or heard about the explosion. The kids almost uniformly claimed they could draw chalk marks on the spots. They knew just where they had been. I could find no way to check out these claims. But the almost ubiquitous incidence of the exact same kind of claim indicated that clear positional memory is associated with psychological shocks. The vast majority of children in the *Challenger* study also remembered two or three people who had been near them at the time they saw or heard about the disaster. About two or three in ten could remember exactly what he or she had been wearing. But "positional" sense was an especially common finding, and this finding was an exciting one. No wonder so many of us can remember just where we were standing or sitting when we heard that John F. Kennedy was shot.

It is apparently the nature of shock-related memory to be set into a certain space. We retain the picture of a position, a place. We may automatically step outside of ourselves for an instant during horrifying events. The shock may be too extreme to allow us to "stay." If we cope by stepping outside of ourselves, we may later see ourselves sitting, standing, or lying in a space. Is this a coping or defensive maneuver or is it a pure act of perception? Whatever the answer, this spatial memory probably best characterizes the memory of a psychological shock originating from outside of oneself.

One wonders why a person—a child, even—retains such a vivid, clear, positional sense in connection with a shock or terrible surprise. Might this sense go back to our primitive origins? In order to survive in the days of caves and of tree-top shelters, might we have needed instantaneously to be aware of where we stood. If suddenly confronted by a woolly mammoth or a saber-toothed tiger, man would immediately have needed to know his routes of escape. Man has moved very far from his origins in those caves and those trees. But perhaps this immediate awareness of position during overwhelming events represents a vestigial trace from man's earliest origins. An extreme external emergency will slow time and create an extraordinary awareness of position. Both emergency perceptions probably serve to preserve the self.

Occasionally, a person is able to rediscover an old trauma through memories relating to this positional sense. The psychiatrist I previously mentioned who, as an adult, slowly began to rediscover a long-forgotten gang rape from his toddler days, was eventually able to recall the whole incident by locating the place where he had been attacked. The psychiatrist drove down to New Orleans, found his old neighborhood, and followed his positional sense to a decrepit shack. At the shack, a flood of memories came back to him—the rape, the pain, and the warnings never to tell. The position of that shack made the whole thing clear to the young man. You see, he had found the shack adjacent to an alleyway. The alleyway ran directly past the house where the psychiatrist had lived until he was six years old. Positional sense—if used by a good therapist—may lead an amnesic patient back to a full memory of a forgotten childhood horror. If one "took" a repeatedly traumatized child back to this "space" inside of his own mind, the child might eventually recover a memory of the entire experience.

I have been curious about how an adult who was traumatized as a child can convey his horror to others. And I have been curious about why we allow ourselves to watch and to listen to these horrors. To satisfy my curiosity, I watched, stared at, and read the post-traumatic creative products of a number of talented people who had apparently been traumatized in their childhoods. And I watched, stared at, and read the post-traumatic play products of a number of ordinary, traumatized children. I found several things in common between these two groups of people. First, both the grown-up geniuses and the traumatized children injected traumatic material into the most ordinary of projects. Horror sat shockingly upon beds of plainness. Magritte painted a train emerging from an ordinary fireplace. And, in her own way, so did Helen Symes, the victim of sex abuse and satanism at her first preschool. A year after her abuses had ended, Helen painted the entirely naked figure of a child inside the usual nursery school cut-out figure made from her full body outline. Helen's teacher was horrifed. It was the first naked child the teacher had ever seen drawn at school. Hitchcock sent in an ordinary crop duster to fumigate a Kansas field and then unleashed it at the scurrying, shocked Cary Grant. In his own way, Jamie Knight, a nine-year-old witness to his mother's shooting of his father, did the same sort of thing. Jamie invented a rather nondescript intergalactic game in which—suddenly—all the galactic nations in the universe turned on him. Jamie was forced to turn "invisible" in this game in order to avoid being shot. And his friends joined in. They began feeling invisible, too. Jamie's creative invention, like Helen Symes's naked figure, carried the simultaneous power of attraction and repulsion. It started out ordinary, but it turned extraordinary quickly enough.

The artistic juxtapositions of plain and terrifying, mundane and mean, smooth and out-of-control—these juxtapositions mimic the sensations of real psychic trauma. Trauma, after all, starts out on a plain, ordinary day. Everything feels "as usual." Then all hell breaks loose and the terror takes hold. The child is traumatized. And his friends may pick up a bit of the trauma through their exposure. A bit of trauma does not make a friend "traumatized." But the bit may enter the workings of a mind, and another, and another.

Stephen King, a traumatized child, closely mimics the sensations of psychic trauma in his terror writing. He gives the reader the sensations of trauma and then leaves the reader dangling alone with these sensations. I looked at King's writing, a childhood traumatic product as we already have seen, and wondered just *how* he could scare so many people, especially children. I decided to watch King's style closely and to try to figure out exactly what he does in order to terrify his young audience. And I think I found a few things.

In general, King's techniques appear unconsciously set up to mimic the sensations of childhood psychic trauma. First, he establishes trust and a feeling of "everyday routine" in the reader's mind. He forces the reader to identify with his about-to-be-traumatized characters. Then King winds up, opens his hatches, and blasts his reader out of his seat with something for which the reader wasn't prepared at all—something that wasn't supposed to happen—something unexpected, shocking, and overwhelming. A trauma.

King also uses masses of detail and slow-motion writing. We already know that this, too, duplicates the perceptions of on-the-spot trauma. King does not hesitate, for instance, to pull out an arm, to impale an eye, or—in "The Body" (Reiner's *Stand By Me*)—to show us initially only a pair of Keds. We see the details slowly, painfully slowly. A death that in reality takes only an instant to accomplish, reads for at least fifteen seconds in King. The details jump out the way the "sunlight" hits the "chrome" of a giant truck about to kill you on a hot Maine afternoon (my paraphrase of Gage's death in *Pet Sematary*). It takes King's teenaged Moochie Welsh four pages to die at the hands of *Christine,* King's vengeful 1958 Plymouth. Gage, a toddler, dies twice on three pages in *Pet Sematary,* and then the little boy's ruined body is reviewed for eight pages more. This time-slowing writing technique obviously makes the detailing more sickening, more "gross."

Stephen King instills "trauma" into the reader's experience by putting supernatural effects into a story *after* his protagonist has been traumatized. He again mimics the perceptions of a trauma victim in this way. Carrie breaks a mirror after her mother abuses her. The tiny boy of *The Shining* develops his prescience after his dad dislocates his shoulder. Johnny of *The Dead Zone* begins telling the future after he awakens from a truck-taxi crash. If one could write schizophrenic language into a book that made sense, the reader would feel schizophrenic as he read it. By writing traumatic and post-traumatic sensations into a book, Stephen King forces his reader to feel traumatized. We already know that by feeling traumatized, a normal person may pick up a post-traumatic symptom or two. This, of course, is what Stephen King wishes for his reader. "I like to scare people," he says. "I really enjoy that."

Artists traumatized in their childhoods carry an innate understanding of how post-traumatic contagion works. They know mass hysteria. They want to scare people because *they* were scared themselves. They want to make sure others feel traumatized, too. A woman once wrote to Stephen King complaining that after reading *'Salem's Lot* she had not been able to sleep for three whole nights. "I wish it had been six," replied King. Alfred Hitchcock had been terrified when he was "no more than six years old" by a wrongful confinement in jail. When the successful director's star Tippi Hedren told him her little girl, Melanie, was six years old, Hitchcock sent the child a little surprise. The young girl excitedly opened her package only to find a small coffin inside. Within the coffin lay a tiny doll—a perfect replica of the little girl's mother. The little girl grew up to become the successful film actress Melanie Griffith, the star of *Working Girl*. Hitchcock's "sick" behavior, one subject of an interview Griffith gave in 1989 to *People,* still lingers in her mind. One swallow of somebody else's terror had stayed with Melanie Griffith for a couple of decades.

Artists who have been traumatized as children do not bother much trying to stir up inner concerns, such as oedipal conflicts, in their audiences. They are far more interested in stirring up external concerns. They know that threats in the direction of the total loss of human control are the way to move a group toward hysteria. Stephen King has outlined a list of what he says worries most people today: nuclear war, radiation, communists, cancer, plagues, terrorists, and machines. King is right. People *are* afraid of these. I'd add: running out of food and water, world population problems, toxic contaminants, and an end to the solar system. King has written almost his entire list into his novel *The Stand*. But he has also realized that he does not have to mention the list out loud to inspire the sensation of panic. His reader will become hysterical over the implications alone. In speaking of films, King says he knows that if one in his audience laughs, many will laugh—if one screams, everyone will scream. There are advantages to films, King says, because "the panic jumps from one person to the next." In a sense, King enjoys this group response. He realizes that he can exert a contagious effect upon masses of people, choir boys and murderers alike.

As far as I can tell, rather opposite forces draw young audiences to the creative products of artists who are expressing traumas from their own childhoods. An audience achieves some reassurance by looking at a traumatic product and failing to be destroyed. The audience may actually feel titillated. The reader or viewer challenges his own sense of macho and ends up feeling relieved. Many children exposed to a traumatized artist probably achieve reassurance simply by being able to get through a horror story or a session at the ghoulie matinee. Just as a Freudian "examination dream" relieves the dreamer as he awakens to find everything to be the opposite of the nightmare, a child may walk out of the afternoon movie happy to find nothing as it was depicted on film. Nothing could be *that* bad, in other words. What a relief. And, in a sense, like sex, it's fun to watch.

But there is a different faction in the traumatized artist's audience, too, a large terrified faction. A few of this faction have been traumatized already. Their exposure to the axe of *The Shining* will remind them of the time their own leg was amputated (Tama Whittaker). Their viewing of the bloody faces in *Halloween* will remind them of their own bloody face after an outboard motorboat accident (Faith Goodman). Most of this frightened part of the audience, however, was never directly traumatized before. The members of this part of the crowd will feel hopped up, overexcited, and wired after experiencing a trauma-inspired show. As in the "traumatic dream," where the dreamer wakes up feeling worse than he felt before, this kind of viewer (or reader) will catch some of the traumatized artist's anxiety after the exposure. He may have a string of bad dreams. She may be forced to play.

Children, who are willing to accept small doses of traumatic anxiety at the movie theater or under the reading lamp, probably do so as a way to develop a modicum of control. A fear of losing control is probably what leads the young audience to a terror or horror production in the first place. If an artist introduces you to a lady in a coffin, a killer train, or a ghost, you think, then perhaps you will learn something about your own traumas-to-be. Maybe you won't figure out exactly what to do, but you might know a little that you didn't know before. In other words, a kid goes to the horror movies, not for the reassurance, but for information. How do you handle a chimera? You might find out by reading *It*. What if you leave a body in your basement? You might find out in *The Telltale Heart*. If you marry a man and his dead first wife "spooks" him back to her, what do you do? You might read Edith Wharton. The quest for control drives a number of fans to the traumatized writer. And in that quest, some fans become a tiny bit traumatized themselves.

Human beings master the earth, in part, because they have acquired more "controls" than have other species. Humans plan for their futures, even after death. They understand tactics and power plays. They picture demographics and mass movements. Children grow up actively clamoring for information regarding how to control their worlds. And those who discover that they cannot control events become traumatized, at least a little. If the discovery of utter helplessness is made early in life, it will wield a big influence, perhaps bigger than if this discovery is made later in life. Whenever the discovery comes, however, a hurt will most likely follow. A scar will most likely form. The scar will become part of the person's psychology. All of us are bothered by the idea of losing control. And so we grow up trying to put our losses into some sort of context, some sort of perspective.

I remember a twelve-year-old boy who came to me a couple of times because he had slept through a moderate-sized earthquake. What had bothered young Ian Ward most, he told me, was that he had slept through such a dangerous thing. Now he could not allow himself to sleep. He must be vigilant whenever possible, he said. In case another event came along to threaten him, he must be awake. You see, the idea of losing control had frightened young Ian so much that he could not allow himself to give up his consciousness. He could not control things, he felt, if he slept. Ian Ward had realized, by implication, that someday he might be rendered utterly helpless. The boy had become a little traumatized simply by understanding this implication. Ian had traumatized himself by sleeping through an earth-quake. He also frightened himself into a couple of visits to my office. He achieved quick relief. Ian Ward, in fact, left psychotherapy feeling "back in control."

Children cringe at the thought of passing directly from sleep to death without having a chance to "do" anything about it. The Bogeyman repre-sents the kind of horrifying figure who robs a child of this kind of control. So does the character Freddy Krueger from *Nightmare on Elm Street.* Freddy tears up children with his pointy steel claws as they lie sleeping in their beds. Freddy's victims die, in other words, failing to awaken as they pass from sleep to death. I know of two youngsters who developed terrible sleep problems once they were exposed to the fictional Freddy Krueger. One of them, a boy, suffered repeated nightmares. The other child, a girl, could not sleep in her own bed. For three years from the time she saw the movie, the little girl demanded that somebody sleep near her. These were post-traumatic symptoms. But nobody had been traumatized—at least, not all the way.

Films like *Nightmare on Elm Street* may have been created by writers traumatized in their own childhoods. But knowing that somebody else's terrors created these movies would not stop most ordinary children from attending them. Children are drawn, as ants are drawn to warm kitchens, to another viewing, another scary exposure. *Nightmare II, Nightmare III, Nightmare IV,* and so on, have done fabulously well at the box office because of childhood needs to repeat exposures to terror. Perhaps, as a child follows Freddy Krueger in variously scripted films, Freddy finally becomes manageable. Similar to the child who lives for years in an alco-holic household or who stays with a schizophrenic parent, the Freddy Krueger-obsessed youngster may eventually get used to it. The youngster may gain some control by repeated exposure. "Dad is drinking again to-night," a child says to himself as he quietly tiptoes to his own room. "Mom is acting crazy. I'll stay away for a while." The Freddy follower may conclude in a similar fashion, "The makeup job on Freddy *this* time isn't so good," or "Maybe they're using another actor instead of the old one."

Children eventually find flaws in the artistic products that have frightened them. After all, kids eventually spotted the seams on the scary rubber shark in the Jaws movies. It was sort of a game—to find those seams. I know of children who have looked into magazines for pictures of the stars without their make-up on. These are the real people who were frightening them, they conclude. Kids also look around the theater—at the naked ladies on the fantastic horses that circle the screen or the men holding up the world on the ceiling. They study the cracks in the walls and the defects of the screen, itself. They often rent a videotape and watch from the safety of their own well-lit homes. Kids do better with their fears, in other words, when they can put their horrors into context. Context helps.

The more I think about the difference between being traumatized and not being traumatized, the more I realize that context, or perspective, makes the major difference. If you're old enough to realize that other people have sex with their fathers—after all, François Sagan talks about it, and so does Sophocles—then you may be able to gain a little perspective on your own dad's caresses when he used to tuck you into bed. Or, if you're widely traveled enough to have visited France, or China, or even browsed through a travel book or two in the library—then you might realize that children are taken away from their parents in other lands to live with wealthier relatives. Or they are apprenticed out to teachers or tradesmen. When you know about other cultures, you realize that Indian boys sat out upon the Great Plains enduring great ordeals without the least sign of psychic trauma. It was expected of them. And other children have their genital tissues cut or their faces scarred in order to achieve mature status in their societies. Children lie in rooms aware of others' sexual practices, and they seem to survive. What I am saying here is that context, perspective, may help the child to tolerate the Freddy Kruegers of this world as well as the terrible events that happen.

With perspective, you can take what you know about history and apply it to your own story—that things are better now, for instance, than they were during the Great Plagues, that the majority of Europe died in the fourteenth and fifteenth centuries of contagious diseases and the Hundred Years War, that even the AIDS epidemic has not yet reached the fearsome dimensions of the 1920 flu epidemic.

Children unfortunately develop perspective late in their journeys through childhood. The lower into childhood one goes, the less perspective one finds. What do preschoolers know of François Sagan, Sophocles, France, China, the Sioux, the Africans, the Great Plagues, AIDS, or flu? There's the rub. If your father in his dotage grabbed the wrong part of your forty-year-old anatomy, you'd gently slap his hand and tell him, "Bug off." It wouldn't traumatize you—most likely. You'd be able to put the experience into a broad context. On the other hand, if you were four years old and the same thing happened, you'd be trapped. You could not escape into musings on the ordeals of the adolescent Sioux warrior. You could not grab for your own copy of *Lolita*.

Many of us store memories that, if we could uncover them, visualize them, and compare them to what we now know as adults, we could beat. We could lick those horrible memories because of our adult perspective. The trouble is—sometimes the memories are too deep, too buried. We've tried too hard to pretend the memories are not there at all. And sometimes we never went on to compare our traumatic memories with what we have learned since. In some cases, we have kept ourselves from learning much since.

The Chowchilla kids—after their kidnapping—lost their interest in world events. They were deliberately failing to add context and perspective to their experience. They did not seem to care. They were actually too scared to "know" much of what was happening in the world. In fact, in 1980–1981, when I last saw the Chowchilla group, most of them were not actively following the first parole hearings of their own kidnappers. They did not read the papers, they said. Later that year I realized that they had also blanked out on their own personal futures. They had no context any longer, no perspective in which to tie the trauma.

The children of Chowchilla were inadvertently giving up something that would have helped them. Other deeply traumatized children also give this up. They renounce perspective, context, or a broader view. As I have already postulated in this chapter, perspective probably saves most children who are indirectly exposed to trauma, as well.

We are improvising treatments today for childhood trauma. And we are trying to improvise things for large populations of children exposed at a distance to horrifying events. My guess is that the answers will lie in helping children achieve some sort of context in which to place their terrors. The context must be emotionally meaningful, not just intellectual. And it must be achieved by the child himself, not just by some friend or representative.

I think of a patient of mine, Charlene Lu, in this "context." Charlene sums up for me how much damage can be done in childhood psychic trauma and how long the damage may last. But Charlene demonstrates, too, that a broader perspective will help the childhood trauma victim rise from the ashes of personal disaster.

You have already briefly met Charlene. Charlene Lu was eight years old when she was traumatized. As she walked home from her after-school Chinese language class, she was lifted bodily by a man from a Chinatown sidewalk. He grabbed Charlene and took her to a quiet garage where he put her into a car and pushed a pair of chopsticks into her vagina. The man perforated holes between Charlene's vagina and her anus and between her intestines and the peritoneal space beyond. The man had shoved hard, high, and bloody. He then let Charlene go.

The child staggered slowly back to her house, bleeding as she went. She lay down on her bed. She then waited until her parents came home at ten in the evening from their small Chinese restaurant. They found Charlene nearly dead. The little girl was rushed to a well-equipped hospital, where she was given blood transfusions and underwent emergency surgery. She was treated with massive doses of antibiotics. Charlene stayed in the hospital for three months. The doctors had to repair Charlene's organs and to quiet all that infection. In the three months' time that Charlene recuperated, nobody at the hospital called in a child psychiatrist. It was the 1970s, and physicians didn't know much about childhood trauma then. But they should have thought of child psychiatry anyway. After all, the psychiatrists were right upstairs. And what had happened to Charlene had been horrible beyond belief.

Charlene Lu went home. She was still eight. Nobody at home thought of psychiatry. Her parents were Chinese immigrants and barely could speak English. Also, because the family was Asian, they wished to handle the problem quietly, silently perhaps. Nobody spoke much to Charlene about her trauma.

The child made a decision. It made sense in a way. The man with the chopsticks had "chosen" her, she thought, because she "showed." She had been a bubbly, effervescent, talky, and showy sort—maybe. She would be different now. Charlene retreated. She would not volunteer at school. She would speak in a whispery, breathless voice. She would turn away from the jokes, the songs, and the school-yard games. She would do her business at school and disappear as much as she could. Despite the fact that the Lus told Charlene that "the man" had been deported, Charlene "spotted" her Oriental tormentor on Chinatown streets about once a year. But "the man" would not have recognized his old victim. All of her "bubbles," after all, had gone flat.

Charlene lived quietly for eight years. She earned her way into an academically acclaimed high school. But then her personality and the school requirements came into conflict. The teenaged Charlene could not get all As at a school where they grade partly on classroom participation. Excellent student that she was, Charlene Lu could garner only B pluses.

An American-born teacher of Charlene's suggested that she see a psychiatrist. Charlene was too backward, too retiring, the teacher thought, for a normal sixteen year old. The Lus brought Charlene to see me, and the job, I realized, would have to be done entirely between Charlene and myself. The Lus did not speak enough English to assist me. Following that first meeting, I did not see the elder Lus again.

Charlene and I worked once a week for one and one-half years. I insisted that Charlene join a teenage club. She liked it, but it was extremely difficult to make her go regularly. I told her she must eat lunch with a group of girls. But it was a struggle to make her talk with these new friends. She frequented the shopping malls. But she stayed tight. Charlene understood why she had retreated from human contact. And she agreed that it would be better for her to "come out." But our struggle was extreme, and the reenactments of "hiding from the man" came along so frequently that each one of them could not be dissected in a once-weekly session.

I think we were getting somewhere—but it felt similar to slogging through a swamp. Then something happened. Mr. Lu incurred a dose of psychic trauma himself. He was carrying home the restaurant payroll when somebody stopped him on a Chinatown street, held him up with a gun, and demanded the money. He turned the money over, called the police from a phone booth, and then came home. But Mr. Lu had made an immediate decision. He would take his family to see the place where he had been born and raised. They must see rural China. Now. Perspective. After all, you never know when you are going to die. Mr. Lu suddenly felt old. He felt he might die at any time, at any moment.

Each year, Charlene Lu had a one-week Presidents' holiday break. The Lus would go then, Mr. Lu decided. Mr. and Mrs. Lu, Morton and Sandra Lu, the Lu's oldest son and daughter-in-law, James Lu, a teenager two years younger than Charlene, and Charlene traveled by air to Hong Kong. They rented a van when they arrived and drove straight to Mr. Lu's old village deep in the rural part of Canton. They stayed for three days. And then they returned home to San Francisco.

The next time I saw Charlene she described her three days in China. Sparks flew from her eyes as she talked, and her voice somehow had taken on a new sound. Four things had impressed Charlene in China, she said. First, the villagers had picked up every piece of old clothing that the Lus had tossed from the windows of their van when they drove into town. The villagers wanted the Lus' old castoffs, in other words. Second, the Lu family in China kept a photo of the American Lus eating dinner at a Grant Avenue restaurant. The photo was placed over their couch in Canton. Just a plain old photo—and it sat in the best spot of the house. Third, Charlene met a seventeen-year-old cousin in China—the same age as Charlene. Charlene's cousin had been working the fields for three years. School had stopped for her after ninth grade. She looked "old." Her father and Mr. Lu discussed the possibility of the girl becoming a mail-order bride for one of the dishwashers in Mr. Lu's restaurant. She was a good cook, a hard worker, and a sturdy girl for childbearing. She might want to live in America. The two men asked Charlene's cousin for her response. And she said "Yes." *That* amazed Charlene. Finally, Charlene's Chinese uncle took the girl aside to tell her something. He had heard that Charlene had been accepted as a freshman at Stanford. She would be starting in September. He wanted Charlene to know that he had kept track of the Lu family history. In two thousand years of Lus, he said, nobody had ever gone to university. She would be the first. They would always remember Charlene Lu. She held a special place in the family archives.

Well, you know the rest, don't you? Charlene changed. Fast. She "showed." She went on to Stanford, lived in an apartment, made a ton of friends, and did very well. She did not need me any longer. Her new perspective from those three days in China had cured the terror and had fixed her damaged personality.

Charlene comes back to visit us a couple of times a year—she likes my secretaries and they like her. And, I guess, she likes me, too. At any rate, I've kept track of Charlene for the four years since her trip to China, and her character changes have stayed permanent. The bubbles are back. This June, Charlene will graduate, the first Lu in two thousand years. Charlene has not dated seriously yet. I would not be surprised if she comes back to me when she considers using that traumatized organ of hers. We may have to improvise some treatment then, too. But I think it will be easier than undergoing a robbery and spending three days in a Chinese village.

We are just getting started helping traumatized children and almost-traumatized children. It will be a huge job. But I feel hopeful. Very hopeful.

Notes

CHAPTER ONE

The first names of children in this book correspond to the first names used in all other Terr professional writings. Nonessential details, however, are changed and may not be consistent with those in the professional papers.

The Ernst Kris quote comes from his "The Recovery of Childhood Memories in Psychoanalysis," *Psychoanalytic Study of the Child* 11:54–88, 1956. Most analysts contemporary to Kris accepted his argument that "reconstruction," the use of childhood memories and/or amnesias to understand the patient's past, is a weak therapeutic tool. Phyllis Greenacre and Marie Bonaparte argued the opposite point, however. Greenacre's "A Contribution to the Study of Screen Memories," *Psychoanalytic Study of the Child* 3/4:73–84, 1949; "On Reconstruction," *Journal of the American Psychoanalytic Association* 23:693–712, 1975; and "Reconstruction: Its Nature and Therapeutic Value," *Journal of the American Psychoanalytic Association* 29:386–402, 1982; and Bonaparte's "Notes on the Analytic Discovery of a Primal Scene," *Psychoanalytic Study of the Child* 1:119-125, 1945, take strongly positive positions on reconstruction as therapy.

Clouzot's *Les Diaboliques* was released in 1955.

The paper describing retinal damage after psychic trauma is Gelber, G. S., and Schatz, H., "Loss of Vision Due to Central Serous Chorioretinopathy Following Psychological Stress," *American Journal of Psychiatry* 144:46–50, 1987.

Hitchcock's *Spellbound* (David O. Selznick, 1945) and Joseph Mankiewicz's *Suddenly Last Summer* (1959) set up amnesias that automatically follow from psychic traumas. Hitchcock's *Marnie* (1964) makes the same assumption.

Before 1896, Freud considered his neurotic patients to be victims of actual childhood seductions. In 1897 Freud abruptly changed his mind, writing that neuroses were the result of *fantasized* childhood seductions. This shift led Freud and his followers deep into the "interior" of the mind. Jeffrey Masson, a lay psychoanalyst who had been given access to Freud's unpublished letters, claimed in 1984 that Freud had abandoned his original ideas about actual childhood seduction because he had feared his peers' disapproval (Masson, J.,

Assault on the Truth: Freud's Suppression of the Seduction Theory, New York, Farrar, Straus & Giroux, 1984). Janet Malcolm, a journalist and essayist, published a book dealing in part with Masson's relationships with his own psychoanalytic peers (*In the Freud Archives*, New York, Knopf, 1984). These two books taken together stirred up enormous controversy. The point remains, however, that after 1897 analysis did "give up" on psychic trauma and has only recently begun to show renewed interest.

Freud remained a great definer of trauma-related concepts despite his preference for the "internal." His 1920 definition of trauma comes from "Beyond the Pleasure Principle," *Standard Edition* 18:7–64, and his 1926 definition was printed in "Inhibitions, Symptoms, and Anxiety," *Standard Edition* 20:77–175. The Sigmund Freud *Standard Edition* is translated and edited by James Strachey, London, Hogarth Press, 1953–1974.

World War II writings considering children's traumatic responses to be reflections of parental responses include Carey-Trefzger, C., "The Results of a Clinical Study of War-Damaged Children Who Attended the Child Guidance Clinic, The Hospital for Sick Children, Great Ormand Street, London," *Journal of Mental Science* 95:535–559, 1949; Mercier, M., and Despert, L., "Effects of War on French Children," *Psychosomatic Medicine* 5:226–272, 1943; and Solomon, J., "Reactions of Children to Black-Outs," *American Journal of Orthopsychiatry* 12:361–362, 1942.

During World War II, Anna Freud and Dorothy Burlingham published their "Report 12" from the Hampstead Nurseries as *War and Children*, Medical War Books, New York, 1943. Later, an expanded version of all of their wartime reports, *Infants Without Families*, was published (Volume 3, *The Writings of Anna Freud*, New York, International Universities Press, 1968–1974). Anna Freud also wrote a paper with Sophie Dann, "An Experiment in Group Upbringing," *Psychoanalytic Study of the Child* 6:127–168, 1951, describing the behavior of a small group of youngsters raised in Nazi concentration camps and then evacuated to a group home in Great Britain.

The Vicksburg tornado study is Block, D., Silber, E., and Perry, S., "Some Factors in the Emotional Reaction of Children to Disaster," *American Journal of Psychiatry* 113:416–422, 1956.

Some of the best-known childhood stress research of the 1960s and 1970s was conducted by Lois Murphy, E. J. Anthony, Michael Rutter, and Norman Garmezy. Lois Murphy and Alice Moriarty's *Vulnerability, Coping, and Growth*, New Haven, Conn., Yale University Press, 1976, is a good example.

David Levy's classic paper showing how hospitals may traumatize children is entitled, "Psychic Trauma of Operations in Children," *American Journal of the Diseases of Childhood* 69:7–25, 1945.

For child psychoanalytic projects done in the 1940s, 1950s, and 1960s emphasizing the effect of realities in young children's lives, see Barnes, M., "Reactions to the Death of a Mother," *Psychoanalytic Study of the Child* 19:334–357, 1964; Kennedy, H., "Cover Memories in Formation," *Psy-*

choanalytic Study of the Child 5:275–284, 1950; and Furman, E., *A Child's Parent Dies: Studies in Child Bereavement*, New Haven, Yale University Press, 1974.

Cortázar's "Blow Up" is published in *Blow Up and Other Stories*, New York, Pantheon, 1985. Antonioni's film *"Blow-Up"* was produced in 1966.

Gaynor Lacey's paper on the disaster in Wales is entitled "Observations on Aberfan," *Journal of Psychosomatic Research* 16:257–260, 1972. C. Janet Newman's Buffalo Creek report is entitled "Children of Disaster: Clinical Observations at Buffalo Creek," *American Journal of Psychiatry* 133:306–312, 1976.

The rush to hypnosis by American police departments after the Chowchilla investigation eventually created major problems for the legal system. Two leading forensic psychiatrists wrote influential articles on the distortions that could occur when witnesses were hypnotized. These are Bernard Diamond's "Inherent Problems in the Use of Pretrial Hypnosis on a Prospective Witness," *California Law Review* 68:313–349, 1980, and Martin Orne's "The Use and Misuse of Hypnosis in Court," *International Journal of Clinical and Experimental Hypnosis* 27:311–341, 1979. The California Supreme Court in 1982 overturned a case in which a previously hypnotized witness's testimony had been instrumental in the lower court's decision. This case, People v. Shirley, Cal.3d 18,53(1982), started significant trends in the states away from hypnosis. A somewhat odd decision, however, from the U.S. Supreme Court, Rock v. Arkansas, 483 U.S.44:107 S. Ct. 2704, 97 L. Ed. 2d. 37, 55 U.S.L.W. 4925 (1987), held that although it would not be acceptable to use the hypnotically obtained testimonies from other witnesses, defendants could bring into court what they had learned under hypnosis.

Hugh Pentecost's short story "The Day the Children Vanished" was first published in *This Week Magazine* in 1958. It was re-released as a novel by Pocket Books, New York, in October, 1976, two months after the Chowchilla kidnapping. The publisher stated on the inside cover that the Chowchilla school-bus kidnapping had so resembled the Hugh Pentecost story that a new expanded version was being offered.

Sala Hunter's "rumor" that the Chowchilla kidnappers had acted out of revenge for a speeding ticket could not be confirmed or disproved. An attorney in the Madera County district attorney's office had heard the story but said it played no significant role in the kidnappers' criminal trial. An FBI agent checked out the "story" in 1989 using bureau computers. There was no record of a ticket, but the Department of Motor Vehicles routinely expunges records of traffic violations after ten years.

The Woods-Schoenfeld appeal is People v. Schoenfeld et. al., 111 Cal. App. 3d 671(1980).

The Chowchilla studies appear as four publications: Terr, L., "Children of Chowchilla: A Study of Psychic Trauma," *Psychoanalytic Study of the Child* 34:547–623, 1979; Terr, L., "Psychic Trauma in Children: Observations Following the Chowchilla Schoolbus Kidnapping," *American Journal of Psychiatry* 138:14–19, 1981 (a brief summary of the first paper); Terr, L., "Chowchilla Revisited: The Effects of Psychic Trauma Four Years After a Schoolbus Kidnapping," *American Journal of Psychiatry* 140:1543–1550, 1983; and Terr, L., "Life Attitudes, Dreams, and Psychic Trauma in a Group of 'Normal' Children," *Journal of the American Academy of Child Psychiatry* 22:221–230, 1983 (the McFarland-Porterville control study).

CHAPTER TWO

Sydney Furst published an edited group of psychoanalytic papers on trauma entitled *Psychic Trauma*, New York, Basic Books, 1967. His essay "Psychic Trauma" is printed on pp. 3–50 and includes the quote used in this chapter. Anna Freud's "Comments on Trauma," from which her quote is taken, appears at the end of the Furst book as well as in *The Writings of Anna Freud* 5:221–241.

The Memory of Eva Ryker (1980) was directed by Walter Grauman and produced by Irwin Allen.

The Charles Michener interview of V. S. Naipaul appears in *Newsweek*, November 16, 1981.

Stephen King's ranking of terror, horror, and the gross-out appears in *Danse Macabre*, New York, Berkley, 1983.

Franklin Roosevelt's "nothing to fear but fear itself" quote comes from his first inaugural address, March 4, 1933.

Sandor Rado's "Pathodynamics and Treatment of Traumatic War Neurosis" appears in *Psychosomatic Medicine* 4:362–368, 1942.

The Baltimore conference on terrorism was sponsored by the American Psychiatric Association and was reported in Eichelman, B., Soskis, D., and Reid, W., eds., *Terrorism: Interdisciplinary Perspectives*, Washington, D.C., American Psychiatric Association Press, 1983.

Rob Reiner's *Stand By Me* was released in 1986.

Faith Goodman refers to the original film *Halloween* (1978), directed by John Carpenter and starring Donald Pleasance and Jamie Lee Curtis.

The main sources on Hitchcock's life and works used for this book are Donald Spoto's *The Dark Side of Genius*, New York, Ballantine, 1984, and Spoto's review of Hitchcock's films, *The Art of Alfred Hitchcock*, New York, Doubleday, 1979. I also referred to J. R. Taylor, *Hitch*, London, Sphere Books (Abacus), 1981. Neither Spoto nor Taylor appear impressed with the truthfulness of Hitchcock's childhood trauma story despite Hitchcock's sister's verification to Taylor.

The Alfred Hitchcock gravestone story was told to a Boston audience by a psychiatrist commenting upon a talk I had given at McLean Hospital, Harvard University, December, 1987.

Hitchcock's *Thirty-Nine Steps* was produced by Michael Balcon and Ivor Montagu, Lime Grove, 1935. *Young and Innocent* was produced by Edward

Black, Lime Grove and Pinegrove, 1937. *Saboteur* was produced by Frank Lloyd and Jack Skirball, Universal, 1942. *I Confess* was produced by Hitchcock, Warner Bros., 1952. *Dial M For Murder* was produced by Hitchcock, Warner Bros., 1953. *The Wrong Man* was produced by Hitchcock, Warner Bros., 1957. *Strangers on a Train* was produced by Hitchcock, Warner Bros., 1951. *To Catch a Thief* was produced by Hitchcock, Paramount, 1955. *North by Northwest* was produced by Hitchcock, MGM, 1959. And *Frenzy* was produced by Hitchcock, Pinewood, London, 1972.

CHAPTER THREE

René Spitz's "No" developmental milestone is presented in his *No and Yes: On the Genesis of Human Communication*, New York, International Universities Press, 1966. Erik Erikson's *Childhood and Society*, New York, Norton, 1950, gives Erikson's eight developmental stages of man, including the "basic trust" and "autonomy" achievements of early childhood.

Several psychiatric authors have pointed out how enraged people become following humanly instigated disasters. Mardi Horwitz's *Stress Response Syndromes*, New York, Jason Aronson, 1976, provides a review of this. Judith Herman tackles the subject in terms of *Father-Daughter Incest*, Cambridge, Harvard University Press, 1982. Judith Herman and Bessel Van Der Kolk consider the self-destructive anger of "borderline" adult patients as a special psychological sequel to early childhood trauma (see their "Traumatic Antecedents of Borderline Personality Disorder" in Van Der Kolk, B., ed., *Psychological Trauma*, Washington, D.C., American Psychiatric Press, 1987, pp. 111–126). R. Walsh may be the first psychiatric writer to draw the connection between adult borderline personality disorder and early, multiple, childhood abuses (Walsh, R., "The Family of the Borderline Patient," in Grinker, F., Werble, B., eds., *The Borderline Patient*, New York, Jason Aronson, 1977).

My own research on child abuse is published in two articles: Terr, L., and Watson, A., "The Battered Child Rebrutalized: Ten Cases of Medical Legal Confusion," *American Journal of Psychiatry* 124:126–133, 1968, and Terr, L., "A Family Study of Child Abuse," *American Journal of Psychiatry* 127:665–671, 1970.

Larry Silver, along with C. Dubliner and R. Lourie, wrote an interesting paper on child abuse more than twenty years ago showing the connection between being a childhood abuse victim and becoming an adult abuser. It is entitled "Does Violence Breed Violence? Contributions From a Study of the Child Abuse Syndrome," *American Journal of Psychiatry* 126:404–407, 1969.

For a good review of carbamazapine (Tegretol) as a treatment for rapid cycling mood disorder and borderline personality, see Post, R. M., and Uhde, T. W., "Clinical Approaches to Treatment-Resistant Bipolar Illness," in R. Hales and A. Frances, eds., *Psychiatry Update* 6:125–150, 1987.

My sources of Greek legends and myths are Grant, M., and Hazel, J., *Gods and Mortals in Classic Mythology*, Springfield, Mass., G. & C. Merriam, 1967, and Graves, R., *Greek Myths*, Hammondsworth, Middlesex, England, Penguin, 1955 (2 volumes).

Shangri-La is the locale of James Hilton's *Lost Horizons* (1922), New York, Buccaneer Books, 1983.

The Gail Miller and Sandy Tompkins book on the Chowchilla kidnapping is entitled *Kidnapped at Chowchilla*, Plainfield, Logos International, 1977.

The defenses are best described in Anna Freud's *The Ego and the Mechanisms of Defense* in *The Writings of Anna Freud*, vol. 2. For a more modern view on coping and defense, see Vaillant, G., *Adaptation to Life*, Boston, Little, Brown, 1977, and Vaillant, G., *Empirical Studies of Ego Mechanisms of Defense*, Washington, D.C., American Psychiatric Press, 1986.

Martin Wangh's paper "A Psychogenic Factor in the Recurrence of War" takes the theoretical position that war effects group revenges for nationally perceived traumas. It is printed in *American Journal of Psychoanalysis* 49:319–323, 1968.

Kai Erikson, a Yale University sociologist, demonstrates in his book *Everything in Its Path*, New York, Simon and Schuster, 1976, that the Buffalo Creek communities lost their cohesive purpose due to ongoing rage and long-lasting depression.

CHAPTER FOUR

Kurosawa's classic film *Rashomon* (1951) tells the story of a rape from four different points of view. The unusual sensation of hearing about one event from several different viewpoints characterizes psychiatric field research.

Adult denial and psychic numbing are put into context with the entire post-traumatic syndrome by Horowitz, M., Wilner, N., Kaltreider, N., and Alvarez, W., in "Signs and Symptoms of Posttraumatic Stress Disorder," *Archives of General Psychiatry* 37:85–92, 1980.

The Byron quote is taken from a letter to John Murray in Leslie Marchand, ed., *Lord Byron: Selected Letters and Journals*, Cambridge, Mass., Belknap Press, 1982, pp. 160–161.

Robert Jay Lifton's *Death in Life: Survivors of Hiroshima*, New York, Basic Books, 1982, gives several of the best examples of psychic numbing available today. Lifton, in addition to defining and exemplifying psychic numbing, develops the concept of "survivor's guilt."

Arata Osada's *Children of Hiroshima*, New York, Taylor and Francis, 1981, consists of a loosely organized collection of children's essays written after the atomic bombings of Japan.

Psychiatry has recently become very interested in the personality disorders. Otto Kernberg's *Borderline Conditions and Pathological Narcissism*, New York, Jason Aronson, 1985, presents the psychoanalytic point of view. T.

Widiger and A. Frances, "Personality Disorders," in Talbot, J., Hales, R., and Yudofsky, S., eds., *The American Psychiatric Press Textbook of Psychiatry*, Washington, D.C., American Psychiatric Press, 1988, pp. 621–648, present the general psychiatric viewpoint.

The two personality styles I found to be precipitated by childhood physical abuse, "withdrawn" personalities and "hail fellow well met" personalities, are described in Terr, L., "A Family Study of Child Abuse."

René Spitz described withdrawn Central American babies in his classic paper "Hospitalism," *Psychoanalytic Study of the Child* 1:53–74, 1945.

Medical treatments and traditions occasionally change abruptly. A "charge nurse" in the cancer unit at Children's Hospital at Stanford told me in the spring of 1989 that nobody she knows presently teaches hypnosis to dying children. The group that taught self-hypnosis moved on with Jordan Wilbur, M.D., to Presbyterian Medical Center, San Francisco. Josephine Hilgard, M.D., and Sam LeBaron, Ph.D., originally part of this group, wrote a book that remains currently in use, *Hypnotherapy of Pain in Children with Cancer*, Los Altos, Calif., William Kaufman, 1984.

Louis Fine, M.D., of Denver still uses hypnotherapy for debilitated children. Although Fine has not published papers on the subject, he employs these techniques for children immobilized in full body casts, children requiring chemotherapy, and children about to undergo painful medical procedures.

Robert Stoller, M.D., an extremely interesting psychiatric researcher in the field of sexual disorders, presented a paper at the winter meetings of the American Psychoanalytic Association, New York City, 1988, in which he theorized that some children who are unable to dissociate during long, painful illnesses "displace" their pain, moving the painful perceptions into association with more pleasurable feelings in their genitalia. Such children may go on to indulge in painful sadomasochistic sexual activities in adult life, Stoller suggests. He also told an audience at the American Psychiatric Association annual meetings, 1989, that the child who was abused or who suffered from a massive physical disease might become sadomasochistic as an adult in order, unconsciously, to "triumph" over his old victimization (*American Psychiatric News*, June 16, 1989).

For an English language description of Despine's work (1840) with his patient Estelle, see H. F. Ellenberger's *The Discovery of the Unconscious*, New York, Basic Books, 1970. Richard Kluft's article "Multiple Personality in Childhood," *Psychiatric Clinics of North America* 7:121–134, 1984, gives a good general introduction to the disorder as it is expressed in young people.

The best trade books available today on adults with multiple personality are Thigpen, C., and Cleckley, H., *The Three Faces of Eve*, Augusta, Ga., Cleckley-Thigpen, 1955, and Flora R. Schreiber, *Sybil*, New York, Warner Books, 1974. The films made from these books were directed by Nunnely Johnson, 1957, and Daniel Petrie, 1976. Eugene Bliss, M.D., a long-time researcher into multiple personality, has recently written a general review of the subject, *Multiple Personality, Allied Disorders, and Hypnosis*, New York, Oxford University Press, 1986. Herbert and David Spiegel, a well-known father-son team in psychiatry and hypnosis, published *Trance and Treatment: Clinical Uses of Hypnosis*, New York, Basic Books, 1978, a useful review of hypnotherapy.

The Terminator was directed by James Cameron, 1984. *Black Widow* was directed by Bob Rafelson, 1986. *Darling*, 1965, was directed by John Schlesinger and starred Julie Christie. Simon Gray's play *Otherwise Engaged* is printed in *Otherwise Engaged and Other Plays*, Portsmouth, N.H., Heinemann Educational Books, 1984. *River's Edge*, based on the Milpitas High School incident, was directed by Tim Hunter, 1986.

Robert Jay Lifton's thoughts about problems in the world's psychology resulting from atomic war are expressed in *The Future of Immortality and Other Essays for a Nuclear Age*, New York, Basic Books, 1987.

W. Beardslee and J. Mack's "The Impact on Children and Adolescents of Nuclear Development" is printed in R. Rogers, ed., *Psychosocial Aspects of Nuclear Development*, Task Force Report 20, Washington, D.C., American Psychiatric Association Press, 1982.

CHAPTER FIVE

Most of the Poe history in this chapter comes from Marie Bonaparte's exploration of Poe's life and psychology, *The Life and Works of Edgar Allan Poe: A Psycho-Analytic Interpretation* (Tr. J. Rodker), London, Imago, 1949. The 1829 version of Poe's poem "Preface," rewritten in 1831 as "Introduction" and eventually discarded when "Romance" was published (1843–1845), is in James A. Harrison, ed., *The Complete Works of Edgar Allen Poe* (also known as the *Virginia Edition*), 7:164, New York, Thomas Y. Crowell, 1902.

The process of mourning in childhood is discussed by John Bowlby in the monumental three-volume *Attachment, Separation, and Loss*, New York, Basic Books, 1973–1983. There is also an excellent book entitled *Bereavement: Reactions, Consequences, and Care*, published by the National Academy of Sciences, National Research Council, Washington, D.C., 1984, that demonstrates how much more we still need to know to understand normal grief. The Cleveland, Ohio, psychoanalyst Marion Barnes provides an excellent description of two young children in the process of mourning in "Reactions to the Death of a Mother," and Erna Furman, another Cleveland psychoanalyst, wrote a monograph on this same subject, cited earlier. Furman also considers the combination of psychic trauma plus grief in the paper "When Is the Death of a Parent Traumatic?" *Psychoanalytic Study of the Child* 41:191–208, 1986.

Spencer Eth and Robert Pynoos discuss the interactions of trauma and grief in "Interaction of Trauma and Grief in Childhood," in Eth and Pynoos, eds., *Post-Traumatic Stress Disorders in Children*, Washington, D.C., American

Psychiatric Press, 1985. Two papers, Kinzie, J. D., Sack, W., Manson, S., and Rath, B., "The Psychiatric Effects of Massive Trauma on Cambodian Children, I. The Children," and Sack, W., Angell, R., Kinzie, J. D., and Rath, B., "The Psychiatric Effects of Massive Trauma on Cambodian Children, II. The Family, the Home, and the School," *Journal of the American Academy of Child Psychiatry* 25:370–383, 1986, report simultaneous grief and traumatic responses in a group of Cambodian children who came to America after surviving the Pol Pot regime's reign of terror.

Stephen King's "Gramma" appears in *Skeleton Crew*, New York, Signet, 1986. *The Exorcist* was directed by William Friedkin in 1973 and won an Oscar for Peter Blatty's screenplay.

The Poe letters are quoted by Marie Bonaparte, *op. cit.*

Mary Shelley's *Frankenstein* (1818), New York, Bantam, 1981, Bram Stoker's *Dracula* (1897), New York, Bantam, 1983, and Robert Louis Stevenson's *Doctor Jekyll and Mister Hyde* (1886), New York, Bantam, 1981, remain classics of the horror genre. Of course, *The Complete Tales and Poems of Edgar Allen Poe*, New York, Modern Library, 1938, remains the great "wonder" of the horror world.

CHAPTER SIX

George Vaillant's *Adaptation to Life* describes his long-term studies of Harvard men as they progressed into middle age. His paper emphasizing "suppression" as a commonly used defense is entitled "Theoretical Hierarchy of Adaptive Ego Mechanisms," *Archives of General Psychiatry* 24:107–118, 1971.

The idea of psychologically exchanging guilt for shame after psychic trauma is my own. There are several old articles in the anthropological literature, however, that separate "shame societies" from "guilt societies."

Donald T. Regan's book on his political life and friendship with the Reagans, *For the Record: From Wall Street to Washington*, New York, Harcourt Brace Jovanovich, 1988, exposed Nancy Reagan's obsession with astrology. It placed the timing of this obsession to the immediate aftermath of the 1981 Hinkley assassination attempt.

Stockholm Syndrome is reviewed by Frank Ochberg in "Hostage Victims," in Eichelman, B., Soskis, D., and Reid, W., eds., *Terrorism: Interdisciplinary Perspectives*, Washington, D.C., American Psychiatric Press, 1983, pp. 83–88.

The brothers Grimm tell the tale "Rumpelstiltskin." Homer's *Odyssey* is printed in the Richard Whitmore translation by Harper & Row, New York, 1968. Stephen King's *Carrie* was published by Doubleday, New York, in 1974. This is King's first novel. Hawthorne's *The Scarlet Letter* (1846–1849) is available in the New York, Bantam, 1981 edition.

The *American Medical Association News* article noting that doctors failed thoroughly to examine the alleged McMartin preschool victims is entitled "In Wake of Sexual Abuse: Unraveling a Nightmare," March 22, 1985.

CHAPTER SEVEN

For a review of the psychological literature on children's responses to controlled perceptual input, see Chance, C., and Goldstein, A., "Face-Recognition Memory: Implications for Children's Eyewitness Testimony," *Journal of Social Issues* 40:69–86, 1984.

Gordon Allport reported that children exhibit a relative lack of racial and cultural bias. His psychological experiments on perception are summarized in Allport, G., and Postman, L., *The Psychology of Rumor,* New York, Henry Holt, 1947.

A. D. Yarmey's *The Psychology of Eyewitness Testimony,* New York, Free Press, 1979, refers to several good studies on children's eyewitness perceptions.

The psychologist Elizabeth Loftus is a leader in the field of perception, memory, and eyewitnessing as it applies to the courts. Her *Memory,* Reading, Mass., Addison-Wesley, 1980, summarizes various studies that she and her group have accomplished.

Steven Ceci currently does psychological research on children's perception and memory. His (edited with coauthors) book, *Children's Eyewitness Memory,* New York, Springer-Verlag, 1987, presents up-to-date work on this topic.

Jean Cocteau's tale, "Death and the Gardener" (1923), is available in A. Manguel's horror collection, *Black Water,* New York, Clarkson N. Potter, 1983. John O'Hara's *Appointment in Samarra* (New York, Random House, 1934) tells a similar but less literal tale of a meeting with Death.

M. E. Seligman reviews his work on unavoidable shock in animals in the article "Learned Helplessness," *Annual Reviews of Medicine* 23:407–412, 1972.

Because his comments about traumatic neurotransmitter release were entirely speculative, my "neuroscientist" colleague asked not to be identified.

Marilynne Robinson's *Housekeeping* was originally published in 1980 and is presently available in paperback through Bantam, New York, 1987.

Neisser's study, "The Control of Information Pickup in Selective Looking," in A. D. Pick, ed., *Perception and Its Development: A Tribute to Eleanor Gibson,* Hillsdale, N.J., Erlbaum, 1979, pp. 201–219, reveals children to be better at picking out important but seemingly irrelevant details than are adults.

Children's confusions with masks and disguises are summarized by Chance, C., and Goldstein, A., *op. cit.* This paper also includes a discussion of "retention intervals," the length of time memories remain in storage, as a factor in children's ability to remember.

The medical-legal problems connected with parental suggestion as it influences children's testimony, especially in cases of divorce, are discussed by

Elissa Benedek and Diane Schetky in their "Allegations of Sexual Abuse in Child Custody and Visitation Disputes," Schetky and Benedek, eds., *Emerging Issues in Child Psychiatry and the Law,* New York, Brunner/Mazel, 1985, pp. 145–156.

I have published some professional papers about loyalty conflicts, immaturity, perception, and memory as they influence children's participation as witnesses in court proceedings. See Terr, L., "The Child as Witness," in D. Schetky and E. Benedek, eds., *Child Psychiatry and the Law,* New York, Brunner/Mazel, 1980, pp. 249–265; Terr, L., "The Baby in Court," in J. D. Call, E. Galenson, and R. Tyson, eds., *Frontiers of Infant Psychiatry* 2:490–494, New York, Basic Books, 1984; and Terr, L., "The Child Psychiatrist and the Child Witness: Traveling Companions by Necessity, If Not By Design," *Journal of the American Academy of Child Psychiatry* 25:462–472, 1986.

The current controversy about whether or not to use anatomically correct dolls with child witnesses is aired in a debate by Yates, A. (affirmative), and Terr, L. (negative), "Anatomically Correct Dolls: Should They Be Used as the Basis of Expert Testimony," *Journal of the American Academy of Child Psychiatry* 27:254–257, 1988. The rebuttals are printed on pages 387–388.

Firefox was based on a novel by Craig Thomas of the same name, New York, Bantam, 1978. The film was directed by Clint Eastwood, 1982.

For possibly the best description of adult war neurosis ever printed, see Abraham Kardiner, *The Traumatic Neuroses of War,* New York, Paul B. Hoeber, 1941. For more modern collected works emphasizing recent findings from Vietnam, see Charles Figley, ed., *Stress Disorders Among Viet Nam Veterans,* New York, Brunner/Mazel, 1978, and Sonnenberg, S., Blank, A., and Talbott, J., eds., *The Trauma of War: Stress and Recovery in Viet Nam Veterans,* Washington, D.C., American Psychiatric Press, 1985. A good single book, nonedited, on this subject is Herbert Hendin and Ann Haas's *Wounds of War: The Psychological Aftermath of Combat in Vietnam,* New York, Basic Books, 1984.

The connection between terrible external events and supernatural experience was cued for the first time at Chowchilla. This link became more apparent later when I wrote "Remembered Images in Psychic Trauma: One Explanation for the Supernatural," *Psychoanalytic Study of the Child* 40:493–533, 1985. This paper on the effects of external anxiety makes an interesting trio with Sigmund Freud's two papers on the supernatural as it relates to internal anxiety (Freud, S. [1907], "Delusions and Dreams in Jensen's 'Gradiva,' " *Standard Edition* 9:1–95, and Freud, S. [1919], "The 'Uncanny,' " *Standard Edition* 17:217–256).

Pliny's letter to Sura as well as Cortázar's short story "House Taken Over" can be found in the *Black Water* collection of supernatural writings edited by A. Manguel.

The Carter haunted-house story is told in Richard Hyatt's *The Carters of Plains,* Tomball, Tex., Strode, 1977.

The film *Stand By Me* had been cited in the notes on Chapter Two. It is taken from Stephen King's novella "The Body," published in King's *Different Seasons,* New York, Viking Press, 1982. *Christine,* by Stephen King, New York, Viking Press, 1983, was made into a film of the same name, directed by John Carpenter and released in 1983.

Alberto Manguel, the collector of horror stories, *op cit.,* reprints Hawthorne's 1868 *American Notebooks,* pp. 950–951.

Stephen King's *Pet Sematary* is published by Doubleday, Garden City, N.Y., 1983. *The Tommyknockers* was published in New York by Putnam, 1987. *The Shining* was printed in 1977, Doubleday, Garden City, N.Y. "Trucks" is printed in King's collection of short stories, *Night Shift,* New York, Signet, 1979.

Edith Wharton's collection of ghost stories as well as her autobiographical note regarding the supernatural effects of her bout of typhoid fever as a child, are published as *The Ghost Stories of Edith Wharton,* New York, Scribners, 1985. For the details of Wharton's life, I relied on R. W. B. Lewis's biography, *Edith Wharton,* New York, Harper & Row, 1975.

Dr. John B. de C. M. Saunders served as chancellor of the University of California at San Francisco from 1964 to 1966 and went on to serve as Regents Professor of Medical History at the same university.

CHAPTER EIGHT

Piaget's 1927 book on "time" is entitled *The Child's Conception of Time,* New York, Ballantine Books, 1971.

Freud's definition of psychic trauma is cited in the notes on Chapter One. His two "hints" at "time" as a central theme in his "protective shield" concept are: (1) "our abstract idea of time seems to be wholly derived from the method of [on-off] working of the system Pcpt.-Cs. and to correspond to a perception on its own part of that method of working. This mode of functioning may perhaps constitute another way of providing a shield against stimuli" (p. 28 in "Beyond the Pleasure Principle," *Standard Edition* 18:7–64) and (2) his idea that a "discontinuous method of functioning . . . [which] lies at the bottom of the origin of the concept of time" also characterizes the protective shield (p. 231 in "A Note Upon the Mystic Writing-Pad," *Standard Edition* 19:225–332).

The case of Little Hans was published by Sigmund Freud as "Analysis of a Phobia in a Five-Year-Old Boy" (1909), *Standard Edition* 10:3–149.

R. Ornstein suggests a four-part breakdown of "time functions": short time (rhythm), duration, sequence and simultaneity, and perspective. See *On the Experience of Time,* New York, Pelican Books, 1975.

Holubar's *The Sense of Time,* Cambridge, Mass., MIT Press, 1969, presents data on biorhythms and animal migration.

Infantile rhythm sense was demonstrated in Kleitman, N., and Englemann, T., "Sleep Characteristics of Infants," *Journal of Applied Physiology* 6:269–

282, 1953. The same data were then interpreted psychoanalytically by Gifford, S., "Sleep, Time, and the Early Ego," *Journal of the American Psychoanalytic Association* 8:5–42, 1960.

For a good early review of the science of chronobiology see Halberg, F., "Chronobiology," *Annual Review of Physiology* 31:675–725, 1969. For some applications of rhythm sense to psychological relaxation techniques, see Miller, N., "Applications of Learning and Biofeedback to Psychiatry and Medicine," in Kaplan, A., Freedman, A., and Sadock, B., eds., *Comprehensive Textbook of Psychiatry* III, 1:468–484, 1980.

P. Fraisse's landmark book on "time," *The Psychology of Time,* New York, Harper & Row, 1963, takes the position that time sense can be independent of speed or distance judgments. Piaget did his studies on time, on the other hand, in response to a question Albert Einstein had asked him as to whether children judged time with "relativity" to speed and distance. Piaget's answer, as put forth in *The Child's Conception of Time,* takes the relativistic side of this "debate." An interior, innate sense of time does, however, probably dominate time sense despite proven distance and speed influences. See Siffre, M., *Beyond Time,* London, Chatto & Winters, 1965, for a description of human time sense under prolonged conditions of isolation and sensory deprivation.

Peter Hartcollis has put psychoanalytic interpretations to time sense, especially to durational experience and to temporal perspective, in such papers as "Time as a Dimension of Affects," *Journal of the American Psychoanalytic Association* 20:92–108, 1972, and "On the Experience of Time and Its Dynamics, With Special Reference to Affects," *Journal of the American Psychoanalytic Association* 24:363–375, 1976.

Bonnie and Clyde was directed by Arthur Penn and released in 1967. *The Wild Bunch* was directed by Sam Peckinpah and released in 1969.

Anna Marie Conrad's statement on her sense of time while buried alive was reported by Erica Goode in the *San Francisco Chronicle,* April 6, 1982.

Fifty-two Americans were taken on November 4, 1979, by Iranian radicals who stormed the American embassy in Tehran. The American hostages remained in captivity for 444 days.

The Hawthorne *Scarlet Letter* quote comes from the Bantam edition, New York, 1981. The novel was written between 1846 and 1849.

"Omens" are a psychological concept I developed during the Chowchilla project, and they are explained in Terr, L., "Children of Chowchilla," and in Terr, L., "Chowchilla Revisited." I also explain "time skew" for the first time in these papers.

Dirty Harry was directed in 1971 by Don Siegel. In the climactic scene at the end, Clint Eastwood rescues a school bus full of kids held hostage by the film's villain.

Stephen King's *The Dead Zone* was published in New York by Viking Press, 1979.

García Márquez's *Chronicle of a Death Foretold* was translated by Gregory Rabassa and published by Ballantine Books, New York, 1984.

Fischhoff's psychological experiments on retrospective rethinking appear in "Hindsight = Foresight," *Journal of Experimental Psychology, Human Perception and Performance* 1:288–299, 1975, and Fischoff, B., and Beyth, R., " 'I Knew It Would Happen,' " *Organizational Behavior and Human Performannce* 13:1–16, 1975.

Superman turns back time in the first Superman film, directed in 1978 by Richard Donner.

My Dinner With André was written by Wally Shawn and André Gregory and was directed by Louis Malle in 1981. The film script is available through Grove Press, New York, 1981. The quotes I use are on pp. 99–100.

I have written two professional papers on time sense and psychic trauma, Terr., L., "Time Sense Following Psychic Trauma: A Clinical Study of Ten Adults and Twenty Children," *American Journal of Orthopsychiatry* 53:244–261, 1983, and Terr, L., "Time and Trauma," *Psychoanalytic Study of the Child* 39:633–666, 1984.

Alain Resnais' *Last Year in Marienbad* was released in 1962 in French with English subtitles.

Peter Cowie's biography is entitled *Ingmar Bergman,* and was published in New York by Scribner's, 1983. I relied upon this biography for my "analysis" of Bergman. Ingmar Bergman himself has recently published an autobiographical sketch, *The Magic Lantern,* New York, Viking Press, 1988. This book does not mention the closet incident, although it tells of punitive lock-ups in cupboards of the Bergman family kitchen. Whatever the "reality" of Bergman's early experience with lock-ups, this type of experience repeats itself in Bergman's various statements about his childhood, in his films, and in the "time" problems that he conveys to his audience.

Bergman's *Hour of the Wolf* was written and directed by Bergman and released in 1968. *Fanny and Alexander* was also written and directed by Bergman and released in 1982. The script was translated by Alan Blair and published in New York by Pantheon, 1982. *The Magician* was written and directed by Bergman and released in 1958. *Through a Glass Darkly* was witten and directed by Bergman and released in 1961. The script is available as Bergman, I., *A Film Trilogy: Through A Glass Darkly, The Communicants (Winter Light) and The Silence,* Austin, Paul (tr.), New York, M. Boyars, 1988. *Persona* was written and directed by Bergman and released in 1966. It is also available in script form in Bergman, I., *Persona and Shame: Two Screenplays,* Blair, Alan (tr.), New York, M. Boyars, 1984. *The Seventh Seal* was written and directed by Bergman and released through Svensk Filmindustri in 1957.

CHAPTER NINE

For reviews of memory manipulation experiments on children, see Loftus, E., and Davies, G., "Distortions of Memory in Children," *Journal of Social Issues*

40:51–67, 1984, and Johnson, M., and Foley, H. A., "Differentiating Fact From Fantasy: The Reliability of Children's Memory," *ibid.*, 33–50.

Stephen Ceci of Cornell has conducted a number of psychological experiments on children's memories in storage. He and his colleagues found that 182 children (ages 3 to 12) were susceptible to misleading information given them after they had been asked to remember something. The three and four year olds were particularly susceptible. In another experiment with 102 children, Ceci's group found that if the delayed misleading information was given by a child rather than by an adult, the children (mean age 4.6) would tend less to remember this misinformation. This suggests that some false memories are caused by childrens' desire to conform to adult wishes (see Ceci, S., Ross, D., and Toglia, M., "Suggestibility of Children's Memory: Psychological Implications," *Journal of Experimental Psychology: General* 116:38–49, 1987).

Yarmey, A. D., *op. cit.*, reviews the effects of uniforms on child witnesses' memories. G. Goodman and C. Aman presented a paper at the annual meetings of the Society for Research in Child Development, Baltimore, 1987, "Children's Use of Anatomically Correct Dolls to Report an Event," in which they stated that normal three year olds playing with either ordinary dolls or anatomically correct dolls tended to misremember what had happened a week before in a play session with an adult male from the researchers' team.

Bob Barklay's and Alison Adams's statements are taken from interviews an NBC national television news team recorded nine years after the Chowchilla kidnapping.

John Boorman's autobiographical film *Hope and Glory* was released in 1987. His screenplay of the same name is published by Faber and Faber, London, 1987. Louis Malle's *Au Revoir Les Enfants* was also released in 1987. Although Malle has produced several films in English, this one, his childhood autobiography, is done in his native French. The screenplay is published in an Anselm Hollo translation by Grove Press, New York, 1988.

Stefan Zweig's *Marie Antoinette: The Portrait of an Average Woman* is translated by Eden Paul and Cedar Paul (1933) and published by Harmony Books, New York, 1984.

Jean Piaget's *Play, Dreams, and Imitation in Childhood* was translated by C. Gattegno and F. M. Hodgson, New York, Norton, 1951.

My own study of early memory is entitled "What Happens to the Early Memories of Trauma? A Study of Twenty Children Under Age Five at the Time of Documented Traumatic Events," *American Journal of Child and Adolescent Psychiatry* 27:96–104, 1988.

The spurt in left brain development occurring at around age three is reported by Thatcher, R., Walker, R., and Giudice, S., "Human Cerebral Hemispheres Develop at Different Rates and Ages," *Science* 236:1110–1113, 1987. Robert Miller notes that children begin to construct grammatically ordered phrases at around age three in "Development From One to Two Years: Language Acquisition," in J. Noshpitz, ed., *Basic Handbook of Child Psychiatry* 1:127–144, New York, Basic Books, 1979. Anny Katan noted that at around age three children begin to put words to their emotions, especially negative emotions such as anger and fear, in "Some Thoughts About the Role of Verbalization in Early Childhood," *Psychoanalytic Study of the Child* 16:184–188, 1961.

Perceptual behavioral memory in very young children is proposed in several reports from psychoanalysis. See, for instance, Anthi, P., "Reconstruction of Preverbal Experience," *Journal of the American Psychoanalytic Association* 31:33–58, 1983; Dowling, S., "Dreams and Dreaming in Relation to Trauma in Childhood," *International Journal of Psycho-Analysis* 63:157–166, 1982; Anthony, E. J., "A Study of Screen Sensations," *Psychoanalytic Study of the Child* 16:211–245, 1961; and Isakower, O., "A Contribution to the Patho-Psychology of Phenomena Associated With Falling Asleep," *International Journal of Psycho-Analysis* 19:331–345, 1938.

My main sources of information on Magritte's life and work are Suzi Gablik's *Magritte,* New York, Thames & Hudson, 1985, and Milton Viederman's psychoanalytic exploration, "Rene Magritte," *Journal of the American Psychoanalytic Association* 35:967–998, 1987. I also used Hammacher, A., *Magritte,* New York, Abrams, 1973, and Torczyner, H., *Magritte,* France, Draeger, 1977.

CHAPTER TEN

Freud's "love and work" concept of normality dominates his "Civilization and Its Discontents" (1930), *Standard Edition* 21:55–145 (see especially p. 101).

Norman Garmezy, a psychologist at the University of Minnesota, uses "grades" and "achievement testing" to measure the coping skills of children exposed to stress. For a recent example of this kind of work, see Garmezy, N., "Stress, Competence, and Development: Continuities in the Study of Schizophrenic Adults, Children Vulnerable to Psychopathology, and the Search for Stress-Resistant Children," *American Journal of Orthopsychiatry* 57:159–174, 1987. Michael Rutter, M.D., a well-respected British child-psychiatrist who has conducted large-scale epidemiological studies of English children on the Isle of Wight and in inner-city London slums, finds that schools function to protect children from stress. Rutter's group also uses grades, attendance records, and proficiency scores as their measures of children's abilities to cope. The group's primary work on this subject is Rutter, M., Maugham, B., Mortimore, P., Ouston, J., and Smith, A., *Fifteen Thousand Hours: Secondary Schools and Their Effects on Children,* London, Open Books, 1979. Because of their methods, neither Rutter's nor Garmezy's research groups detect real psychic trauma in youngsters. Their conclusions about "invulnerable children" or "stress resistant" children do not relate, as far as I can tell, to childhood trauma.

In an early controlled study on World War II and Korean War veterans who were seen at variously long intervals after the wars, Herbert Archibald and Read Tuddenham found that one half of the soldiers who had been diagnosed "combat fatigued" (today's "post-traumatic stress disorder") were not working at the time of the follow-up. (The study is "Persistent Stress Reaction After Combat," *Archives of General Psychiatry* 12:475–481, 1965.) More recent studies of war veterans do not necessarily replicate Archibald and Tuddenham's numbers, but they confirm the general idea that adult trauma victims have problems with work.

M. Horowitz's *Stress Response Syndromes,* New York, Jason Aronson, 1976, proposes that flashbacks function as the negative to massive denial. When there is denial, there are flashbacks. I found at Chowchilla (Terr, L., "Children of Chowchilla") that the kidnapped youngsters denied external reality minimally, if at all. Perhaps this lack of denial contributed to the absence of flashbacks in these children.

The paper reporting the school performance of Cambodian child refugees, Sack, W., Angell, R., Kinzie, J. D., and Rath, B., "The Psychiatric Effects of Massive Trauma on Cambodian Children, II. The Family, the Home, and the School," indicates that psychic trauma does not ordinarily interfere with school work.

It is impossible to cite any one publication that illustrates phase-specific fantasy—the child psychoanalytic literature is replete with examples. See, in particular, *The Psychoanalytic Study of the Child,* New Haven, Yale University Press, all volumes.

Henry James's "The Jolly Corner" is included in the anthology, Pronzini, B., Malberg, B., and Greenberg, M., eds., *The Arbor House Treasury of Horror and the Supernatural,* New York, Arbor House, 1981.

CHAPTER ELEVEN

Selma Fraiberg's *The Magic Years,* New York, Scribners, 1984, is possibly the best available book on children's internal development up to the age of six. For a thorough compendium of Selma Fraiberg's professional writings, see *The Selected Writings of Selma Fraiberg,* edited by her husband, Louis Fraiberg, Columbus, Ohio, Ohio State University Press, 1987.

My thanks to Tina Goldfine and her child-psychiatrist husband, Peter, for allowing me to tell Tina's story.

Freud's division of anxiety into two types, traumatic (actual) and anticipatory, is explained in "Inhibitions, Symptoms, and Anxiety" (1926), *Standard Edition* 50:77–172.

William Manchester's *Good-bye Darkness: A Memoir of the Pacific War* (1979) was published by Dell, New York, 1987.

Stephen King's *Misery* was published in New York by Viking Press, 1987.

John Donne's poem "Devotions" is published in Donne, J., *Complete English Poems,* A. J. Smith, ed., Penguin, New York, 1977.

The best book on dreams that I know is Sigmund Freud's "The Interpretation of Dreams," (1900), *Standard Edition,* volumes 4 and 5.

I write about children's post-traumatic dreams in several of my papers on psychic trauma, especially in the Chowchilla studies and the McFarland-Porterville control study, the study of early childhood memories of trauma, and the paper on the connection between remembered traumatic images and supernatural phenomena. All of these have been cited previously. My ranking of verbal ability in children as associated to nonremembered terror dreaming appears in "Children of Chowchilla." I have also published a review chapter on children's nightmares in Guilleminault, C., ed., *Sleep and Its Disorders in Children,* New York, Raven Press, 1987, pp. 231–242.

The psychiatrist John Mack gives a description for professionals of how dreams change as children grow up in "Nightmares, Conflict, and Ego Development in Childhood," *International Journal of Psycho-Analysis* 46:403–428, 1968. He also wrote a dream book for lay readers, *Nightmares and the Human Conflict,* Boston, Little, Brown, 1970. Selma Fraiberg also wrote a piece on early nightmares and other sleep problems, "On the Sleep Disturbances of Early Childhood," *Psychoanalytic Study of the Child* 5:285–309, 1950.

For interesting, nonpsychoanalytic works on dreams, see Devereux, G., "Pathogenic Dreams in Non-Western Societies," in Devereux, G., ed., *Basic Problems of Ethnopsychiatry,* Chicago, University of Chicago Press, 1980, pp. 274–288, and Hobson, J. A., and McCarley, R., in "The Brain as a Dream State Generator," *American Journal of Psychiatry* 134:1335–1348, 1977. David Foulkes, a cognitive psychologist, has published a number of well-conceived studies of how normal children dream, *Children's Dreams: Longitudinal Studies,* New York, Wiley, 1982. Foulkes's sleep-lab studies do not directly relate, however, to the kind of dreaming that follows from childhood traumatic experience.

The unremembered terror dreams of psychic trauma and the dreams of ordinary infant and toddler development hold a great deal in common. For descriptions of early dreaming, see Niederland, W., "The Earliest Dreams of a Young Child," *Psychoanalytic Study of the Child* 12:190–208, 1957; Dowling, S., "Mental Organization in the Phenomena of Sleep," *Psychoanalytic Study of the Child* 37:285–302, 1982; and Hirschberg, J. C., "Dreaming, Drawing, and the Dream Screen in the Psychoanalysis of a Two and a Half Year Old Boy," *American Journal of Psychiatry* 122:37–45, 1966.

Freud's statement "in the unconscious everyone of us is convinced of his own immortality" comes from his "Thoughts for the Times on War and Death" (1915) *Standard Edition* 18:271–300, p. 289.

My McFarland-Porterville control study is cited in the notes on Chapter One.

Freud saw dream interpretation as possibly predictive (in Chapter Two of "The Interpretation of Dreams"). He considered character, impelled by the drives, to be predictable from a person's dreams. Because dreams at their deepest levels express wishes (the drives), the dream interpreter might correctly guess at a person's future behaviors, and thus at the dreamer's future. Robert Michels, M.D., a well-known contemporary psychoanalyst, has expanded on this idea in a lecture on Joseph's "correct" analyses of his prison-mates' dreams. Joseph's interpretation, Michels says, was based upon what Joseph knew of the men's characters from their dreams.

Shakespeare's *Julius Caesar* is available in the Folger Library Edition, Wright, Louis B., and LaMar, Virginia, eds., New York, Washington Square Press. John Irving's *The World According to Garp* was published by Pocket Books, New York, 1984. Charles Dickens's *A Christmas Carol* (1843) was published in New York by Bantam, 1986. Martin Luther King Jr.'s "I have a dream" speech was delivered on August 28, 1963, in Washington, D.C. He also gave a prophetic-sounding speech about his visions—"I have been to the mountain"—in Memphis, Tennessee, the night before he died. King was assassinated in Memphis on April 4, 1968.

Virginia Woolf's "A Sketch of the Past" is published in *Moments of Being,* New York, Harcourt Brace Jovanovich, 1985. The Woolf quotes I used in this section come from this autobiographical book. Quentin Bell's book on Woolf, *Virginia Woolf: A Biography,* San Diego, Harcourt Brace Jovanovich, 1974, minimizes the possible effects of childhood sexual abuse in Virginia. A new book on Virginia Woolf, on the other hand, puts the sexual abuse into the forefront (Louise De Salvo's *Virginia Woolf: The Impact of Childhood Sexual Abuse on Her Life and Work,* Boston, Beacon Press, 1989). Leon Edel, a literary-psychoanalytic scholar, includes an interesting essay on Woolf's psychology in his *Stuff of Sleep and Dreams: Experiments in Literary Psychology,* New York, Harper & Row, 1982.

Carl Sagan's *The Dragons of Eden* was published by Random House, New York, 1977.

CHAPTER TWELVE

The first paper I published on post-traumatic play is entitled " 'Forbidden Games': Post-Traumatic Child's Play," *Journal of the American Academy of Child Psychiatry* 20:740–759, 1981.

War and Children by Anna Freud and Dorothy Burlingham was cited in the notes on Chapter One. The story of "Bertie's" play appears on pp. 68–69 of the 1943 edition. Gaynor Lacey's and David Levy's papers are also cited in the notes on Chapter One.

"Nursery Chairs" (1927) can be found in A. A. Milne's *The World of Christopher Robin,* New York, E. P. Dutton, 1958.

E. Boyer's *The Secret Game* was published in 1950 in New York by Harcourt Brace & Co. The film *Jeux Interdits* was directed in 1952 by René Clément.

Milton Rokeach's *The Three Christs of Ypsilanti: A Psychological Study* (1964) remains in print today through Columbia University Press, New York, 1981.

Stephen King's *Danse Macabre* was published in New York by Berkley, 1983. The autobiographical quote about King's four-year-old trauma appears on pp. 83–84 of that edition. Douglas Winter's book entitled *Stephen King* was published in New York by New American Library, Plume, 1986. J. Underwood and C. Miller edited a book of Stephen King interviews, most of which originally appeared in various newspapers and magazines or were delivered as lectures. It is entitled *Bare Bones,* New York, McGraw-Hill, 1988.

I know about the Stephen King spiderweb gate from a waitress in Kennebunkport, Maine, who described King's house in minute enough detail for me to find it if I ever were to visit Bangor.

The story about King's abandonment by his father is told in Underwood and Miller, *op cit.,* and Douglas Winter's biography, *op cit.* King's lack of any idea about his father's whereabouts is on p. 35 of Underwood and Miller. His discovery of his father's paperbacks is described in *Danse Macabre,* p. 94. The other childhood stories about King's mother's behavior and his seven-year-old first story of a dinosaur are told by Winter, *op cit.* King says that the Bible is unbeatable as horror literature in Underwood and Miller, *op. cit.,* p. 187, and he tells of his Sodom and Gomorrah game in the same book, same page.

King's "symptoms" were told by Stephen King to various reporters and to audiences at a Billerica Library lecture and at the World Fantasy conference. They are quoted by Underwood and Miller, *op. cit.,* pp. 24–56, 169, 177. King's quotes about a foreshortened future are in *ibid.,* pp. 19, 177, 193.

The "phony" Bachman biography is printed in *The Bachman Books,* New York, New American Library, NAL Books, 1985.

King's experiences with abusive substances in college are given by him in Underwood and Miller, *op. cit.,* pp. 32 and 43. His comments about sixty psychedelic trips are on p. 43. He admits to drinking two and one half quarts of beer on the average day *ibid.,* p. 169. He speaks of Ray Bradbury *ibid.,* p. 163.

Stephen King's *It* was published in 1986 in New York by Viking Press. *Pet Sematary* was published in 1983 by Doubleday, Garden City, N.Y.

King's comments on whether or not he needs to write terror fiction are quoted from Underwood and Miller, *op. cit.,* p. 124. His quote about *Stand By Me* comes from the same page.

King's *The Dead Zone* was published in 1979 in New York by Viking Press. His *Cycle of the Werewolf* was published in 1985 by New American Library, Plume, New York. The film *Silver Bullet* (1985) was directed by Daniel Attias. The Mark Dinning rock quote comes from *Christine,* New York, Viking, 1983, p. 421. *Thinner,* a Stephen King novel written under the Bachman pseudonym, was published by New American Library, NAL Books, 1984. "Uncle Otto's Truck" appears in *Skeleton Crew,* New York, Putnam, 1985. "Battleground" is printed in *Night Shift,* New York, Signet, 1979. The King novel *The Stand* was published in 1978 by Doubleday, Garden City, N.Y. "The Mangler" is in *Night Shift,* New York, Signet, 1979. The film *The Shining* was directed by Stanley Kubrick and starred Jack Nicholson and Shelley Duvall, 1980. King's quoted complaint about Kubrick's film story comes from Underwood and Miller, *op. cit.,* p. 96f. "The Breathing Method" is one of four King novellas published in *Different Seasons,* New York, Viking Press, 1982. The film *Carrie* (1976) was directed by Brian de Palma, starring Sissy Spacek and Piper Laurie. *Cujo* was directed by Lewis Teague in 1983.

For Elie Wiesel's own personal nonfiction horror story see *Night* (1960), New York, Bantam, 1982.

I have written a paper about horror writing, horror reading, and Stephen King entitled "Terror Writing by the Formerly Terrified: The Life and Works of Stephen King," *Psychoanalytic Study of the Child* 44:369–390, 1989.

CHAPTER THIRTEEN

Melvin Reinhart, M.D., currently practices psychiatry in Ann Arbor, Michigan, and teaches psychiatric trainees. I have lost track of "Victor Martin."

G. Grass's *The Tin Drum* was translated by Ralph Manheim and published in New York by Random House, 1971.

The "classic" pediatric monograph on failure to thrive in childhood is Patton, R. G., and Gardner, L. I., *Growth Failure in Maternal Deprivation,* Springfield, Ill., Thomas Publishing, 1963.

Marie Bonaparte's book on Poe, *op. cit.,* relates the West Point story of the bleeding gander and the supposedly axed-off head of Poe's professor.

Creepshow was directed by George Romero and released in 1982. *Pet Sematary* was directed by Mary Lambert and released in 1989.

The Stephen King quote about his behavior with his own children at the movies comes from Underwood and Miller, *op. cit.,* p. 57. His quote about the "ultimate triumph" is *ibid.,* p. 50. His list of King-inspired murders is *ibid.,* p. 51. His comment about Tylenol poisonings is *ibid.,* p. 52.

Magritte's tamperings with his chronologies and with the dates of his paintings are described by Milton Viederman, *op. cit.* His day at the coffin-maker's shop was related by Hammacher, *op. cit.* Hitchcock's pranky reenactments are recounted by Donald Spoto in the Hitchcock biography, *op cit.*

My thanks to Diane Schetky, M.D., Rockport, Maine, for telling me about Madeleine Carroll's dinner table talk and for allowing me to print the tale.

CHAPTER FOURTEEN

The film *Jaws* was directed by Steven Spielberg and released in 1975. It is based on the novel by Peter Benchley.

The newspaper article that quotes Johnny Johnson shortly before he died is S. Tomkins, "Sadly Silenced," *Fresno Bee,* June 28, 1981.

Steven Stayner's story was presented as an NBC television miniseries, "I Know My First Name is Steven," May 22 and 23, 1989.

Dorothy Otnow Lewis, a New York City child psychiatrist, conducts long-term follow-up studies of violent juvenile delinquents. Lewis and her group find that early child abuse along with bad role-modeling from parents, chronic rage, brain damage, hyperactivity, and impulsivity lead to aggressive adult criminality. See Lewis, D. O., Lovely, R., Yeager, C., and Della Femina, D., "Toward a Theory of the Genesis of Violence: A Follow-Up Study of Delinquents," *Journal of the American Academy of Child and Adolescent Psychiatry* 28:431–436, 1989, and Lewis, D. O., Moy, E., Jackson, L. D., Aronson, B. A., et al. "Biopsychosocial Characteristics of Children Who Later Murder," *American Journal of Psychiatry* 142:1161–1167, 1985.

I have written several pieces on possible treatments for childhood psychic trauma. See, for instance, "Play Therapy and Psychic Trauma," in C. Schaefer and K. O'Connor, eds., *Handbook of Play Therapy,* New York, John Wiley, 1983, pp. 308–319; "Children at Acute Risk—Psychic Trauma, Fright, and Unexpected Events," in L. Grinspoon, ed., *Annual Review of Psychiatry* 3:104–120, 161–164, Washington, D.C., American Psychiatric Press, 1984; "Treatment of Psychic Trauma in Children," in J. Noshpitz, ed., *Basic Handbook of Child Psychiatry* 5:414–421, New York, Basic Books, 1985; and "Treating Psychic Trauma in Children," *Journal of Traumatic Stress* 2:3–20, 1989.

My article about the thirteen medical-legal cases I saw that involved childhood trauma is entitled "Personal Injury to Children: The Civil Suit Claiming Psychic Trauma," in D. Schetky and E. Benedek, eds., *Child Psychiatry and the Law,* pp. 249–265.

The new preliminary study on propranolol (Inderal) on childhood post-traumatic stress disorder is Famularo, R., Kinscherff, R., and Fenton, T., "Propranolol Treatment for Post-Traumatic Stress Disorder, Acute Type: A Pilot Study," *American Journal of the Diseases of Children* 142:1244–1247, 1988.

The general group-therapy and family-therapy literature is too extensive for me to cite any special article. The ideas I mention about whether or not to conduct family therapy with abusers and their children come from my own work with abusive families, some of which is published in "A Family Study of Child Abuse." The minimarathon group techniques I mention in Chapters Seven and Fourteen come from Isaiah Zimmerman, Ph.D., a Washington, D.C., psychologist who introduced me to the idea at a 1983 Southern California Group Psychotherapy Association meeting. Dr. Zimmerman, in consulting to the U.S. State Department, created this minimarathon program for the eventuality of American embassy workers and their families being taken hostage.

The idea of "chaperones" for parentally snatched children, as far as I can tell, comes from the Association of Family Courts, a group that represents court workers, referees, and judges handling divorce and custody disputes.

Safeguards for abused children who are to stay in their own homes are proposed in my and Andrew Watson's article "The Battered Children Rebrutalized."

Silverman, I., and Geer, J., wrote "The Elimination of Recurrent Nightmare by Desensitization of a Related Phobia," *Behavioral Research and Therapy* 6:109–111, 1968. Garfield's book *Your Child's Dreams,* New York, Ballantine, 1984, recommends a different type of behavioral modification, redreaming corrective endings to nightmares.

Trance treatments for children and adults who have dissociated after multiple early abuses are described in *Psychiatric Clinics of North America* (Symposium on Multiple Personality), Vol. 7, March 1984, Philadelphia, W. B. Saunders, and Braun, Bennett, ed., *Treatment of Multiple Personality Disorder,* Washington, D.C., American Psychiatric Press, 1986.

David Levy's abreactive technique is published as "Release Therapy in Young Children," *Psychiatry* 1:387–390, 1938, and "Release Therapy," *American Journal of Orthopsychiatry* 9:713–736, 1939. The Levy idea of "preset play" is described in "Release Therapy," *ibid.* Shapiro, S., "Preventive Analysis Following a Trauma: A Four-and-One-Half-Year-Old Girl Witnesses a Stillbirth," *Psychoanalytic Study of the Child* 28:249–285, 1973, describes a type of "preset" play. MacLean's "tiger" play is described in "Psychic Trauma and Traumatic Neurosis: Play Therapy With a Four-Year-Old Boy," *Canadian Psychiatric Association Journal* 22:71–76, 1977. Theodore Gaensbauer's use of preset play with a two-and-one-half-year-old boy traumatized by a dog attack was presented at a symposium on "trauma" cosponsored by the Denver Child Psychiatry Council and the University of Colorado Department of Psychiatry, 1985.

As far as I can tell, the two "classic" works that "invented" play therapy are Melanie Klein's *Psycho-Analysis of Chidlren* (1932) (tr. Alix Strachey), London, Hogarth Press, 1937, and Robert Waelder's "The Psychoanalytic Theory of Play," *Psychoanalytic Quarterly* 2:208–224, 1933. Although Anna Freud disavowed any interest in "play therapy" (in "Indications for Child Analysis" [1945], *The Writings of Anna Freud* 4:3–38) she made an enormous contribution to play as therapy with her "Four Lectures on Child Analysis" (1927), *ibid.* 1:3–69, and "The Ego and the Mechanisms of Defense" (1966 revision), *ibid.* 2.

Erik Erikson's great contribution to an understanding of play was published under his original name, Erik Homburger ("Configurations in Play," *Psychoanalytic Quarterly* 6:139–214, 1937). Erikson also gave several new interpretations to the meaning of young children's play in *Childhood and Society.* Selma Fraiberg described the play and seeking behaviors of totally blind children in *Insights from the Blind,* New York, Basic Books, 1977.

Erikson's coffin play description is in *Childhood and Society.* "Bertie" is cited by A. Freud and D. Burlingham in *War and Children.*

Erna Furman's "filial therapy" is discussed in her "Treatment of Under-Fives by Way of Parents," *Psychoanalytic Study of the Child* 12:250–262, 1957, and "Filial Therapy," in J. Noshpitz, ed., *Basic Handbook of Child Psychiatry,* 3:149–158.

The psychological radio call-in show conducted after the Los Angeles earthquake is described in Blaufarb, H., and Levine, J., "Crisis Intervention in an Earthquake," *Social Work* 17:16–19, 1972.

Madelyn Gould and David Shaffer published "The Impact of Suicide in Television Movies: Evidence of Imitation," in the *New England Journal of Medicine* 315:690–693, 1986. In the same issue of the *New England Journal,* David Phillips and Lundie Carstensen published "Clustering of Teenage Suicides After Television News Stories About Suicide," pp. 685–689. It appeared that fictional or factual media representations of teenaged suicide could spark epidemics. Phillips, however, challenged Gould and Shaffer's data in Phillips, D., and Paight, D., "The Impact of Televised Movies About Suicide: A Replicative Study," *New England Journal of Medicine* 317:809–811, 1987. Although Gould and Shaffer's statistics on the rise in suicides had been correct for New York, other cities did not exhibit such an increase, Phillips and Paight found.

CHAPTER FIFTEEN

The percentages of people in the population-at-large who experience some post-traumatic symptoms come from projects called the Epidemiological Catchment Area (E.C.A.) studies (many of these studies remain unpublished at this time). The figure of 8 percent comes from an unpublished North Carolina study. The figure of 15 to 16 percent prevalence of post-traumatic symptoms comes from a published St. Louis study conducted by Helzer, J. E., Robins, L. N., and McEvoy, L., "Post-Traumatic Stress Disorder in the General Population: Findings of the Epidemiological Catchment Area Survey," *New England Journal of Medicine* 317:1630–1634, 1987.

Alison Lurie's *Foreign Affairs* was published in New York by Random House, 1984.

The bibliographical references to Stephen King's *Pet Sematary, Christine, The Shining, The Dead Zone,* and *The Stand* are cited in the notes on Chapter Twelve. *'Salem's Lot* was published in 1975 by Doubleday, Garden City, N.Y.

My comment, "if one could write schizophrenic language into a book that made sense, the reader would feel schizophrenic as he read it," is strongly influenced by Evelyne Keitel, a young scholar of comparative literature who teaches at the University of Berlin. Her book *Reading Psychosis: Reader's Text in Psychoanalysis,* Oxford, Basil Blackwell, 1989, places this idea at its center.

The King letter about sleeplessness after reading *'Salem's Lot* comes from Underwood and Miller, *op. cit.*, p. 4, as does his quote about enjoying the act of scaring people.

The Melanie Griffith interview appears in *People* 31:82–89, February 27, 1989.

King's outline of the most common fears in the population-at-large appears in Underwood and Miller, *op. cit.*, pp. 1–24.

Index